KUT 1916

British 60–pounder gun in action. (Author's collection)

KUT 1916

COURAGE AND FAILURE IN IRAQ

Patrick Crowley

This book is dedicated to those British and Indian
soldiers who never made it home

They shall not return to us, the resolute, the young,
The eager and wholehearted whom we gave:
But the men who left them thriftily to die in their own dung,
Shall they come with years and honour to the grave?

Extract from Rudyard Kipling's 'Mesopotamia 1917'

First published 2009

By Spellmount, an imprint of
The History Press
The Mill, Brimscombe Port
Stroud, Gloucestershire, GL5 2QG
www.thehistorypress.co.uk

© Patrick Crowley, 2009

The right of Patrick Crowley to be identified as the Author
of this work has been asserted in accordance with the
Copyrights, Designs and Patents Act 1988.

British Library Cataloguing in Publication Data.
A catalogue record for this book is available from the British Library.

ISBN 978 0 7524 5447 4

Typesetting and origination by The History Press
Printed in Great Britain

CONTENTS

LIST OF MAPS

ACKNOWLEDGEMENTS

This book has taken a long time to construct, as I have worked at it in the margins of a series of busy jobs. I began collecting reference material from the library of the Defence Academy, Shrivenham, in 2003 and took a particular interest in Mesopotamia whilst on operations in Iraq in 2006/07. My prime thanks go to my father-in-law, John Rule, who has been enthusiastically investigating various references for me over a two-year period. Without his 'reconnaissance' of archives at Kew, the National Army Museum, the Imperial War Museum and some regimental museums, this book would never have appeared. My second thanks go to the patient staff of the Prince Consort's Library, Aldershot, and the Royal Military Academy Sandhurst – both institutions hold a fascinating and invaluable collection of books and have been extremely helpful in finding rare references. I am also particularly grateful to two busy and influential individuals, Professor Gary Sheffield and Lieutenant-General Graeme Lamb, for their written contributions. Thanks also to Brigadier Mark Armstrong and Lieutenant-Colonel Bede Strong for their modern pictures from Iraq. Other patient helpers have been the staff at the Royal Hampshire Regiment Museum at Winchester. Aggie Smith provided invaluable practical help in putting the initial drafts together and the Indian Army Liaison Officer at Headquarters Infantry, Colonel Mohit Seth, helped identify Indian Army heritage. Finally, my thanks to my wife, Jane, for being so patient when we might have been doing other things!

Colonel Patrick Crowley, Iraq 2006.

Foreword by Gary Sheffield

The Mesopotamia Campaign of the First World War remains a neglected facet of that terrible conflict – although events of recent years have given it additional currency. The campaign was a product of two interweaved factors: the deadlock on the Western Front, and British imperialism. Once it became clear that the fighting in France and Flanders was going to be long drawn out, bloody and indecisive, decision-makers began to search for strategic alternatives. The ill-fated Gallipoli Campaign of 1915 was the principal product of this thinking, but other secondary theatres were also developed as a consequence.

Mesopotamia, modern day Iraq, was in 1914 a province of the Ottoman (Turkish) Empire. British and Indian troops were landed at Basra, at the head of the Persian Gulf, at the end of 1914. This was a limited and sensible move to secure oil supplies. Under the pressure of events, the aims of the British forces in the area became increasingly ambitious. Although primarily a struggle to prevent German domination of Europe, the war was also seen as an opportunity to strengthen and expand the Empire. Turkey had been the 'sick man of Europe' for decades, and the time seemed to have arrived for the Ottoman Empire to be partitioned between Britain, France and Russia. It has been said that the British Empire was acquired in a fit of absent-mindedness. Much the same can be said of the conquest of Mesopotamia. Almost as a reflex, bit by bit, the British forces advanced deeper into the interior. The defeat at Kut, a story well told by Patrick Crowley in this book, was a disaster waiting to happen.

'Mespot' lacked the romance and glamour, however spurious, of the campaigns at Gallipoli and in Palestine. Post-war debates raged on whether the opportunity for a major victory had been thrown away at the Dardanelles (the answer, almost certainly, is no). Similarly, the remarkable success of Allenby's forces and the already legendary exploits of T.E. Lawrence drew writers to the Palestine Campaign. By contrast, little was written about Mesopotamia, which has remained the least known of the major 'sideshows' fought against the Turks. In the short term, the defeat at Kut was a damaging blow to British prestige. It came a few months after the final evacuation of Gallipoli, and around the same time as the naval battle of Jutland (which disappointed a public expecting a new Trafalgar), the Easter Uprising in Dublin, and the death of Lord Kitchener, and a few months before the armies of the Empire began the long-drawn out agony of the Somme. Kut was thus one of a series of pieces of bad news in mid-1916. In the longer term, Kut proved to be a setback in the Mesopotamia Campaign, but little more. The war ended with military victory in the region and the poisoned chalice of Iraq passing to Britain. For those who suffered as a result of Kut, either during the campaign and siege or as a prisoner of war, the consequences of the defeat were of course serious indeed.

I am very pleased that Patrick Crowley has re-examined the Kut campaign in this book. He is a serving officer with experience of the current 'Mesopotamian campaign' and an accomplished historian, and his account brings the campaign to life. I particularly admire his concentration on the human dimension of war. *Kut 1916: Bravery and Failure in Iraq* is a very welcome contribution to the literature on the war against Turkey, and a fine tribute to the men who served, fought, and suffered in that terrible campaign.

Professor Gary Sheffield BA MA Leeds PhD London
Professor of War Studies
University of Birmingham

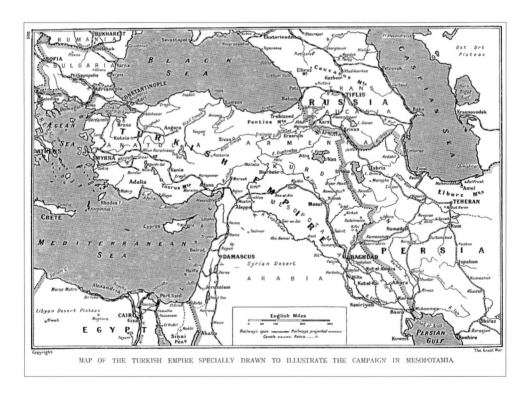

MAP OF THE TURKISH EMPIRE SPECIALLY DRAWN TO ILLUSTRATE THE CAMPAIGN IN MESOPOTAMIA.

Map of the Turkish Empire. (*Times – The Great War*)

PREFACE

I am an infantryman, and proud of it. My regiment is the Princess of Wales's Royal Regiment, which recruits from the counties of Surrey, Kent, Hampshire, Sussex and Middlesex; it is the same regiment that, at the time of writing, has already clocked up three battalion operational tours in Iraq since 2003. The deployment of 2004 resulted in the award of the Victoria Cross to Private (now Lance-Corporal) Johnson Beharry, along with many other gallantry awards – but that is another story, already told.[1]

In 2006/2007 I found myself, as a staff officer, on an operational tour in Baghdad – part of the Multi-National Force-Iraq Headquarters, composed mainly of American, British and Australian officers. My tour was fascinating, exciting and stimulating and I was lucky enough to be able to travel a little, due to my liaison role.

I have always had an interest in the culture and military history of the areas in which I have served and I soon began to make connections with some of the names around me. I was aware of the historical importance of Basra in the south and its occupation by British forces from India in 1914. It remains strategically important, both for its oilfields and its position dominating the route from the coast to Baghdad. I had passed through Basra, but also visited the British base of Shaiba, a location of one of the earlier clashes with the Turks in 1915. I was inquisitive about other names, such as 'Maude House', the British Deputy Commanding General's and British Support Unit's location in Baghdad. Lieutenant-General Sir Stanley Maude marched into Baghdad in 1917 and was one of the key commanders in the third failed attempt to relieve the siege of Kut-al-Amara (henceforth known as Kut). It was at Kut in 1916 that the British forces suffered one of their worst defeats in military history.

There were a flurry of personal accounts, analyses and history books concerning the Mesopotamia (now Iraq) Campaign published during the 1920s and further excellent books were produced around the fiftieth anniversary of the siege. Little has been written since about the siege. This book recounts the tragic experience of our forebears at Kut and their subsequent captivity.

Colonel Patrick Crowley

Notes

1. Read Holmes (2006), Beharry (2006) and Mills (2007).

Lower Mesopotamia. (Candler)

Part One

TO THE FALL OF KUT

To the Garrison of Kut

Battle and toil survived, is this the end
Of all your high endeavour? Shall the stock
That death and desert braved be made the mock
Of gazing crowds, nor in the crowd a friend?
Shall they who ever to their will did bend –
From Zain to Ctesiphon – the battle-shock
Fall prey to lean starvation's craven flock
And the dark terrors that her train attend?

You leave the field; but those who, pressing by,
Take up the torch, whene'er your name is named
Shall fight more stoutly, while your company,
Its task performed, shall carry unashamed
Into captivity a courage high:
The body prisoner, but the mind untamed

R. W. Bullard[1]

Chapter One

THE SCENE IS SET

This modest venture led to a British military disaster so total yet unnecessary, so futile yet expensive, that its like did not occur again until the fall of Singapore in 1942.[2]

The town of Kut in Mesopotamia, now Iraq, surrendered to the Turkish Army on 29 April 1916. The occupying British-led and mainly Indian Army force had been besieged for four months. 12,000 soldiers were taken into captivity and were to suffer almost as much as their countrymen did in different circumstances under the Japanese nearly thirty years later. There had been 3,776 casualties during the siege, 23,000 men were killed or wounded during the unsuccessful relief attempts and a further 4,000 were to die, subsequently, as prisoners. It was, arguably, Britain's worse military defeat since the surrender of Cornwallis's army in 1781 during the American Revolutionary War and came only a few months after the evacuation from Gallipoli.

The campaign in Mesopotamia was India's main contribution to the First World War. It spawned two major enquiries, the resignation of Austen Chamberlain, the Secretary of State for India, and the offer of resignation from Lord Hardinge, the Viceroy of India. It is now a little-known affair, overshadowed by the scale of the First World War and the attention that is given to the Western Front and Gallipoli. However, it was an expeditionary campaign fought over ground to which the British Army was to deploy again in the 1920s and 1940s and assault through in 1991 and 2003. Many Britons, both military and civilian, have seen service in the area, so the fascinating story of Kut is currently of great pertinence. Foresightedly, in his analysis of the campaign in 1926, Major Evans commented: 'Unless these difficulties are studied, unless they are met before, and not after, they occur; unless the essentials of the problem are appreciated before the solution is begun, the mistakes in 1914–18 will occur.'[3]

This chapter provides an overview of the British campaign in Mesopotamia, whilst the subsequent chapters are devoted to the human story of those besieged in Kut; the failed relief attempts, surrender, captivity and freedom.

The Campaign Summarised

The First World War reached Mesopotamia just twenty-four hours after conflict formally began between Britain and Turkey. Mid-morning on 6 November 1914, a landing force disembarked from a British flotilla led by HMS *Ocean* and the sloop, *Odin*. The objectives, reached by the Shatt-al Arab waterway at the head of the Persian Gulf, were the fort and telegraph station on

Field Marshal Sir Arthur Barrett. (Wilson)   Lord Hardinge. (Wilson)

the Fao Peninsula. Lead elements of Indian Expeditionary Force 'D', consisting of British, Indian and Royal Naval troops, commanded by Brigadier-General Walter Delamain, were immediately successful. His 16th Infantry Brigade of the 6th (Poona) Division conducted a second landing two days later at Sanniya, unopposed. By 24 November, Basra had been secured and two brigades, commanded by Lieutenant-General Sir Arthur Barrett, were firmly established in the theatre of operations. The British forces had totally surprised and overwhelmed the enemy, seizing all of their objectives – and, particularly, securing the oil.

Oil

Mesopotamia was an ancient name used by the British to conveniently describe the three Turkish provinces (*vilayets*) of Basra in the south, Baghdad in the centre and Mosul in the north. The southern vilayet had recently become increasingly important, because of the local oilfields and pipeline leading to Abadan. Winston Churchill, as First Lord of the Admiralty, had encouraged the development of oil-fired ships for the Royal Navy and in 1913 the Anglo-Persian Oil Convention secured a British controlling stake in this critical asset. Without the intervention of Indian Expeditionary Force 'D', the oil would have been controlled by the enemy. As Sir Arthur Hirtzel, Political Secretary to the India Office stated: 'The political effect in the Persian Gulf and in India of leaving the head of the Gulf derelict will be disastrous, and we cannot afford, politically, to acquiesce in such a thing for an indefinite period while the main issues are being settled elsewhere.'[4]

General Sir Edmund Barrow, Military Secretary to the India Office, agreed and was concerned about British influence in the region with the Arabs. Turkish presence would mean 'Our allies the Sheikhs of Mohammera and Kuweit will be threatened and ... either attacked or seduced, in which case our prestige and all our labours of years will vanish into air and our position in the Gulf itself will be precarious.'[5]

Strategic Importance

Mesopotamia's geographical position was important in 1914, as Iraq's is now. The British Empire had to protect the Persian Gulf, particularly because of its proximity to India. An overland route from Europe to Asia had been considered by the British and partially constructed by her rival, Germany, who planned a Berlin to Baghdad railway to assist its '*Drang nach Osten*' (drive to the east).[6] German economic activity in the region had been increasing before the war and was seen as a threat to British interests and, by the time of the Fao Peninsula landing, many Turkish regiments were advised or even commanded by German officers. The British Empire, specifically India, could not afford this area to be dominated by her new enemy despite the primacy of the Western Front. The capture of the oilfields was a great success achieved by an Allied army given limited goals within the 'art of the possible'. It marked the first of the four phases of the Mesopotamia Campaign, the others being the successful advance towards Baghdad; the disaster at Kut coupled with the failure of the Relief Force; and the successful advance to and capture of Baghdad in 1917.

Basra

By the end of November 1914, 6th (Poona) Division was complete in the Basra (or Busrah) area. Basra had been captured at the cost of 489 British dead (170 men from the Dorsetshire Regiment) compared with 1,500 Turks killed. These ratios sound impressive, but the Turks had, mistakenly, recently withdrawn three out of their four divisions based in Mesopotamia and only left the 38th Infantry Division in the country – The Iraq Area Command (*Irak ve Havalisi Komutanligi*) was no match for the Allied assault or for the subsequent operations.[7] Prior to the Fao landings, 'Mesopotamia was the backwater of the Ottoman Army' with no supporting aircraft, limited logistics and less than normal establishment levels of artillery.[8] However, Expeditionary Force

'D', commanded from India, was only equipped to support the initial operation. The campaign was to suffer from changing objectives and purposes, what is now known as 'mission creep', and confused command and control arrangements between London, Delhi and commanders in the field; this confusion helped to bring about the disaster at Kut.

Already, the contingent's political officer, Sir Percy Cox, was recommending an advance to Baghdad to the Viceroy of India, including in his telegram:

...Turkish troops recently engaged with us were completely panic-stricken and very unlikely to oppose us again ... Effect

Sir Percy Cox. (Graves)

of the recent defeat has been very great, and if advance is made before it wears off and while the cool season lasts Baghdad will in all probability fall into our hands very easily[9] ... After earnest consideration of the arguments for and against I find it difficult to see how we can well avoid taking over Baghdad.[10]

Lieutenant-General Barrett approved the telegram, but Force 'D' was certainly not equipped for anything like this ambitious aspiration and the Official History stated that the idea 'was at that time obviously beyond our military capacity and offered no strategical advantage.'[11] This suggestion was rejected by the India Office in London, but a move forty miles further up the Tigris, at its junction with the River Euphrates, to Qurna was recommended, despite the objections of Lord Crewe, Secretary of State of India.

Qurna

Qurna (or Kurnah/Kurna) was captured on 9 December 1914 and it was felt that the Shatt-al-Arab waterway was more secure as a result. A small brigade-size force – supported by the fire from two warships and a mix of five armed river steamers and launches – succeeded in capturing over 1,000 men and seven guns. The advance had been vindicated and, once again, it seemed that Turkish weakness had been confirmed.

As debate began as to what should happen next, General Barrett, the Force commander, was superseded by General Sir John Nixon in April 1915, as the occupying force expanded its size to army corps level. The Allied army's main elements were now based on three main formations:

• The 6th Division recently placed under command of Major-General Charles Townshend, who would end up surrendering his besieged force at Kut.
• The newly formed 12th Division under Major-General George Gorringe, who would later attempt to relieve Townshend at Kut.
• The 6th Cavalry Brigade commanded by Major-General Sir Charles Melliss VC, who was also to be in the besieged town.

However, although the force was increasing its strength to over 20,000 men, the combat service support and, in particular, the medical elements were not increased enough to meet new requirements, despite the appointment of Surgeon-General H. Hathaway, instead of a colonel, to run the medical support. In fact, the Mesopotamia Commission of 1917 reported: 'We endorse the finding as regards Surgeon-General Hathaway, who in our judgement showed himself unfit for the high administrative office which he held.'[12]

Shaiba

The Turkish threat had grown in the meantime and during the period 12–14 April 1915, two Turkish divisions from Nasiriya attacked the British at Shaiba. 15,000 men were supposedly involved in the assault, along with twenty-one guns, though more recent Turkish accounts mention about 4,000 assaulting troops.[13] Shaiba is ten miles west of Basra and was held by a British force in an isolated fort cut off from Basra by the worst floods in thirty years. It was quickly reinforced by Major-General Melliss and the 30th Brigade to give the defenders about 7,000 in strength. He described his success:

General Sir John Nixon. (*The Illustrated War News*, 17 November 1915)

Major-General Charles Townshend. (Candler)

Lieutenant-General Sir George Gorringe. (Wilson)

Major-General Sir Charles Melliss. (Wilson)

Next morning, 13 April we drove the enemy back from the vicinity after ten entrenchment sorties. On 14 April, I moved out with my forces to attack the Turkish camp at Borglsiyeh, after a desperate fight lasting from 10.20 am to 5 pm. The Turkish entrenchments were carried as darkness fell, but our force was too exhausted to follow.[14]

This was a significant battle, which removed the main Turkish threat to Basra and the oil supplies. It was reported that, in this assault, there were 2,435 Turkish casualties, compared with the 1,257 British. The Turks recorded that they had lost 6,000 men killed or wounded over the three days of fighting with 700 taken prisoner.[15] Once again, commanders were convinced about the weakness of their enemy. The Turks fled ninety miles to the north-west and the Turkish commander, Suleyman Askeri Pasha, committed suicide, probably because of the setback at Shaiba and the fact that his previous Arab allies had turned against him. However, the British success had not been easily won as troops struggled through the waterlogged landscape and extremely hot conditions. It had depended on some luck, as the Turks had only withdrawn after mistaking the movement of supply carts and mules towards the battle as a major reinforcement. There was also a glimpse of the considerable weakness in the Allied medical support system, which was to plague the early years of the campaign and, particularly, Major-General Townshend's later advance towards Baghdad. The flooding meant that wheeled ambulances were inoperative and stretcher bearers struggled through waterlogged areas in order to reach a limited number of canoes used for casualty evacuation.

Ahwaz

A second threat to the oil came from an enemy force to the north of Basra consisting of eight Turkish battalions, 10,000 Arabs and eight guns under command of Mohammed Daghestani Pasha in the area of Ahwaz on the River Karun. Major-General Gorringe was despatched with the 6th Cavalry Brigade and 12th Division to deal with them, and after a difficult advance, again across waterlogged terrain and in hot conditions, the enemy withdrew towards Amara before contact was made. General Nixon was pleased – from his perspective, the enemy were weak, the oil was secure and there was now the opportunity to exploit his generals' successes.

Amara

The Allied advance continued in late May 1915. General Nixon had informed Major-General Townshend that Amara needed to be captured so that the British position in Mesopotamia could be secured. India did not disagree with the proposal and London supported the advance on 24 May, however, the Secretary of State required General Nixon to guarantee that Amara would be sufficiently garrisoned to avoid a successful attack by the enemy from Baghdad.

The advance began from Qurna, which was surrounded by floods. This town was reputed to be the site of the Garden of Eden, but the hot and oppressive weather conditions made it one of the least popular locations in the country: 'In the stifling heat the men were continually in a state of dripping perspiration and had no means of keeping cool or clean, for the air was full of dust and thick with flies.'[16] The objective was three miles north on the Tigris River – Turkish positions, which were also partially flooded, comprising four islands and some isolated outposts. Surprise in that environment was very difficult and Major-General Townshend, who commanded the assault, realised that any outflanking movement was impossible. The flooding,

Captain Wilfred Nunn, Royal Navy. (*The Times History of the War*)

which was to prove difficult to deal with again at Kut, was described by Captain Wilfred Nunn, Royal Navy, who helped plan the attack with the General:

The Tigris that year rose to an abnormal height. As in the days of Noah, Mesopotamia underwent another flood. Almost the entire countryside and the marshes round Qurna were covered by a great spreading sheet of shallow water, dotted here and there with the blunt tops of sandhills and the spiky heads of high reeds. On some of these sandhills and higher pieces of land the enemy had placed gun-positions. The flood-water was in many places very shallow, it is true, but the area was intersected by deep water cuts, ditches, and canals – which, incidentally, were usually invisible until you fell in. Consequently wading became impossible for troops. In fact, as I have said before there was too little water for the sailors and too much for the soldiers.[17]

'Townshend's Regatta' was born on this operation. Local canoes, known as *bellums*, were the main form of transport available, each paddled or punted by an NCO and nine soldiers, eight to fight and two to pole, and the only means by which to assault the enemy. Sixty were allotted to each battalion, 328 for the brigade carrying out the initial assault, and rehearsals were required to allow the troops to gain competency in their handling. Some bellums were armoured and mountain guns were mounted on double bellums. Other guns were placed on barges and river steamers, whilst supplies were on *dhows* or *mahelas*. This unusual 'regatta' also included four sloops (HMS *Espiegle*, *Clio*, *Odin* and *Lawrence*), three armed launches (HMS *Miner*, *Shaitan* and *Sumana*) and four 4.7 inch guns mounted in horse-boats. This was an imaginative use of resources and, as an infantry officer wrote later: 'It was certainly a bold scheme and unexpected, but for these very reasons it was entirely successful.'[18] Local Arabs were offered 400 rupees for every mine they discovered in the waterways.

The assault took place on 31 May 1915, led by battalions of the 17th Infantry Brigade, the 1st Battalion the Oxfordshire and Buckinghamshire Light Infantry on the left of the river and the 22nd Punjabis on the right. The rest of the force included the 16th Infantry Brigade and divisional troops, including 2nd Battalion the Norfolk Regiment and a mix of gunners, sappers and signallers. Major-General Townshend commanded the attack from HMS *Espiegle*. Captain Nunn commented from the same sloop as the day's battle progressed:

We lifted our fire as our troops got close, and could see them swarming up the mound. I particularly watched a big soldier who climbed on to their parapet holding his bayonet as if he were just about to select a big fat Turk to stick it into. Next appeared a row of enemy with their hands up and the position was taken.[19]

However, conditions for the troops were bad, as manoeuvring the bellums was not easy and many of them had to wade through insect ridden water to attack their objectives. Corporal C. Lowman is quoted: 'These insects and flies in Mesopotamia did not merely tickle and sting, they bit hard. Even sandflies and yet smaller insects, which no mosquito net could keep out, joined the larger beasts in their tormented attacks.'[20]

The attacks and advance were successful over the next few days, despite the gunboat *Espiegle* grounding at one point and the command of the expedition transferring to the decks of the *Comet*. Both General Nixon and Sir Percy Cox, the General's political adviser, accompanied the 'regatta' and the Turks appeared to be withdrawing and avoiding contact with Major-General Townshend's force. The successful occupation of Amara, with only limited bloodshed, was a major achievement. Through novel tactics, effective use of firepower and what could be described as 'bluffing gunboat diplomacy', Major-General Townshend forced the more numerous enemy under the command of Halim Bey to withdraw, and he seized Amara. Before reaching the town he had persuaded both the Turk and local Arabs that he had a force of 15,000 behind him. In fact, his immediate force consisted of the gunboats *Comet*, *Shaitan*, *Sumana* and the *Lewis Pelly*. On board were four marines, seventeen sailors and twelve soldiers from the Queen's Own Royal West Kent Regiment and the 1/4th Hampshires!

About 1,000 enemy troops on both banks were seen retreating north out of the town. Captain Singleton, the captain of the *Comet*, earned the Distinguished Service Order for his handling of his ship, the encouragement of the 2,000 Turks to head north and the capture of over 250 enemy soldiers. Lieutenant Palmer, another naval officer on the *Comet*, then went on with two other members of his ship and an interpreter to take the surrender of a complete Turkish battalion. At one point, over 1,000 prisoners were being held captive by the small Allied force amongst a potentially hostile population of 10,000. There was a sense of relief on the morning of 4 June when a river transport arrived with the 2nd Battalion of the Norfolk Regiment on board. As an aside, the soldiers of the West Kents and Hampshires clearly enjoyed their time onboard ship, as Captain Nunn stated that they asked to see him and 'mustered on the quarterdeck their senior

Medical bellum. (Birch Reynardson)

A mountain gun on a raft. (Birch Reynardson)

put forward the request that they might be permitted to change over from the Army to the Navy.' He suspected 'that they preferred yachting on the river to foot-slogging in the desert!'[21]

In all, about 2,000 prisoners, twelve field guns and five naval guns had been taken, whilst the advancing force only lost four killed and twenty-four injured throughout the advance from Qurna to Amara. In addition, two enemy boats were sunk and six boats and ten barges captured. Major-General Townshend had displayed audacity and initiative in this operation and had been lucky. He had outwitted the enemy and boosted the confidence of his subordinates both in their capability and his. It is easy to forget these successes in the light of the later surrender of Kut and the criticism heaped on Major-General Townshend. Soldiers can put up with a commander's eccentricities if they know that he is a winner and he had proved his credentials during this engagement. Even the critical Mesopotamia Commission Report recorded: 'As a military operation this action was audaciously planned and well timed, and it deserves high praise, as it achieved great objects with comparatively small loss of life.'[22] At this point Major-General Townshend leaves the scene for sick leave in India, suffering from fever.

Nasiriya

The next objective, Nasiriya (or Nasiriyeh) was twenty-eight miles west from Qurna, up the River Euphrates. Major-General Gorringe was to lead the 12th Division in this advance, the aim being again to secure approaches to Basra, as this was seen as an exposed left flank. The objectives included the town of Suk es Sheyukh en route to Nasiriya, and the suppression of strong local tribes.

General Nixon was keen to secure Nasiriya on the Euphrates and had also suggested to India the seizing of Kut on the Tigris, otherwise a British garrison based at Nasiriya could be threatened by Turks based at Kut. Sir Percy Cox also supported a move to Nasiriya in order to secure the heartland of the Arab Muntafiq group of tribes. Sir Harry Beauchamp-Duff, Commander-

Armoured Protection for Bellums. (Birch Reynardson)

in-Chief India, Lord Hardinge, the Viceroy, and Austen Chamberlain, the Secretary of State for India, were against the taking of Kut at this stage, as the proposed seizure of the town was seen as a commitment too far. However, India approved this advance on 22 June, without receiving the Secretary of State's approval. This was evidence of potential 'mission creep', as each new objective was suggested by General Nixon in order to secure the previous captured objective. His argument for the seizing of Nasiriya was flawed; it was not possible for the Turks to proceed south from Kut by boat, as the waters were so low on the connecting river, the Shatt al Hai, for most of the year. The argument against further advances was expressed by an accompanying political officer of the time, Captain Arnold Wilson, who was on Major-General Gorringe's staff: 'Basra was easily defendable, and once we held Amara and Qurna the narrow strip of land along the Tigris was unlikely to be the scene of serious fighting.'[23]

Major-General Gorringe's force was based on 30th Indian Brigade under command of Major-General Melliss, two batteries of guns, various divisional troops and, similar to Major-General Townshend's advance, a 'regatta' of boats. The water was lower than it had been on the Tigris. Smaller river-steamers were employed: the *Shushan*, with Captain Nunn on board, and the *Massoudieh* and *Muzaffri* armed with re-distributed guns. Three other river-steamers carried the troops and each carried two 18-pounder guns on their decks and there were two more tugs, some towing mahelas carrying stores. The mounted guns were on bellums.

At this stage of the campaign, the 12th Division had already taken about fifty per cent casualties, fought at Ahwaz and marched great distances in pursuit of the enemy for an unpopular commander nicknamed 'Blood Orange'. Major-General Gorringe proved his leadership as he personally took charge of mining operations on the waterways and, later, the author Russell Braddon wrote that:

Gorringe was the ideal man for a relentless slog. A big man, highly coloured, deeply tanned, officious and utterly without tact, he reminded those less insensitive than himself of an enormous he-goat, and allowed nothing – not Turks, Nurretin, counter attacks, casualties, swamps, Marsh Arabs or deeply entrenched redoubts – to stop him.[24]

These characteristics did not mean success, however, when he was attempting to relieve the besieged force at Kut a few months later. The same author described Major-General Melliss, who had the nickname of 'Old Blood and Thunder' as 'given to roaring like a bull when enraged; and when in doubt he attacked.'[25] Many of the British commanders in Mesopotamia appear to have been lively characters.

The *Shushan* and *Massoudieh* led the flotilla to the west of Lake Hammar on 27 June. The force would have to contend with six weeks of shallow waters, deep mud, oppressive heat of between 115 and 120 degrees Fahrenheit and aggressive local Arabs as well as the Turks. The troops were suffering from the conditions and medical facilities were inadequate, as one officer described: 'Sickness of all kinds became rife, sun-stroke and heat-stroke were common, fever and dysentery and para-typhoid – ample warning was given to those responsible of the difficulties to be expected if they should ever have to deal with the rush of a casualty list.'[26]

Suk es Sheyukh was captured on 6 July, but the main Turkish position was located about six miles south-east from Nasiriya on both sides of the River Euphrates. Approaches to the positions were marshy and any manoeuvring with the various boats was extremely difficult. The initial frontal attack on 14 July faltered with heavy casualties amongst the 24th Punjabi Infantry and there was some concern about the security of the British position. The same officer wrote that 'Probably seldom before have British, or, for that matter native, troops been required to fight under such terrible conditions of weather and climate, in a difficult country, against a resolute enemy.'[27]

Allied reinforcements arrived, including one brigade, a battery of guns and, for the first time, two Caudron/BE2C aircraft primarily available for reconnaissance. Another assault was made on 24 July. 2nd Battalion the Queen's Own Royal West Kent Regiment, leading the attack for 12th Brigade on the left bank, takes up the story:

> The bombardment opened punctually at 5 a.m. on 24 July. About 5.20 our scouts crept over our parapet and went forward to the margin of the wood, about 200 yards to the front. At 5.30 a.m. Nos 1 and 3 Companies commenced their advance, and reached the edge of the wood referred to. There they were held up, and, as the enemy's fire seemed stronger than our own, the remaining two companies were called up. The reinforcing companies gave fresh impetus to the leading line and carried them forward. In the open they could not make much ground, but on the extreme left Major Kitson led portions of Nos 3 and 4 right into the enemy's flank trench and carried it. A few moments afterwards the whole line surged forward and reached the trenches. One company of the 90th Punjab Infantry was close behind Nos 1 and 2, and took part in the close fighting in the trenches. The bayonet was brought into play in a few cases, but as a rule the enemy were either shot down at a few yards' distance or, throwing down their arms, were taken prisoners.[28]

The battalion began the attack with seventeen officers and 470 other ranks. They suffered thirty-three per cent casualties, similar statistics to the 1/4th Hampshires and the 17th Sapper Company. Both sides, British and Turk, had begun with about 4,500 men each, but the British had over twenty more guns and made effective use of them from their boats. 1,000 Turks had been captured with 2,000 killed and wounded. Total British casualties were 104 killed and 429 wounded.[29]

The 30th Brigade had assaulted on the right bank of the river, once the parallel initial assault had begun. The 1/4th Hampshires and the 2/7th Gurkhas succeeded in driving the Turks out

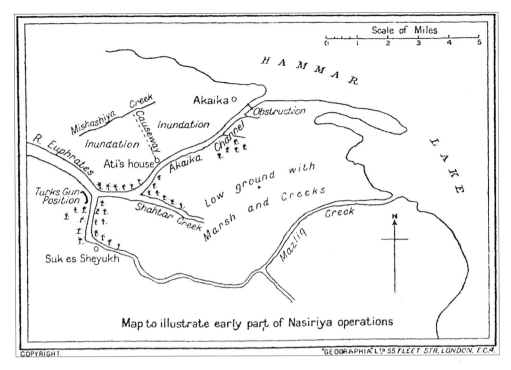

Early part of Nasiriya Operations. (Nunn)

2nd Battalion the Queen's Own Royal West Kent Regiment at Nasiriya, 24 July. (*Queen's Own Gazette*)

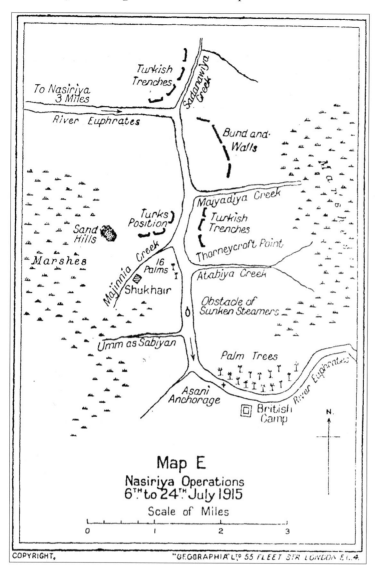

Map E
Nasiriya Operations
6TH to 24TH July 1915
Scale of Miles

Nasiriya Operations,
6–24 July 1915. (Nunn)

of those trenches, supported by the 67th Punjabis and fire from the *Shushan, Massoudieh* and the *Muzaffri.* The fighting all took place with temperatures at 110 degrees Fahrenheit in the extremely humid shade. The Turks eventually withdrew north in the afternoon and Nasiriya was occupied on 25 July 1915. However, British medical treatment and evacuation procedures were seen, again, to be wanting, as Captain Wilson's account explained:

> After the battle, as after the preceding engagement, I spent some hours assisting in the evacuation of the wounded. I was horrified at what I saw, for at every point it was clear that the shamefully bad arrangements arose from bad staff work on the part of the medical authorities, rather than from inherent difficulties. The wounded were crowded on board to lie on iron decks that had not been cleaned since horses and mules had stood on them for a week. There were few mattresses.[30]

The poor state of medical support was not to be rectified by the time of the siege of Kut.

The Move to Kut

General Nixon was keen to push on to Kut and make the most of the Turkish defeats. He was supported by Sir Percy Cox. Consequently, on 27 July, a telegram was sent from the Viceroy to the Secretary of State saying that 'Now that Nasiriya has been occupied the occupation of Kut-el-Amara is considered by us to be a strategic necessity.'[31] London was not convinced, because of the long fragile lines of communication and the administrative challenges, combined with the weather conditions and the health and lack of troops. Lord Hardinge, the Viceroy, supported General Nixon and the Secretary of State was persuaded to support the advance. Approval was given on 23 August and Baghdad appeared to be in their sights. A weak Turkish division was reported to be at Kut (the 35th Division) with one withdrawing to the town from Nasiriya (the 38th Division); another enemy division was in Baghdad (the 45th Division). Success would offset the increasingly depressing messages coming from the Dardanelles. Nasiriya, which was situated in a useful position to defend the Basra vilayet, would be protected whilst the advance would separate the Turks from their allies, the Arab Beni Lam tribe. The British position in Mesopotamia would be consolidated.

The Turkish Army

The Anglo-Indian force had achieved great successes so far in the campaign, though the enemy had been limited in strength. A number of measures were being put in place by the Turkish Army to rectify this situation, though their effect would only begin to be felt at Ctesiphon in November 1915. A new Mesopotamia-based Turkish Army, the 6th, was formed in April, based on the existing XII and XVIII Corps and a new commander was appointed – Nurretin Pasha (or Nur ud Din Pasah). Nurretin was not staff-trained, but had an impressive intellect and a great deal of practical operational experience. He had fought in the Ottoman-Greek War of 1897, dealt with guerrillas in Macedonia in 1902 and served in a counter-insurgency campaign in the Yemen in 1911–13. Following divisional command, he had: 'arrived in mid-June to take over a badly battered army.'[32] Initially, Nurretin had to rely on what remained of the 35th and 38th Turkish Divisions, about 7,000 men. However, the 45th Division would be available at Ctesiphon and two more experienced war-fighting divisions from the Caucasus, the 51st and 52nd Divisions, would arrive in due course.

Townshend's Doubts

On sick leave in India, Major-General Townshend discovered that the Foreign Department and Sir Beauchamp-Duff, the Commander-in-Chief, were against another advance unless more forces were available. On 8 August 1915 he wrote to a friend, General Sir James Wolfe Murray in England, expressing a number of concerns about an advance to Kut.

> I believe I am to advance from Amarah on Kut-al-Amara directly I get back to my division … The question is where we are going to

Nurretin. (Braddon)

stop in Mesopotamia? I stayed with the Viceroy last month, but could not get anything out of him as regards our policy in Mesopotamia … We have certainly not got enough troops to make certain of taking Baghdad … We can take no risks of a defeat in the East. Imagine a retreat from Baghdad and the consequent instant rising of the Arabs of the whole country behind us, to say nothing of the certain rise in that case of the Persians and probably of the Afghans in consequence … I consider that we ought to hold what we have got and not advance any more-as long as we are held up, as we undoubtedly are, in the Dardanelles. All these offensive operations in secondary theatres are dreadful errors in strategy: the Dardanelles, Egypt, Mesopotamia, East Africa![33]

The following day he received a letter from a friend in the Foreign and Political Department at Simla, India. This included the comments:

There is no doubt that there are many good military reasons for seizing Kut, and politically I think there are no objections. But I entirely agree that we should be very careful before we go any further. I do not think there is an idea at present of an advance to Baghdad, and unless the forces at our disposal were more than adequate for the purpose, this Department would very strongly deprecate such a move.[34]

Major-General Townshend lunched with Sir Beauchamp Duff on 10 August. He was told that he would probably advance to Kut on his return to Mesopotamia, though London had not yet sanctioned the proposal suggested by General Nixon and supported by Sir Percy Cox. Major-General Townshend said that he could take Kut, but:

It was not for me, I said, to point out to him the grave risks of continuing the strategic offensive with inadequate forces and with no troops on the lines of communication behind me. He fully agreed with me, and said with emphasis: 'Not one inch, Townshend, shall you go beyond Kut-el-Amara unless I make you up to adequate strength'. I mentioned that I ought to have fully an army corps to take Baghdad and hold it.[35]

These three quotations reveal a great deal about Major-General Townshend, who later was blamed for the situation at Kut. He had identified the limitations of the army in Mesopotamia and was not happy to be over-stretched; reinforcements were required for victory. However, he was the victim of his previous successes along the Tigris – the advance was to continue.

Before travelling to Amara, Major-General Townshend told General Nixon that 'If I routed the Turks in the battle and stampeded them, as at Qurna, I might follow them into Baghdad. That is, if they were well on the run.' General Nixon offered to enter the city with him and Sir Percy Cox mentioned that: 'If I went into Baghdad it would have almost the same political significance and importance as if I were to enter Constantinople. The news would go through all Asia.'[36] There was quite an incentive for Major-General Townshend to succeed after his form so far and his superiors were expecting more of the same.

Es Sinn: The Battle of Kut

6th Division concentrated at Ali-al-Gharbi in early September 1915, whilst Major-General Gorringe's 12th Division became responsible for lines of communication between Amara and Kut. By 25 September, Major-General Townshend's 6th Division was at Sunnaiyat and had been reinforced by two more battalions. He now had at his disposal about '11,000 rifles, 28 guns and

40 machine-guns. The Turks were estimated at approximately 6,000 with 38 guns.'[37] These were the 35th Division with six infantry battalions on the right southern bank of the Tigris and the 38th Division with six battalions on the left northern bank. They had four battalions and some cavalry in reserve. However, according to Erickson's research: 'most of these soldiers were local Arabs, who had been drafted into the Turkish Army, and their morale was not high.'[38]

On the morning of 27 September, the assault began at 'Horse Shoe Marsh'. The advance and fight were difficult; navigation proved tricky, whilst the ground was marshier than expected and the Turks were dug in with excellent fields of fire between the Suwaikiya (or Suwacha/Suwachi) and Suwada Marshes and had built a boom across the Tigris. Also, the attacking forces were always going to have difficulty engaging their targets accurately: 'Such mistakes were constantly occurring owing to the difficulties of observation, for, in addition to mirages, there was nearly always a sand-storm blowing which made it almost impossible to see any distance.'[39]

This was a problem throughout the campaign and would hamper the progress of the later Kut Relief Force. Of note, in this battle, was a brave bayonet charge by the 104th Indian Rifles; 111 Turks and one of their officers were captured, and the attempt by Lieutenant-Commander Edgar Cookson, Royal Navy, to destroy the boom – he was awarded the Victoria Cross post-humously for this action. The three main Turkish redoubts had to be taken by similar assaults. The enemy had been driven from their positions by the end of the following day and the 18th Infantry Brigade was ordered to pursue. It reached Aziziya (or Aziziyeh), over sixty miles beyond Kut, on 5 October. By that time, the Turks had lost 4,000 men compared with the 1,230 British troops, but they were regrouping and had not been routed.

The pursuit was not successful, mainly due to a two-day delay at Kut caused by ships becoming stuck in the mud of an extremely shallow Tigris. Also, Major-General Townshend was not impressed by the lack of initiative displayed by two Indian cavalry regiments, who were unable to make contact with the retreating Turks because the Sikh and Hindu cavalrymen were delayed. They had not been fed and would not use Arab cooking pots; he did not dispute their valour, but was frustrated by the fact that their culture had limited their effectiveness in that situation. Even today, when multi-national operations are the norm, commanders have to take into consideration national and cultural idiosyncrasies before allocating tasks. On this occasion, a British cavalry regiment may have been more effective in this pursuit role, but none was available.

There is no doubt that this battle, known as the 'Battle of Kut', was a significant victory for Major-General Townshend's division. The initial feint had deceived the enemy, who thought that the attack was taking place on a different flank and the British columns' movement at night and the 'turning manoeuvre' had contributed to the enemy's surprise. Major-General Townshend, never an immodest commander, later stated:

> The Battle of Kut-el-Amara can be said to have been one of the most important in the history of the British

Lieutenant-Commander Edgar Cookson, Royal Navy. (Wilson)

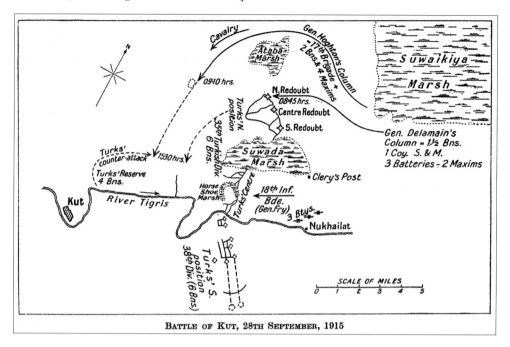

BATTLE OF KUT, 28TH SEPTEMBER, 1915

Battle of Kut, 28 September 1915. (Mesopotamia Study)

Army in India. There had been nothing of its magnitude either in the Afghan War or the Indian Mutiny, for it was fought against troops equally well armed and of equal numbers to ourselves. In addition, we ejected them from a very strong and up-to-date position commanding ground as flat and as open as a billiard-table with nothing to check their fire-sweep.[40]

Captain Wilson, the political officer, expressed with his informed hindsight:

Had General Townshend's plans been successfully developed on the lines laid down by him, the main portion, if not the whole, of the Turkish force then in Mesopotamia would have been captured or destroyed and Baghdad might have been entered without further resistance.

The failure or inability of the British forces to pursue the enemy was interpreted by him as 'a turning point, perhaps decisive, in the whole of the campaign.'[41]

However, General Nixon's army was spread thinly in garrisons throughout the occupied country and he was short of modern equipment, ammunition, transport and combat service support troops. At Kut, he now had 6th Division with its three infantry brigades, mixture of artillery, signals and engineers, eight cavalry squadrons and one battery of horse artillery. This force amounted to about 10,000 personnel, which was less than the Turks in the Kut and Baghdad area, yet the campaign's successes so far encouraged General Nixon to advance further.

More Doubts

Baghdad was still another 213 miles by water from Kut, and there were doubts in both Delhi and London that a British force in Baghdad would be able to rebuff a Turkish counter-attack. The

British troops were tired, suffering from the intense heat and inadequate logistic support, Turkish reinforcements were reported to be moving towards the area and the long lines of communication were fragile. Interestingly, the German General Colmar Von Der Goltz, who was a Field Marshal in the Turkish Army, becoming the overall commander besieging Kut a few months later, had written in 1899:

> The lines of communication should be made secure before everything. The longer they are, the more difficult they are to guard, and the more vulnerable do they become. It is easier for the enemy to intercept them, and more difficult also for us to forward supplies to our army by them. Advances along very extended lines of operations, which render similar lines of communications necessary, are therefore always productive of trouble.[42]

He goes on to refer to Napoleon's march on Moscow – an historic event well-known by Major-General Townshend, who was a much-publicised student of Napoleon. Even back in England, Field Marshal Horatio Kitchener, Secretary of State for War, believed that a march on Baghdad 'could be made with less risk, less cost and equal value later on.'[43]

The Dorsets at the Battle of Kut-al-Amara, 28 September 1915. (*The Times History of the War*)

Political reasons for success supported General Nixon's aspirations and outweighed other military advice. Sir Percy Cox's biography acknowledged that 'Cox had never disguised his belief that the occupation of Basra logically entailed the capture and permanent occupation of Baghdad, if the Arabs of Iraq were to give the British any large measure of support against the Turks.' It is also pointed out that 'In any case it was not his business to give advice or express opinions on a purely military problem.' However, this latter comment could be described as a 'cop out', as it was written in hindsight.[44]

To his credit, Major-General Townshend did, again, express concerns to General Nixon about a move towards Baghdad. He wrote in his diary, on 3 October: 'The Army commander does not seem to realise the weakness and danger of his lines of communications.'[45] He also wrote in his appreciation of the situation that 'a defeat would mean possibly a great disaster, which would shake the stability of India, and anyone advocating such a step would show in my opinion that he was utterly ignorant of the art of war.'[46] He sent a telegram to General Nixon on the same day, from Aziziya, which included the comment:

> Should it not be considered politically advisable by the Government to occupy Baghdad at present on account of the doubtful situation at the Dardanelles, and the possibility of our small force being driven out of Baghdad by strong forces from Anatolia, which would compel us to retire down a long line of communications (Baghdad to the sea is some 400 miles), teeming with Arabs, at present more or less hostile, whose hostility would become active on hearing of our retreat, then I consider that on all military grounds we should consolidate our position at Kut.[47]

He goes on to say that two divisions, not just his one, would be required to seize Baghdad and that he had a duty to warn General Nixon of his rashness. In addition, he still had in his mind the comments made by the Commander-in-Chief in India a few months previously which had supported his view that many more troops were required to secure the city.

General Nixon responded to the telegram on the same day. He believed that the Turkish force was 'inferior' both in strength and morale to the 6th Division and he attached four more squadrons of cavalry and a battery of guns to Major-General Townshend's command. He also stated that the Turkish position, reported near Ctesiphon, was not that strong. He thought that he would be better placed to defend the Allied position against Turkish reinforcements from Baghdad rather than from current positions. Major-General Townshend commented: 'It seemed to me that it was useless to try to argue any longer.'[48]

His force was given six weeks to prepare for the next advance from Aziziya, as debate and appreciations continued about the merits of the move. London had set up a war committee to consider the next stage in this campaign and General Nixon informed Austen Chamberlain that forces were sufficient to capture Baghdad, but that an extra division and a cavalry regiment would be needed to defend it. No mention was made about the limitations of transport.[49] The strength of the Turkish Army, commanded by Nurretin, and its speed of reinforcement was consistently underestimated and, consequently, the occupation of Baghdad was recommended. There were other strategic considerations. In India, the Punjab was fragile and there were new concerns about Afghanistan. Both London and Delhi had seen impressive victories in Mesopotamia and wanted the campaign to end quickly. A successful occupation of Baghdad was appealing at a time when, elsewhere, the War was not going well. General Nixon was authorised to order the advance to Baghdad on 24 October 1915.

Ctesiphon, Umm-al-Tubal and the Withdrawal to Kut

The 6th Division won a small engagement at Kutuniya (or Kutunie) and then advanced to Zor, concentrating at Lajj on 20 November. News had arrived that 30,000 Turkish troops were marching from Anatolia to Mesopotamia, under Halil Bey, and that General Von Der Goltz was taking charge of the Turkish forces in the country. The enemy at Ctesiphon, which was only eighteen miles south-east of Baghdad, were dug in on two main lines of defensive positions and were estimated at 11,000; in fact they had 16,000 to 18,000 troops there. For the first time, they had been able to reinforce their depleted 35th and 38th Divisions with the 45th Division. In addition, the newly-arrived and combat experienced 51st Division was in reserve. This was the first time that the Turks had secured a significant advantage in numbers. Colonel William Beach, then serving as an intelligence officer, wrote in 1924:

> Thus, at Ctesiphon, although the Turkish order of battle was foretold with almost complete accuracy … the strengths of these newly-arrived formations were much in excess of those of their predecessors and the personnel of almost immeasurably greater individual value.[50]

The British force consisted of 14,000 troops, thirty-five guns (some of which were on six supporting ships) and five airplanes.[51] In logistic support, it had 1,000 mules, 620 camels, 660 carts, 240 donkeys, 5 river transport steamers and 2 hospital ships. These assets could cope, in theory, with 1,500 casualties.[52] However, there was no reserve available to support the isolated 6th Division. Major-General Townshend was not happy with the quality of Indian reinforcements at this time and wrote about: 'a widespread unwillingness [by the Indians] to advance against the holy place of Selman Pak, the tomb of a devoted servant, [the barber], of the prophet [Mohammed], at Ctesiphon.'[53] Captain Wilson disputed the General's comment about 'widespread unwillingness', though he acknowledged that one Indian battalion was sent back to Basra because of its high rate of desertion.[54] Also, beri-beri had decimated one British unit based

The arch at Ctesiphon. (Moberly)

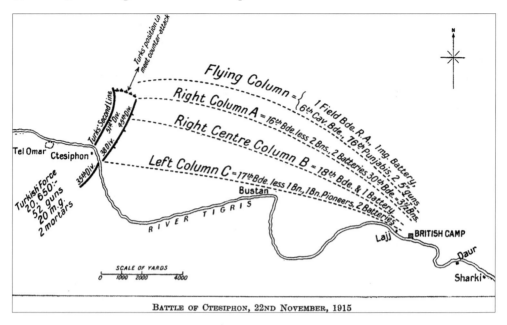

Battle of Ctesiphon, 22 November 1915. (Mesopotamia Study)

at Aziziya. Relative strengths and capabilities were, therefore, not good from Major-General Townshend's point of view and he realised that he could only win the next battle by 'exploiting the principle of economy of force' with minimum forces attacking part of the enemy's defences, whilst employing 'Principal Mass' to his flank and rear.[55]

The Battle of Ctesiphon, called 'Pistupon' as only the English soldier could simplify foreign place-names, began on 22 November 1915 with a British attack in three columns on the left bank of the Tigris. It followed another night advance in order to surprise the enemy. Casualties were extremely heavy on both sides, particularly amongst British commanders of Indian units – for example, at the end of the battle, the 110th Mahrattas had only one officer standing. Forward positions, including the apex of the enemy position, known as 'Vital Point' or 'VP' by the British and Strong Point 11 by the Turks, were taken, but many units gained little ground and the Allied force regrouped about 5,000 yards east of the ancient Ctesiphon Arch.

The Turks partially withdrew to the River Diala (or Diyala) having suffered double the casualties of the British, but then launched an unsuccessful counter-attack during the night of the 23rd. However, with further casualties, Major-General Townshend withdrew to Lajj, reaching there in the early morning of the 26th only to hear from aerial reconnaissance reports that the enemy probably numbered '12,000 rifles and 400 sabres'.[56] The evacuation of wounded, again, was difficult: 'The medical personnel were insufficient, stores were inadequate, and means of transport insufficient.'[57] Other comment was: 'The four field ambulances available were equipped to deal with 400 casualties: they had to cope that day with almost ten times that number.'[58]

Major-General Townshend claimed in his book, *My Campaign in Mesopotamia*, that he would have 'swept the Turks into the Tigris' if he had been equipped with another brigade and that 'victory was slipping from my grasp for the want of a few troops.'[59] He may have been right, but his memoirs were written after the War at a time when he was fighting for his reputation. His communiqué to British and Indian troops sent at the time stated: 'You have added a brilliant page to the glorious battle roll of the Army in India, and you will be proud to tell them at home that you fought at the Battle of Ctesiphon.'[60] The reason stated for the withdrawal was to be in a better position for the re-supply of food and the reception of reinforcements, which were expected soon. What Townshend did not know was that 'Nurretin was equally discouraged and was also considering withdrawal' after such heavy losses.[61] Surprisingly – even after their recent 4,000 casualties, which had particularly cut down the infantry and their officers – morale in the 6th Division was still high.

The decision was made to retire to Aziziya, passing through Zor and Kutuniya, and on 28 November it was decided to withdraw to Kut via Umm-al-Tubal. On 1 December, 6th Division attacked the 12,000-strong Turkish force that was now pursuing them and succeeded in forcing them to retreat. In particular, the British artillery, coupled with the fire from the gunboats, wreaked havoc amongst the enemy, inflicting heavy casualties on the Turkish 45th and 51st Divisions. Unfortunately, the ships *Comet* and *Firefly* were put out of action and had to be abandoned. In this engagement, the Turkish XIIIth Army Corps, under command of Nurretin, lost 748 killed compared with the thirty-seven British fatal casualties.

It can be argued that at both Ctesiphon and Umm-al-Tubal, Major-General Townshend's division had won tactical pyrrhic victories, but it was forced to withdraw in an operational failure. As an observer wrote: 'It seemed that Ctesiphon was a great victory; but bought at a price.'[62] From the Turkish point of view, they had achieved a significant victory and succeeded in stopping the Anglo-Indian advance through Mesopotamia at Ctesiphon. Nurretin's defensive position had been strong, he had manoeuvred his reserve at the decisive point in the battle and his artillery had performed exceptionally well.

Townshend's force was exhausted and as he reached Kut on 3 December 1915, his strength was only '1,305 sabres, 39 guns and 7,411 bayonets.'[63] He had suffered nearly fifty per cent casualties and each of his brigades was down to battalion strength. However, he had kept the Advanced Guard of the Turkish 6th Army at bay for ninety miles, captured and retained 1,200 prisoners and kept his force in good order, despite inadequate supplies of food or water – what he later called: 'an honourable retreat.'[64]

The Decision to Stand at Kut

The 6th Division was tired, hungry and thirsty. They had just marched forty-four miles in thirty-six hours and were in need of a rest. The British would have to delay a Turkish advance on Basra somewhere and it was optimistically anticipated that reinforcements – in the shape of Major-General Sir George Younghusband's 28th Brigade from Egypt and an additional two Indian divisions from France – should be able to reach Kut within a month. These were some of the factors that had to be considered by Major-General Townshend during the first few days of December 1915. He was also aware that there were large amounts of supplies and ammunition stockpiled in Kut, in preparation for an Allied push towards Baghdad, which should not be lost to the enemy and he did not want the prestige of his force to be further damaged by successive retreats.

A debate about the pros and cons of staying put in the town had already begun on 1 December when the acting commander of the town, Brigadier-General J. Rimington, delivered the message that it would be difficult to

… make an entrenched defensive position covering Kut which cannot be turned. Enemy will certainly surround us in a very confined camp and will hold us with a small force while he will occupy Es-Sinn position against our reinforcements. Alternative would be to retire on Es-Sinn.[65]

Townshend was also told that there were some boats which could help the withdrawal. Brigadier-General Rimington reiterated his concerns about defending Kut, with hindsight, in an article in *The Army Quarterly* magazine of 1923. He mentioned that Townshend had, wrongly in his view, put political and strategic factors before the Brigadier-General's military judgement. He left, 'knowing that all these fine fellows were destined to undergo a rigorous siege, especially as, to my mind, the future looked very black.'[66] Rimington thought that a defensive position at Es Sinn would have been more beneficial and that a withdrawal to that location would have been successful:

> In the result, the view given in my telegram was amply justified, as the enemy closed the neck of
> the peninsula with a semicircle of trenches, held by a small portion of his Army, and from that time
> Townshend was sealed up as surely as the Genie in the jar of the Arabian Nights tales.[67]

He also wrote, 'It can never be sound to shut oneself up in a tight hole, when any other course is available, even though the most definite promise of relief has been received.'[68] However, he does not blame Townshend for the decision. Instead, he identifies the commander and his staff at fault for not seeing 'the bigger picture' and failing to provide better direction to their divisional commander. Despite contrary views, once he had considered the state of his troops, the limited mobility of the force, the possibility of being overwhelmed in a weaker defensive position at Es Sinn and the strategic position of Kut securing a main route to Basra, Townshend said that he would stay and defend the town.

On 3 December, Major-General Townshend wrote in his diary: 'I mean to defend Kut as I did Chitral.'[69] (The General had successfully defended the town of Chitral, in the North-West Frontier region of India in 1895. (See Appendix V)) He informed General Nixon of his decision and mentioned that he had plenty of ammunition and a month's rations for British troops and two month's rations for Indian personnel. This message generated a quick response:

> The army commander is glad to hear of your decision, and is convinced that your troops will
> continue to show the same spirit in the defence as they have shown throughout your operations.
> Reinforcements will be pushed up to you with every possible speed.[70]

Morale was high, General Nixon had provided his blessing and optimism reigned. Major-General Townshend issued a communiqué to his troops:

> I intend to defend Kut-al-Amara and not to retire any further. Reinforcements are being sent at
> once from Basra to relieve us. The honour of our mother country and the Empire demands that we
> all work heart and soul in the defence of this place. We must dig in deep and dig in quickly, and then
> the enemy's shells will do little damage. We have ample food and ammunition, but commanding
> officers must husband the ammunition and not throw it away uselessly. The way you have managed
> to retire some 80 or 90 miles under the very noses of the Turks is nothing short of splendid, and
> speaks eloquently for the courage and discipline of this force.'[71]

The scene was set for the Siege of Kut.

Notes

1. Published in the *Basra Times*, 25 May 1916 and Wilson (1930) p.128.
2. Dixon (1976) p.95.
3. Evans (1926) p.134.
4. Graves (1941) p.175.
5. Ibid p.176.
6. Blaxland (1969) p.442.
7. For a detailed analysis of Turkish strength and capabilities during the First World War, two books by American Lieutenant-Colonel Edward J. Erickson are excellent references. They are the only detailed analyses published in English and one is endorsed by the Chief of the Turkish General Staff. See Bibliography.
8. Erickson (2007) p.68.
9. Quoted in Wilcox (2006) p.13.
10. Graves (1941) p.182. 22 November telegraph from Cox to Viceroy.
11. Moberly (1924) p.1.
12. Mesopotamia Commission (1917) p.93.
13. Erickson (2001) p.110.
14. Neave (1937) p.8.
15. Figures from Erickson (2001) p.110.
16. Neave (1937) p.11.
17. Nunn (2007 Reprint) p.99.
18. Birch Reynardson (1919) p.140.
19. Nunn (2007 Reprint) p.104.
20. Neave (1937) p.16.
21. Nunn (2007 Reprint) p.122.
22. Mesopotamia Commission Report (1917) p.18.
23. Wilson (1930) p.52.
24. Braddon (1969) p.51.
25. Ibid p.51.
26. Birch Reynardson (1919) p.164.
27. Ibid p.182.
28. Quoted from author unnamed short *History of the Queen's Own (Royal West Kent Regiment)* p.20.
29. Statistics from Wilson (1930) p.60.
30. Ibid p.60.
31. Mesopotamia Commission (1917) p.18.
32. Erickson (2007) p.75.
33. Townshend (1920) p.84 and 85.
34. Sherson (1928) p.269.
35. Townshend (1920) p.86.
36. Ibid p.91–92 (both quotations).
37. Figures from *The Campaign of the British Army in Mesopotamia* (1930) p.26.
38. Erickson (2001) p.112.
39. Birch Reynardson (1919) p.197.
40. Townshend (1920) p.121.
41. Wilson (1930) p.82.
42. Von Der Goltz (1899) p.105.
43. Arthur (1920) Vol III, p.301.
44. Graves (1941) p.195.
45. Townshend (1920) p.124.
46. Ibid p.125.
47. Ibid p.124–125.
48. Ibid p.130.
49. Wilson (1930) p.83.
50. Moberly (1924) p.537.
51. Figures from Nunn (2007 reprint) p.168.
52. Figures from *The Campaign of the British Army in Mesopotamia* (1930) p.31.
53. Townshend (1920) p.143.
54. Wilson (1930) p.84.
55. Townshend (1920) p.167.
56. Figures from *The Campaign of the British Army in Mesopotamia* (1930) p.33.
57. Nunn (2007 Reprint) p.175.
58. Wilson (1930) p.86.
59. Townshend (1920) p.176.
60. Ibid p.185.
61. Erickson (2007) p.76.
62. Birch Reynardson (1919) p.263.
63. Figures from *The Campaign of the British Army in Mesopotamia* (1930) p.34. The Quetta Report states 1,505 sabres p.227.
64. Townshend (1920) p.200.
65. Ibid p.198.
66. Rimington (1923) p.22.
67. Ibid p.23.
68. Rimington (1923) p.26.
69. Sherson (1928) p.297.
70. Townshend (1920) p.200.
71. Ibid p.212–3.

Chapter Two

KUT

We arrived at the unanimous opinion that, although from a political point of view the further ahead that our front was, the better for stability among the tribes behind it, yet from a purely military point of view Kut bend was a death-trap …

Sir Percy Cox[72]

The Town

The small peninsula of Kut-al-Amara was about two miles long and one mile wide – a horse-shoe-shaped feature along the Tigris facing south-east. Initially, the Official History provides an almost romantic description of a town that consisted mainly of over 600 mud and brick houses, animal dung and sewerage running along the streets: 'In its south-western portion lies the small town of Kut, flanked on either side by palm groves, fruit orchards and the remains of former extensive vegetable gardens.'[73] However, it does go on to state that 'the whole place was indescribably filthy, owing to the insanitary habits of the inhabitants and to the accumulations of refuse and filth on the thoroughfares, the riverbanks and the immediate confines of the town'[74] and Colonel P. Hehir, 6th Division's senior medical officer, later described it as 'the most insanitary place we occupied in Mesopotamia.'[75] Major Charles Barber, another medical officer, recorded his arrival in the town, just before 6th Division's withdrawal:

> Our first impression of Kut was not a pleasing one. Approaching it from the east, almost the first thing that caught the eye was the gibbet – almost a gruesome looking object – and on the dirty, untidy portion of the bank around it, backed by an irregular row of squalid-looking, mud-coloured houses, lay a heterogeneous collection of oil tins, a decrepit native boat, some old Turkish carts, a rubbish heap, and a wireless station, with a tent or two for the operators: a veritable East End.[76]

The few best brick houses were on the west river side at Kut, as an observer wrote: 'A few brick houses on the river front and on the streets leading to it are the only civilized dwellings in the place.'[77] There was also a *Serai*, a small Turkish administrative building, with barrack square and flagstaff, a mosque with a turquoise-domed minaret, two bazaars, a sheikh's house and some wool presses.

  This was to be the home of the 6th Division for the next five months.

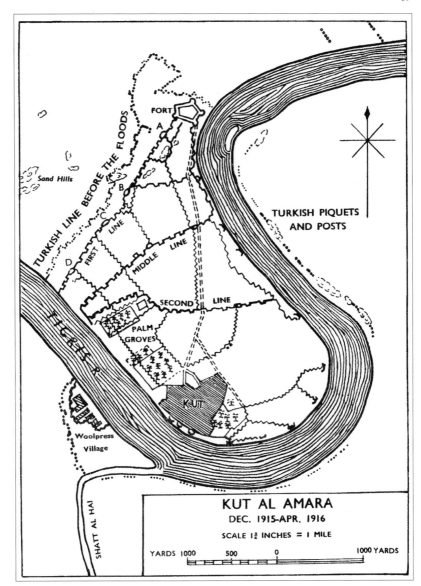

Kut – general.
(Qureshi)

The Resident Population

The population of Kut was about 7,000, comprising mainly Arabs and much smaller numbers of Jews, Sabeans[78] and Nestorian Christians. Their livelihoods were dominated by the grain trade whose traffic ran though the town on two caravan routes. On arrival of the British force, women could be seen beside mud ovens, 'winnowing or grinding their corn, cooking their 'kabaabs', which resemble thick pancakes, or playing with their grubby children.'[79]

One significant decision that Major-General Townshend had to make during the first few days of his arrival was whether he should allow the population to stay in the town; 700 'visitors' were expelled, due to the levels of food supplies, but a debate concerning the future of the remaining civilians occurred between the divisional commander, General Nixon and Sir Percy Cox. Townshend was inclined to expel the whole population, for military expedience reasons and considering his past experiences at the Chitral siege. However, Sir Percy Cox, the senior political officer, reminded him that: 'We had to remember that winter conditions prevailed and the nights were bitterly cold and it was a serious step to turn out four or five thousand people into the blue.'[80] Relief was expected, by now, within two months and it was reported to Major-General Townshend that there was enough food for the population to survive for three months. He allowed them to stay, later blaming Sir Percy Cox's intercession for this decision. Captain Arnold Wilson, the junior political officer, stated in his memoirs that Townshend never really understood how to handle the Arab population and made the error of sending Captain Gerald Leachman – the only other officer with experience of the locals – out of the town with the cavalry on 6 December: 'and in consequence had no independent political adviser of experience and adequate status whom he could consult in dealing with the Arab population.'[81] He went on to say that much of the population were thieves or in communication with the Turks. The decision to leave the population in situ was to have a significant effect on the availability of rations during the siege. With hindsight, The Quetta Report of 1923, compiled by officers of the Staff College Quetta in India, stated its view, very clearly, about the decision to keep the Arabs in Kut: 'It may have been humane to keep the Arabs in Kut and allow them to eat their own grain and ours, but when the terrible results of this solution of the problem in soldiers' lives are considered it is hoped that in a similar situation the plan adopted in Kut will be avoided at all hazards.'[82]

Major-General Townshend later revealed in his book that he was anxious about the local population and knew that they were in contact with the enemy. He took some of their prominent personalities into custody and told the inhabitants that he would shoot them if there was any sign of treachery. To stop looting he made an example of twelve men who had been caught stealing by putting them on trial and having them shot, as he put it: '*pour encourager des autres.*'[83]

The Quetta Report of 1923, further stated that:

In all sieges there are four main considerations for a commander –
(1) Defences,
(2) Food Supply,

On the banks of the Tigris at Kut. (*The Illustrated War News*, 9 February 1916)

(3) Ammunition Supply and

(4) High morale and good health of the troops.[84]

These four headings are useful to help set the scene when describing the situation in Kut at the beginning of December 1915.

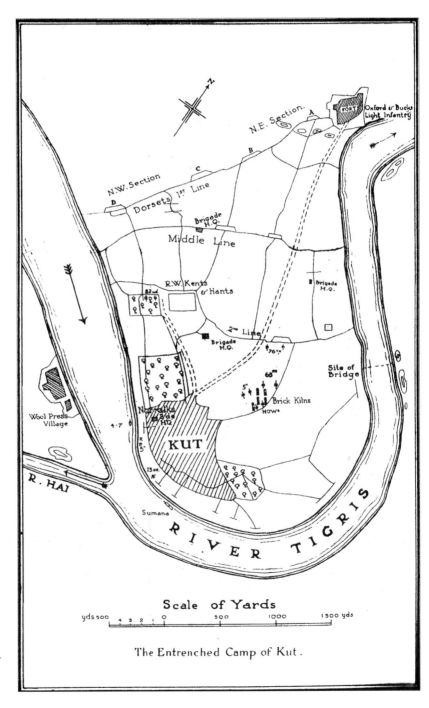

The Entrenched Camp of Kut.

Kut – friendly
dispositions.
(Townshend)

The Defences

Kut was vulnerable, surrounded on three sides by water leaving little space for the defenders to manoeuvre, prone to flooding and an easy target for artillery. The defence became based on three existing features: the village of Yakasub or Elhan, known by the defenders as the 'Woolpress Village' on the opposite bank of the river, which included the liquorice factory; the small town at the base of the horseshoe; and the old mud fort at the neck of the peninsula. The fort was connected by a barbed wire fence to four blockhouses, which could accommodate about a dozen men each. A group of sandhills lay to the north, which were too far away to be occupied by the defenders, but ideal as cover for the enemy. The Woolpress Village was to be connected to the town by a bridge made of boats. These features provided limited protection, so the first priority for the defenders was to 'dig in' and strengthen the perimeter. Lieutenant G. Heawood, commanding Q Company of 1st Battalion the Oxfordshire and Buckinghamshire Light Infantry, commented:

> Of the next few weeks the chief memory that remains is one of digging. We seem to have dug all day and every day – in the glare of the sun, in the darkness of the night, and in the moonlight. We commenced these labours on our first afternoon, for although we were not technically surrounded for another three or four days, we prepared for the siege which was known to be inevitable.[85]

These comments could have been written by an infantryman in a defensive position today. Kut was divided into three areas of defensive responsibility, backed up by the General Reserve:

Aerial view of Kut. (IWM Q 45884)

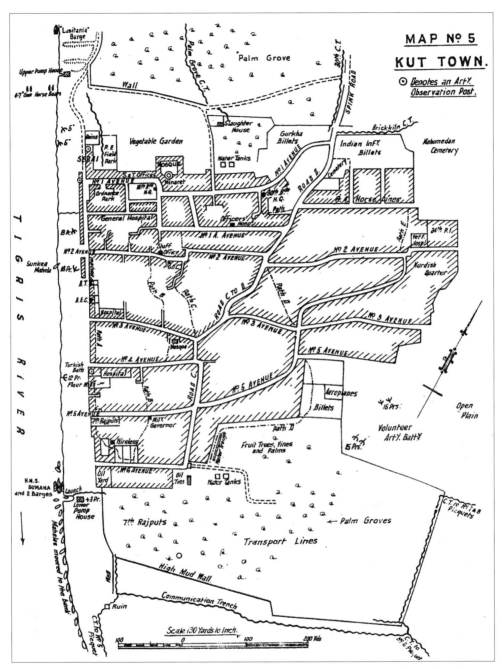

Kut town – detail. (Sandes)

• **The North-East Sector.** The 17th Infantry Brigade was responsible for this sector under command of Brigadier-General Frederick Hoghton. It included the fort, the east part of the first line and the right of the river line and second line. The fort was an easy target for the Turks throughout the siege. It was placed in the charge of Lieutenant-Colonel Walter Brown with his 103rd Mahrattas and the support of an all-arms grouping of two 15-pounders of the Volunteer Battery, the six machine-guns of Captain Charles Stockley's Maxim Battery, fifty 'bombers' of

Lieutenant-General Sir Walter Delamain. (Wilson)

the 1st Oxford and Buckinghamshire Light Infantry, the Sirmur Company of Sappers and Miners and the 119th Indian Infantry.

• **The North-West Sector.** Initially, the 16th Infantry Brigade held this sector under the command of Major-General Walter Delamain. It then rotated responsibility of the sector and General Reserve with 30th Infantry Brigade. The North-West Sector included the west part of the first line and the river line on the west as far as the left of the second line.

• **The Southern Sector.** The 18th Infantry Brigade held this sector under command of Brigadier-General William Hamilton The 110th Mahrattas and 120th Indian Infantry was responsible for the Woolpress Village under command of Major Philip Pocock. This force was supplemented, when necessary, by half a battalion of British infantry. The Southern Sector included this village on the opposite bank of the Tigris from the town, the second line and the river line south of it. Communications and re-supply were provided by the six launches and the gunboat *Sumana*; the latter also provided fire support.

• **The General Reserve.** This Reserve was provided by the 30th Infantry Brigade, under command of Major-General Sir Charles Melliss, at the beginning of the siege. Later, it rotated its responsibilities with the 16th Infantry Brigade. The Brigade was based in the north of the town at night and stationed in Kut during the day.

The bulk of the artillery was positioned 500 yards to the north-east of the town amongst some brick kilns. This included the six 18-pounders of 63rd Field Battery, two 5-inch guns of 86th Heavy Battery and the four howitzers of 1st/5th Hampshire Battery. Elsewhere, a battery was placed in the palm groves and 4.7-inch guns were put on board horseboats on the Tigris. In addition, two infantry units, the divisional and brigades' headquarters, general hospitals, field ambulances and the Indian stationary hospital were located in or near the town.

   Extra defences had to be dug to reinforce the existing obstacles and to provide protection. Initially, the 'First Line' was dug along the line of wire and the blockhouses were removed, as they provided aiming marks for the Turkish artillery. Work began on 4 December and the First Line was completed by the 15th. Four new redoubts, 'A', 'B', 'C', and 'D', were built into the First Line later. The 30th Infantry Brigade had dug the 'Second Line' by 12 December and the 'Middle Line' was finished by Christmas 1915. Trenches were dug around Woolpress Village and interconnecting trenches sprung up all over the defensive position in order to ensure some security from sniping and protected re-supply and reinforcement routes. In all, thirty miles of trenches were dug.[86] For the infantry, these trenches dominated their lives, as the History of the 1/4th Battalion of the Hampshire Regiment described:

> It is interesting to recall that A Company lived underground in open trenches and dug-outs through-
> out the whole period of the siege, a total of 145 consecutive days and nights; this was the experience,
> also, of other infantry units.[87]

It is to the credit of the defenders that, despite the moderate defensive position of Kut, the town was not taken by direct force.

Food Supply

Throughout the siege, the food supply situation was to dominate a great deal of the decision-making processes of both the besieged British, the Allied relief force and the besieging Turks. Major-General Townshend believed he had 'ample' food supplies in early December to both feed his troops and the local population, though those calculations were based on relief arriving in the town within one, then two months.

Rations were spread throughout a town that was virtually constantly under fire and, therefore, difficult to count. Theft was common and whilst grain was ground, no one seemed to know how much food was produced. The estimation of rations seemed to be inconsistent as the siege progressed. Lieutenant-General Sir Fenton Aylmer, the commander of relief forces from mid-January, thought that he would have to reach Kut by mid January. This was because of the perceived shortage of food and this could be said to have led 'to the premature battles of Shaikh Saad, Wadi and Hanna.'[88] On 22 January, Townshend had informed Aylmer that he had twenty-two days of food left, but three days later stated that there was eight-four. Aylmer replied:

> I am delighted that his [Townshend's] food supplies are now found much better than I could know from previous telegrams. This information had it been communicated to me before, would certainly have modified much of what I have unsuccessfully attempted to do.[89]

Another challenge for the defenders was to keep the Indian troops fed, when they would not, for the majority of the siege, eat any of the readily-available horsemeat; it was not until 13 April that the Indians agreed to this irreligious act. All ranks became more and more under-nourished as the weeks progressed and by the end of the siege about fifteen soldiers were dying each day, mainly from starvation.[90] Ultimately the lack of food was one of the deciding factors determining the surrender of the 6th Division in April 1916.

Ammunition Supply

Major-General Townshend told the garrison in his first communiqué that he had 'ample' ammunition. However, he also told his commanding officers that:

> We must husband our ammunition carefully; we have 800 rounds per rifle, and roughly 600 rounds per gun, but with night attacks ammunition runs away like water. Therefore, I ask commanding officers to be careful and to impress the men with thrift in this direction.[91]

Despite this anxiety, the combination of only a small number of Turkish assaults and the lack of aggressive forays out of Kut meant that by the end of the siege, there was still an adequate supply of ammunition available to the defenders.

Morale and Health

The high state of British morale before the siege, despite the withdrawal from Ctesiphon, has already been described. The halt at Kut was seen as a pause before reinforcement and counter-attack and the 6th Division had absolute confidence in their leader, who had led them through a series of victories.

This situation was to change gradually, as later chapters will describe. Trench warfare was depressing and dangerous when each soldier was an easy target for enemy artillery and the ever-present sniper threat. The recurrent failure of the Relief Force to reach Kut meant frequent disappointment. Rations became scarce and the heat and flooding meant that living conditions became increasingly intolerable.

The Indian troops were thought to be particularly vulnerable. Attempts were made by the Turks to encourage fellow Moslems to desert, and morale was not helped by the lack of British Indian Army officers available to maintain discipline in units, due to their earlier high casualty rate.

Morale and health may have begun at a high level, but this was not maintained as the siege progressed – as the Quetta Report commented: 'The hospitals appeared fuller than they ought to have been.'[92] Colonel Hehir commented that general health:

> remained fair to the end of February, after which it gradually declined to the end of March, particularly in Indians. Up to this time the men were moderately cheerful and in fair spirits. One saw, however, how deeply they were disappointed each time the relief failed. From this time onwards there was a rapid lowering of stamina, vitality, physical condition and health generally to the end of the siege. When Kut capitulated the whole garrison was in an exceedingly low state of health.[93]

He mentioned that Indian troops suffered badly from scurvy, partly because they were not prepared to eat horse flesh, and that there were 1,050 cases. There were also 551 cases of malaria, 528 of gastroenteritis and diarrhoea, 684 of dysentery and 487 admissions of pneumonia.[94]

Morale and health were, therefore, key factors when surrender was being considered.

The Garrison

The list of units defending Kut can be found in Appendix I. Colonel Hehir provided the following garrison figures, recorded on 8 December 1915, which divide the population of the garrison into effectives, sick and wounded and civilians:[95]

British officers   206
British rank and file   2,276
Indian officers   153
Indian rank and file   6,941
Followers (about)   3,500
Total (*fighting*) Effectives = 13,076

British officers   12
British rank and file   258
Indian officers   22
Indian rank and file   1,176
Followers   42
Total Sick and Wounded = 1,510
Total to be Rationed = 14,586

Men 1,538
Women and children 3,803

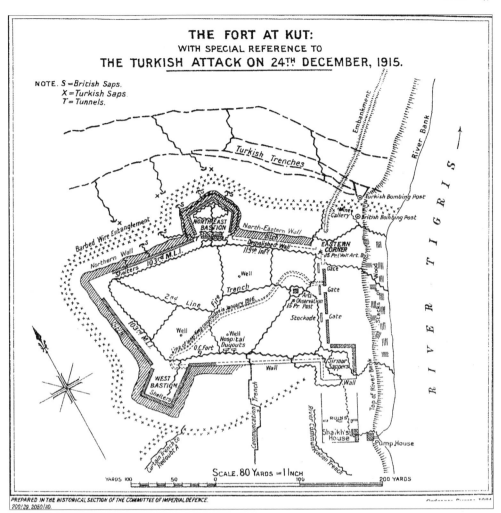

Fort at Kut, December 1915. (Moberly)

Immigrants from Woolpress village 504
Maheillah men *(for the boats)* 316
Coolies 64
Total Civilian Population = 6,225

These figures indicate that 20,811 people were trapped in Kut, of which about 7,000 were effective infantry. All of the infantry battalions were under-strength, such as the 2nd Battalion of the Norfolk Regiment within 18th Infantry Brigade, which numbered only seven officers and 234 other ranks. Interestingly, Colonel Hehir does not consider the need to ration the civilian population, which is presumed to be looking after itself at this stage.

Nevertheless, December was to be a month of hope and successful defence against the only determined Turkish attack of the siege.

Notes

72. Graves (1941) p.195. Notes from a discussion between Cox, Brigadier-General Rimington, then responsible for the town, and his staff officer, Captain Julius, on 2 December 1915.

73. Moberly (1924) Vol 2 p.157.

74. Ibid p.157.

75. Mesopotamia Commission Report (1917) p.169.

76. Barber (1917) p.31.

77. Birch Reynardson (1917) p.221.

78. Also known as Mandeans. A small sect, still in Iraq, who are known as the last disciples of St John the Baptist.

79. Barber (1917) p.40.

80. Graves (1941) p.196.

81. Wilson (1930) p.92.

82. General Staff Army Headquarters, India (1925) p.236.

83. Townshend (1920) p.227.

84. General Staff Army Headquarters, India (1925) p.227.

85. Mockler-Ferryman (undated) p.98.

86. Figure from General Staff Army Headquarters, India (1925) p.228.

87. Wheeler (undated) p.14.

88. General Staff Army Headquarters, India (1925) p.228.

89. Ibid p.228.

90. Figure from General Staff Army Headquarters, India (1925) p.229.

91. Townshend (1920) p.216.

92. General Staff Army Headquarters, India (1925) p.230.

93. Mesopotamia Commission Report (1917) p.170.

94. Ibid p.171.

95. Ibid p.169.

Chapter Three

December 1915 – Hope and Successful Defence

During the first few days of the siege the Relief Force was expected by the New Year and at the end of December we thought we were certain to be out of Kut by 10 January.

Lieutenant Harry Bishop[96]

The Beginning

7 December 1915 marked the official first day of the siege of Kut, as the Turkish forces surrounded the town, cutting off the garrison from land and water-borne re-supply. The only communication between Major-General Townshend and General Nixon was now by wireless.

The day before, the first Turkish shells had fallen on the town and the Cavalry Brigade and 'S' Battery of the Royal Horse Artillery were sent across the Tigris on a hastily constructed bridge back from Kut south to Ali-al-Gharbi where they would form a covering force for the relief column. This column would eventually concentrate at Amara, its lead element consisting of Major-General Younghusband's 28th Brigade. Townshend anticipated that the move south of the cavalry along with his aeroplanes, spare transport and gunboats would mean fewer mouths to feed in Kut and better support for the Relief Force. The only cavalry left at Kut was a squadron each of the Indian 7th and 23rd Cavalry. The remaining forty-three guns listed in Appendix I included the 12-pounder and two 3-pounders mounted on the gunboat *Sumana* and the four 4.7-inch guns on horseboats.

On the same day, Major-General Townshend suggested to General Nixon that the whole Division could move from Kut to Ali-al-Gharbi in order to hasten the link up with the 28th Brigade, as he recognised that his position was vulnerable and his troops had now had a chance to rest. This prompted a seven-point response from his commander that concluded with the final comment: 'Taking all of these points into consideration, Army Commander does not approve of your proposal to fall back on Ali-al-Gharbi.'[97] It had been pointed out that:

• Relief could be even less than two months away.
• The 28th Brigade should be at Ali-al-Gharbi and Shaikh Saad, and that supplies should be on the move towards Kut within the next week.
• A retirement would increase the Turkish threat along the waterways and that the Turkish boats

The British headquarters at Kut. (*The Times History of the War*)

and artillery were not as numerous as Major-General Townshend thought.

• The overall Turkish strength needed confirming from the air.

• Any retirement from Kut should be a last resort and that the situation would be helped by the Russians who were pressurising the Turks as well.

• More reinforcements were on the way and that the 6th Division was holding up superior numbers.

As a result of this exchange, Major-General Townshend concluded in his autobiography: 'Thus it was finally settled that I was to stand at Kut.'[98] Although his comments were made in hindsight and his views seem at odds with decisions made about defending the town a few days before, there is no doubt that General Nixon misunderstood the British position at Kut and Turkish capabilities. Relative strengths had not been considered adequately and there were no substantial reinforcements in Mesopotamia.

As the Turks closed in on Kut on 7 December, they were estimated at divisional strength with eight guns on the right bank of the Tigris north-west of the town, a force of 1,500 troops and guns on the left bank to the north-west with a further two divisions a few miles upstream. They advanced as close to the northern defences as possible and began digging in, beginning the construction of a network of trenches that eventually sealed off the Kut peninsula and they began to sap (dig entrenchments) towards the town. Simultaneously, the Turks were bypassing the town in order to block any potential reinforcement to Kut from the south. The day also marked a demand from General Nurretin, the local Turkish commander, for Major-General Townshend to surrender. The response was predictable:

Hoisting of the British flag at Kut. (*The Times History of the War*)

I sent a reply that I had no answer to give to such an absurd demand as the laying down of my arms. But I thanked him for his courtesy in conforming to the usual custom in war in summoning the commandant or governor of a town to surrender before starting bombardment of it.[99]

Snipers

There were thirty British casualties that afternoon from Turkish shelling, and enemy snipers were already becoming more than a nuisance; they were to hone their skills during the siege. Captain Edward Mousley, a gunner officer who wrote a detailed account of his experiences in Kut, commented at this early stage of the siege:

One evening I stood at the mouth of the dug-out giving orders. Some snipers from over the river must have seen me. A volley whistled past, one bullet cutting through the pocket of my tunic close to the hip. More extraordinary was the escape of the Commanding Officer of the 63rd Battery, Major Broke-Smith. One morning he had a bullet through his topee and one through a pocket. In the afternoon another bullet got another pocket. Someone suggested his requiring a new outfit at an early date.[100]

Snipers always have a far greater effect on their enemy than their numbers would suggest, not just in physical casualties, but also in the way they dent the enemy's morale, creating uncertainty and fear. Another defender of Kut, Sergeant A.C. Munn of the Oxfordshire and Buckinghamshire Light Infantry, summed up this threat: 'It was courting death to show one's head above ground level.'[101] Sterilized water was a premium throughout the siege and bottles were relayed to the trenches by the native *bhisties* (water carriers) – they suffered particularly high casualties from enemy snipers.

Communiques

The defenders received a communiqué from their commander stating that the Relief Force would be concentrating only thirty-five miles away at Shaikh Saad within the week and that they should conserve their ammunition. Major-General Townshend used communiqués throughout the siege in order to boost morale; unfortunately, they were to prove to be false promises.

Shelling

The first major artillery bombardment began on 8 December and continued into the following day, severely damaging the fort, which increasingly became a favourite target for the enemy. At 1500 hours on the 9th the First Line trenches were attacked, for the first time, from the north-west by massed Turkish infantry of the 35th Division between Posts 'B' and 'D', but they were successfully kept at bay. However, the retreating enemy did manage to dig trenches within 600 yards of the First Line, thus helping to tighten the noose around the town. Shelling quickly became part of normal day-to-day life, as Major Barber of the Indian Medical Services described:

> Those of us who had never been under shell fire before were inclined to take it very coolly at first. But after being nearly hit once or twice, we developed a healthy respect for an approaching shell, and ceased to take unnecessary risks.[102]

It was not long before he had to move his hospital, because of the artillery threat.

Humour played an important part in maintaining the garrison's morale and the enemy artillery gained nicknames as the siege progressed. 'Frolicsome Fanny' and 'Frolicsome Flossy' were the names given to two enemy gun positions and the slang descriptions of 'Windy Lizzie' or 'Whizz-Bangs' applied to incoming shells.[103] Even some of the British weapons were given names – The Queen's Own Royal West Kent's improvised mortar gained the title 'grasshopper' as every time it was fired it jumped.[104]

Gallantry

A significant action of gallantry occurred on 9 December, following the withdrawal of the 67th Punjabis who had been covering a dangerously exposed boat bridge. Three officers of the 67th Punjabis were killed as the battalion attempted to maintain its position under intense sniper fire and the 2nd/7th Gurkhas, another battalion of Major-General Melliss's 30th Brigade, provided covering fire. Orders had been given to destroy the bridge that night, despite the proximity of the enemy that had now occupied the old trenches of the 67th Punjabis. Lieutenant Alec Mathews, Royal Engineers, and Lieutenant Roy Sweet, 2nd/7th Gurkhas, took a group of volunteers from the Gurkhas and Sappers and Miners and crossed over to the enemy-held bank to lay the explosive charges. Their dangerous mission was successful; the officers were recommended for Victoria Crosses, though later received Distinguished Service Orders, whilst their men received the Indian Order of Merit. Major-General Townshend commented:

> They volunteered for what appeared certain death, for the enemy had this bridge at the mercy of their rifles at 300 to 400 yards range and were firing down on to it. They waited all day to carry out the operation under cover of darkness – a very different proceeding from doing it on impulse of the moment.[105]

Lieutenant-General Sir Fenton Aylmer. (*The Times History of the War*)

This was to be the first of many gallant actions during the siege. British casualties amounted to 199 men on this day. Lieutenant Sweet was to demonstrate his bravery again, in captivity, but eventually died from ill health in a prison camp.

The Relief Force

10 December marked the introduction of another commander to the army of Mesopotamia, as Lieutenant-General Sir Fenton Aylmer took charge of the Tigris Corps and relief forces. He was a Royal Engineer, had served with the Bengal Sappers and Miners and had been in the force that relieved Townshend at Chitral twenty years before. He was also a brave man who had been awarded the Victoria Cross in 1891, but had little charisma. His first telegram to Kut encouraged the garrison: 'Have utmost confidence in defender of Chitral and his gallant troops to keep flag flying till we can relieve them. Heartiest congratulations on brilliant deeds of yourself and your command.'[106]

His force was rushed to Mesopotamia in an attempt to relieve Kut and maintain British prestige in the country. They started to arrive in Basra during the first week of December 1915 and were pushed north towards Ali-al-Gharbi as soon as possible. River transport remained scarce, so many troops had to conduct a fourteen-day march to reach the concentration area. The 7th (Meerut) Division would eventually be complete in Mesopotamia by the end of December, though its 28th Brigade had arrived by 6 December. It arrived with mixed experience – some of the division having been at the battlefields of Neuve-Chapelle and Loos on the Western Front – and the formation was placed under command of Major-General Younghusband. Unfortunately, its main medical support did not arrive until the third week of January 1916. By this time, the bulk of the second reinforcing division, 3rd (Lahore) Division had arrived at Basra. Lieutenant-General Aylmer's advance for the relief of Kut was, officially, to begin on 4 January 1916.

Back in Kut

A heavy bombardment continued at Kut during 10 and 11 December as the Turks attempted to push closer to the northern defences, attacking with the troops from the 38th, 45th and 51st Divisions. There was a high rate of British casualties of about 150 soldiers per day compared with an even higher Turkish toll of about 400 as they crossed open ground enfiladed by fire from the fort.[107] The Turks launched further attacks on the First Line in the early daylight of the following two days, suffering high casualties, possibly 2,000 men, with little gain. Turkish casualties were particularly concentrated on one exposed sandhill just to the north of the First Line, which gained the name of 'Corpse Hill'. Four battalions were sent to attack the Woolpress Village, but they were also beaten off with heavy casualties. The American soldier and author, Erickson, puts the Turkish failure to achieve success down to a lack of surprise, frontal attacks across exposed ground and a lack of artillery ammunition. The Turks were also tired after their attempts to pursue the enemy and they, like the defenders, lacked reinforcements at that stage.[108]

Indian troops in front line trenches. (IWM Q 69757)

Major-General Townshend sent some important observations to Lieutenant-General Aylmer:

- Casualties were roughly 150 to 200 a day
- A strong division was required to relieve Kut
- The danger of a determined Turkish assault
- The shortage of British officers in Indian regiments
- The concern about the amount of artillery ammunition available
- Morale dropping[109]

The following day, it was estimated that Kut was surrounded by about 12,000 Turks with thirty-three guns, but the next few days were relatively quiet apart from continuing sniper activity. To help counter this ever-present threat, Major Booth from the Army Signal Company set up an enterprising counter-sniper detachment. This period of relative peace allowed the defences to be strengthened, as both the First and Second Line were completed, along with additional communication trenches. Friendly casualties were down to forty to fifty a day. Fortifications were improved within the town and there were even two small successful sorties from the fort, which drove some Turks out of nearby trenches. These attacks were led by Lieutenant-Colonel Brown and succeeded in bayoneting thirty Turks at the expense of one man wounded. The official history of the 103rd Mahrattas records these events, but acknowledges that the raids did not stop the determined sapping by the enemy:

> On the 17th two raids, carried out simultaneously by parties of this battalion and the 119th, captured several enemy trenches and prisoners and, to some extent, relieved the fort of the fear of mines; but

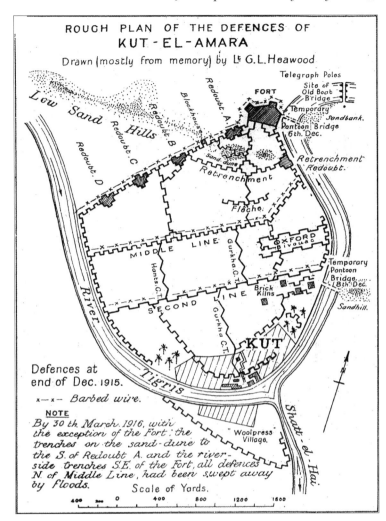

ROUGH PLAN OF THE DEFENCES OF
KUT-EL-AMARA
Drawn (mostly from memory) by L⁺ G.L.Heawood

Defences at
end of Dec. 1915.
x—x— Barbed wire.

NOTE
By 30th March 1916, with
the exception of the Fort: the
trenches on the sand-dune to
the S. of Redoubt A. and the river-
side trenches S.E. of the Fort, all defences
N. of Middle Line, had been swept away
by floods.   Scale of Yards.

Rough plan of
the defences.
(Mockler-Ferryman)

in no way arrested or intimidated the Turkish sappers. Every night brought their sap heads closer to the short listening trenches we had pushed out under the fort walls, and our barbed wire entanglements, never very strong, were shattered nightly by the cannon ball bombs which the Turks rolled into them. It was easy to see where the next attack might be expected.[110]

Nevertheless, this combination of activities improved the defenders' state of morale; though the Turks had managed to dig within fifty yards of the First Line on the north-west front, where both sides could hear each other working. The generally quiet situation was also improved for the besieged by the withdrawal of 2,000 Turkish troops and four guns back to Baghdad.

The Turks

Knowledge about the enemy improved in this period because of information received from reconnaissance aircraft via Lieutenant-General Aylmer and the capture of a number of prisoners. The Turkish force was based on their 6th Army, which was divided into two corps. The 51st

Division began the siege and was joined by the 38th and 45th. The 35th Division completed the encirclement of the town and proceeded downstream to form the block to stop reinforcement from the south. It was also responsible for penning in the British troops at Woolpress Village. This rapid Turkish movement and its effect prompted Erickson's view that 'this action by Nurretin was to prove of decisive significance as the campaign matured.'[111] In all, four Turkish divisions were besieging 6th Division – the 35th, 38th, 45th and 51st, and two more – the 52nd and 26th – were expected soon. This could amount to over 40,000 troops, rather than the 12,000 estimated a few days before. The number and capability of the enemy were consistently underestimated during the Mesopotamia Campaign. The garrison's fighting strength was recorded as 9,185[112] and, in fact, by 23 December there were about 25,000 Turks surrounding the town supported by fifty guns.[113]

Their numbers notwithstanding, the Turkish Army was not particularly healthy; during the four years of war 10,000 were to die from infectious diseases on the Mesopotamia front, compared with 5,934 killed in battle. Like the British forces, there was a shortage of doctors and medical supplies. In addition,

> The enormous need for tents, greatcoats, clothes, shoes, and the like could hardly be met. The insufficiency of food supplies further contributed to the bleak health conditions throughout the War.[114]

According to an account by a young German officer serving with the Turks, Field Marshal Von Der Goltz was not confident that he could take Kut and keep both the Russians and British at bay. His best plan was to invest the town, keep most of his force as a block south of Kut and hope to starve out the defenders.[115] Erickson's analysis concurs with this, Nurretin being told to 'shift from direct assaults to grinding down the English in Kut.'[116]

The garrison quickly began to realise the determined spirit of some of their enemy. In the first week of the siege the Turks had succeeded in digging lines of trenches close to the British lines by day and night over flat and exposed terrain despite the failure of their attacks and the effective defensive fire.

Some strategic news arrived in the town on 19 December, as it was reported that Field Marshal Von Der Goltz was about to invade Persia with 40,000 men. The Russians were reacting to this threat, but Major-General Townshend had been hoping that they would help relieve the pressure on Kut, rather than conduct a defensive action many miles away. Russian activity was not going to help his situation in the short term.

One practical message was sent to Lieutenant-General Aylmer at this stage. Townshend had calculated that if he wanted to link up with any relief force, it would not be practical to build any more bridges across the Tigris to move his troops across. He therefore urged the corps commander to relieve him on the left northern bank of the river, where their forces could meet.

The Big Assault

Christmas Eve 1915 was not to be a night of celebration for the Kut garrison. Instead, it marked the most determined assault on the town to date as the Turks and Nurretin made the most of the newly arrived and combat-experienced 52nd Division. Attempts had been made during the previous night to cut the wire entanglements in front of the fort, known by the Turks as the Kudeyra Kale, in the north-east sector. Then heavy rifle fire lasted between 0515 and 0830 hours against the liquorice factory and the Woolpress Village on the other side of the river. Heavy shelling began battering the fort following a large landmine explosion under the defender's wire at about 0700 hours and, as the day progressed, the barrage easily created breaches in the mud walls and shells fell in the town and within the First Line. However, the bulk of enemy fire was being concentrated against the fort in preparation for an assault. Nurretin was preparing to attack the British 17th Brigade with his 52nd Division, commanded by Kaimakam (Lieutenant-Colonel) Bekir Sami.

Communications were broken between the fort and the rest of the defences and the two 15-pounder guns of the Volunteer Artillery Battery were disabled. One shell was responsible for killing the acting Commander Royal Artillery, his staff officer and an officer of the Ordnance. Sergeant Munn was observing the barrage of the fort from a trench further to the rear:

> For hour after hour the enemy poured hundreds of shells into the fort with scarcely a reply from our people; in fact, I thought they had all been killed in the first half hour. It seemed to me impossible that anyone could have lived through such a bombardment.[117]

The walls of the north-eastern corner and bastion of the fort were systematically destroyed by up to 22 enemy guns, despite the limited amount of ammunition available, and the garrison was forced to pull back from its forward positions.

At this stage, between 1100 and 1200 hours, the bombardment ceased and the Turks launched their assault against this north-eastern sector from their positions only 100 yards away. The area was held by two Indian regiments; the 103rd Mahrattas and the 119th Infantry, thirty men of the Oxfordshire and Buckinghamshire Light Infantry and the artillery crews from the two disabled guns. The enemy did, initially, achieve a lodgement as a furious hand-to hand fight ensued. Bayonets and improvised grenades were to the fore, as the 103rd Mahrattas' history recorded:

> The North-East bastion was almost entirely in ruins, and in the outer end of this the Turks effected a lodgement from which they were gradually bombed and shot out by cross fire from men of this battalion in the side galleries of the bastion and by the Oxfords who held a stockade across the neck of it.[118]

The story from the stockade was of soldiers pouring

> … 'mad minutes'[119] of rapid fire into the compact masses of the enemy, while the bombers of the 43rd, 103rd and volunteer gunners hurled bomb after bomb where none could fail to find a billet. Four machine-guns on the flanks ploughed through the enemy ranks while all the available guns plastered the Turkish trenches.[120]

Despite the onslaught, the Turks held on in the fort for about thirty minutes, supported by waves of reinforcements, before they were driven out. One hundred of their dead were left within the crumbling walls, as Major-General Townshend reinforced the fort with the remaining 200 men of the Oxfordshire and Buckinghamshire Light Infantry.

Further along the wall, the 119th Infantry had been forced to pull back. Major Alexander Anderson, of the Royal Field Artillery, who commanded the two guns, saw that they had lost most of their officers. He rallied the Indian battalion, along with his gunners, and led the eviction of the remaining Turks. 'His manservant, Gunner Chakharia, rushed forward, picked up a wounded gunner and carried him back safely and returned to his side.'[121]

The afternoon was spent removing the wounded and repairing defences. As it became obvious that the Turks would attack again, the defence of the north-east sector was quickly rearranged. The sector was now commanded by Colonel Ernest Lethbridge, commanding officer of the 1st

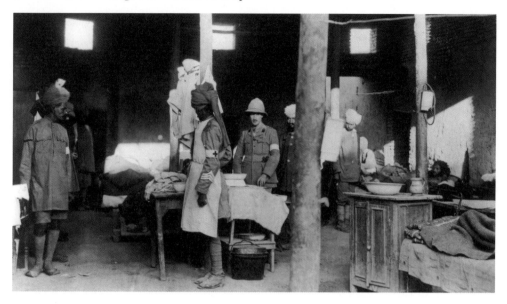

Ward in Indian hospital. (IWM HV 51391)

Battalion Oxfordshire and Buckinghamshire Light Infantry. What was left of his battalion was split between supporting the Volunteer artillerymen on the stockade in the neck of the north-east bastion and the remainder on the wall to the east of the bastion. The 103rd Mahrattas were in front of them on the outer ruins of the bastion and, in case of an attack, they were ordered to 'retire right and left to the side galleries thus uncovering the stockade and allowing of a cross fire from three directions to bear on the assailants.'[122] On the eastern corner, the Rajput Company of the 119th Infantry held the line.

The second assault came at 2000 hours accompanied by an intensity of enemy machine-gun and rifle fire, complemented by the British howitzers dropping shells immediately in front of the fort to catch the Turks as they began their attack. The moon was rising and helped create confusing shadows as the 103rd Mahrattas completed their move into the galleries under a deluge of Turkish hand grenades. This battalion was virtually destroyed.

> A party of 'D' Company of this battalion, under Subedar Ramchander Rao Mohite, in the gallery to the right of the stockade, was destroyed man by man; but not before it had achieved its purpose and saved the stockade and the fort and possibly the whole front line from capture.[123]

Confusion reigned in the darkness, as smoke and dust, explosions and rifle and gun fire, all occasionally lit by a friendly illuminating 'star shell', combined to create a living hell. An hour into the debacle, the machine-gun in the centre of the stockade was disabled, the Turks closed in and the successful defence of the position was in doubt. A grenade killed or wounded most of the defenders on the right of the stockade and Major Anderson and one of the Oxfordshire and Buckinghamshire company commanders were hit. The 48th Pioneers arrived as reinforcements at a critical time at about 2300 hours and, despite their immediate engagement and high casualties, the position held and the Turks withdrew at about midnight.

A third assault began at 0230 hours on Christmas Day, but without the same intensity and it was quickly repulsed. The defenders in the sector were reinforced from the town by 2nd Battalion the Norfolk Regiment at 0300 hours.

The Turkish 52nd Division had launched these attacks and the defenders believed that the enemy had suffered over 2,000 casualties; a later Turkish estimate was 907[124]. As daylight came, masses of Turkish dead could be seen around the besieged walls. There were also many wounded and, although bread and full water-bottles were thrown over to them, no successful break in battle or armistice was agreed to allow them to be evacuated. Lieutenant Heawood of the Oxfordshire and Buckinghamshire Light Infantry commented:

> Turkish dead and seriously wounded lay thick right up to our trenches. We made an attempt to bring them in; but the Turks from their trenches barely a hundred yards away, opened a heavy rifle fire on us until we desisted. Our men succeeded in passing out water and food to them, but many died within a few yards of us, without our being able to do anything for them. For some reason the Turks themselves would not succour their wounded, as we saw some of them crawl back and get right onto their parapet, only to remain there for want of a helping hand from their friends. Presumably, they were afraid that we would fire on them if they showed themselves, though, of course, we had no such intention.[125]

Both sides did manage to recover some of the Turkish wounded but, consequently, the bodies in the area began to decompose and the stench was to remain as the siege continued.

The British casualties in the fort alone were 315 including seventeen officers; sixty-seven had been killed elsewhere in Kut during the same period. All of the units involved had suffered considerably and the company of the 103rd Mahrattas based at the north-east bastion had lost seventy per cent of its number. Major-General Townshend commented upon the valour of his troops, particularly praising Lieutenant-Colonel Brown, the commanding officer of the 103rd Mahrattas, and then the British Light Infantry:

> The repulse of the Turkish assault proved afresh the valour of the troops composing the Sixth Division, and especially did the men of the Oxford Light Infantry add more glory to this history of that famous regiment, so renowned in the Peninsular War.[126]

This was the only significant attack on Kut by the Turks, who preferred to follow the earlier mentioned advice of Field Marshal Von Der Goltz; to isolate Kut and block off any potential relief. Von Der Gotz was absent from the scene when the assault took place under the command of Nurretin and Von Kiesling states that it was against the Field Marshal's orders.[127] Whatever the reasoning behind the assault, it failed and the Turks realised the strong defences of Kut and the high loss of life that would be associated with any further attacks, probably for little gain. The Turkish 6th Army was to follow Field Marshal Von Der Gotz's intent for the rest of the siege; there was no need to launch any more costly failures, particularly as reinforcements were still limited in numbers, as the 6th Army remained a lower priority than other Turkish forces located in Gallipoli and the Caucasus. However, orders were given at the end of the month to despatch another division, the 2nd Infantry Division, from Gallipoli to Mesopotamia, allowing each of the two corps to have three infantry divisions.

Christmas

The rest of Christmas Day was quiet and the garrison attempted to make the most of the event in spite of the need to remain alert, repair defences and gather the dead and wounded. Reverend Harold Spooner, the Anglican padre, ran an unusual church service:

To Dot.

I.E.F. "D."

With Best Wishes

for

A Bright and Happy Christmas

and

A Prosperous New Year

from

Will.

Greetings from Mesopotamia,
Your knowledge of which should
    shame yer,
In this the so called Garden of Eden
Our troops have done some doughty
    deeds in.
We're not in the lime-light view,
Flies, such heat, you never knew ;
Fevers, Arabs, Turks, thirst, boils,
Shells and bullets are our toils.
But now its getting somewhat cold,
Now we think of friends of old,
And hope that when this reaches you
Huns and wars are finished too.

Mesopotamia,
Xmas, 1915.
The last card from Billy

Last Christmas card sent by Regimental-Sergeant-Major 'Billy' Leach. The improvised arms of the Indian Expeditionary Force 'D' are: a shark rampant preparing to snatch the unsuspecting Territorial from the Tigris; mosquito couchant; eight fleas gules doing squad drill; beri-beri bug incognito; two sandflies proper in bivouac and one turtle proper not in consommés! Note thermometer 130 degrees in shade of date palm. (Royal Hampshire Regiment Museum)

Christmas card from A. Dade, Queen's Own Royal West
Kent Regiment. (*Queen's Own Gazette*)

But what an extraordinary service. 18 officers and men in
a dugout. A milk box for an Altar - my big wooden cross
made by the Norfolk's Pioneers on top of it. A flask for
Chalice – ordinary plate for pattern – bullets whizzing
overhead. We sang two hymns – 'While Shepherds watch
their flocks' and 'Hark the Herald Angels sing'. Never
have I heard such devout and earnest singing – never
have I seen a congregation so thoughtful and devout.[128]

Captain Mousley mentions visiting his gunners' dug-
outs and seeing their Christmas decorations, whilst
noting their improvised special meal of plum and
date duff. As usual, the British soldier's humour was
evident:

Rush curtains hung over the entrance, and matting
purchased from the bazaar was on the ground. Tonight, decorations of palm-leaves were spread out gaily on both sides,
and the artistic talent of the various sub-sections had com-
peted in producing coloured texts: 'God Bless our Mud Home', 'Merry Christmas and plenty of Turks',
'Excursions to Kut on Boxing Day'. One humourist had hung up a sock without a foot, and suspended a
large bucket underneath to catch his gifts.[129]

Mousley also recounts an improvised officers' Christmas dinner for twelve, where a few rare luxuries were available. Limited amounts of gin and whiskey were quaffed and a tongue-in cheek
menu of 'Tigre Creme, Turques Diablees, Nurr Eddin Entree, Donkey a la Lambe and Alphonse
pouding' was enjoyed.[130] He also participated in a sweepstake on when the garrison would be
relieved and a short game of football.

Major Barber managed to eat some duck and plum pudding sent by 'a fond mother', whilst
other troops had a dinner of beef, potatoes, tinned fruit, bread, jam and tea. Major Edward
Sandes, who was the Royal Engineer officer in charge of the Bridging Train at Kut, ate a five-
course meal at the Royal Engineer Officers' Mess. However, he also made more melancholy
observations:

Our hospitals were filled with suffering wounded; our gallant dead were being borne to their last
resting place; and the Turkish wounded lay in their agony around the ruined fort amid their more
fortunate comrades who had met a sudden end while bravely attempting to do their duty. It is
at such occasions that one realises what a senseless and brutal thing is modern warfare, in which
thousands of men set forth to kill their fellow-men against whom they feel no personal enmity, and
whose bravery and endurance they in many cases actually admire.[131]

It is clear that the officers had a more bearable experience than their troops. Modern soldiers
who have served in Iraq or any other operational area will recognise the humour revealed, the
importance of making some days special and different when away from families and friends –
and the critical role of food when aiming to maintain morale.

1915 Concludes

There was little fighting during the remainder of 1915, though enemy sniping continued and their shelling increased at night. Time for the defenders was spent improving the defences. Trenches were re-dug and fresh barbed wire laid – Lieutenant Heawood summed up the routine: 'The days and night were now all much the same – by day, deepening old trenches, clearing out after rain, or digging new trenches; by night, completing work which could not be done with safety in daylight.'[132]

Weather conditions began to change in late December, as temperatures dropped by night making life even less comfortable for the garrison. As the year came to an end, Sergeant Munn recalled living conditions for the infantry.

> At this time the weather was bitterly cold, the nights especially. We used to dress to go to bed. I used to put on a pair of long trousers over my putties and shorts, a British warm coat round my body, a balaclava cap and scarf round my head, mitts and woollen gloves on my hands, all this besides two blankets. For a long time no man was allowed to take his boots off. I had mine on continuously from 24 December till 23 January. We lived in the trenches: some never left them until we surrendered (29 April). About this time foodstuff was getting a bit short, but as we expected to be relieved any day, nobody troubled much.[133]

By 31 December the garrison had suffered 1,774 casualties, been harassed continually and subjected to increasingly difficult living conditions. In addition 'pneumonia was becoming serious amongst the troops.'[134] Elsewhere, in Gallipoli, Allied troops were withdrawing from the bays of Suvla, Anzac and Cape Helles after that disastrous adventure against the Turks.

Nevertheless, the only significant Turkish assault at Kut had been driven off, the Relief Force was expected soon, rations were available at normal levels and so confidence and morale were still remarkably high. Major-General Townshend was not complacent, though. He telegraphed Lieutenant-General Aylmer that he was concerned about the potential flow of Turkish reinforcements from the Baghdad area and hoped that relief would come much sooner than 10 January. He asked for news about the movement of British reinforcements up river and of the Russian allies. He was also preparing plans for defending the Middle Line of his defences if the First Line fell. The garrison was informed, by special order, on 28 December that the Relief Force would start from Ali-al-Gharbi, which was only fifty-six miles away from Kut, on 3 January 1916.

The final words of 1915 go to Major Sandes:

> In the last days of the year 1915 the 6th Division and 30th Brigade were holding their own against the enemy, and were in fairly good health and good spirits. All looked forward with confidence to a speedy relief. The defences around Kut were more or less complete; there was abundance of food for a considerable time; ammunition was sufficient for probable requirements; the weather was fine and cold, and the river line fairly low. Optimism prevailed.[135]

Relief was expected in January 1916.

Notes

96. Journal of the United Service Institution of India (1919) p.226. Lieutenant Harry Bishop was an officer in the 66th Punjabis during the siege.

97. Townshend (1920) p.219.

98. Ibid p.219.

99. Ibid p.222.

100. Mousley (1922) p.24.

101. Mockler-Ferryman p.128.

102. Barber (1917) p.57.

103. Windy was an adjective used to describe apprehensiveness of personal danger or trouble, whilst 'whizz-bang' was an onomatopoeic description of the noise of an explosion. Brophy and Partridge (1969) p.163.

104. Mousley (1922) Various references and p.34.

105. Townshend (1920) p.170

106. Ibid p.223.

107. Moberley (1924) p.171/172.

108. Erickson (2007) p.84.

109. Moberley (1924) p.173.

110. Paltan (1930) p.48.

111. Erickson (2007) p.82.

112. Figure from Moberley (1924) p.174.

113. Erickson (2001) p.114.

114. Ozdemir (2008) p.86.

115. Moberley (1924) p.174/175 quoting Oberstleutnant von Kiesling in *Mit Feldmarschall*

von der Goltz Pasha in Mesopotamien und Persien.

116. Erickson (2007) p.86.

117. Mockler-Ferryman (undated) p.129.

118. Paltan (1930) p.48.

119. Brophy (1969) p.119. A phrase used to describe rapid rifle fire of fifteen rounds per minute or the frenzied minute spent charging around an assault course doing bayonet practice.

120. Neville (1938) p.140.

121. Farndale (1988) p.222.

122. Moberley (1924) p.179.

123. Paltan (1930) p.49.

124. Quoted from Turkish Commandant Moukbil Bey — MIllar (1970) p.118.

125. Mockler-Ferryman (undated) p.103.

126. Townshend (1920) p.233.

127. Moberley (1924) p.176.

128. Moynihan (1983) p.23.

129. Mousley (1922) p.41.

130. 'Alphonse' was a nickname given to Major-General Townshend by his troops, because of his obsession with Napoleon. Mousley (1922) p.43.

131. Sandes (1920) p.164.

132. Mockler-Ferryman (undated) p.104.

133. Ibid p.130.

134. Barber (1917) p.94.

135. Sandes (1920) p.166.

Chapter Four

JANUARY 1916 – FALSE HOPES

We now come to a period when the breakdown in the medical arrangements of the campaign was more marked than at any other time.

Mesopotamia Commission[136]

The Relief Force Advances

Major-General Younghusband, now promoted to command the Indian 7th Division, began his advance up the Tigris from Ali-al-Gharbi on 4 January. His Relief Force moved along both banks of the river; on the right bank, Major-General George Kemball with his 28th Brigade, one troop of cavalry, the 9th Field Artillery Brigade and part of the engineers and pioneers. On the left bank, Brigadier-General Gerard Rice with his 35th Brigade, the 16th Cavalry, 1/1st Sussex Battery Royal Field Artillery and some pioneers. Behind them was the General Reserve consisting of the Heavy Artillery Brigade and 19th Infantry Brigade. In addition, the 6th Cavalry Brigade worked on the flanks, helping to ensure routes were clear. The gunboats *Butterfly*, *Cranefly* and *Dragonfly* accompanied the advance, along with the *Gadfly* which housed Major-General Younghusband's headquarters.

Once again, Captain Nunn was in charge of the naval element accompanying 7th Division's commander on the *Gadfly*. The 'fly' or *Butterfly* class of 'small China gunboats':

> were of about 98 tons displacement, 126 feet long, 20 feet beam, and their draft of water was between two and three feet. Their armament was a 4-inch, a 12-pounder, a six-pounder gun, a two-pounder anti-aircraft pom-pom, and four maxim guns. Their crew consisted of two officers and about 20 men.[137]

Their top speed was nine and a half knots and seven of their class were commissioned in Mesopotamia in 1916. Captain Nunn said that their main weakness was a lack of redundancy in the engine and screws; there was no reserve boiler. Nevertheless, the boats gave invaluable assistance to the Relief Force by providing additional firepower, reasonable communications and transport between riverbanks.

The Indian 3rd Division, under command of Major-General Henry D'Urban Keary, was still assembling at Basra. The Tigris Corp Commander, Lieutenant-General Aylmer, sent an Order of the Day:

Major-General George Kemball. (*The Times History of the War*)

Major-General HenryKeary. (*The Times History of the War*)

> We have now to relieve our brother soldiers at Kut-al-Amara, who for a month have most gallantly repulsed every hostile assault, inflicting great losses on the enemy. Such a task must appeal very deeply to us all, and I feel the utmost confidence that, whatever the difficulties we may encounter, every man will do his utmost to ensure a glorious result.[138]

On the face of it, 7th Division was an impressive grouping of about 13,330 men and thirty-six guns.[139] Everyone in this force realised the urgency of their mission, particularly as, according to Major-General Townshend, the defenders of Kut would run out of rations in mid January. Unfortunately, there were some considerable obstacles in the way of this hastily improvised advanced guard of the Relief Force. The political officer, Captain Wilson later summed up the challenge of the situation:

> The problem facing General Nixon as Commander-in-Chief and General Aylmer as Corps Commander was thus one of extreme difficulty: they were burdened with immense responsibilities and with the need for a whole series of makeshifts and improvisations with the scanty material and personnel at their disposal. They were particularly deficient in information as to the ground over which they would have to fight, and as to the dispositions of the enemy; of the true state of General Townshend's supplies they were completely ignorant.[140]

The Enemy

The Turks blocked the route of the advance and intelligence concerning their exact positions and strength was sketchy, a situation not helped by limited numbers of Allied reconnaissance aircraft. 2,500 enemy were, supposedly, astride the river three miles south-east of Shaikh Saad, but

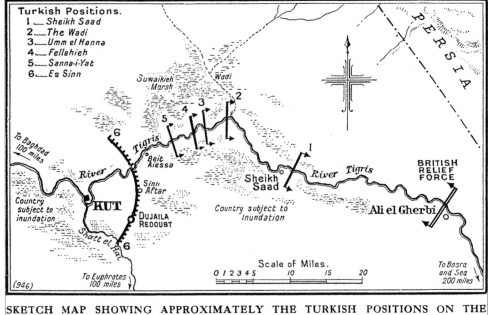

SKETCH MAP SHOWING APPROXIMATELY THE TURKISH POSITIONS ON THE TIGRIS.

Turkish positions on the Tigris. (*The Times History of the War*)

there was confusion about the overall numbers of Turkish troops surrounding Kut and blocking the Relief Force; the 'best guess' was probably 30,000 men and eighty-three guns.[141] In fact, at Shaikh Saad, there were four battalions and 2,000 mounted men and at Es Sinn there were 2,500 men and eighteen guns. 11,500 men and forty-one guns from the 45th and 36th Divisions were at Shumran Bend, nine miles west of Kut, and on the left bank near to the town 12,900 men and twenty-four guns from the 5th, 31st and 38th Divisions.[142] The situation was not helped by the fact that there was a lack of knowledge and mapping of the area over which the Relief Force was about to cross. These were not good odds from a British perspective, but there was a great sense of urgency to relieve the siege. Lieutenant-General Aylmer considered that the combination of Major-General Townshend's garrison at Kut and Major-General Younghusband's 7th Division and 6th Cavalry Brigade should be enough concentration of force to relieve the town. However, he knew that there were risks, as illustrated by an extract from his telegram to Major-General Townshend, copied to General Nixon, on 30 December 1915:

> Our relieving force can only be organised as it arrives at Ali Gharbi and dates of starting from there allowed for this. These dates also depend on arrival of ships from Basra. There are objections to pushing forward troops prematurely from Ali Gharbi for your relief and using forced marches, but I am of course ready to take very great risks in this matter should your condition absolutely require it.[143]

He went on to say that he would prefer to advance with his whole corps, once complete. This would be slower, but more guaranteed to succeed. Nevertheless, urgency was required, despite his reservations, as reflected in this extract from another telegram to General Nixon on 4 January 1916: 'On numbers given he [The Turks] can detach a force sufficient to keep Townshend secure in Kut and still engage my force in superior numbers, say at Es Sinn position on our nearer approach.'[144]

Lines of Communications

There were also problems in the rear at Basra. Facilities for off-loading at the port were not good at this stage of the campaign, so the much-needed reinforcements did not disembark and move inland as quickly as required. A great deal of work was done to improve this situation, but even so progress was slow. General Gorringe had instigated the rapid building of five more wharves in the port, which helped, but they did not meet the full requirement. A request had been made by General Nixon, back in August 1915, to construct a railway from Basra to Nasiriya, but the suggestion was turned down because of the expense.[145]

The importance of boats in this campaign had been realised for some time, particularly after the success of 'Townshend's Regatta' and the difficulties in providing supplies upstream, whilst bringing casualties back to Basra. However, production in England was slow and the new ones ordered were not expected to be despatched until March. The India Office, the Admiralty and authorities in Egypt all attempted to identify existing vessels and move them to Mesopotamia as soon as possible, but this was not quick enough to meet the immediate requirement of the Relief Force. Seventy-two boats were expected from England, ten river steamers from Egypt and forty from India; unfortunately, the bulk of these vessels only arrived during May 1916, too late for Kut. The Relief Force had to make do with the existing fleet, which had limited capacity and was generally in poor condition. The Connaught Rangers were not impressed by their transport when they travelled up the Tigris, as the rain fell. Their padre, Father S. Peal recorded:

> The steamer had the ordinary canvas awning, but this was quite insufficient as we were crowded on deck. Those on the barges were worse off. A few loose mats tied to poles were the only protection. When a barge is crowded and men move about on an iron floor with hob-nailed boots in wet weather it is easy to slip and fall into the river. Many a poor fellow has found his grave in the river while attempting to draw water on deck for making tea. Some corpses of such victims may be seen

General Sir John Nixon and his staff. (*The Illustrated War News*, 1 December 1915)

sticking in the reeds near the bank. Two of our boys in full uniform slipped off one night, but fortunately they escaped drowning as we were anchored at the time.[146]

Land transport was also lacking, as there was insufficient river transport to position and supply carts and animals along the Tigris in key lines of communication positions. In addition, camels were difficult to procure and maintain and there were not enough engineers in the Relief Force to deal with mobility challenges. Medical support and supply arrangements were inadequate both on land and water and, because of dependence on the river, Lieutenant-General Aylmer had only limited scope for manoeuvring away from the Tigris. Available assets were only a quarter of what his force needed, so maintaining supplies of food and clothing was difficult, let alone dealing with potential massed casualties. Artillery ammunition was particularly difficult to supply, because of its bulk and the lack of available high-explosive shells. This constraint, along with old equipment and poor communications would limit the British rates of fire and artillery effectiveness during the relief attempts.

Medical support for the Relief Force was considered in the Official History only to be enough to support one third of its strength.[147] Weaknesses in this area had already been realised and they spawned an initial report from Surgeon-General MacNeece, Director of the Indian Medical Services, and, subsequently, a more detailed report from the Vincent-Bingley Commission, which in time became part of the Mesopotamia Commission's report.

Command and Control

There were a further three command and control challenges that the Relief Force had to contend with: General Nixon's health; the lack of staff in the various headquarters; and the absence of a divisional signal company. The commander of all troops in Mesopotamia was not a well man and his decision-making abilities must have been affected at this stressful time. As the Official History stated: 'The strain on him since the Battle of Ctesiphon had been very great and within a day or two of his arrival at Basra on 6 December his health became much worse.'[148] Nevertheless, his request to India, in early January, to be relieved came as a surprise to the authorities.

The lack of staff in both Lieutenant-General Aylmer's 'Tigris Corps' headquarters and the newly arrived 7th Division did not help rapid planning or the efficient dissemination of orders. Staff were improvised from existing officers already in Mesopotamia, appointments were gapped and, consequently, many of the appointed officers had no staff training. Thus they were not used to working as a team, as an efficient headquarters should be, they did not know their commanders' methods of leadership, and all of their procedures would be slower than normally expected and required. This would have been a huge frustration for both Lieutenant-General Aylmer and Major-General Younghusband, made worse because there were inherent inefficiencies created in two levels of command – corps and division. Further improvisation of communications was required because 7th Division's signal company had not arrived prior to the advance. Cobbled-together headquarters, supported by a communication system run by personnel unfamiliar with each other and the procedures required, were not a good recipe for clear and swiftly executed orders and the efficient movement of troops on the battlefield.

The situation was not helped by the piecemeal arrival of 7th Division at Ali-al-Gharbi. Many of the arrivals were separated from their headquarters and without their full equipment. None of the three brigades had worked together before and, therefore, were not best trained, particularly as what training they had received was based on slightly differing systems from within the Empire.

The 28th Brigade was considered efficient, had served for sometime in Egypt and its units were used to working together. 35th Brigade was recently formed in India, but had little experience, whilst the 19th Brigade had a new commander and staff along with all newly-assigned units, apart from the 1st Battalion Seaforth Highlanders (Seaforths). Some of the personnel had been sent from France, considered by many the place 'where the real fighting is happening', so there was some animosity, as they did not want to be in this particular 'sideshow'. Morale was therefore mixed. The official embedded 'Eye Witness', Edmund Candler, travelling with 2nd Battalion the Black Watch commented:

> Nothing could exceed the muddle at Ali Gharbi. Regiments were thrown into new brigades as they came up the river. There were brigades made up of units which had never been brigaded before, an improvised staff both in the Tigris Corps and the 7th Division, brigadiers who do not know their regimental commanders, and a Corps commander who did not know his divisional commanders and brigadiers … The substitution of a new and improvised staff at the last moment invited disaster.[149]

Even basic equipment was not ideal in the increasingly wet and miserable conditions. The History of the 62nd Punjabis described the situation.

> The whole country soon became a mass of soft, deep clinging mud and there was a constant icy gale blowing straight off the Pusht-i-Kuh mountains. The troops had no adequate shelter and no fuel to dry their clothes; moreover, they were on reduced rations and unlike the troops from France with their serge uniforms, they were still shivering in khaki drill. The 62nd Punjabis, fortunately, owing to the remarkable foresight of Colonel Geoghegan, then commanding the Battalion, had been equipped. Each officer and man, with a suit of serge uniform, purchased out of the regimental funds before the Battalion left Cawnpore to embark for the war.[150]

The key point was that it was not only the Kut garrison that was suffering from the poor conditions. It is no surprise that the Official History described the Relief Force in this manner:

> It is thus sufficiently clear that General Aylmer's force, lacked, at this period, the standard of organisation and cohesion which is desirable for a body of troops undertaking an offensive in a difficult country against an entrenched and determined enemy, operations which would depend primarily upon combination and unity of effort.[151]

But in spite of these considerable challenges of structure and transport, speed was deemed essential and the risks associated with the advance of the Relief Force were accepted. Different decisions may have been made if Lieutenant-General Aylmer and General Nixon had known that Kut actually had enough food to hold out for four months.

12th Division

At this point, it is worth remembering Major-General Gorringe's 12th Division, which had responsibility for the 'Euphrates Line' when Major-General Townshend was advancing to Ctesiphon in December 1915. Reported Turkish threats to this area and Nasiriya meant that some of the newly arrived units in Basra had to be sent to a reorganised 12th Division, despite the need to relieve Kut. This dissipated the fighting power of the Relief Force, but General Nixon did not want an increased threat to his flanks and the oilfields. 12th Division, based now

Major-General Sir Charles Melliss in Kut. (Kut dinner menu card 1939)

on the 12th and 34th Brigades, therefore, advanced to Butaniya, about twelve miles north of Nasiriya, on 7 January, providing a demonstration up the River Hai towards Kut, over 100 miles to the north, whilst the Relief Force fought their first battle near Shaikh Saad. The 12th Division was to remain north of Nasiriya until 7 February, successfully repulsing an attack on one occasion by about 3,000 Arabs.

Kut

For the defenders of Kut, 1 January 1916 began inauspiciously. Major-General Townshend reported a sepoy of the Indian 103rd Light Infantry deserting his sentry post, firing two shots at an officer and attempting to escape to the enemy. The miscreant was sentenced to death by a general court martial and shot at sunset.[152] He also reports of a 'close shave' from shelling on his headquarters and another shell exploding amongst the wounded at the one of the hospitals in the town.

Generally, morale was good in the town because of the successful defence so far and the optimistic rumours about relief arriving soon. Reverend Spooner held a communion service for men of the Queen's Own Royal West Kent and Hampshire Regiments, commenting that the service 'seemed to mean a great deal to these men facing death daily – sometimes hourly.' He went on to say that the soldiers that he was talking to 'seemed very cheery and in no way depressed.'[153] Conditions were turning for the worse, however, as the temperature was dropping and the rainy season was expected.

On 5 January a Turkish column of about 8,000 men was reported marching towards Es Sinn. By 6 January, Townshend was already telegramming advice to Aylmer on how he believed the Relief Force should manoeuvre. However, news arrived in Kut on 8 January about the Battle of Shaikh Saad.

Shaikh Saad

The first Turkish blocking position two and a half miles below Shaikh (or Sheikh) Saad was well defended. Air reconnaissance reported 10,000 Turks split evenly for about 2,000 yards on both banks of the Tigris, but news was also heard about the possible arrival in the area of an additional 8,000 Turks. Major-General Younghusband intended to contain the enemy until Lieutenant-General Aylmer was able to reinforce him with more troops on the evening of 6 January. He planned to threaten the enemy's left, whilst launching his main attack on his own left, the right bank of the river, using Major-General Kemball's 28th Brigade. Younghusband was optimistic about success, telegramming to the Tigris Corps commander that he would build a bridge across the river, that the enemy were not well dug in and would probably withdraw and remarking that his artillery was probably more effective than theirs.

The assault began quietly at 0900 hours, partly in a dense mist which cleared an hour later. There was a brief skirmish on the southern bank between 1,000 Arabs and the 28th Brigade, which was divided into two columns. The British came under heavy fire at midday and the 28th Brigade began to realise that the Turkish trenches extended a lot further south from the riverbank than expected. Its main units, the 56th Rifles, 53rd Sikhs and the 2nd Battalion Leicestershire Regiment (The Leicesters) were being split up from each other and, instead of outflanking the enemy, they found themselves outflanked. The 6th Cavalry Brigade, on the same flank, ran into heavy fire and aggressive counter-attacks by the Turks, which were only just held off by their 'S' Battery of artillery. The Allied cavalry came to a standstill under the pressure of a large body of Arab horsemen. The Leicesters were within 500 yards of the enemy trenches, but were suffering heavy casualties. As it started to get dark at about 1710 hours, the Battalion was ordered to dig in

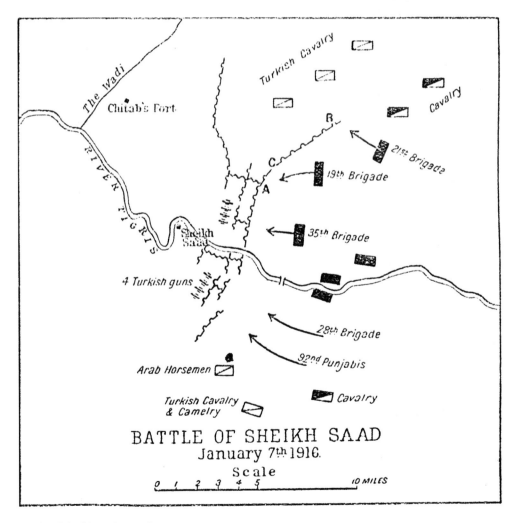

Battle of Shaikh Saad. (Candler)

as best they could so they could resume the assault in the morning. More casualties were caused as they attempted to re-supply ammunition and remove casualties, but 'the battalion stretcher bearers, under Lance-Corporal Queenan, did excellent work throughout and brought in the killed and wounded of the Battalion and other units.'[154]

On the left northern bank of the river, a mirage prevented the accurate locating of the enemy and Brigadier-General Rice's force came under attack at 1100 hours. The 37th Dogras came under heavy fire and the 16th Cavalry, on their right flank, was brought to a standstill by Turkish cavalry. The Indian 97th Infantry and 102nd Grenadiers came to support the 37th Dogras, as they dug in about 800 yards from the enemy trenches, whilst the other battalion of the 35th Brigade, the 1/5th (The Weald of Kent) Battalion the Buffs (East Kent Regiment) (known as 1/5 Buffs), remained in reserve.

The 2nd Battalion of the Black Watch were also in the fight on the left bank. An anonymous author, who called himself 'one of its officers', commented that no clear orders or direction of assault had been issued to his regiment prior to the attack. Also, there was only limited artillery support. He wrote:

> But without covering fire, and there was little artillery fire available to cover our attack, such an attack over bare open plain cannot succeed unless the enemy be few in numbers or of poor heart. The Turk was neither weak nor faint-hearted, and poured in so deadly a fire that before the leading lines were within 20 yards of the enemy, 500 of the battalion had been killed or wounded. 19 officers and two-thirds of the men had been hit.[155]

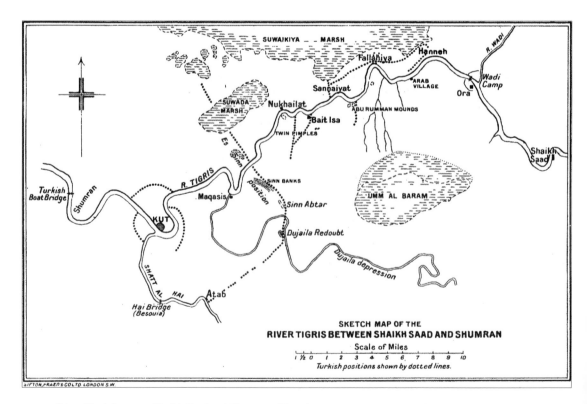

River Tigris between Shaikh Saad and Shumran. (Evans)

High levels of casualties had been sustained on both banks of the Tigris as darkness fell. The Turkish defence may have only consisted of about 3,000 men — the 35th Division, a cavalry brigade and a camel corps regiment — though this figure had risen to 9,000 men by the following day.[156] However, locating the enemy on the featureless landscape when they were dug in, was difficult and it was too easy for the Turkish defenders to pick off the advancing infantry on the flat ground, particularly with machine-gun fire. Candler reported, dramatically, that:

> The Turks are adept in trench work. They dig deep and narrow; moreover the mirage and the flatness of the ground helped them. The first thing one saw of the enemy position was the glint of their bayonets.[157]

Therefore, it was extremely difficult to support the Allied troops with accurate artillery fire from either the ground or the river-boats. A soldier of the 1/5th Buffs commented on the landscape just before the battle.

> One can see a horizon all around you, the country is so flat. All trees were left behind at Amara. Not seen a bush or blade of grass since.[158]

The Relief Force had suffered 600 casualties on 6 January.

Whilst the battle raged on that first day, Lieutenant-General Aylmer started to move up the Tigris with further reinforcements to link up with Major-General Younghusband and improve the odds against the Turks. This grouping consisted of the 7th Lancers, some artillery, the 21st Brigade and an improvised 9th Brigade. They were supported by five more steamers and tugs. The two friendly forces were united at 0730 hours on 7 January. There was some debate between the two generals as to what should happen next. Younghusband was, initially, not keen to rush into an attack as he was uncertain of the enemy dispositions. He did, however, favour applying pressure on the smaller enemy force on the right (southern) bank. Aylmer wanted to attack as soon as possible to avoid further Turkish reinforcement and improvement to their defences. The decision was made to attack with the main effort on the left (northern) bank; Younghusband commanded the force there based on the 16th Cavalry, 19th, 21st and 35th Brigades. Major-General Kemball had command of the right bank with the 28th Brigade, 92nd Punjabis and one-and-a-half batteries of guns. The 9th Brigade, most of the Heavy Artillery Brigade and some sappers were held in reserve. The intent was to conduct a turning movement with the 16th Cavalry Brigade and the 19th Brigade on the left bank. Re-grouping on either side of the river was achieved through the construction of a bridge by engineers in the columns linking both banks. The attack began at midday.

A bloody engagement ensued as the 19th Brigade, commanded by Colonel A. Dennys, ran into heavy enemy crossfire from well-defended positions. Candler commented on the effect of the enemy fire: 'Troops who had been through Loos and Givenchy described it as equal to any rifle fire they had come under on the Western Front.'[159] Colonel Dennys' units became intermingled, but the Brigade successfully repulsed a Turkish counter-attack in the early afternoon. The remainder of the British forces on the left bank also came under heavy enemy fire; their artillery was particularly effective. Mirages again hampered Allied visibility and the troops were facing into the sun. As daylight ended, the troops on this side of the Tigris were still 300–400 yards from the Turkish trenches and had suffered tremendous losses. For example, 2nd Battalion the Black Watch and 6th Jats each had lost their commanding officers and 400 men.

Transport cart in the mud. (Moberly)

The attack on the south bank began at about 1400 hours. Intense enemy fire kept the 28th Brigade pinned down, but at 1600 hours the Leicesters, the 51st Sikhs, 53rd Sikhs and 92nd Punjabis rose and drove the last 300 yards to take the first line of enemy trenches. Candler observed:

> The Leicesters on the left sustained the reputation of dash and fearlessness earned in France. Sixteen officers of the Regiment fell in the attack – seven killed and nine wounded, and 298 of the rank and file. The 51st Sikhs on the right of the Leicesters were the first to secure a footing in the enemy lines, and it fell to them to capture the two mountain guns and three maxims which were opposite their position. The 53rd Sikhs and 56th Rifles on the right advanced with the same resolute elan.[160]

There were 350 Turkish dead and 600 prisoners were taken, but at a cost of 1,106 casualties in the 28th Brigade alone. As a result, three company sergeant-majors of the Leicesters were commissioned, only to die a week later.

The 28th Brigade remained in the enemy trenches during 8 December, whilst orders were delivered from Lieutenant-General Aylmer for the whole of the Relief Force to resume the attack the following morning. Following a number of minor skirmishes and surprising reports from the cavalry that the enemy had withdrawn, at 1400 hours on the 9th, the 28th Brigade advanced to and occupied Shaikh Saad.

The battle had been won, but the relief troops were too tired to follow up their success and pursue the enemy. Weather conditions had worsened and the force was wet, as a bitter wind and heavy rain swept through their increasingly muddy position and poor visibility reduced the effectiveness of the reconnaissance aircraft and cavalry. The nearest Turkish forces were now reported to be in an area known as the Wadi, however, they had successfully delayed Aylmer, disengaged from the action and were preparing to block the advancing forces again. Captain Nunn commented that 'This army was pitted against a skilful, entrenched enemy, who was, furthermore, fighting in his own country and under conditions to which he was accustomed'.[161] To make matters worse, British and Indian morale was not helped by the medical situation.

Medical Support

Victory at Shaikh Saad had been won at a high cost. There had been just over 4,000 friendly casualties during the battle of whom 417 were killed.[162] All units had suffered; the Seaforths had lost twenty officers and 380 men, whilst the 6th Jats began the action 485 strong and finished with just 150. The condition of the wounded was made worse by the cold and wet weather.

In a telegram sent from Lieutenant-General Aylmer to General Nixon on 11 January he admitted that his 'medical establishments, as you may calculate, are deplorably low and wounded cannot receive proper attention.'[163] The scale of casualties at Shaikh Saad revealed some of the risk that the Tigris Corps commander had taken when he advanced so quickly from Ali-al-Gharbi. As the Vincent-Bingley Committee commented: 'On January 3rd, when the force marched from Ali-al-Gharbi, no part of the medical establishments of these divisions was available for service at the front.'[164] Seven field ambulance sections were cobbled together for the 7th Division, eight for Corps Troops and two sections placed on the *Julnar*, as a boat hospital to receive the wounded. However, they were all short of personnel and equipment and not all properly trained. A court of enquiry even took place in the field, because a significant re-supply of locally purchased stores did not arrive at the front in time for the battle.

The medical system could not cope with the volume of casualties on 7 January. The *Medical History of the War* estimated that 90 British officers, 900 British other ranks and 2,500 Indian troops were admitted to medical units over the period 6–9 January 1916.[165] Drugs and dressings ran short and there was not enough space on the *Julnar* or in the reception tents for the wounded. A soldier in 1/5th Buffs observed:

Those that were wounded too bad had to lie where they fell, in the open, and some had first aid dressings and some had not … There were no hospital carts, only the company stretchers (two to a company) and no hospital and only one doctor to each regiment. The wounded natives and officers came back and lay on the bank of the river near where the boats were anchored. Some terrible sights too … The tents were soon full, then we emptied 20 transport carts to go and fetch the wounded. Terrible rough ground, iron laths for bottoms of the carts and no springs and careless drivers, so you can guess what the wounded had to suffer that could not walk, or with internal injuries … many that were alive when first in the carts were dead when they reached here … Went over to the hospital tents and oh, the sights. Men that had died in the tents were dragged outside and left there, others that had been there all night were soaked and sitting in the mud, no other alternative.[166]

An officer in the Leicesters stated:

It rained heavily and was freezing cold and the mud was awful. Medical arrangements had completely failed and the sufferings of the wounded were horrible. At times men lay out all night in pitiless icy rain, dying from exposure. Many were found dead without a mark on them; others were picked up and slowly jolted, petrified and sodden with freezing mud, in springless carts to the dressing station. Later, a man arrived at Amara with wounds which for eight days had remained unattended – wounds which were putrifying, gangrenous and full of maggots.[167]

Many of the wounded only survived though the extra efforts made by regimental officers and their soldiers providing comfort, food, blankets and tents rather from the medical staff. The condition of the makeshift camps at Shaikh Saad and Musandaq was poor and unsanitary. Wounds remained undressed and many of the patients had dysentery. One of the hospitals for a time only had three medical officers for 1,200 patients and the Mesopotamia Commission commented that the limited number of river steamers 'were short of equipment, sweepers, orderlies, bandages, medical comforts, blankets , bedpans, urine bottles, cutlery and crockery'.[168]

Travel by boat down to Basra was also a harrowing experience for the wounded. Major Carter of the Indian Medical Services had watched the arrival of the *Mejidieh* at Basra early during the siege:

> The stench that rose from its human cargo and its soiled boards baffles description. The patients were crowded and huddled together, and only a few could stand, others had to kneel to get out of the filth in which those lying flat on their backs were covered, some with blankets, some without. With no protection from sun or rain for 17 days, with fractured limbs, many with their skins perforated in five or six places by broken bones, they had been left unattended writhing in the cramped space allowed them on the deck of the ship, which was covered with dysentery and swarming with flies and vermin.[169]

Conditions were compared with the Crimean War.

The terrible state of medical support in Mesopotamia was not over yet and spawned the Vincent-Bingley Commission, which was later subsumed into the Mesopotamia Commission Report of 1917. This attempted to learn lessons from the campaign. The main causes of the breakdown were put down to:

• The lack of proper hospital river steamers
• The lack of river transport
• The insufficiency of the medical and subordinate staff and of medical stores and accessories
• The weather conditions
• Ambulance land transport[170]

However, Lieutenant-General Aylmer was not blamed for the medical deficiencies because they were partially unavoidable due to the pressure that was being placed on him to relieve Kut as soon as possible, and the unexpected resistance put up by the Turks. Medical support could have been placed onboard ship in a better desired order of arrival for Mesopotamia, though that would have delayed the arrival of the General's combat power in the country. He was attempting the relief of Kut in difficult circumstances and, undeterred, he issued congratulatory orders to his troops on 11 January:

> Though deploring the heavy losses which have taken place, the Corps Commander wishes heartily to congratulate all ranks under his command on the great gallantry they have shown during the recent operations and on the success which they have gained.[171]

The Wadi

There was still a great deal of pressure on the Tigris Corps to relieve Kut. Major-General Townshend had reported that Turkish reinforcements were expected on the town's perimeter on or around 20 January and rations were running out. Aylmer realised that his tired force only had a short period to recover, but had to continue the advance, despite it being a 'precarious undertaking'.[172]

The next Turkish position was nine miles upstream from Shaikh Saad on the left bank of the Tigris, on the line of the Wadi stream, stretching north two-and-a-quarter miles from the riverbank. This time, the enemy strength was estimated to be 11,000 and they were reported to

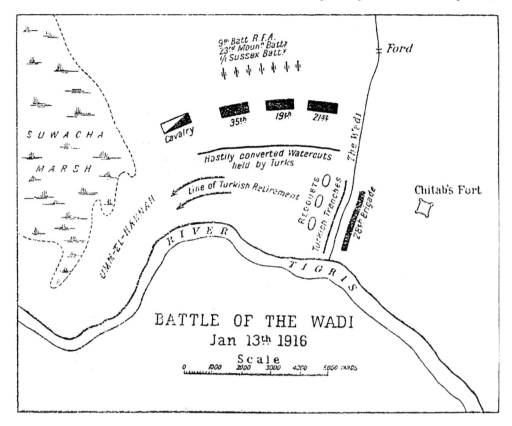

Battle of the Wadi, 13 January 1916. (Candler)

be under a new commander – Halil Bey. They mainly comprised their cavalry brigade, 35th and 52nd Divisions.

Aylmer was optimistic of success as the Turkish flanks could be exploited in a 'turning manoeuvre' and the Wadi stream was reported to be easily fordable. Outflanking the Turkish forces was estimated to be a more formidable task further towards Kut, where they were dug in positions in the Hanna area with the impenetrable Suwaikiya (or Suwacha) Marsh on one side and the Tigris on the other. The advance to attack began on the evening of 13 January.

The 7th Division and the 6th Cavalry Brigade had the task of enveloping the left flank of the enemy after a wide turning movement north. The 28th Brigade was to fix the enemy in their trenches from a central position, as the Corps Artillery pounded the enemy positions and then supported a general frontal assault. 9th Brigade was in reserve. A much smaller column protected the right southern bank, with the gunboats that would support the attack. Aylmer's headquarters was on the river in the *Mejidieh*.

By midday of 13 January, the 28th Brigade had secured the forward Turkish trenches which were just east of the Wadi, following a successful artillery and gunboat engagement. However, they were still 3,000 yards from the main enemy positions. Meanwhile, 7th Division crossed the Wadi at about 1000 hours, but the steep banks proved a difficult obstacle for the artillery and transport. Progress was slowed, as support for the guns was awaited and the transport was not able to cross until darkness, so again, the medical support, due to lack of available ambulances on the Wadi position where the fighting took place, proved inadequate. 21st Brigade came under

Sepoy Chatta Singh digging cover under fire. (*Deeds That Thrill the Empire*)

fire at 1100 hours as 1/9th Gurkhas were brought to a halt and the remaining troops in that brigade gradually came in contact with the enemy. Major-General Younghusband attempted to outflank the Turks to the right of 21st Brigade, with 19th Brigade, which soon came under fire, whilst 35th Brigade remained in Divisional reserve. Three gunboats, the *Gadfly, Cranefly* and *Dragonfly* were shelling the Turkish right.

As the 7th Division threatened the Turkish left flank, Major-General Kemball ordered a frontal assault by the 28th Brigade at 1600 hours, just over an hour before sunset. There was no ground cover and, despite support from the Corps Artillery, the lead battalions came under accurate withering enemy fire when they were about 600 yards from their trenches. The campaign's Official History reports that 'The attack was pushed forward with speed and determination' and 'in spite of these heavy losses, the 28th Brigade responded grandly'.[173] The troops had a different view at the time as overlapping and interlocking enemy machine-gun fire decimated their ranks on the banks of the Wadi and in a small irrigation cut.

Candler described the bravery of the 56th Rifles, 28th Brigade, who attempted to seize their objective. He provided the example of Sepoy Boota Singh who:

> brought in man after man under heavy fire. Of enormous physique himself and devoid of fear, he went out five times, lifted the wounded man on his back and carried him in. On the sixth journey he was shot dead ... It would be a long roll of chivalry that recorded a tithe of the gallant deeds performed by a single battalion in a day's action, many of them unnoticed, or witnessed only by others who have fallen.[174]

The Indian regiments generally displayed great bravery, a behaviour not always appreciated by Major-General Townshend in Kut. The most noticeable act of bravery in this battle was the winning of the Victoria Cross by the Indian, Sepoy Chatta Singh, of the 9th Bhopal Infantry of the 21st Brigade of the 7th Division. He saved the life of his commanding officer, Lieutenant-Colonel T. Thomas, who had been shot whilst moving forward to one of his companies to issue orders. His left leg had been shattered and he later died from his wounds at Amara and was buried there. The sepoy went into 'no-man's land', bound up the wound and dug cover for them both, whilst exposed to enemy fire. He remained with him for five hours until it became dark, when he helped bring his commanding officer to safety.

648 casualties were taken including three out of four of the battalion commanding officers. The remnants of the Brigade were withdrawn as darkness fell. The Leicesters had four officers wounded and 197 other ranks killed and wounded. Both the flanking movement by the 7th Division and the assaults at the enemy centre had been checked and it was not feasible for another attack to take place on the centre the following day.

After a wet and cold night, it was reported that the enemy had evacuated its forward eastern positions at the Wadi. The 6th Cavalry Brigade reconnoitred west and the 35th, 19th and 21st Brigades were ordered south to the river and ordered to advance west upstream. The 'inertness' of the cavalry in this action was adversely commented on by the Quetta Staff College Critical Report of 1923, but their numbers were low, the horses were particularly vulnerable on the open terrain and there was the continuing problem of lack of maps and intelligence. Candler commented that:

> There is little doubt that we could have broken through had we known our country. The truth is that the map is at fault. In this flat, featureless country there are no landmarks. We were quite in the dark as to the enemy's position.[175]

The 14th Hussars' History commented that any opportunity for exploitation was left too much to the initiative of individual units, with limited knowledge of the bigger picture. However, ground and aerial reconnaissance did confirm that the Turks had withdrawn four miles west to the eastern end of the Hanna defile. The Wadi was in British hands on 14 January, but at a high cost.

As at Shaikh Saad, once again, the Turks had fought a successful delaying operation without becoming decisively engaged by the British. They had received heavy casualties, estimated at 2,000, but the Relief Force had also suffered 1,613 concentrated in the ranks of 28th Brigade. Some Allied reinforcements had arrived and the column now had a strength of 9,000 men made up of Corps Troops, the 3rd Division under Major-General Keary and the 7th Division under command of Major-General Younghusband. However, Lieutenant-General Aylmer's Corps had suffered 6,000 casualties so far in its relief attempt and the Turks were occupying and strengthening an extremely strong position which blocked the way to Kut.

As the Relief Force reconstituted, the wet weather, which was to debilitate the defenders in Kut, closed in and hampered all movement: 'In fact it is no exaggeration that at this period the best allies the Turks could have were the rain, the gales and the floods.'[176] Aerial reconnaissance was halted, there were difficulties evacuating the wounded and it was not possible to maintain flexibility by bridging the Tigris, because of the strong and widening waters and damage to bridging equipment.

Communication continued between Major-General Townshend and the Corps Commander. The defenders were concerned that 15 January had been reached without relief, as Townshend said that he would not have stayed put in the town if he had known he would not have been relieved by then. He was informed about the reasons for delay and told Lieutenant-General Aylmer that he had enough rations left for twenty-one day's British and eighteen day's Indian requirements. This was a longer period than he had reported before, but there were further concerns that, after the evacuation of Gallipoli and the anticipated difficulty of pushing through the Hanna position, further significant Turkish reinforcements could be on the way.

On 16 January, Aylmer relayed his concerns about the next stage of the operation to both Nixon and Townshend. He mentioned the strong and deep defensive position, which was probably getting stronger, well supported by artillery. It included comments such as:

> The position of affairs must be frankly faced. The enemy is blocking the entrance of the Wadi-Nukhailat defile with very strong works and, judging of his dispositions within them, they have been designed to resist a heavy bombardment from across the river as well as attack in front … It is impossible in my opinion to take the first position by a coup de main from this side alone without losing half the force … The best plan seems to me for Townshend to cross river during the night, with such able-bodied men as he has got, in the mahailas (*boats*) and other river transport available and march well round the Es Sinn position (right bank). I would cross about one division and cavalry brigade at same time and march to meet him and bring him back here. The opportunity is now favourable.[177]

General Nixon, whose health was deteriorating, quickly responded and disagreed with his Corps Commander's estimate. He could not accept that, after two victories, the Relief Force would not continue its success. He did not agree with the likely reinforcement of the enemy and would not condone any movement out of Kut by the defenders.

> The course you now propose for Townshend in your telegram under reply would be disastrous from every point of view to Townshend's force, to the whole of the forces in Mesopotamia and to the Empire, and I cannot sanction it.[178]

Whilst Townshend stated that he would not be able to cross the river with any significant strength to link up with the Relief Force and that he would fight to the last until his ammunition was exhausted if the relief failed, Aylmer acknowledged Nixon's direction. His response included the following comment: 'The only way to relieve Townshend without the necessity of his breaking out is for me to force the defile and join hands with him on the left bank.'[179]

He realised that options were limited. He would attempt to ferry guns across the river and

enfilade the Turks whilst conducting a frontal assault on the Hanna position. The weather was deteriorating, his combat power was limited, his supply system was poor and he had a shortage of medical and bridging equipment and ammunition. He had little opportunity to surprise the enemy and Kut appeared desperate for relief. At this critical stage, his superior commander was replaced.

General Sir Percy Lake Takes Overall Command

19 January marked the day of General Sir Percy Lake's assumption of the Mesopotamia command. His previous appointment had been Chief of the General Staff in India

Lieutenant-General Sir Percy Lake. (Wilson)

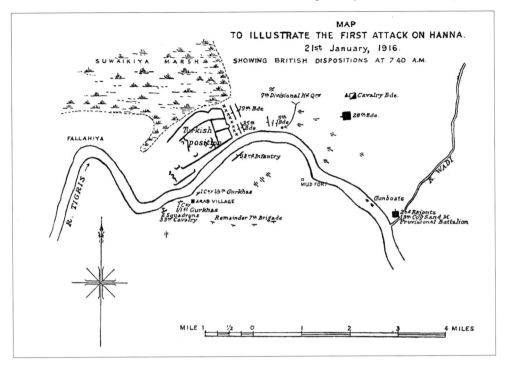

First attack on Hanna, 21 January 1916. (Neville)

so he knew the situation well. General Nixon had asked to be relieved, because of his ill health.

During his six months in command, Nixon had had some success and there had been a string of victories, but these had been pyrrhic; Baghdad had not been captured, 6th Division was bottled up in Kut, whilst the Relief Force was struggling to relieve it amidst considerable casualties. The Mesopotamia Commission made two important comments concerning his part in the build up to the Kut disaster after describing him as a successful and dashing cavalry officer.

> … the military successes which he had achieved induced him to under-estimate the full risk involved in an advance from Kut to Baghdad' and 'He underrated the difficulty of transporting reinforcements, as they arrived from the port of embarkation to the scene of action, and he seriously under-estimated the number of his opponents and miscalculated the dates at which they should arrive. The extreme difficulty of the first task and the lack of reliable information do not seem to have been properly appreciated by those controlling the conduct of the campaign.[180]

The Official History kindly points out that he never had the opportunity to retrieve his failure and re-establish his reputation and that no commander succeeds without taking risks.

His replacement was taking over command at a difficult time as the success of the Relief Force could not be guaranteed. General Lake, an infantryman, had served in Afghanistan and the Sudan, commanding an Indian division prior to his appointment as Chief of the General Staff, India in 1912.

Coincidentally, Nurretin, the Turkish commander, was replaced by Colonel Halil Bey on 20 January, though he did not change dispositions and recognised the need to continue his predecessor's policy of starving out the garrison at Kut.

The Hanna (or Umm-el-Hannah) Defile

Between 18 and 20 January, the Relief Force manoeuvred amongst the thick mud in order to attempt the assault on the Hanna position, five miles west of the Wadi. This period allowed the Turks to strengthen their positions further, including a second depth location at Sannaiyat. Major-General Keary had command of the right riverbank with two squadrons of 33rd Cavalry, a reinforced 7th Brigade and fourteen guns which would be able to enfilade the Turks in their defensive positions on the opposite bank. Meanwhile, on the left bank, immediately in front of the enemy, 7th Division placed their lead elements within 600 yards of their trenches. The enemy position was a mile deep with five lines of interconnecting trenches each 200 yards behind the other and had both flanks protected by either the Suwaikiya marsh or the Tigris and the water level was rising; there was no space for manoeuvre and a frontal assault was inevitable.

Candler was not impressed by the series of frontal attacks that had occurred so far in the attempt to relieve Kut.

> In the actions of January 5th and January 13th impatience, faulty intelligence and an unjustifiable contempt for the enemy resources had cost us dear. We had played into his hands with our frontal attacks; and now, it seemed, necessity compelled us to repeat the manoeuvre.[181]

His observations certainly hit the mark and in the case of the Hanna defile there was no choice. There was little opportunity for surprise, though flanking fire from the southern bank of the river could be achieved. This fire, however, was only to last a few minutes compared with the much longer bombardments seen as essential for success on the Western Front. Also, the assault was again to be in daylight probably because of the command and control limitations, and yet a night attack might have caught the enemy partially unprepared. In the commanders' defence, darkness had been used during the previous few nights to at least ensure that the attackers had reached positions 250 yards from the enemy trenches undetected.

The friendly bombardment from the artillery and gunboats *Cranefly* and *Dragonfly* began on the morning of 20 January. In the evening, the 7th Division edged closer to the Turkish trenches until they were about 300 yards away. The 19th Brigade and 35th Brigade were in the front line prepared to attack in the early morning of 21 January. The 21st Brigade had been split up and attached to the two forward brigades. The 9th Brigade was just behind. The depleted 28th Brigade was in reserve after its tribulations from the Shaikh Saad and Wadi attacks. On the left bank, Lieutenant-General Aylmer had thirty guns and twenty-one battalions, about 7,600 troops.

The next bombardment began at 0745 hours, 'zero hour', and the 35th Brigade assaulted ten minutes later into a hail of enemy bullets – the friendly artillery fire appeared to have had little affect. The 41st Dogras could not penetrate the enemy's barbed wire entanglements. On their left, the 2nd Battalion Black Watch and the 6th Jats managed to get through some depleted wire and into 150 feet of the enemy trenches, though there were only sixty of them left to hold the newly acquired position. The 60 were a mixed group; 40 from the Black Watch, 4 from the Hampshire Regiment, 5 from the 97th Infantry and 11 from the 6th Jats. The assault by the Black Watch was described, in a somewhat jingoist style:

> No pause had been made for firing for the bayonet was the weapon our men trusted. More and more it is proved that the bayonet is the weapon that wins the trench, the rifle the weapon that holds it ... only four officers reached the objective and of these three were wounded ... the Regiment added

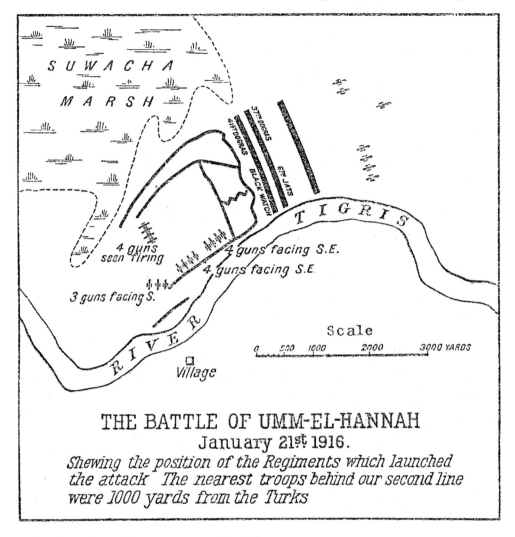

THE BATTLE OF UMM-EL-HANNAH
January 21st 1916.
*Shewing the position of the Regiments which launched
the attack The nearest troops behind our second line
were 1000 yards from the Turks*

Battle of Um-El-Hannah, 21 January 1916. (Candler)

a very glorious page to its history. Great gallantry was displayed and Lieutenant MM Thorburn who
was severely wounded by a bayonet thrust received the Military Cross as an immediate reward.'[182]

9th Brigade attempted to reinforce these troops, but had some distance to cover in difficult conditions. The 62nd Punjabis lost direction and suffered 372 casualties, which included a company
commander and their commanding officer who was shot through the head. Another one of this
Brigade's smaller battalions was the 1/4th Hampshires; they were particularly keen to do well,
because part of their unit was incarcerated in Kut with 6th Division. Four of them had managed
to make it through to the Black Watch, but after 'about an hour and a quarter the Turks counter-
attacked in overwhelming strength' and drove the composite group of defenders back.[183] Most of
the attacking 7th Division reached no further than 100 yards from the enemy trenches.

Confusion reigned throughout the attack, as communications and visibility were poor. Most
of the reports on progress were relayed from the right bank, opposite to the attack. A Turkish
counter-attack was expected and 19th Brigade was reinforced on the right flank by elements

Left Captain Sinton VC. (Card – Gallagher Ltd)

Right Lance-Naik Lala VC. (Card – Gallagher Ltd)

of 28th Brigade to halt it. The attack had been checked and a further artillery bombardment was ordered. At about 1130 hours, the weather grew considerably worse: 'The whole area was transformed into a morass of deep and glutinous mud, which almost paralysed movement and intercommunication.'[184] The new artillery barrage began ten minutes before another assault at 1300 hours. The troops were bogged down in the mud, having already suffered heavy casualties, whilst wet, cold and tired and attempting to negotiate intact barbed wire entanglements. The cavalry had not been significantly engaged throughout the battle.

Major-General Younghusband decided in mid-afternoon that the time had come to withdraw to more stable positions before reconstituting and continuing the attack once conditions had improved. Orders were issued for a withdrawal shortly after dark and the troops began moving back to positions 1,300 yards to the rear where they had been two days before. They were, fortunately, not pursued by the Turks, who were also tired and depleted at this point. However, Lieutenant-General Aylmer saw a copy of these orders and disapproved, as from his perspective there were still four fresh battalions ready for the assault. However, he was too late to change things, as by the time his subordinate received counter-orders, his division was already retiring.

The heavy casualties from 21 January amounted to 2,741 of which seventy-eight were British officers. The rates varied between fifty per cent and ninety per cent and 1/4th Hampshires, who had started the battle in 9th Brigade with sixteen officers and 339 other ranks had casualties of thirteen and 275 respectively. Candler dramatically described their advance:

> A small batch of the Hants were seen to advance at a walking pace some 1,800 yards without taking cover. At 400 yards from the enemy one officer and two men were left. They walked coolly on and were within 300 yards of the Turkish trenches when the officer, the last of that forlornest of forlorn hopes, fell.[185]

The Black Watch had also been hit hard: 'When muster roll was called 99 men remained of this gallant regiment, out of the 950 who had landed in Mesopotamia less than three weeks before.'[186]

Two more Victoria Crosses were awarded as a result of the Hanna attack on 21 January – an officer and a soldier from the Indian Army. Captain John Sinton, Indian Medical Services, was the Medical Officer of the 37th Dogras of the 35th Brigade. During the battle he went forward to tend to the wounded, but was shot both through the side and arms. However, he continued his medical duties despite his wounds, refusing to go to the hospital. In three previous actions he had also displayed great bravery. Captain Sinton outlasted the War and was an accomplished man. A ward in the Musgrave Park Military Hospital, Belfast was named after him in 1987.

Lance-Naik Lala was then a sepoy in the 41st Dogras, attached to the 35th Brigade. He saw the adjutant of the 37th Dogras, Captain Nicholson, wounded in No Man's Land so he dealt with his wounds and dug a trench to provide cover from the enemy fire. He later rescued his own adjutant, Captain Lindop, as well. Lala's name became well known as his bravery was recognised in books written later by Major-General Younghusband, his divisional commander, and Edmund Candler.[187] The citation in the *London Gazette* of 13 May 1916 concluded with the words: 'He set a magnificent example of courage and devotion to his officers.'[188]

Matters were again made worse by the poor medical support and the battle was described by Candler as 'a twentieth century battle with eighteenth century medical arrangements.'[189] He went on to say that events showed 'that the most cruel sacrifice which war can demand is to ask men to face the modern machinery of destruction without the resources of alleviation which modern science can provide.'[190] Major Evans described the situation thus:

> Men lay out all night in pitiless, icy rain, dying from exposure because the medical personnel – heroic in its efforts – was hopelessly inadequate to succour them. In the morning many sepoys were found dead without a mark upon them; others were picked up and were slowly jolted, petrified and sodden with freezing mud, in springless carts to dressing stations which for hours had been nothing better than a shambles. Still later, men arrived at Amara with wounds which for eight days had remained untended – wounds which were putrefying, gangrenous and full of maggots.[191]

Lance-Naik Lala drags a wounded officer, whom he found lying close to the enemy, to a shelter. (*Deeds That Thrill the Empire*)

Father Peal of the Connaught Rangers commented: 'Next morning some men were found dead, stark and stiff, without a scratch or wound, victims of exposure and cold.'[192] A two-hour truce allowed most of the wounded to be extracted, but he goes on to describe their experience:

> The wounded had to be carried about three miles on transport carts through slush and mud across country without any sign of a road. The poor men were coated and caked in clay. They shivered with cold and their teeth chattered. Arrived near the *Jalnar*, the improvised hospital ship, they had to wait before they could get on board. Everything was deficient. The stretchers were few, the bearers fagged out, the ground near the boat worked into a paste, the passage on board along a wet, slippery plank. Going on deck, the scene was heart-rending. Wounded and dying, European and native, all huddled together soaked to the skin, coated with clay. The medical arrangements were nil. The medical officers, though most devoted, were too few to cope with such a rush. The boat accommodation was very limited and very leaky, scarcely a dry spot aboard. Even the medical comforts, blankets and razais sent from India; were soaked and wet resembling sponges. And our wounded shivering with cold, had to be covered with these. No one who had seen this could believe that such things were possible. There was some comfort in helping our men. Several, in spite of their pain, smiled at meeting a priest, and gladly made their peace with God and received the last sacraments.[193]

Fortunately, the medical support did improve in time for the subsequent actions. However, it is clear that maintaining high morale within the Relief Force when the physical conditions and medical support were so poor was a considerable challenge. What the British and Indian troops achieved is incredible.

Initially, Lieutenant-General Aylmer hoped that he would renew the attack the next day, despite the two unsuccessful assaults, but told Major-General Townshend that his task would be made easier if a sortie could be made from Kut. However, the latter responded that, because of the poor flooded condition around the town, a foray would probably lead to a weakening of the position and his defeat.

There was no doubt that it would be a significant task to oust the Turks from the Hanna defile. General Lake acknowledged the sacrifices that had already been made, but was confident that a renewed assault could take place when 'circumstances admit'.[194] He was frustrated, particularly because at Basra there were 10,000 men and twelve guns, which might have been available for the attack if there had not been such a dire shortage of river transport and unloading facilities. Despite the failure, Major-General Younghusband was proud of his troops and the courage they had shown.

> I cannot speak too highly of the splendid gallantry of the Black Watch, aided by parties of officers and men of the 6th Jats, 97th Infantry, and 41st Dogras, in storming and occupying the enemy's trenches. Their advance had to be made across a perfectly open bullet-swept area against sunken loop-holed trenches in broad daylight, and their noble achievement is one of the highest.[195]

Meanwhile, the water levels were rising and floods were causing even greater challenges both for the defenders of Kut and the Relief Force. The two pyrrhic victories of Shaikh Saad and the Wadi, followed by the rebuttal at the Hanna defile marked the end of the first major attempt to relieve Kut.

The morale of the Relief Force was not helped by the worsening weather conditions. Diaries of the time feature frequent comments about the mud and its effect. For example, a 1/5th Buffs diary:

- 17 January – 'The rain has been our worst enemy lately. Not many wounded, but plenty sick. Dysentery is playing havoc with the men. It's the river mud water they have had to drink.'
- 18 January – 'We are living in a foot or two of mud in places. Here the roadways made by the carts are a mud stream, the mules are one mass of mud and dying wholesale.'
- 21 January – 'It has been raining for days now and the mud is indescribable.'
- 23 January – 'The men are covered with mud and unshaven, nor washed, and so haggard, all done up, so you have a job to recognise them. They are lying about as if they were on the sands at the seaside instead of the mud.'[196]

The right bank of the Tigris was overflowing and gradually increasing the discomfort, as shown by the experience of the 14th Hussars:

> Thanks to the deficiencies in food, clothing and equipment, the hardships endured by the troops were indescribable. The camp occupied by the 14th Hussars from 15 to 23 January was forever afterwards referred to by those who had the misfortune to experience its horrors as 'The Wet Wadi Camp'. The ground was low-lying and the rain soon turned it into a morass. Horses stood up to their hocks in sticky mud, with water in places several inches deep. The men having nowhere to sit down stood about with blankets thrown over their heads, their feet buried in mud, or moved about with difficulty in a mixture of slime and manure water. And over all the pitiless icy rain beat down. Very little wood was available for lighting fires.[197]

Reorganisation and further preparation was required before a further assault. A little more time seemed to be made available, because of the revised assessment of rations available in Kut. Townshend reported that the town had twenty-two days on half-rations left on 22 January and then stated three days later that a store of food had been discovered! If he killed horses and mules this would mean that he could hold out for another eighty-four days. This revised assessment must have caused considerable annoyance to both Aylmer and Lake, who had driven the Relief Force hard, with such heavy casualties and poor lines of communications, in order to ensure that Kut did not starve.

The Relief Force was still twenty-five miles from Kut and extremely tired, as illustrated by a description of the 28th Brigade:

> The Brigade was now rested, and none too soon. The Battalions had marched and fought most gallantly and in the most difficult conditions against a staunch and resolute enemy until only a fraction of their initial strength remained. Indeed whole battalions totalled little more than a company at full strength, and all were near exhaustion.[198]

By the end of January, the Turks were believed to consist of five divisions; two at Hanna, two at Kut and one at Es Sinn. This amounted to a force of 24,500 and seventy-eight guns.[199] Meanwhile, yet another Allied division, the 13th Division, was ordered to move from Egypt to Basra.

Back in Kut

A hint about the forthcoming deteriorating conditions within Kut during January 1916 comes from Major Barber's account of the siege:

2/7th Gurkhas at Kut. (IWM Q 92661)

On the 3rd we got the first shower of rain, which was to cause us much discomfort in the future. It was very cold and fuel was getting very scarce, but our greatest problem at this time was the myriads of lice that infested clothes and bedding.

He goes on to make more general comments about conditions, which will be familiar to those who have served in hot arid climes.

But it is the way of the East to provide every season with its special pest wherewith to irritate and chide its human guests. If it be not lice, then its fleas, and if not fleas, then mosquitoes, or in addition thereto, the sand-fly is provided. If a much-prayed-for wind springs up and blows them away, it brings with it a dust-storm and chokes you, or it blows so swiftly over a sun-baked desert that it scorches you and heats you till your head is like to burst. And if for some unaccountable reason none of these pests is in the ascendant, there is always the snake, the centipede, or the scorpion to fall back upon. And over and above all is the common fly, to whom, I suppose, in his myriads, pride of place should be given, for his numbers in the East sometimes are almost incredible to those who have not experienced him, and his persistence wears one out.[200]

The importance of the defenders of Kut being able to survive in such poor conditions could not be underestimated. The Turks had succeeded in isolating the garrison and making life extremely difficult for it with constant sniping and intermittent shelling, but the everyday seemingly mundane challenges of eating, sleeping, keeping clean and free from disease, whilst coping with poor weather, were often greater than the enemy threat. Major Sandes commented on the resilience of the British, Indian and Gurkha soldier.

The cheeriness of the British private soldier in the trying circumstances prevailing in January must have been seen to be believed. Almost up to his waist in water, drenched to the skin by rain, frozen during the night, and sniped continually by a vigilant foe, he would turn everything onto a joke, would sing his well-known musical hall ditties, and the more trying the situation the more, apparently, would he enjoy it. Never surely did the character of the British soldier undergo a more searching test, and never did it survive that test with greater honour than during the siege of Kut. A tribute is also due to the patient endurance of the Indian ranks and the dogged pluck of the Gurkhas which backed up the untiring efforts of our small force of British troops, so that together, British and Indian, these men withstood the best troops in the Turkish Empire for five long months.[201]

Key to maintaining morale was hope that the Relief Force would succeed and throughout January optimism reigned, as Major Barber put it, 'we never doubted the ability of the Relieving Force to get through …'[202] As the month progressed, Turks were seen heading east to confront the Relief Force and gunfire was heard in the distance. Reports filtered through to the defenders on 12 January about the victory at Shaikh Saad and on the 16th the news about the costly victory at the Wadi arrived. Morale was boosted, but soon partially quashed on 17 January when the garrison realised that progress towards them was slow. Even then, however, the defenders still expected relief within a few weeks. Within Kut, attention was now being focussed on the lack of food and the effects of torrential rain.

Food

A number of Major-General Townshend's assessments about the availability of rations in Kut have already been made in the text and it can be seen how the Relief Force and its commanders were confused about the true situation. In summary, the availability of food appears to have been reported as follows:

- 3 December 1915 – one month's full rations for British troops and two months for the Indian personnel was available, feeding the whole garrison until early January. This estimate was then pushed to mid-January 1916.
- 7 December – sixty days food reported for both British and Indian troops.
- 11 December – fifty-nine days estimated for all ranks, except for meat. It was also assessed at this time that the local population could feed themselves for three months.
- 16 January – twenty-one days of food, on half rations, left for the British and eighteen for Indians, which would feed the garrison until 18 February.
- 22 January – it was announced that twenty-two days half rations were left, but there was more food available in the town.
- 25 January – a food store was discovered following house-to-house searches, which meant that eighty-four days of half-rations were left. This should feed the defenders until 17 April. 3,000 horses and mules were also available.

Assessments appear to have been inconsistent and whilst Townshend could have been more accurate, he was certainly badly served by his supply staff. Apart from confusing the Relief Force and instigating their risky rapid advance along the Tigris and the ill-supported attacks at Shaikh Saad, the Wadi and the Hanna defile, the availability of food did became an issue for the defenders of Kut during January.

By 10 January, both Major Barber and Lieutenant Harry Bishop stated that rations were down to two-thirds normal.[203] Between 13 and 21 January, the garrison was put on half rations for the first time, though fresh meat had already run out on 26 December. In addition, according to Captain Mousley, there had been only limited amounts of tinned or fresh milk, bacon and bread available for some time.[204] Major Sandes reported, however, that some fresh beef became available on 7 January, as the oxen from the artillery heavy battery's trains had been put down. He also commented on the need to eat horseflesh and stated that on 29 January:

> the less valuable horses began to provide the British troops with meat, but a large proportion of the Indian troops (including most of the Mohammedans) refused to eat it. I was very agreeably surprised when I first tasted horseflesh. Except for a slightly novel flavour it was quite as good as the beef obtained usually in India, though in no way comparable to English beef. Some of our mess were slightly prejudiced against it at first – chiefly on sentimental grounds – but hunger soon altered their views, and all came to enjoy the food in a remarkably short time.[205]

The most was made of tinned meat, corned and bully beef. Half a pound each day was allowed and the corned variety was favoured. Captain Mousley describes his breakfast consisting of rice, bully beef and tea and goes on to mention his preference for donkey over mule for his dinner.[206]

The type and amount of rations issued to the Indian troops was different to the British requirements and the rationing situation was going to become worse for the Indian troops in late January and early February. After that the choice of food lessened and religious restrictions led to difficult decisions about their diet being made. Some form of meat was needed to maintain a healthy diet, but the Official History of the 7th Rajputs commented that 'Townshend did not handle the matter very tactfully.'[207] It goes on to state that the General did not understand the 'peculiar mentality of Indian troops', as he did not just issue an order but advised the soldiers that it was their duty to King and Country to eat horsemeat.

This became a critical issue so, for Mohammedans, advice was sought of the Imam of Delhi, whilst for the Hindus from panchayats[208] of the various castes and maharajahs and panjits.[209] Despite permission being granted by these influential characters to eat the meat, the sepoys believed that if they ate horseflesh nobody would marry their daughters! In the 7th Rajputs, two Indian officers and a non-commissioned officer of their battalion ate a meal of horseflesh in public in order to encourage the rest of the unit to do the same. This example only partially worked, however, and one soldier reportedly blew 'out his brains rather than obey'.[210] Many soldiers became used to mule steaks supplemented by pies made from starlings, sparrows or the occasional partridge and mud fish.

Fresh water supplies were maintained under difficult conditions. Four large tanks were dug and lined with tarpaulins for storage and pumps brought water from the Tigris to fill them up. There were upstream and downstream pump-houses, which had to be maintained under sniper fire and, somehow, they continued to work during the siege.

The Official History of the Dorsetshire Regiment sums up the overall situation for the defenders in January 1916.

> Thus from the beginning of 1916 onwards the story of the 2nd Dorsets in Kut is a one of gradual starvation, of patient endurance of monotonous hardships and hunger, unrelieved by any chance of activity. Fighting the floods was the chief demand on the men who, enfeebled as they were, had to put in 'hours of back-breaking work on those awful bunds' [dug out, elevated sand mounds] as one observer describes it, and to watch the rising river, knowing what little chance the bunds stood against a really bad flood.[211]

Rain

The effect of the onset of the rainy season on the Relief Force has already been described. It was also to make conditions particularly miserable for both the defenders of Kut and the besieging Turks. Major Sandes states that the heavy and continuous rain began on 8 January and the water level of the Tigris began to rise significantly.

> Every road became a river; every trench became well nigh impassable; men slipped and fell continually as they attempted to stagger along in the treacherous mud; and in the lines of defence around the town the troops tried in vain to get some slight shelter from the deluge under their waterproof sheets.[212]

As one of the key engineer officers, Sandes' men now had to spend a great deal of time keeping the routes in Kut passable. This was not an easy task, as the ground was flat and it was quickly discovered that drainage ditches dug on the side of the tracks did not work. Instead, wells were dug in corners and natives were employed to bale out the ponds in the roads with empty fuel cans and then empty them into the wells. It did not take long for the wells to become unsanitary. The half battalion of the 1/4th Hampshire Regiment in Kut described the lot of the infantry:

> This flooding extended to every part of the besieged town, causing great hardship and misery, and necessitating much hard work bailing out water and re-conditioning the defences. Living under these mole- and frog-like conditions permitted of no relaxation for the infantry, having little or no option but to sleep in their webbing equipment with pouches and haversack well stocked with ammunition, in open trenches or dug outs, often disturbed by gunfire and threatened attack. At night men felt the cold very keenly especially after rain and flooding – clothed as they were in khaki drill jackets and shorts.[213]

Conditions in the hospitals worsened and Major Barber commented that:

> The next few days it rained steadily and the lanes of Kut became indescribably filthy. The hospital main Bazaar street became a stream; many of the wards leaked, and the patients were miserable and cold. The trenches were abominable, and the Tommies were in some cases up to their waist in liquid mud.[214]

Reverend Spooner also commented on the hospitals.

> Hospital in appalling state – rain all dripping through the roof where great holes have been made by shells, on to patients' beds and into their cubicles where some poor beggars are lying on the ground, and it is impossible to stop it … Spent whole day in trying to cheer up patients in hospital, not so easy a task as there is nothing cheerful to tell them.[215]

The rain became even heavier on 17 January and the trenches were becoming increasingly uncomfortable. Standing water increased in depth, there was little scope for any drainage and the situation was made worse by the Turks who were on slightly higher ground and were able to divert some of the water into the British lines.

Serious flooding may have been prevented if the defenders had been able to construct a bund, or bank, to protect the town, but the besieging Turks made sure that practical protective measures were not feasible; their fields of fire were too effective for any work to be conducted in the open. Disaster struck overnight on 20/21 January, when at 0630 hours the water burst into the north-west sector of the First Line trenches. Barber says that 'our men were washed out of the front line trenches'[216] but also states that the Turks were in an even worse state, having to withdraw 1,000 yards.

21 January was not a good day for Major-General Townshend. Apart from the weather and the forced abandonment of the First Line he had heard from Lieutenant-General Aylmer that the Relief Force had been repulsed at the Hanna defile.

> After great exertions, with an enemy attacking us, we managed to dig ourselves in at Kut. As soon as the defences began to be respectable, and two decisive assaults by the enemy had been repulsed, rain came to swell the river, to aid the dreaded flood of the Tigris, to delay and hamper our relief force. Finally, the floods came – to wash us out of our trenches, to force the men to live standing in water up to their knees, and consequently to fill the hospitals with disease and sickness. What worries, what trials, what anxiety were experienced by me in that Siege![217]

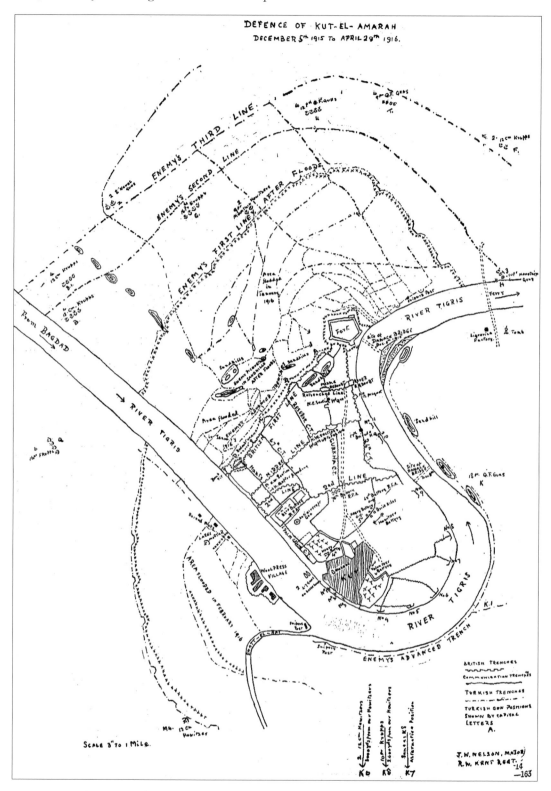

Major Nelson's map of Kut. (*Queen's Own Gazette*)

Major J. Nelson, commanding 2nd Battalion the Queen's Own Royal West Kent Regiment, recorded more detail in his diary:

> Bomb pit near river on western end of our line flooded out at 0400 hours. At 0600 hours water suddenly appeared through the middle of the Turkish trenches in front of us and broke into the left of our line. Bunds were made in seven places and successfully broken by the water. Eventually, we saved about 80 yards of the support trenches by means of two 30 feet bunds, and also filled in two traverses of the Hampshire Command Trench stamping it well in. By this time the 2/7th Gurkhas and 67th Punjabis on our right were flooded out. Eventually the battalion had to withdraw to the Middle Line across the open, having sustained 12 casualties (Royal West Kents and Hampshires) from snipers, leaving a strong piquet in the piece of the support trench that had been saved. Luckily the enemy were also flooded out of their front trench in front of us, and we managed to knock over a considerable number of them … It poured with rain all day and night, and everyone was soaked to the skin and covered with mud as there was no shelter in the Middle Line. Quite the worse day of the siege so far … Unfortunate wounded had an awful time as we could not get them to hospital.[218]

The evacuation of part of the First Line led to some casualties from enemy fire and then the need to strengthen the Middle Line with three new echelon trenches. The Turks, however, became more exposed, suffering casualties from British fire and being drowned in the water as they withdrew. Captain Mousley mentioned that: 'We shelled his ragged masses with great glee.'[219] Captain Walter Morland of the Oxfordshire and Buckinghamshire Light Infantry counted forty enemy corpses on the morning after the flood rose and some amusement was provided by a plague of frogs around the fort.[220]

The conflicting lines had been only forty yards apart in places before the flood, but the distance had now been increased to 1,000 yards. The History of the 24th Punjabis commented that morale was slightly improved because the gap had increased. Prior to the floods, nights were much noisier and more dangerous with small arms fire and sniper activity in that sector being particularly deadly. The 103rd Mahrattas

> worked up to their ankles in mud and water, while the trenches became so slippery that it was almost impossible to move without falling. Infested with lice as the result of never getting their clothing off, soaked to the skin day and night and already seriously short of fresh food, the number of sick began to increase alarmingly, throwing an extra strain on the remainder and although morale, as yet, showed no deterioration, it was obvious that under such conditions it must, before long, suffer.[221]

Lieutenant Bishop recorded that for two days after the 21st, the 66th Punjabis were able to walk in the open and examine the enemy trenches. Spare scarce firewood was collected and they found documents, which encouraged the Indian troops to 'murder their British officers and join the Turks' as their comrades had done at Gallipoli.[222] An example of psychological warfare or information operations, these leaflets seem to have had little effect on the defenders.

Other Activity

Shelling and sniping continued throughout the month, as fears were raised at times about further attacks. Heavy gunfire occurred on the 5th and 20th against the Woolpress Village and more 'hate', as it was called, happened more generally on the 10th. On 12 January, after heavy supporting fire, the Turks attempted to charge a friendly-held crater on the First Line, but they were driven back.

Firewood was becoming scarce and buildings were being dismantled in order to allow food to be cooked and to supply the engine room of the *Sumana*. Fortunately, there was a barge full of crude oil from the Anglo-Persian oilfields that had been left beside the town and that was quickly utilised. However, Captain Mousley reported that

> We are awfully short of firewood, only enough being available to cook one meal a day for the men, and provide hot water besides for breakfasts. Sometimes there is not even that. Theft of wood is punishable with death.[223]

The End of January

Morale in Kut was still good at the end of January 1916, despite the worsening physical conditions and the mental anguish of the uncertainty of relief. The Relief Force had been stopped, but was tantalisingly close to Kut. The garrison was still reasonably fit, adequately fed and supplied with enough ammunition. It was, as Major Sandes put it, 'hopeful in spite of previous disappointments'. Their commander now issued a communiqué to explain the situation.

COMMUNIQUE NUMBER ONE[224]

26 JANUARY 1916

The Relief Force under General Aylmer has been unsuccessful in its efforts to dislodge the Turks entrenched on the left bank of the river, some 14 miles below the position of Es Sinn, where we defeated the Turks in September last, when their strength was greater than it is now. Our relieving force suffered severe loss and had very bad weather to contend against. They are entrenched close to the Turkish position. More reinforcements are on their way up the river, and I confidently expect to be relieved during the first half of the month of February.

I desire all ranks to know why I decided to make a stand at Kut during our retirement from Ctesiphon. It was because, so long as we hold Kut, the Turks cannot get their ships, barges, stores and munitions past this place, and so cannot move down to attack Amarah. Thus we are holding up the whole of the Turkish advance. It also gives time for our reinforcements to come up river from Basra and so restore success to our arms; It gives time to our allies, the Russians, who are now overrunning Persia, to move towards Baghdad. I had a personal message from General Baratoff, commanding the Russian Expeditionary Force in Persia, the other day, telling me of his admiration of what you men of the 6th Division and troops attached have done in the past two months, and telling me of his own progress on the road from Kirmanshah, to Baghdad.

By standing at Kut I maintain the territory we have won in the past year at the expense of much blood, commencing with your glorious victory at Shaiba, and thus we maintain the campaign as a glorious one instead of letting disaster pursue its course down to Amarah and perhaps beyond.

I have ample food for 84 days, and that is not counting the 3,000 animals which can be eaten. When I defended Chitral some 20 years ago, we lived well on atta and horseflesh, but, I repeat, I expect confidently to be relieved in the first half of the month of February.

Our duty stands out plain and simple. It is our duty to our Empire, to our beloved King and Country, to stand here and hold up the Turkish advance as we are doing now, and with the help of all, heart and soul with me together, we will make this defence to be remembered in history as a glorious one. All in England and India are watching us now and are proud of the splendid courage and devotion you have shown. Let all remember the glorious defence of Plevna, for that is what is in my mind.

I am absolutely calm and confident as to the result. The Turk, though good behind a trench, is of little value in the attack. They have tried it once, and their losses in one night in their attempt on the

Fort were 2,000 alone. They have also had very heavy losses from General Aylmer's musketry and guns, and I have no doubt that they have had enough.

I want to tell you now, that when I was ordered to advance on Ctesiphon, I officially demanded an army corps, or at least two divisions, to perform the task successfully. Having pointed out the grave danger of doing this with one division only, I had done my duty. You know the result, and whether I was right or not; and your name will go down to history as the heroes of Ctesiphon, for heroes you proved yourselves in that battle. Perhaps by right I should not have told you of the above, but I feel I owe it to all of your to speak straightly and openly and to take you into my confidence. God knows I felt our heavy losses, and the sufferings of my poor brave wounded, and I will remember it as long as I live. I may truly say that no general I know of has been more loyally obeyed and served than I have been in command of the 6th Division. These words are long, I am afraid, but I speak straight from the heart, and you see I have thrown all officialdom overboard. We will succeed; mark my words. *Save your ammunition as if it is gold.*

Charles Townshend

Kut-al-Amarah   Major-General
26th Jan, 1916   Commanding 6th Division

Major-General Townshend recorded, in his usual immodest manner, that this communiqué: 'had a most excellent effect on the garrison. The Brigadier-Generals told me of the fine spirit it had aroused in the troops.' He went on to mention a message from General Lake which stated that 'I am always glad to have your ideas, and your suggestions are most valuable, whilst your undaunted spirits are most encouraging.'[225]

Personal accounts support their commander's comments, Barber commented: 'Thus spake Townshend, and all were pleased with the confidence he placed in them.'[226] Lieutenant Heawood records that 'In spite of these various troubles we were neither miserable or gloomy; in fact we were in the best of spirits.'[227]

Optimism was to prevail in February.

Notes

136. From the Vincent-Bingley Report Appendix 1 (1917) p.156.
137. Nunn (2007 reprint) p.200.
138. Wylly (1928) p.149.
139. Figures from Moberly (1924) p.212.
140. Wilson (1930) p.105/106.
141. Figures from Townshend (1920) p.239.
142. Figures from *The Campaign of the British Army in Mesopotamia 1914–1918* (1930) p.40.
143. Moberly (1924) p.199.
144. Ibid p.203.
145. Ibid p.45.
146. Jourdain and Fraser (1924) p.491.
147. Moberly (1924) p.207.
148. Ibid p.187.
149. Candler (1919) Vol 1 p.40.
150. Qureshi (1958) p.176.
151. Moberly (1924) p.205.
152. Townshend (1920) p.237.
153. Moynihan (1983) p.25.
154. Wylly (1928) p.150.
155. Anonymous (1918) p.17.
156. Moberly (1924) p.220 and 226.
157. Candler (1919) Vol 1 p.47.
158. The Great War (1991) Vol 1 No 4 p.151.
159. Candler (1919) Vol 1 p.49.
160. Ibid p.46.
161. Nunn (2007 reprint) p.204.
162. Moberly (1924) p.242
163. Ibid p.240
164. Mesopotamia Commission (1917) p.156.
165. Referenced in Wylly (1928) p.152.
166. *The Great War* (1991) Vol 1 No 4 p.152 and 153.
167. Wylly (1928) p.153
168. Mesopotamia Commission (1917) p.69.
169. Quoted in Neave (from Vincent-Bingley evidence) (1937) p.39.
170. Mesopotamia Commission (1917) p.68 and 93.
171. Wylly (1928) p.154.

172. Moberly (1924) p.240.

173. Ibid p.251.

174. Candler (1919) p.80.

175. Ibid p.76.

176. Moberly (1924) p.256.

177. Ibid p.260/261.

178. Ibid p.262.

179. Ibid p.263.

180. Mesopotamia Commission (1917) p.108.

181. Candler (1919) p.83.

182. Anonymous (1918) p.20.

183. Hailes (1938) p.111.

184. Moberly (1924) p.273.

185. Candler (1919) p.94.

186. Anonymous (1918) p.21.

187. *A Soldier's Memories* (1917) (Younghusband (London. Herbert Jenkins)) and *The Sepoy* (1919) (Candler (London. John Murray)).

188. *London Gazette* and Gliddon (2005) p.61.

189. Candler (1919) p.101/102.

190. Ibid p.102.

191. Evans (1926) p.60/61.

192. Jourdain and Fraser (1924) p.496.

193. Ibid p.497.

194. Moberly (1924) p.277.

195. Candler (1919) p.95.

196. Quotations from *The Great War* (1991) Vol 2 No 1 p.22–24.

197. Anglesey (1995) p.36 and 37.

198. Condon (1962) p.108.

199. Figures from *The Campaign of the British Army in Mesopotamia 1914–1918* (1930) p.44.

200. Barber (1917) p.99–100.

201. Sandes (1920) p.167.

202. Barber (1917) p.101.

203. Ibid p.122 and Bishop (1920) p.17.

204. Mousley (1922) p.38.

205. Sandes (1920) p.178–179.

206. Mousley (1922) p.52.

207. Rawlinson (1941) p.162.

208. Hindu village councillors.

209. A learned man in India.

210. Rawlinson (1941) p.163.

211. Anonymous (1933) Chapter V. No page numbers.

212. Sandes (1920) p.171.

213. Wheeler (undated) p.13.

214. Barber (1917) p.125.

215. Moynihan (1983) p.26.

216. Barber (1917) p.126.

217. Townshend (1920) p.256257.

218. Nelson (1918) p.3941.

219. Mousley (1922) p.52.

220. Neville (1938) p.163.

221. Paltan (1930) p.50–51.

222. Bishop (1920) p.21.

223. Mousley (1922) p.50.

224. Townshend (1920) p.265–266.

225. Both references; Townshend (1920) p.266.

226. Barber (1917) p.135.

227. Mockler-Ferryman (undated) p.108.

Chapter Five

FEBRUARY 1916 –
UNCERTAINTY AND ROUTINE

The bravery and endurance with which you and the troops under your command have resisted the attacks of the enemy have excited admiration of all, and I am confident resistance will be maintained until help reaches you in the near future. India thinks of you and your troops all the time.

His Excellency the Viceroy of India to Major-General Townshend, 4 February 1916[228]

A 'Quiet' Month

February 1916 could be described as a 'quiet' month, both for the defenders of Kut and the Relief Force, as there were few significant events, bar the transfer of strategic command of the whole Mesopotamia Campaign from India to the War Office in London. Conditions worsened in the town, as all troops were on half rations, disease became rife, there were still flooding problems, it was cold and the enemy sniping and shelling continued relentlessly. Meanwhile, hope of relief still prevailed as Lieutenant-General Aylmer received further reinforcements and prepared for the second attempt at breaking through the enemy defences; this would occur in March.

Dispositions

British intelligence at the beginning of February estimated that the Turks were now grouped as follows:

• Around Kut, 4,000 to 5,000 troops of the 45th Division.
• In the Hanna defile, 12,000 personnel and over 26 guns from the remnants of the 38th Division, incorporated in the 35th, and the 51st and 52nd Divisions.
• In the Es Sinn position on the right bank of the Tigris, 2,000 cavalry and two battalions of infantry, being reinforced by the 2nd Division.

The estimate was about right, though the Turkish 2nd Division was only just beginning to arrive. The Turks were ferrying elements of 35th Division across to the right bank opposite Es Sinn where they anticipated that the Relief Force would attack next time.

The Turks were proving a hardy enemy, despite their own supply difficulties. Major Sandes commented that they only had five large boats, supplemented by camel and pony-cart convoys to ferry supplies to the besieging troops and withdraw the wounded. He put their hardiness down to their ability to survive on only meagre rations, their disciplined handling of Arabs which produced a high level of work and extra resources, and the fact that the failure of the Relief Force gave them time to reinforce and re-supply their positions unharrassed.[229]

Meanwhile, Aylmer had about 4,500 troops and 20 guns on the right bank of the Tigris and 9,000 personnel and 26 guns on the left bank. In addition, 12,000 reinforcements were on their way.[230]

The New Relief Plan

General Lake approved a new plan for the continued British offensive on 4 February and the month became a time for reorganisation. The first relief attempts were during a period when Lieutenant-General Aylmer had been forced to cope with inadequate staff, scarce resources and poor supply and medical systems because of the emphasis on speed to relieve Kut. The situation had been exacerbated by the poor weather and a lack of trench mortars, heavy artillery, howitzers, verey lights to illuminate the battlefield at night, and machine-guns. There was also still a shortage of boats, aircraft, observation balloons and bridging equipment which, if available, would have helped to make the Relief Force better aware of the enemy situation and provide better manoeuvrability and unpredictability.

The new plan, based on reinforcement and better resources, was fourfold:

• Fix the enemy on the left bank of the Tigris, march across the desert with the remainder of the Relief Force and strike against the Turkish right at Es Sinn.
• Cross the Shatt al Hai.
• Attack the enemy's boats and bridges at Shumran, crossing to the left bank.
• Relieve Kut.

Major-General Townshend was to support the attack with a foray on the right bank of the river. There were significant challenges with this new plan, as there was still only limited land transport of 1,000 transport carts and about 3,000 mules,[231] so the marching soldiers would only be able to carry one day's food supply with an additional day's rations carried on the transport. If the Shatt al Hai bridgehead proved difficult, then the Relief Force would be required to make a tricky crossing of the Tigris south-east of Kut. It could be necessary to evacuate the Kut garrison from the left bank.

Aylmer believed that he would have 12,000 troops on the right bank to start the advance that could begin in the middle of the month and he communicated to Townshend that 'Whatever happens, your cooperation is essential to the fullest extent possible.'[232] Emphasis was put on the need to construct bridges across the Tigris and Hai and the possibility of supporting the Relief Force from the Woolpress Village. Townshend, in response, stated that he would do his best to support the advance, but that he would only be able to help construct bridges once the Relief Force had arrived on the right bank. His reasons were sound; his stock of roadway planks, needed for constructing a bridge, was limited and the river was nearly 500 yards wide. The current was swift, up to five knots, and any effort at constructing a bridge would be hampered by shell and sniper fire, even at night.[233] He also queried the decision to advance so early with only 12,000 troops, suggesting that it would be worth waiting for the 13th Division from Egypt, rather than risk another failure to relieve him.[234]

The Tigris Corps was to be reinforced by two infantry brigades and one artillery brigade in order to make the new plan work. A time imperative was that the main floods were expected by mid-March, so any relief attempt after that date would be even more difficult. Eventually, after much debate and communication between all of the senior commanders and the Chief of the Imperial General Staff, it was agreed that the Relief Force would not resume the offensive until further reinforcements and transport were available and that the relief attempt should take place before the floods resumed in mid-March.[235]

Considerable effort was underway to improve the logistics system and supply bases in the Basra and Shaiba areas, though these improvements were to come too late to have a significant impact on the situation in Kut. Twenty-four miles of embankments were raised to protect areas from flooding as roads and accommodation was improved. These measures were desperately needed in the muddy areas; British humour was evident in one of the sodden camps – Makina Masus, which was renamed 'Muck in the Marshes'.[236] Progress was steady, but not helped by the shortage of local and reliable labour. Medical arrangements in the south were slightly improved and materials were ordered to provide a light railway in the Basra port and Shaiba area to help shift supplies more quickly. The Indian Government had provided Sir George Buchanan, as Director-General of Port Administration and River Conservancy in January to help sort out the port facilities, so steady improvements were being made.

Change of Strategic Command

The debacle in Mesopotamia – and in particular Kut – was receiving increasing attention from London. In January, Lord Hardinge, Viceroy of India, had been extremely optimistic about Allied progress. In letters to the British Prime Minister he did not appear concerned with Major-General Townshend's predicament, as he expected the relief to be successful and he failed to appreciate the shortages of resources in the theatre of operations.[237] His military staff were not so sanguine. The Battle at Shaikh Saad proved that Turkish resistance was tough and, following a Cabinet War Committee Meeting on 13 January, India was ordered to prepare three more brigades for Mesopotamia. In addition, the Commander-in-Chief in Egypt was warned that he might have to send a complete division to the country and this force was likely to come from those troops recently evacuated from Gallipoli.

The repulse of Lieutenant-General Aylmer's Relief Force at Hanna on 21 January again prompted discussion by the War Committee and it was agreed that General Sir William Robertson, the Chief of the Imperial General Staff in London, would conduct an appreciation of the situation. General Robertson then sent a series of questions to General Sir Beauchamp-Duff, Commander-in-Chief India, to gain his views. At this stage, both commanders were not aware that Kut had enough rations to hold out until April.

General Beauchamp-Duff estimated relative strengths; the Turks, who probably numbered 32,000 men and 50 guns, could have increased their strength to 80,000 men and 132 guns by the beginning of March. By the middle of the same month, British forces advancing towards Kut should number about 38,500 men and 86 guns if the extra three brigades arrived. He admitted that an early advance on Baghdad was unlikely, that an attack by the Russians in the Khaniquin region would be beneficial to divert some Turkish assets and, if Kut fell, the Tigris Corps should hold a line on the Tigris as high up the river as possible. There, it would be better placed for subsequent actions.

General Robertson's estimate of the situation and a second paper on the control of operations in Mesopotamia, together with General Beauchamp-Duff's comments, were examined on 3 February by the War Committee. General Robertson was not convinced that Kut would be relieved and believed that contingency plans were required. He agreed with General Beauchamp-Duff's view that the British troops should remain as far up the river as possible, but believed that the Russians would be better attacking in the Erzerum (or Erzroum) area. As for future control, the War Committee agreed with General Robertson's recommendation, namely, to control Mesopotamia from London, as India could no longer provide adequate command or resources for the situation. In order to achieve success, resources had to be coordinated from throughout the Empire and only London could carry out that function efficiently. It had been acknowledged that whilst the early successes in Mesopotamia, including the seizure of the oilfields and the advance of 'Townshend's Regatta', were achieved under Indian control, later developments in the campaign had suffered due to the weak strategic command.

The new system of command was welcomed and clarified for General Lake on 10 February; General Robertson would henceforth issue orders for both Mesopotamia and Persia to the Commander-in-Chief India in the same way as other theatres of war. India was still responsible for commanding forces in the country and providing their administration, but subordinate to London. The War Office would supply assets that were not available in India from other parts of the Empire. Greater efficiency was the goal and the Official History states that 'The assumption of control by the War Office forms a landmark in the history of the campaign in Mesopotamia.'[238]

In the meantime, a possible threat from Afghanistan to India was delaying the despatch of the extra three brigades to Mesopotamia, whilst the 13th Division and 7th Mountain Artillery Brigade, in Egypt and recently returned from the evacuation of Suvla Bay, Gallipoli, were ordered to move to Basra. They were to arrive there between 27 February and 12 March. News of the forthcoming arrival of the 13th Division prompted the ever-ambitious Major-General Townshend to ask General Lake whether he could be put in command of the new 'corps', thus seeking further promotion![239]

Life in Kut

Major-General Townshend reported that at the end of January, the second phase of the siege began, as the garrison went on half-rations. He calculated he had 13,421 mouths to feed.[240] His figures were based on 10,513 troops, of whom 8,356 were combatants, and 2,908 camp followers. His defenders had suffered 2,240 casualties by the end of January and they had only '756 rounds per rifle', though plenty of gun ammunition.[241]

Rumours inevitably circulated amongst the garrison, as the weather improved slightly and the ground seemed better going for the movement of the Relief Force. Major Anderson, the commander of the Volunteer Artillery Battery in the town, described the rumour mill in his notes:

> The officers' hospital was the great centre for collecting and disseminating news – true or false. Visitors were frequent and any officer who had a friend in a General or staff officer, was cross-questioned, after their departure, as to anything he had heard and unending were the discussions as to our position and the prospects generally. A few pessimists were already in evidence but were promptly squashed and optimism fully prevailed, though it was tempered with considerable discounting of the passages in the communiqué which forecasted early February relief.[242]

He went on to say that the garrison was confident that it could defend Kut, but that, realistically, relief was not expected until 13th Division had arrived in the country from Egypt and

Lieutenant-General Aylmer's force had been fully reinforced. Captain William Spackman of the Indian Medical Services provides another perspective:

> It is very hard to keep up one's spirits sometimes, with the relieving force failing to get through and not much hope of relief for another two to three weeks unless the rain stops. We can hear their guns most days thundering away 16 miles off, but they don't get any nearer. They must be having it pretty rotten too, I guess.[243]

The enemy continued to improve their trenches, especially to the east of Kut along the Tigris in order to block any link up operation between the garrison and the Relief Force. Major Sandes described the situation as follows:

> Kut was now surrounded by a maze of hostile trenches and redoubts, often strengthened by barbed wire, and backed up by well-protected artillery at a safe distance in rear. Any attempt by the garrison to break out and attack the Turks – unless the latter were badly shaken or on the point of retirement – would have entailed enormous losses to our force, even if successful at the time.[244]

Some of the garrison succeeded in leaving the fort at night and destroying the old enemy saps, evacuated when the floods arrived, but now partly visible as the water level of the Tigris had begun to fall. Lieutenant George Naylor, the only Oxfordshire and Buckinghamshire Light Infantry officer left in the fort, reported in his diary that:

> It was an eerie time; dead bodies were lying about all over the place, reminders of 24 December, and as it was now nearly six weeks since that day the still night was heavy with the sickly smell of decomposing bodies.[245]

Further work was required to construct a dyke to ensure that the town was protected when the floods arrived again. As evening fell, each day, 300 Arabs gathered under the control of Lieutenant W. Snell of the Dorsetshire Regiment and were divided into gangs for the night's work. Once equipped with shovels and picks they headed off to improve the flood defences under control of an engineer officer or an NCO, earning themselves a rupee for about four hours work. Similar work went on around the Turkish lines and both sides harassed each other with artillery fire. A brother officer of Lieutenant Naylor, Lieutenant Heawood, who was not in the fort, described the ongoing improvements.

> During the first fortnight of February we started in earnest to fight the floods, by making bunds. It was decided that, if the floods became impossibly bad, we should hold in strength only Middle Line and the Fort, with, perhaps, the near sand-dunes (which would of course be above flood level).[246]

Lieutenant Heawood was to occupy 'Redoubt B' for the rest of the siege with Q Company, the Oxfordshire and Buckinghamshire Light Infantry. His troops worked night and day strengthening their defences to put up new wiring, assisted by working parties from other regiments and sappers. He describes the period of these preparations as perhaps the most rewarding of the siege, though the Redoubt was not tested, and with improvements in the weather he stated 'I think that I may truly say that we almost enjoyed life for the time being.'[247] However, the river began to rise again on 13 February.

Sergeant Munn of the same regiment was not happy about the increasing scarcity of rations.

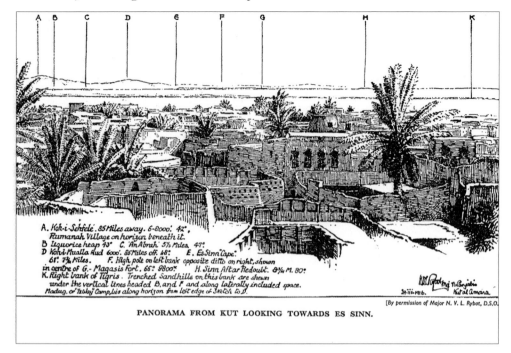

A. *Koh-i-Sehfele. 85 Miles away. 6-8000: 42°,*
Rumanah Village on horizon beneath it.
B *Liquorice heap 43°* C. *An Abrah: 5½ Miles. 47°:*
D *Koh-i-Mualla Rud 6000'. 85 Miles off. 48°:* E. *Es Sinn Cape:*
61°. 7½ Miles. F. *High pole on left bank opposite ditto on right, shown*
in centre of G.- *Magasis fort. 65° 9800°.* H. *Sinn Aftar Redoubt: 8¾ M. 80°:*
K. *Right bank of Tigris. Trenched Sandhills on this bank are shewn*
under the vertical lines headed B, and F and along laterally included space.
Madug, or Ilibay Camp, lies along horizon from left edge of Sketch to D.

[By permission of Major N. V. L. Rybot, D.S.O.]

PANORAMA FROM KUT LOOKING TOWARDS ES SINN.

Panorama from Kut looking towards Es Sinn. (Neville)

About half-way through February the rations were sadly diminishing. Tobacco was out first, and we were smoking anything that would smoke, and green leaves (dried over a fire), tea leaves and sawdust mixed, ginger cut up into small lumps. Tea ran out, and we had ginger water instead (ginger crushed and steeped in boiling water). Milk and sugar had given out long ago, likewise beef and mutton, and all the bully was gone with the exception of two day's emergency rations which were kept back until the very last.[248]

Captain Spackman also commented about the food in February.

Food is now getting an acute problem. I killed our last-but-one chicken yesterday to prevent its being stolen. A great find among my precious tinned stores (I run the messing) was two tins of snails, 'escargots', and jolly good too! Sugar is now one teaspoonful each per day. Luckily, I have a lot of jam and tinned meat saved up (and butter) so am not entirely dependent on our ration. Bread is only 12 ounces each, which is a blow, with meat at eight ounces only.[249]

There was enough food, but most items had to be carefully rationed. Improvised flour mills were organised by Captain Stephen Winfield-Smith of the Royal Flying Corps, but the bread was brown, rather than white, because of its constituents of two-thirds fine flour and one-third atta (coarse flour) and it became increasingly difficult to ensure a balanced diet for everyone, especially as vegetables had run out. Major Sandes commented that on 4 February 'our only three camels in Kut were slain to provide meat for the Indian troops' as many would still not eat the horseflesh, while the tinned milk ran out on 6 February, other than for patients in the hospitals.[250] Eggs were also becoming rare items, reserved for those in the hospitals, and on 6 February the wood ration, which was needed for cooking, was reduced to half a pound per

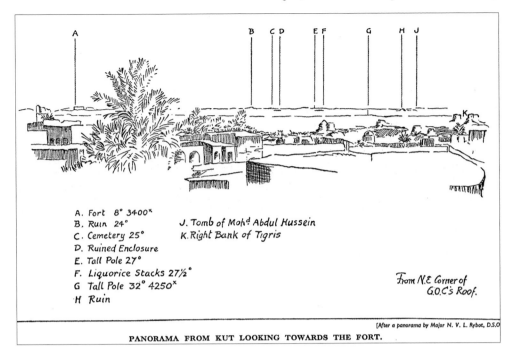

A. Fort 8° 3400ˣ
B. Ruin 24°
C. Cemetery 25°
D. Ruined Enclosure
E. Tall Pole 27°
F. Liquorice Stacks 27½°
G Tall Pole 32° 4250ˣ
H Ruin

J. Tomb of Moh.ᵈ Abdul Hussein
K. Right Bank of Tigris

From N.E. Corner of
G.O.C's Roof.

[After a panorama by Major N. V. L. Rybot, D.S.O]

PANORAMA FROM KUT LOOKING TOWARDS THE FORT.

Panorama from Kut looking towards the Fort. (Neville)

man.[251] Fortunately, as mentioned earlier, some crude oil was available and, once the garrison had become experienced in using it and dispersing the fumes, it became vital for cooking.

The horses were also hungry. Captain Mousley wrote about them eating their tails, whilst 'Don Juan' had eaten three blankets and a companion's head collar.[252] Starlings became a useful source of extra food, though the garrison's enthusiasm had to be tempered by Divisional Orders on 11 February:

> Shooting. Persons shooting starlings etc should do so on edge of gardens or edge of town, and must
> be careful not to shoot into the palm trees or over streets and houses, whence glancing pellets might
> strike people beneath. Yesterday afternoon two officers were struck by pellets apparently fired from
> General Reserve Headquarters.[253]

The garrison, particularly the Indian personnel, was becoming weaker and the hospitals consequently grew crowded. Scurvy and dysentery increased and most troops suffered from the latter to some degree or another. Major Sandes put this down to silt in the river water, which his unit tried to filter and then always boiled before drinking.[254] He also commented on the predominantly Indian troops with scurvy: 'The hospitals were full of previously able-bodied soldiers, now mere bags of skin and bone and with all their former energy gone.'[255]

13 February marked the first bombing from an enemy aircraft, much to the chagrin of Major Sandes, whose birthday it was. In contrast, Major Barber's account for the month starts with 'February brought us novelty in the form of aeroplanes.'[256] The pilot of the German plane was promptly nicknamed 'Fritz', whether he be a German or a Turk. He succeeded in causing quite a stir after the previous relatively dull weeks living in the town, though little damage was done. The incident spurred a frenzy of anti-aircraft precautions, in spite of the fact there was no

Indian Troops manning anti-aircraft gun at Kut. (IWM HV 51386)

specialist dedicated equipment or weapons for the task in Kut. Early warning air sentries were established, along with improvised alarm gongs made from empty brass shell-cases. Six maxim machine-guns were strapped to barrels and elevated to engage the enemy, whilst a 13-pounder Quick Firing field gun was also secured and elevated and placed in a circular pit from where it could be fired skyward with a 360 degrees arc of fire. Major Sandes reported that the pilot was once hit in the thigh with a bullet and twice hit by shrapnel from the field gun.[257]

'Fritz's' routine became quite predictable, as there was plenty of warning; his take off in the distance could be seen, his airplane was slow and noisy and he usually dropped four bombs on each fly past. However, this new threat from the air was not popular; Major Barber:

> We didn't like it. Cooped up in a small mud town we felt rather like rats in a trap, and very helpless against this new form of frightfulness. Your bomb comes down with a vicious scream and bursts with a nasty flame and an equally unpleasant bang[258] … It was a nuisance this bombing, and we all heartily cursed it.[259]

The bombing quickly became a new routine and, by the next day, Captain Mousley was commenting in his diary, the 'Turkish aeroplane bombed us again today. Yesterday 35 people including Arabs were wounded.'[260] Some of the soldiers' enthusiasm for shooting at aeroplanes had to be controlled. Major Nelson, commanding the half battalion of the 2nd Battalion Queen's Own Royal West Kent Regiment, reported that some firing was so wild and dangerous that only ten picked shots from every unit were allowed to engage the aircraft.[261] Following a number of civilian casualties, it was discovered that people on the ground were usually safe if they made sure that they took shelter in the bottom of two-storied buildings as the bombs would explode on the roof.

Friendly aircraft dropped newspapers, items such as rifle pull-throughs, vital millstones for grinding the corn and messages for the hierarchy, but there was no mail from families and friends. Major Barber commented that the 'ordinary man' was not happy about the lack of mail: 'He groused bitterly in consequence as time went on, 'it never seemed to strike them down below that we were simply pining for news from our people at home.'[262] Even today, the morale of troops is significantly affected by the ability to communicate with loved ones and satellite communications have not totally replaced the value of a letter.

There was a less lethal irritation in Kut that dominated many soldiers' lives, and featured more and more as the weather gradually became warmer – lice. Major Anderson:

> The trenches were full of them, from a very early stage, and being in constant contact with the native troops and having such rare opportunities for baths and a change of clothes or even a wash, it was impossible to keep clear of them. They are not only loathsome things but are also a danger as they are understood to be carriers of typhus and we heard about this time that the Turks were having a bad time from this.[263]

Sergeant Munn was less subtle, as his regiment suffered from 'millions of 'em, which caused us more trouble than all the Turks on earth.'[264]

The Turks were discomforted, but they had the upper hand in Mesopotamia at this stage and learned, about this time, of German successes at Verdun. The Kut garrison heard them give three cheers, but the British displayed their usual streak of grim humour; the troops were reputedly informed by their commander that the Turks must be either having a pay day, being inspected by 'von Pilsener' or celebrating the death of their leader, Enver Pasha![265] Morale was partially improved in Kut on 16 February, when the defenders heard that the Russian General Baratoff had captured Erzerum from the Turks. Any Allied action, despite its distance away in the Caucasus and Northern Persia, which might affect the Turkish hold in Mesopotamia, was welcomed. As Lieutenant Bishop recorded: 'In particular, the taking of Erzerum by the Russians cheered us up, and made us hope that the Russian force approaching Baghdad from Persia would be equally successful.'[266] There were even discussions amongst the defenders about whether the Russians might relieve Kut before the British.

Another feature of life in Kut were auctions of dead officers' belongings, described by Major Barber as 'very sad affairs, though necessary.'[267] They appeared to become almost social occasions where brother officers from around Kut seized the opportunity to gather above ground and meet each other.

Enemy snipers were still very active. Major Barber described one of his patients being hit.

> The usual evening hate [Turkish gun barrage] took place on the 5th, and a sniper succeeded in hitting one of my patients. The poor wretch was basking in a square yard of sunshine, and picking innumerable lice off his blanket, when a bullet came round some corner and hit him in the leg. He was very depressed over it; said he had no luck in this war. He had lost two brothers in France, and this was the third time he had himself been hit.[268]

There was also no let up from the shelling. As Major Barber stated, 'the 'hates' became more intense, and night bombardments became regular and annoying features. We supposed they were trying to wear out our nervous systems.'[269]

The rain returned in the middle of February and, as Major Barber described, 'the roads again became rivers of mud.'[270] Whilst the sappers worked on the bunds at night, as described earlier, the wet conditions made work difficult for the medical staff and patients.

> Hospital life was made miserable by it. Roofs leaked, rafters broke, and walls here and there collapsed, and it was difficult to keep anything clean; but the patients bore it all with most extraordinary patience and never groused.

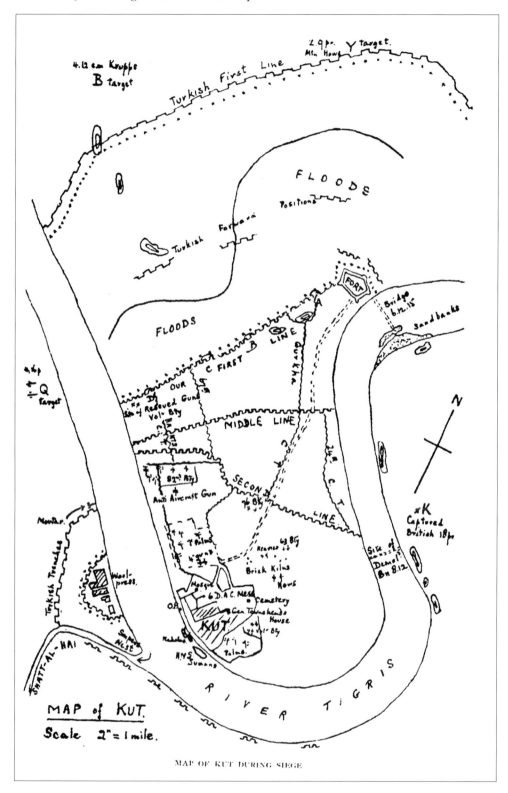

Captain Mousley's map of Kut. (Mousley)

Men of the half battalion of the 1/4th Hampshire Regiment avoided hospitalisation if they possibly could.

> Conditions in the hospitals were appalling, and no man sought admission except in the most extreme circumstances; anywhere out in the open trenches was preferable to being tortured by bugs, fleas and mosquitoes (the devil's trinity) in overcrowded hospitals devoid of most medical requirements and grossly under-staffed.[271]

There was increased excitement in Kut on 21 and 22 February in expectation of supporting a relief effort and the garrison was stood to arms. Captain Mousley described himself as 'booted and spurred'.[272] Friendly guns were heard in the east at about 0700 hours on the morning of the 22nd and Major-General Townshend noted: 'Apparently much confusion was caused in the enemy's main camp behind the Hanna position; but they did not retreat.'[273] More of this action by the Relief Force later, though hopes faded, as Major Barber wrote, 'Hour by hour went by and found us still waiting and tense with excitement.'[274]

Also on the 21st, Major-General Townshend mentioned in his diary the increased frequency of desertions by some of his Indian troops. He reports a sepoy of the 119th Infantry being shot for killing his adjutant, and soldiers from the 66th Punjabis, 76th Punjabis and 120th Infantry deserting.

Darkness on the 22nd heralded a major bombardment and increased levels of enemy fire directed at the Woolpress Village. For Captain Mousley, this was an exciting and dangerous experience:

> I ran to the observation station, river front, in case the field-guns were required to go into action. For 40 yards I had to run the gauntlet from the street end to the door. There was not an inch of cover and the bullets were splashing on the road and into the buildings on my left. The fire was swishing as thick as water from a powerful fire hose. Goodness knows how I got through.[275]

This fire lasted almost an hour and the garrison expected an attack, but as the commander commented: 'evidently the Turks could not make up their minds to rush into the open and carry the village with the bayonet, and eventually the fire died out.'[276]

Morale was slightly improved on 26 February when four British aircraft were seen to fly up-river and bomb the Turks at Shumran. As Major Sandes put it: 'We knew to our great joy that the enemy was being paid back in his own coin by bombs from our aeroplanes.'[277]

Patience was being pushed to its limits within the garrison, but humour and optimism prevailed. On 28 February, two sweepstakes were started based on the anticipated date that the first ship from the Relief Force would pass the fort, one by Lieutenant Mathews, Royal Engineers and one by Lieutenant Clifton, East Surrey Regiment, aide de camp to Major-General Townshend. On the same day, a dinner was held to celebrate the sixteenth anniversary of the Relief of Ladysmith in the South African War (See page 112). Perhaps the Kut garrison might be relieved soon?

The Relief Force

The aim of the action at Hanna on 22 February, which had been delayed by rain for twenty-four hours, was to wear down the enemy, particularly in their main camp, identify their main positions by demonstration and possibly induce them to vacate the defile. The 28th Brigade was to engage the enemy at Hanna, whilst the 21st Brigade feinted a crossing at the Suwacha (or

Suwaikiya) Marshes to the Turks' left. Major-General Gorringe marched up the right bank of the Tigris with the Cavalry Brigade, 36th Brigade and two batteries of guns.

The Turks were surprised, but their position was strong and Gorringe's force did not have the ability to cross the river as pontoons were not available. Firing continued and he was wounded during the following day, having to be replaced by Major-General Keary. The right bank was reinforced by another brigade. Although the Turks showed no signs of being dislodged, Lieutenant-General Aylmer had identified many of the enemy positions and 'softened them up'. He had also positioned the Relief Force in better start points ready for the next main assault. However, only limited objectives were achieved and Candler observed in frustration that 'to the very end, and in spite of all the experience, the Staff persisted in regarding the Turk as a timid character who might be frightened out of his bolt-hole by a noisy demonstration of force.'[278]

The maxim of 'never underestimate the enemy' again seemed to be forgotten, but Candler agreed with Gorringe's assertion that if their force on the right bank had been equipped with pontoons, they could have achieved a great success that day.

The hardships that the Relief Force had suffered had a continuing impact. A number of units found themselves having to join together in order to regain their fighting power. In early February, the 1/4th Hampshires amalgamated with the 1/5th Buffs to form the 'Territorial Composite Battalion' on the left bank of the Tigris. This new battalion became more popularly known as the 'Huffs' with a Royal Sussex Regiment officer in command, Major Foster Newton Thorne, and a new strength of 730 men.

At the same time, the 'Highland Battalion' was formed from two decimated battalions – 2nd Battalion of the Black Watch and 1st Battalion the Seaforth Highlanders. Five officers and 178 other ranks were all that was left of the Black Watch and they formed the first two companies of the new unit. The ensuing esprit de corps was described as producing 'a tradition worthy of the spirit and fighting record of both regiments.'[279] Other depleted regiments, such as the 37th Dogras and 41st Dogras, were also amalgamated in the field. In their case they became the 'Composite Dogra Battalion'.[280]

With the Royal Flying Corps in Mesopotamia. (*The Illustrated War News*, 7 June 1916)

Captain Murray and aircraft. (National Army Museum 1983-12-72-32)

Air Support

At this point it is worth mentioning the use of aircraft in Mesopotamia. 'Air power' had not yet developed and the first flight of 30 Squadron of the Royal Flying Corps did not arrive in the country until May 1915. However, many soldiers were anticipating their importance: 'Many of us had never seen an aeroplane, and probably none of the enemy had, while among the Arabs, such magic would have a great effect.'[281] Another observer wrote, romantically: 'In Ahwaz I saw my first aeroplane, and it really did look nice. I rather envied the men in the machine, up in the cool air, getting a lovely breeze, and sailing along like a gigantic bird.'[282]

Initially, the Squadron's mixed British, Indian, Australian and New Zealand air and ground crews only supported four Maurice Farman aeroplanes and, most of the time, there was just one aircraft serviceable. They did carry out useful reconnaissance prior to the actions at Qurna and Amara and a sketch map was produced for Major-General Townshend's use during the first battle at Kut. In addition, they successfully ranged artillery on the enemy trenches at Nasiriya, gaining praise from General Nixon. 'I have to place on record the excellence of the work performed by officers and men of the Royal Flying Corps, whose valuable reconnaissance materially assisted in clearing up the situation before the battle of the 24th July.'[283]

As the advance up the Tigris continued, other aircraft arrived to support the effort. By January 1916 three flights had been established. Aircraft were a mixture of Maurice Farmans, Caudrons, Martynside Scouts, Sunbeam Short seaplanes, BE2Cs and Voisins. As well as reconnaissance and artillery spotting tasks, a number of bombing raids took place, mainly on the enemy aerodrome at Shumran. On 1 October 1915, there was even a first reconnaissance over Baghdad. The future potential of air power was illustrated by the effects of a bombing raid conducted in October.

> On the 22nd a bombing raid was carried out by three machines on a hostile Arab village five miles south-west of Fraser's Post. Sixteen two pound, two 20 pound, Hales High Explosive and three 30 pound bombs were dropped. On the 27th the village flew the white flag.[284]

However, as the Indian Staff College commented on aircraft and air cooperation in its *Critical Study of the Campaign*:

> All slow and except for the last type (BE2Cs), with a very poor performance. Aerial photography had not reached Mesopotamia. The only maps available were produced by officers sketching from the air and were therefore quite inaccurate.[285]

The technology was basic, though lessons concerning the use of aircraft were being learned fast. Unfortunately, the aircraft were extremely unreliable, vulnerable and dangerous. Examples of aircraft being forced to land because of magneto troubles, damaged on the ground by bad weather, wrecked on landing or shot down by rifle or machine-gun fire were numerous, and on 1 December only one aircraft was available for reconnaissance. Also, airfield support was not helped by the floods and mud. Their basic capabilities meant that it was often difficult to believe some of their sightings and so commanders were wary about their use. An example of this occurred before the Battle of Ctesiphon. Initially, a seaplane observer reported to Major-General Townshend that the position was unoccupied, but he decided to confirm the situation with another flight. The second pilot reported 'that the position was undoubtedly occupied; that he had seen four large paddle-steamers, lighters, mahelas, storehouses and at least 3,000 or 4,000 men.'[286]

Despite the aircrafts' shortcomings, their reconnaissance missions, artillery spotting tasks and later attempts to relieve Kut with food were all important and by the time of the Battle of Ctesiphon they were being employed in a reasonably coordinated manner. The crews showed incredible bravery, as shown by an incident in November 1915:

> On the 13th Captain White and observer Captain Yeats-Brown in Maurice Farman '2' landed and attempted to cut the telegraph wires north and west of Baghdad, but were taken prisoners. Both officers subsequently escaped.[287]

However, individual heroism was not enough; air support was unreliable and there were never enough resources:

> The number of machines available was quite inadequate for even normal reconnaissance purposes. Contact or counter-attack work, which would have been invaluable, was out of the question: and artillery spotting was a rare luxury.[288]

Three damaged aircraft were actually left in Kut during the siege. This unfortunate Royal Flying Corps detachment was commanded by Captain S. Winfield-Smith and included another pilot and three observers. The lack of air capability was to be highlighted in the coming February. At the beginning of that month the Relief Force again only had one serviceable aircraft available, though three more were in the air by 1 March. Air superiority was lost nevertheless and Turkish air capability had increased; the enemy had better aircraft in greater numbers and were to start bombing both Kut and the Relief Force headquarters.

On the River Euphrates

Whilst the main effort continued to be for the relief of Kut, Major-General Brooking ordered the withdrawal of his detachment of 1,600 troops, based on 24th Brigade, from Butaniya in early February, when the enemy threat in that area had abated. A further detachment – which

Above Commonwealth War Graves
in Kut today – Privates W. Cannon
and A. Vinson of the Oxfordshire and
Buckinghamshire Light Infantry and
Private J. Mitchell of the Durham
Light Infantry. (Brigadier Mark
Armstrong)

Right Commonwealth War Grave
Kut, Private E. Paston, Norfolk
Regiment. (Brigadier Mark
Armstrong)

included troops from 12th Cavalry, the other half of the 2nd Battalion Queen's Own Royal West Kent Regiment (the others were in Kut), 1/5th Queen's Royal Regiment (West Surrey) and 114th Mahrattas – was sent from Nasiriya to support this move. The withdrawal was successful but only after continuous harassment by 5,000 Arabs. There were 373 friendly casualties and the commander spoke highly of the conduct of the West Kents. The CO of the latter battalion, Lieutenant-Colonel S. Pedley wrote about his fellow regimental soldiers, who were incarcerated in Kut, in the *Queen's Own Gazette* on 21 February 1916.

> Still I am unable to give any news of our two companies at Kut. They seem to be rather hemmed in, and when accounts of their experiences come to hand there will be more interesting reading than many expect.[289]

He was right.

The End of February

Life continued to be dominated by anticipation of relief and the adverse conditions created by the constant sniping and shelling, the weather, the scarcity of food, and disease. Changes in routine were welcomed and any surprise discoveries of items of food or tobacco were relished. Major Sandes enjoyed a rare delicacy, mule's tongue in aspic, on the last day of the month.[290]

By the end of February, the casualties in Kut had grown to 2,927. Of this number 846 had been killed or died of wounds, 1,608 were wounded, 30 missing or had deserted and 443 died of disease.[291] 'Optimism still reigned supreme, but the prolonged uncertainty was very trying.'[292]

Maintaining Morale

On 28 February 1916, a dinner was held in Kut to mark the anniversary of the Relief of Ladysmith, which took place during the South African War against the Boers. Optimism still prevailed amongst the garrison that it too would be relieved within the next month. The anniversary provided an excuse for a party and the imaginative menu reflects the usual satirical humour of the British Army.

One is reminded of the rendition of 'Is this the way to Amarillo' sung by British troops in Iraq in 2004 and the annual celebration of old battle honours and customs that still prevails even when a regiment is posted abroad and on operations, wherever it may be and under any circumstances.

SIXTEENTH ANNIVERSARY DINNER
RELIEF OF LADYSMITH
To be held at Hotel Optimus, Kut.
February 28th 1916 at 8 p.m.

MENU
HER'S D'OUEVRES

Olives	All Nations
SOUP	
Cheval	D'Artillerie
FISH	
Sole	Trench Sabot

ENTREE

Cutlets   Jaipur Pony Superb

JOINT

Horse Loin   Shell trimmings
Mule Saddle   Bhoosa Sauce
                                                                 Vegetable au Cotton

SWEETS

Windy Lizzie Pudding   Flatulent Fanny Sauce

SAVOURY

Whizz Bangs with Starlings of Toast

DESSERT

Liquorice Root   Mahailah Squares
Coracle-chunks   Bomb shells

COFFEE

S. & T. Special and Arabian

WINES

Liquorice, Tigris Water, Date Juice, etc

Cigars   Relief Special
Cigarettes   Kut Favourites

Bellums, Mahailahs, A. T. Carts, G. S. Wagons at 3 a.m. sharp

GOD SAVE THE KING EMPEROR

By kind permission of Fritz and Franz [the two German aeroplane pilots] the KUT ORCHESTRA
will render the following programme during Dinner.

PART I

1. OVERTURE	'Here we are again'	*Aylmer*
2. WALTZ	'Tantalising Aeroplanes'	*Turco*
3. SELECTION	'Shelling Recollections'	*Windy Lizzy*
4. SONG	'I'm a long way from Kut al Amara'	*'J.N.'*
5. FANTASIE	'The Wizz Bang Glide'	*Woolpress Bill*
6. WALTZ	'Those Tinkling Geggs'	*Observer*
7. SELECTION	'Bombing Memories'	*Miles Running*
8. TWO STEP	'Be quick and get under'	*A. Dugout*

INTERVAL

During the Interval the Anti-Aircraft Squadron, ably supported by 13 pounder, will give a short
sketch entitled 'Aeroplanes and how to scare 'em.'

PART II

1. MARCH	'Over the hills not far away'	Percy Lake
2. CORNET SOLO	'I hear you calling me'	Aylmer
3. SELECTION	'Odoriferous Kut'	A. Smell
4. SONG	'We don't want to lose you, but we think you ought to go'	Von der Gotz
5. WALTZ	'Mail Time Dreams'	I.E.F.
6. ROMANCE	'When shall we three meet again'	Weston-Kee-Craw
7. GALLOP	'The GEE HEE'S Lament' Stewpot	
8. Regimental Marches	R. F.C. Mechanical Transport 'Maxim Gun Battery'	

Notes

228. Townshend (1920) p.268.
229. Sandes (1920) p.183–184.
230. Moberly (1924) p.294.
231. Ibid p.294.
232. Moberly (1924) p.504.
233. Townshend (1920) p.272.
234. Moberly (1924) p.506.
235. Ibid p.299.
236. Ibid p.280.
237. Ibid p.284.
238. Ibid p.288.
239. Townshend (1920) p.273.
240. Ibid p.267.
241. Ibid p.355–356.
242. Anderson (1960) p.55.
243. Spackman (1967) p.4.
244. Sandes (1920) p.182.
245. Neville (1938) p.170.
246. Mockler-Ferryman (undated) p.109.
247. Ibid p.110.
248. Mockler-Ferryman (undated) p.130–131.
249. Spackman (1967) p.5.
250. Sandes (1920) p.186–187.
251. Barber (1917) p.151.
252. Mousley (1922) p.62.
253. Nelson (1918) p.3957.
254. Sandes (1920) p.193.
255. Ibid p.195.
256. Barber (1917) p.136.
257. Sandes (1920) p.191–192.
258. Barber (1917) p.141.
259. Ibid p.142.
260. Mousley (1922) p.61.
261. Nelson (1918) p.3957.
262. Barber (1917) p.137.
263. Anderson (1960) p.61.
264. Neville (1938) p.173.
265. Ibid p.172.
266. Bishop (1920) p.26.
267. Barber (1917) p.144.
268. Ibid p.148.
269. Ibid p.158.
270. Ibid p.155.
271. Wheeler (undated) p.14.
272. Mousley (1922) p.71.
273. Townshend (1920) p.283.
274. Barber (1917) p.165.
275. Mousley (1922) p.72.
276. Townshend (1920) p.283.
277. Sandes (1920) p.194.
278. Candler (1919) p.122.
279. Wauchope (1925) p.222.
280. Atkinson (undated) p.54.
281. Birch Reynardson (1919) p.144.
282. Black Tab (1917) p.88.
283. Anonymous (undated) p.3.
284. Ibid p.5.
285. Quetta Critical Report (1925) p.211.
286. Eady (1930) p.104.
287. Anonymous (undated) p.6.
288. Quetta Critical Report (1925) p.211.
289. *Queen's Own Gazette* (April 1916) p.3480.
290. Sandes (1920) p.197.
291. Moberly (1924) p.308.
292. Barber (1917) p.171.

Chapter Six

MARCH 1916 – THE SECOND RELIEF ATTEMPT

As I write it rains, and with every drop of rain the time within which the garrison, and more important still, the strategic position at Kut, can be relieved, shortens.
Captain Edward Mousley[293]

Anticipation in Kut

March was dominated by the second main attempt to relieve Kut, which occurred at the end of the first week. The defenders became increasingly weak under the attrition of enemy guns and sniper fire combined with the lack of nourishment and return of the floods.

The month started with a heavy bombardment of the town, described by Captain Mousley, who came close to being killed, as 'the biggest artillery bombardment the enemy has yet made.'[294] He went on to explain the routine effects of a Turkish gun being fired, an experience that would have been common to the rest of the garrison.

One counted the usual 12 seconds from the distant boom of these targets and then heard the invisible singers in the mid-air, and then krump-krump-sh-sh-sh-sh as the shells struck with a deep bass explosion followed by the swishing sound of falling earth that had been hurled up aloft.[295]

This shelling was coordinated with a bombing raid of three German planes. There was frustration that the improvised anti-aircraft defences appeared to have little effect and that the hospital seemed to be regularly targeted by the enemy. The civilians and hospital patients appeared to be the main victims from the aerial attacks. Major-General Townshend commented

If any of the German pilots had fallen into the hands of my troops he would have been torn to pieces. It was not fear of their bombs, for everyone treated the aeroplanes as a joke, running to cover at the last moment with shouts of laughter. But the victims were often women and children and our poor wounded in the hospital.[296]

At this time, Major Sandes mentioned the effectiveness of the garrison's guns and praised the fortitude of the often forgotten naval gunners, who were under regular enemy gunfire.

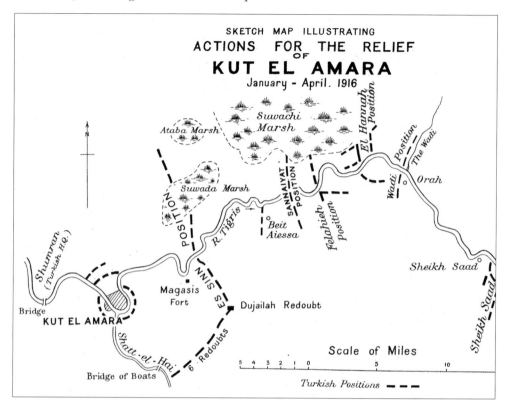

Actions for the relief of Kut, January–April 1916. (Mockler-Ferryman)

The heroism of the naval crews of the 4.7 inch naval guns afloat below the upstream pump-house at Kut was beyond all praise in this bombardment as throughout the siege the sailors manning these four useful long-range weapons were grouped closely around their guns in the tiny horse boats moored out in the river – quite unprotected except by the shields of the guns and a few thin steel side-plates proof only against rifle bullets.

He quoted them as saying 'We know we have got to be killed sooner or later, but we hope it will be later.'[297]

Morale was not improved by the decision to issue gas-respirators on 4 March, because of a rumour that the Turks might employ this relatively new weapon. Strange metal cylinders were seen being unloaded from an enemy ship in the distance, so Major-General Townshend was only being prudent dispite his remark that 'The use of poison gas is a cowardly barbarism worthy of Chinese pirates.'[298]

Incredibly, with the next relief attempt about to begin, Townshend chose this period to send his despatches about the Battle of Ctesiphon and the withdrawal to Kut to General Lake. He was after official recognition of what had been achieved by his command, by encouraging the prompt issue of awards and promotions. Never bashful, he even expressed concern that other major-generals, junior to him and in other theatres of the War, had been promoted to lieutenant-general over his head![299] Perhaps he believed that morale within the town would receive a significant boost if his recommendations were pursued.

Hope was building that the successes of the Russian General Baratoff against the Turks elsewhere would lead to enemy withdrawals and a greater chance of relief. The Russians had launched a force of 15,000 troops and forty-six guns from the Caucasus into Persia in an attempt to cooperate with the British against the Turks, but progress had been slow. It was hoped that the Russian presence and threat would help divert the enemy. Rumour and false hope flourished within Kut and Captain Mousley remembered a hopeful verse:

> The mountains looked at Baratoff
> And Baratoff looked on me;
> And in my evening dream I dreamed
> That Kut might still be free.[300]

There was great anticipation in Kut that the second relief attempt would succeed and the defenders were reorganised into three groups to ensure that they could react to any success. Major-General Delamain had command of the first group in the north-west of the town, whilst Major-General Hoghton controlled the second grouping in the north-east. An additional central grouping was the 30th Brigade under Major-General Melliss with a mixed brigade commanded by Colonel Evans comprising the Norfolks, Dorsets, 22nd Punjabis and 24th Pioneers. The guns were positioned so that they could best cover the most likely approaches of the Relief Force. Overall command was to be from Major-General Townshend in the centre who believed that this new grouping would enable his force to support quickly the relief attempt from different directions and allow him to cross the Tigris if the need arose.

Disappointingly, Lieutenant-General Aylmer's attack was delayed twice due to bad weather and Townshend showed some sympathy for him:

> Throughout the siege the weather conditions were entirely in favour of the Turks. Never had a com-
> mander worse luck than General Aylmer in this respect; he had only to project an attack for driving
> rain and a regular gale to arise, wash away his bridge, and make the ground like a pudding, rendering
> it impossible for his troops to march or move the guns.[301]

However, the defenders' arrangements were in place by 0530 hours on 8 March, the date of the next relief attempt. Major Barber described his soldiers' level of expectation: 'They were in high spirits at the thought of getting a move on at last, and our blood raced through our veins with the anticipation of exciting events.'[302]

Gunfire was heard at 0710 hours from the direction of the Dujaila Redoubt with a lull at 0830 hours. Heavy rifle fire occurred from 1400 to 1600 hours when another bombardment began against the Redoubt for a further hour. From the Kut perspective, all was quiet that night – too quiet for the anticipated success. The Regimental History of the Oxfordshire and Buckinghamshire Light Infantry recalled, as its soldiers stood in the fort at Kut:

> The Regiment hoped on, and the night found all ranks still hoping and still ready to take their
> part. The next morning the bombardment started again to southward but it died away, and left the
> Regiment, if not actually gloomy, at any rate more anxious and pensive as the day dragged on.[303]

The garrison had raised their hopes very high prior to this second relief attempt, so disappointment was felt deeply. Lieutenant Heawood, of the same regiment, illustrates the anticipation.

> We spent that day cooped up in the old stable yard, in a somewhat restless state, occasionally climbing
> up to the one safe coign of vantage on a wall, from which little could be seen, owing to a very thick
> mirage. This entertainment was varied by the receipt from time to time of orders, explanatory of

what we were going to do if General Aylmer did actually break through, and our manner and order of trying to cross the river.[304]

The 24th Punjabis were also poised in anticipation of action and had even spent money on extra food to make themselves as strong as possible in case they were deployed out of the town. That evening, Major Sandes commented: 'We were a very silent mess that night, each one being too busy with his own thoughts to discuss lighter subjects.'[305]

The Battle at Dujaila Redoubt

Prior to the attack on the Dujaila Redoubt, the Relief Force had occupied trenches within 300 yards of the Turkish positions at Hanna on the left, northern, bank of the Tigris. It was the right, southern, bank that offered a greater opportunity for success, according to both Lieutenant-General Aylmer and General Lake. Major-General Keary held a position there, just east of Sannaiyat, but an attack was needed soon otherwise the floods would worsen, more Turkish rein-forcements would arrive and their defences would be strengthened. There was also concern about the improving Turkish lines of communication as their bridging assets in the area of Magasis (or Maqasis) increased. With the imminent arrival of the British 37th Brigade, it was thought that about 25,000 personnel could be manoeuvred against the Turkish force of 11,000 on the right bank. The odds would be further improved with support from a force launched from within Kut.

Aylmer realised that he would only be successful in this enterprise if surprise was achieved. All movement, however difficult, was confined to darkness and during the first week in March he

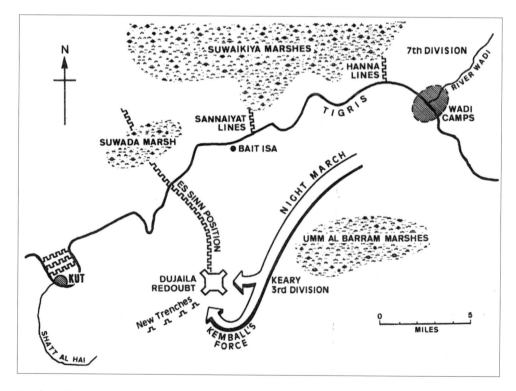

Attack on Dujeila Redoubt, 8 March 1916 – detail. (Candler)

had attempted to reinforce the Turks' perceptions that he would attack at Hanna by issuing false orders and maintaining a bombardment and forward patrols on the northern bank of the Tigris.

The plan was to contain the enemy at Hanna, on the left bank, with the 7th Division under the command of Major-General Younghusband, whilst the southern force, based on the 3rd Division, conducted a night approach march of fourteen miles in two columns and attack the Es Sinn position in the area of the Dujaila Redoubt. One column, under the command of Major-General Kemball, would attack the Redoubt and conduct a flanking attack, whilst the other, under Major-General Keary, attacked the enemy just north of the Redoubt from the east. Nine planes were available to deal with hostile aircraft. The aim of the operation seemed simple, as described by Tigris Corps Order Number 26, issued on 6 March: 'The intention of the Corps Commander is to turn the right flank of the Es Sinn position by seizing the Dujaila Redoubt and following this up by capturing the whole position.'[306] Aylmer kept control of the 7th, 8th and 35th Brigades ready to deal with any Turkish counter attack.

One concern was that Major-General Kemball – whose column was key – had little time for consideration of the plan and was only supported by an improvised staff. Major-General Gorringe would have commanded, but was wounded; Major-General Keary was the next logical commander, as 3rd Division's leader, but he had earlier disagreed with Lieutenant-General Aylmer about his plan.[307] However, the plan went ahead with a fighting strength on the right bank of '1,286 sabres, 18,891 rifles and 68 guns.'[308]

Distances, bearings, formations required and rest periods were calculated and issued and the columns were ordered to be in their final assaulting positions by 0615 hours on 8 March. It was a considerable challenge to coordinate the move of 20,000 troops in column, at night, at distances up to ten miles. Navigation had to be accurate and surprise was critical; many of the troops were tired, having spent the previous night crossing the Tigris. There was also an emphasis on speed, but that was going to be difficult to achieve because of the size of the columns moving at night and their integrated transport, which often moved more slowly than the marching troops. Some of the guns had to be moved seven miles in darkness to reach their rendezvous before the advance and this movement was to take longer than expected, hence delaying the columns.

Captain K. Mason, Royal Engineers, led the night move 'assisted by a small staff who checked the dead reckoning with a bicycle wheel, three pedometers and an improvised pace-stick'.[309] Fortunately, the weather was good and the night clear. By the middle of the night, despite a two-and-a-half hour delay at the start, the move had gone well. Major-General Kemball's lead brigades then had to change formation into line in anticipation of a forward enemy position, which fortunately did not exist. However, they encountered a five-foot deep entrenchment, which took a while to bypass, whilst at the same time there was a delay as Major-General Kemball's staff tried to remove some of the horse-pulled transport from his column: 'Occasionally, too, mules broke loose and careered away into the darkness, flinging their loads far and wide, in perverse contempt of the plans of men.'[310]

The British and Indian troops were extremely fortunate that they did not run into any Turkish piquets; apart from alerting the enemy, the columns would have been thrown into confusion and there would have been even further delays in the advance. However, the march was debilitating, the History of the Connaught Rangers commenting that 'from first to last … the night march was wearisome plodding through swamps and sticky mud, and many of the men were exhausted before arriving at the places of deployment.'[311]

For any experienced modern soldier, the confusion created by these simple activities, at night and without the luxury of image intensifiers, can be appreciated. Dawn was at 0545 hours and at 0600 hours Major-General Kemball's column found themselves about 1,500 yards short of their line of departure for the attack.

Turkish trenches at Dujaila. (Black Tab)

The Dujaila Redoubt was 4,000 yards away to the north-west and, judging by the enemy's inactivity, surprise appeared to have been achieved. The lead battalion, Lieutenant-Colonel G. Walton's 26th Punjabis, was keen to attack, but was held back by Major-General Kemball. This was despite of an earlier reconnaissance by the political officer Major Gerald Leachman, who had reported to Kemball that the enemy position was weakly held and the view of the facing brigade commander, Brigadier-General G. Christian, was that the attack should go ahead immediately. Major-General Kemball was, however, not prepared to take a risk. He wanted to ensure that all was ready before the assault began. By 0700 hours his force was concentrated in a small area, still in column, though hidden in a large depression, whilst his commanders took their bearings. Kemball's troops were not yet dispersed in open order for the attack and the ground between him and the enemy positions was flat and bare. He was extremely vulnerable to enemy artillery fire.

According to later Turkish reports, surprise had indeed been achieved.[312] British artillery fire opened up on the Redoubt at 0700 hours causing total confusion and the death of Fazl Pasha, the commander of the irregular Turkish cavalry. However, it took a long time for Kemball to begin the assault; the delays meant that much of the earlier surprise was lost and the Turks had time to prepare.

It is hard to gauge whether or not the delay was the Generals' fault. Detailed intelligence about the well-concealed Turkish positions was not available, his troops had to extricate themselves from the depression in order to attack and his artillery had to manoeuvre to provide effective covering fire. When the artillery did fire, it continued to engage the Redoubt rather than the enemy positions that were confronting the assaulting troops. It might have been foolhardy to allow an attack to develop without appropriate fire support, but surprise is a force multiplier and Kemball did not appear to display much initiative, preferring to stick with the original orders from Aylmer, described by Candler as: 'inelastic; it [the plan] was not modified to meet new emergencies as they arose.'[313]

Some authors had firm views about the lack of success at the Dujaila Redoubt. In 1917, one officer wrote, bitterly: 'The consensus of opinion is that Dujeila could have been taken almost without a shot having been fired. But individual initiative is not encouraged in the British Army.'[314] In 1937, author Dorina Neave wrote:

As is so well known now, had General Aylmer attacked at dawn on the 8th, instead of giving his men a well-deserved rest on their arrival by the Dujaila Redoubt, the Turks would have been taken unawares and badly beaten. The Redoubt was practically empty … So limited were the troops holding this spot that Leachman was able to walk through the trenches unobserved, and rushing over to the General implored him not to wait till scheduled time for the attack to commence. But once again his eager, excited manner was mistaken for over-agitation and his advice ignored.[315]

The situation was not quite as simple as that. Nevertheless, the lead brigade, the 36th Brigade, did not begin their assault until 0830 hours, three hours later than originally planned. As one regimental history commented, 'The success of the night march was beyond all hopes, the road to Kut lay bare, and yet the opportunity was not gladly seized.'[316] The History of the 26th Punjabis was even more forthright: 'Instead of assaulting an almost unoccupied position by surprise at dawn, our infantry found themselves attacking a strongly-held and well-prepared position across open country in daylight.'[317]

The War Record of the 47th Sikhs concurred: 'Had the attack been delivered without waiting for the artillery, there is little doubt the Dujaila Redoubt would have fallen and the success of the operation have been assured.'[318] A Turkish historian commented:

> The situation of the XIII Corps was truly serious. In rear was the besieged army of General Townshend ready to attack and numbering 6,000–7,000 men and 40 Quick Firing guns. On the left was the Tigris which could only be passed at the Maqasis crossing by a pontoon and 15 rafts and boats. On the right was the Shatt al Hai which could be passed by a light bridge only.[319]

This view is reinforced by Lieutenant Heawood, who spoke to Turkish officers about the battle when he was a prisoner in Baghdad. They told him

> The whole day was touch and go with them, and that if our people had known exactly how the Turks were situated, nothing could have saved them from disaster. Had they been driven from their position on the right bank they could retreat only by the bottle-neck of their bridge over the Hai, and by a ferry across the Tigris, both more or less under artillery fire, and the former the possible objective of the Kut garrison, issuing out to complete the Turkish rout.[320]

There were sound reasons for delaying the attack, but the surprise gained from the night move had been squandered and the Turks responded quickly to reinforce their right flank.

Major-General Kemball sent a report to Lieutenant-General Aylmer at 1100 hours. At that stage it appeared to him that the advance was going well for his 36th, 28th and 9th Brigades, though they were 'hotly engaged'. He had also received reports that some Turks had been seen withdrawing from the Dujaila Redoubt, but these messages were too optimistic and gave Aylmer a false picture of the battlefield. The three brigades were not finding it easy to dislodge the 3,000 infantry of the 1st and 5th Regiments of the 2nd Turkish Division armed with machine-guns. The ground was difficult to read and Kemball himself was receiving inaccurate reports from brigade units who thought that they were closer to the Redoubt than they actually were. The General wanted an assault against the Redoubt as soon as possible, but shortly after 1400 hours he was told by one of his brigade commanders that distances from the enemy had been miscalculated and that 'units have lost heavily and are dead beat'.[321] The 9th Brigade attempted to advance, but for little gain; artillery support was not being targeted at the critical points of assault and the Turks were launching effective counter attacks. By mid-afternoon Aylmer realised that Kemball was unlikely to be successful with his force alone.

Gunboat on the Tigris. (Candler)

Whilst General Lake blamed Major-General Kemball for the failure at Dujaila Redoubt because of the initial delays, Candler blamed the failure on the decision to hold back Major-General Keary's column for so long. Candler said that Lieutenant-General Aylmer and Major-General Gorringe, then his Chief of Staff, were co-located with Major-General Keary and, therefore, they were to blame for the inaction.[322]

3rd Division had been waiting all this time for the opportunity to attack. Another assault on the Redoubt by the majority of 8th and 37th Brigades was planned for 1645 hours with the whole of the Corps artillery in support, and Major-General Keary addressed the 8th Brigade personally to encourage the effort. However, the supporting artillery fire was still inaccurate, as the Turkish positions were not identified clearly and the sun was falling over the objective straight into the artillery observers' eyes.

The final attack took place at 1715 hours, led by a courageous charge of the 1st Battalion of the Manchester Regiment. They occupied two lines of trenches and were joined by the 59th Rifles, 2nd Rajputs and 1/2nd Gurkhas. Nearly 300 men of the 2nd Rajputs were killed on this day and only five of the seventeen Indian officers survived. Afterwards, an officer of the battalion wrote to his mother:

> Then at 4.30 pm, the Manchesters and 2nd Rajputs (us) were ordered to take it (Dujaila Redoubt) at all costs. They (we) had to advance over two-and-a-half miles of absolute flat ground with absolutely no cover and under a terrible fire from enemy rifle and machine-gun. They lost heavily straight away but I hear got into Turk trenches and fought magnificently. Ten officers were with the Regiment in the fight, all were killed or wounded (six killed). Russell, who was in officiating command owing to heavy casualties was hit in the stomach and also twice in the legs afterwards. He was brought in the night quite conscious and lived till noon on the 9th. He was perfectly cool in advance and apparently died very bravely. There is some consolation in thinking that if he had to be killed he could not meet it with a finer death than in command of his Regiment and leading men.[323]

A small British gunboat. (*The Times History of the War*)

For the 1/2nd Gurkhas, this was their first action in Mesopotamia and three out of their four British officers were killed, the other wounded. The Battalion Diary of the Manchester Regiment recorded:

> The trenches were bombed along for some distance, but the supply of bombs being limited was soon exhausted; the sun, moreover, was low and full in the eyes of the attackers, and as they swept over the crest of the redoubt they were enveloped in thick clouds of dust and smoke caused by the shell and machine-gun fire. In the meantime our machine-gunners reached a position about 500 yards from the redoubt and maintained fire until ordered to withdraw by the Battalion Machine Gun Officer. At 5.45pm a heavy counter-attack developed chiefly from the left flank, where, being able to approach under cover, it was not noticed until too late and the Turks were able to use their bombs with great effect. At the same time the flanking fire re-doubled and the position became untenable and the force was ordered to withdraw … All ground gained was finally abandoned at dusk, but all through the night large parties were out collecting and bringing in the wounded.[324]

The Turks launched an effective counter attack on both of their flanks and eventually drove the 8th Brigade out of the position, though it retired in good though depleted order, protected by covering fire from the 47th Sikhs 'who, behaving with great steadiness, drove back two attempts of the enemy to leave their trenches and pursue'.[325]

A Victoria Cross was awarded to a member of the 1st Battalion the Manchester Regiment in this battle, Private George Stringer.

> [He] held his ground single-handed and kept back the enemy till all his grenades were expended. His very gallant stand saved the flank of his battalion and rendered a steady withdrawal possible.[326]

There was huge frustration amongst the men of the 8th Brigade, who were convinced that they could have succeeded in taking the position if there had been more support from other brigades. The Regimental History of the 59th Rifles claimed that 'from reports received from enemy

Carrying the Sick at Amara. (Black Tab)

officer prisoners captured some five weeks later, it appeared that if one more brigade had joined in they would have gone back, and orders had already been issued for a Turkish Retirement.'[327]

The lack of progress against the Dujaila Redoubt led to the decision that evening by Lieutenant-General Aylmer to withdraw the force to the Wadi the following morning. He could see no progress being made to relieve Kut, he had suffered heavy casualties, the troops were shattered, drinking water was short, and he was concerned that his Corps could be cut off from their lines of communication by the enemy. Major-General Kemball was disappointed, as he was convinced that many of the enemy had withdrawn from the Redoubt; however, later Turkish reports stated that there was no Turkish withdrawal. Aylmer probably had no choice but to withdraw his force fifteen miles back to the Wadi.

The second relief attempt had failed and at a high cost. The Official History reported that medical arrangements in the Relief Force were considerably better than in the earlier battles.[328] However, British casualties amounted to 3,474 over the period 8–9 March, whilst the Turkish losses were 3,100. Some units were hit worse than others: within Major-General Kemball's command, the 82nd Punjabis, 1st Highland Light Infantry, 93rd Infantry, 53rd Sikhs and 56th Rifles lost about one third of their number; within Major-General Keary's 8th Brigade, the 1st Manchesters lost forty per cent and the 2nd Rajputs forty-eight per cent. Of the total Allied casualties, 512 were killed, 2,465 wounded and 497 were missing. A high price for relatively little gained. At this stage, the Relief Force had already lost a total of 14,000 casualties in order to relieve the 9,000-strong garrison at Kut. For many, the greatest opportunity to relieve Kut had failed, despite the sacrifices made. The Official History summed up perceptions: 'Thus ended an operation which at certain stages seemed to promise more chances of success than the previous attempt to relieve Kut; and its conduct has probably given rise to more comment and criticism than any other action in the campaign.'[329]

It was up to Major-General Townshend to explain to his garrison what had happened.

COMMUNIQUE NUMBER TWO[330]

10 MARCH 1916

As on a former occasion, I take the troops of all ranks into my confidence again, and repeat the two following telegrams from General Aylmer, from which they will see that our Relieving Force has again failed to relieve us.

First Telegram, March 8th 1916: – Today's operation terminated in a gallant but unsuccessful attempt to storm Dujaila Redoubt. Troops pushed home the attack and carried out the operation with great gallantry, but the enemy was able to mass reinforcements, which arrived from the left bank at Magasis and from Shumran, and we were unable to break through. Unless the enemy retires from his present position from the right bank, which does not seem probable, we shall be unable to maintain ourselves in present positions, owing to lack of water; and unless the enemy evacuate the Es-Sinn position tonight, we shall be obliged to withdraw to our previous positions at Wadi. The Relief Force under General Aylmer has been unsuccessful in its efforts to dislodge the Turks entrenched on the left bank of the river, some 14 miles below the position of Es Sinn.

Second Telegram, March 8th 1916: – We have been unable to break through to relieve you today, and may have to withdraw to Wadi tomorrow, but hope to make another attack before long and relieve you at an early date. Please wire movements of enemy, who in any case suffered most severely as their reported counter attacks have been repulsed with heavy loss.

I know that you will be deeply disappointed to hear this news. We have now stood a three months' siege in a manner which has called upon you the praise of our beloved King and our fellow-countrymen in England, Scotland, Ireland and India, and all this after your brilliant battles of Kut-el-Amarah and Ctesiphon and your retirement to Kut, all of which feats of arms are now famous. Since the 5th of December you have spent three months of cruel uncertainty and to all men and to all people uncertainty is intolerable; as I say, on the top of all this comes the second failure to relieve us. And I ask you to give a little sympathy to me also, who have commanded you in three battles referred to, and who having come to you as a stranger now love my command with a depth of feeling I have never known in my life before. When I mention myself I would couple the names of the Generals under me, whose names are distinguished in the Army as leaders of men.

I am speaking to you as I did before, straight from the heart, and, as I say, ask your sympathy for my feelings, having promised you relief on certain dates on the promise of those ordered to relive us. Not their fault, no doubt, and do not think that I blame them. They are giving their lives freely, and deserve our gratitude and admiration.

I want you to help me again as before. I have asked General Aylmer, for the next attempt, which must be made before the end of this month, to bring such numbers as will break down all resistance and leave no doubt of the issue. Large reinforcements are reaching him, including an English Division of 17,000 men, the leading brigade of which must have reached Wadi by now, that is to say General Aylmer's headquarters.

In order to hold out I am killing a large number of horses, so as to reduce the quantity of grain eaten every day, and I have had to reduce your ration. It is necessary to do this in order to keep our flag flying. I am determined to hold out, and I know you are with me in this, heart and soul.

Charles Townshend

Major-General

Commanding 6th Division

Kut-al-Amarah

10th Mar, 1916

An Offer to Surrender

On the same day that this communiqué was published, an offer was made from Halil (or Kalil) Pasha, the Turkish commander of the 6th Army.

> Your Excellency,
> The English forces that came to relieve you were compelled to retreat after giving battle at Felahieh and suffering 7,000 casualties.
>
> After this retreat, General Aylmer, who was a month and a half in making his preparations, yesterday, when he thought he was strong enough, resumed the offensive with the 5th, 6th, 8th and 12th Brigades of infantry and one cavalry brigade on the right bank of the Tigris, as you saw. But he was again compelled to retreat, with 4,000 casualties, and I am left with adequate forces.
>
> For your part, you have heroically fulfilled your military duty.
>
> From henceforth I see no likelihood that you will be relieved. According to your deserters I believe that you are free without food and that diseases are prevalent among your troops.
> You are free to continue your resistance at Kut, or to surrender to my forces, which are grower larger and larger.
>
> Receive, General, the assurance of our highest consideration.
> Halil   Commanding Turkish Forces in Iraq, Governor of Baghdad

Townshend declined the offer. 'I thanked him for his courtesy and said I was glad to find again as I had found in my operations at Kut-al-Amara and Ctesiphon, that the Turk was a good soldier and a gentleman.'[331]

Consequences

The failure to succeed at the Dujaila Redoubt had a number of consequences. The Turks were able to tighten their hold on Kut, were increasingly confident of success and were given more time to prepare their defences against the next attempt at relief. In Kut, morale reached its lowest levels of the siege and Major Barber wrote that 'the reaction from high hope to bitter disappointment left one rather battered.'[332] From this moment there was an increasing belief within the garrison that the relief might not happen. The Relief Force had suffered a severe setback with heavy losses. In hindsight it is easy to comment that any further relief attempts over the next seven weeks were doomed to failure, but Lieutenant-General Gorringe had no choice but to keep trying.

Apart from explaining the new situation to the garrison, Townshend was obliged to order the slaughtering of another 1,100 animals, which would enable the town to hold out until the middle of April. Major Sandes commented on the new rationing.

> Each British officer and soldier now received a small loaf of about ten ounces weight per diem, the bread being composed of a mixture of wheat and barley – very coarse and very heavy. The Indian troops were given an equivalent of flour and made their chupatties as usual. Those of the garrison who would eat horseflesh received one pound of meat per day, and a small quantity of oatmeal was issued to certain troops. The jam ration had ceased altogether and also the supply of date sand butter.[333]

On 15 March, the rations for British troops were reduced to ten ounces of barley bread and one-and-a-half ounces of horse-flesh, whilst Indian soldiers received eight ounces of barley meal and four ounces of parched barley. Three days later, the bread allowance was reduced to eight ounces and then to five ounces on the 20th. Lord Elton of 1/4th Hampshires:

> Hunger, I suppose, began about the middle of March. Soon we were living on a few ounces of coarse bread and a little horse or mule each day. There was also a little crude lime juice to mix with the water of the Tigris. But that was all.

He went on to describe the psychological effects of the lack of food.

> One thought by day and dreamed by night, not of the victory of the relieving force, but of mutton cutlets, of York ham, above all, of being let loose in a confectioner's … And these hard-bitten warriors were not thinking of corkscrews and bottles of whisky. They were planning to sit down with a tablespoon to a pot of jam.[334]

The garrison was becoming very weak. By 29 March rations were reduced to four ounces of bread and one-and-a-quarter pounds of horseflesh per person. At this time, Captain Mousley described a main meal.

> For dinner we had a very excellent roast joint of horse and some rice. I find that first-class horse is better than second-class mule, and only second to second-rate young donkey. It beats camel and eclipses buffalo altogether.[335]

Tea ran out in March, dried ginger was being used as a tea substitute and dried apricot leaves were being used as tobacco. Major Sandes reported that his girth had reduced by four inches,[336] whilst Captain Spackman wrote 'we are now pretty ravenous.'[337] For many, it was the shortage of tobacco that hit morale the most. Efforts continued to supplement the rations and, in the 2nd Battalion of the Dorsetshire Regiment, Lieutenant Highett is mentioned for his attempts to shoot starlings – as their Regimental History describes, the result was 'Starling on toast' or 'Starling Pie' providing welcome additions to their menu.[338] No one seemed to have much luck in obtaining fish from the Tigris, however, despite the help of explosives!

Major-General Townshend explained that morale was not good.

> The effect of the repulse was soon apparent among my troops. There was a general feeling of gloom and depression, and desertion amongst the Indian troops increased; the Arabs of the town now looked upon our cause as lost. If I had not been lucky enough to find the hidden grain at Kut we should have fallen by the first week in March.[339]

Lieutenant Heawood stated that 'It would be wrong to make out that we were not disappointed; we were bitterly so, for we realised that the failure of so strenuous an attempt meant a very considerable delay before another could be made.'[340] Major Sandes also commented on the situation.

> The failure of General Aylmer's force was a bitter blow to our hope of early relief, and the sorely-tired troops in Kut knew that it must be many a long day before they could expect to shake hands with their comrades from Europe and India, and that meanwhile they must continue once more to fight, dig – and starve.[341]

Optimism did still prevail amongst many however, as Captain E. Jones saw

… the men of the besieged garrison betting quite cheerfully on the next possible date to be relieved, carried on quite hopefully, never for a moment entertaining such a thought as the possibility of not finally being relieved.[342]

However, it was plain that the Kut garrison had certainly reached their lowest state of morale since the siege began.

A New Commander for the Relief Force

The confidence of the Relief Force had also been dented; as Candler opined: 'Good Regiments do not lose morale, but they lose confidence by familiarity with ineptitude.'[343] A key task following the failure at the Dujaila Redoubt was to find a scapegoat. Lieutenant-General Aylmer had already been re-christened 'Faylmer' by the troops.[344] His strict control of the battle had meant a successful night move, but the failure to exploit the surprise gained was seen by many as a missed opportunity to relieve Kut. Some observers pointed to Major-General Kemball's reticence to advance, inaccurate artillery fire and the failure to launch Major-General Keary's 3rd Division into the battle much earlier. Candler pulled no punches: 'I wish that we were not attacking Sinn, whittling away our reinforced strength in more frontal assaults.'[345] However, rations in Kut were short, the spring floods were expected at any time and Turkish reinforcements were anticipated in the area – did Aylmer really have a choice? Should he have planned the attack differently or have delayed the relief attempt until the arrival of 13th Division? Was Kemball's reluctance to seize the initiative and attack without artillery support the reason for failure or could Townshend have been more proactive in Kut and provided more support to the Relief Force? There is no clear answer, but the author Fitzgerald Lee expressed this trenchant view in 1927:

> If, on the 8th March, Townshend had only made a desperate dash to get across two hundred yards of water, to his brother soldiers who were within three miles of him, General Aylmer would have gained a victory at Dujaila and saved Kut. This would have been no more than the gallant Aylmer deserved; for in the whole history of War no commander ever made a nobler attempt to save the troops and the reputation of a brother officer.[346]

This observation is unfair in being too cut and dried, as the situation at the Dujaila Redoubt was extremely difficult to assess, even for the local commanders, and communications and speed of reaction of the troops on the ground were slow. Both London and India were not happy with the failure and decided that Aylmer had to be the scapegoat. Townshend was sad to see him go describing him as 'brave, loyal, just, and a good commander.'[347] He also believed that he had had bad luck through poor weather, floods, lack of transport and inexperienced troops.

Lieutenant-General Aylmer was succeeded by Major-General Gorringe on 11 March 1916, a fellow engineer, who had previously been successful at Nasiriya and

Major-General Sir George Gorringe. (*The Times History of the War*)

Kut bazaar scene during the siege. (Sandes)

made his name in the South African War. Major Anderson commented that 'this was looked upon as very satisfactory by everyone as the latter [Gorringe] from his record in Mesopotamia was known to be very energetic.'[348] Captain Spackman made it very clear what he thought:

> We had a great disappointment on the 8th and 9th when a great attack was made on the right bank. We could see the shells bursting clearly and the Turkish reserves moving about; but old Aylmer muffed it again, and now like Nixon and others is away on account of 'ill health'. So we are condemned to hang on interminably, but are still fairly confident of being relieved at last 'next month', (always 'next month') especially as it is now Gorringe who is directing attack at Wadi River, 20 miles downstream, Gorringe who we know as the successful general at Nasiriya last July.[349]

The new commander believed that the offensive could begin again on 1 April once the reinforcing 13th Division had arrived. For the Relief Force, the rest of March was spent in stalemate, dug in along the Tigris. They were recuperating from the battle, preparing for the next relief attempt and, like the defenders of Kut, coping with the new floods. Bunds had to be repaired and raised along the river-banks and bridges built over waterways to keep roads open and avoid the wide scale flooding of defences. The Black Watch summed up this routine: 'The strain on troops holding these trenches was exceptional, the labour continuous and the hours of rest few.'[350] The Turks were doing the same.

Garrison Routine Continues

As food became scarce, pressure on the garrison continued. On 18 March, the Turks fired eighty shells into the town in the early evening and this was followed by a bombing run by one of their aeroplanes. The same evening, the Turks attempted to disable the gunboat *Sumana*, which was the key means of supply between the Woolpress Village and the rest of the town. Some damage was done by a Turkish direct-firing 18-pounder gun, but the boat survived after supporting fire was brought to bear on the enemy. There were fifty-two casualties that day, mainly within the hospital in town where six were killed outright and twenty-six wounded. Major Barber had to deal with its aftermath.

> As ill-luck would have it, the bomb came through the roof and landed on the side wall of the Bazaar, with the result that it burst before reaching the ground and sent a shower of wicked metal over the devoted sick beneath … The place was a shambles … The wretched victims lay about in all directions amongst the bricks and dust and blood.[351]

Captain Mousley spent some of March in hospital and commented wryly: 'The only advantage to be derived from being in hospital here is that one has facilities for dying under medical supervision.'[352]

Also on 18 March, one bomb fell through the roof of a shelter in which four sepoys of 'A' Company of the 7th Rajputs were sitting. However, it did not go off. 'Captain Lilly's orderly, Sepoy Chandika Singh, carried it into the orderly room, but was told to deposit it in the Tigris with all speed and care!'[353]

This was followed on 22 March by another big bombardment of the town for three-and-a-half hours, which resulted in another sixteen casualties and the false perception that another enemy assault was about to occur. Further gunfire occurred that afternoon and in the evening. In total, 1,000 shells and fifty bombs were dropped on Kut that day. Shell and bullet remained real threats, as Captain Spackman commented:

> We got heavily bombarded one day and had some very narrow escapes, an adjacent dug-out was hit by a 50-pound shell and four men were killed in it. I have many times been nearly hit. Yesterday my leg was missed by six inches and today my head by a bare foot, by casual bullets, but I fancy we shall be relieved soon now.[354]

Note how his optimism remained. The casualties from the bombardments might have been worse, but most of the Turkish shells were shrapnel rather than high explosive, so many did not penetrate the buildings and many were faulty and did not explode.

On 14 March, the Tigris rose two feet eight inches and floods started to cause a major problem again on 23 March. The water came from both melted snow in the hills and the heavy rain and it threatened to flood Redoubt B. It reached its height on the 26th, when it was two feet higher than the previous floods in January. The water had to be continually baled out and Redoubt B and some of the adjacent trenches were evacuated. Lieutenant Heawood described the work that had to be done:

> We baled out the water with old tins, but the place was so low-lying that half the water came back again. Then we tried soaking up the water by throwing down earth into it; but that was not a great success, as digging out the saturated earth was very heavy work. At last we borrowed a pump from the sappers, and got on better, though we had to drain the trenches by sections, filling them up every here and there, and then re-digging them.[355]

Forward trenches had to be abandoned by the end of the month and the Middle Line became the main defence. New positions were dug in the sand hills between the Middle Line and the fort, though this was difficult with the troops busy working all day making mud bricks and then revetting their trenches. Repair work went on until 0100 hours each morning. Soldiers from the Oxfordshire and Buckinghamshire Regiment were in the forefront of this debilitating work. The aim was for each soldier to make 250 mud bricks a day. Conditions were not good.

> Soaked from above by torrential downpours, paddling about in slush, mud and water up to and above their ankles, without dry quarters to sleep in, the men of the Regiment worked by day and night under ceaseless sniping fire until bodily exhaustion and empty stomachs reduced them almost to impotence.[356]

Lieutenant Spencer of the Royal Artillery:

Every road was transformed into a river, and men were trapped in the trenches, waist high in the filthy mire, which was a thick gluey substance, slippery as an eel, hard as iron, with an evil smell, clinging to the feet, clogging every footstep with infernal obstinacy.[357]

Now on limited rations, the work output of the garrison was greatly reduced. Major Barber described the effect.

The men's digging powers too, were very sensibly decreasing. They found by practical experience that the less potential energy you put into the human machine, the less power you'll get out of it.[358]

He went on to say that morale was still good, but mentioned that the possibility of becoming prisoners was beginning to be discussed. Captain Mousley, for the first time in his account, acknowledged that 'the garrison is in a bad way' and 'men go staggering about, resting every now and then up against a wall.'[359] He also mentioned that more soldiers were ending up in the hospitals and many appeared to be in a coma.

Fortunately for the defenders, the Turks were also suffering in their trenches and were kept just as busy as the defenders attempting to keep the floods at bay. Around the Woolpress Village the enemy were forced to pull back some 900 yards, so there were some benefits from the flooding, as the possibility of a Turkish assault was lessened. Also, the level of enemy sniping was reduced. However, most of the village was flooded too. As the floods subsided after 26 March and the weather improved, it was hoped that Lieutenant-General Gorringe would seize the opportunity to attempt a relief again. Life in the trenches was still difficult, as the ground was so wet. Many entrenchments were beyond repair with their sides constantly collapsing and soldiers having to run the gauntlet of sniper fire as they moved from one piece of cover to another over-ground.

The numbers of troops suffering from scurvy, pneumonia and consumption (tuberculosis) was increasing; 560 soldiers were lying in hospital with scurvy by the end of March. Wounds were not healing quickly and most Indian troops were still not eating horse-flesh. Major Barber:

Very few of the Indians were eating the fresh meat that would have helped them, in spite of a comprehensive routine order issued near the end of February, which explained to them that the holy books of the Hindu religion do not forbid the eating of horse-flesh, and that their spiritual heads had wired to say so.[360]

He then mentioned his frustration, as a doctor, when trying to deal with the wounds of his weakened patients.

One of the hardest things the doctor had to bear was the sight sometimes of battered humanity beyond the reach of his art, because he could no longer expect Dame Nature to do her part. Large wounds would sometimes begin by showing promise of healing for a few days, but would then stop and progress no further; would bleed when touched, and by their presence react on the enfeebled body that had no energy to deal with them.[361]

The combination of the floods, lack of food and disease was affecting everyone, as Private C. Hughes saw:

Everybody is feeling the pinch and showing it. There is a dejected feeling that the relieving force will find it a difficult task to reach us now the floods have started again, and the cold and damp makes dysentery very prevalent.[362]

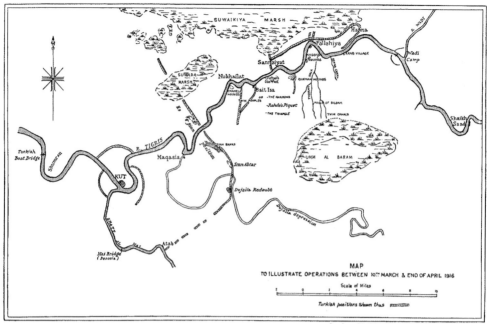

MAP

TO ILLUSTRATE OPERATIONS BETWEEN 10TH MARCH & END OF APRIL 1916

Scale of Miles

Turkish positions shewn thus

Based upon The Official History of the Mesopotamia Campaign
by permission of The Controller of H.M. Stationery Office.

Operations between 10 March and the end of April 1916. (Neville)

The *Sumana*, responsible for keeping the Woolpress Village supplied, was temporarily put out of action on 30 March when an enemy shell destroyed a key valve and junction on the main steam-pipe, but within the week she resumed her duties. She was critical to the village, which, because of its isolation had almost become a 'siege within a siege'.[363] The flood had turned it into an island.

It was becoming warmer by the end of March 1916 and the flies added to the misery in Kut. Captain Mousley said that they swarmed everywhere in billions, describing the Kut fly as a 'pronounced cannibal'.[364] The mental suffering was sometimes as bad as the physical: 'A book is now almost as great a luxury as bread.'[365] This period also saw the return of extremely wet weather and a violent thunderstorm.

> It seemed as though the Creator had let loose the elements to impress on us mortals the greatness of His power in comparison with the puny efforts of man striving against his brother-man. [March 1916 was] a month of sore trial for us all; of hope and bitter disappointment alternating almost from day to day; of hunger, sickness and pain – yet we were buoyed up with the knowledge that, though fate seemed to be fighting against us, we were doing our duty for the Empire, and that our fellow countrymen in far-off England and India, and in Mesopotamia itself, were striving manfully to rescue us from the clutches of the treacherous Tigris and the Turk.[366]

The 13th Division reached Shaikh Saad on 25 March, the same day that Major-General Townshend reminded the Tigris Corps Headquarters that food in Kut would run out on 15 April. The Turks had also received reinforcements.

Time was running out for the garrison.

Notes

293. Mousley (1922) p.92.
294. Ibid p.76.
295. Ibid p.77.
296. Townshend (1920) p.286.
297. Sandes (1920) p.200.
298. Townshend (1920) p.286.
299. Ibid p.287.
300. Mousley (1922) p.87.
301. Townshend (1920) p.288.
302. Barber (1917) p.181.
303. Neville (1938) p.185.
304. Mockler-Ferryman (undated) p.111.
305. Sandes (1920) p.205–206.
306. Moberly (1924) p.517.
307. Moberly (1924) p.318.
308. Moberly (1924) p.319.
309. Moberly (1924) p.320.
310. Neville (1938) p.179.
311. Jourdain and Fraser (1924) p.504.
312. Moberly (1924) p.323.
313. Candler (1919) p.140.
314. Black Tab (1917) p.249.
315. Neave (1937) p.60.
316. Neville (1938) p.179.
317. *A History of the 26th Punjabis 1857–1923* (1924) p.41.
318. 47th Sikhs War Record (1992) p.143.
319. Moberly (1924) p.329 quoting *Baghdad and the Story of its Last Fall* by Captain Mohammed Amin Bey.
320. Mockler-Ferryman (undated) p.114.
321. Moberly (1924) p.335.
322. Candler (1919) p.148.
323. *The History of the Rajput Regiment* (1989) p.132.
324. Wylly (1925) p.152.
325. Moberly (1924) p.341.
326. *London Gazette* 5 August 1916 and Gliddon (2005) p.70.
327. *Regimental History of the 6th Royal Battalion (Scinde)* (1935) p.69.
328. Moberly (1924) p.348.
329. Ibid p.349.
330. Townshend (1920) p.300–301.
331. Ibid p.294–295.
332. Barber (1917) p.187.
333. Sandes (1920) p.209–210.
334. Elton (1938) p.131.
335. Mousley (1922) p.101.
336. Sandes (1920) p.222.
337. Spackman (1967) p.6.
338. *History of The Dorsetshire Regiment 1914–1919* (1933) p.216.
339. Townshend (1920) p.299.
340. Mockler-Ferryman (undated) p.114.
341. Sandes (1920) p.208.
342. Neave (1937) p.61.
343. Candler (1919) p.158.
344. Mousley (1922) p.90.
345. Candler (1919) p.146.
346. Fitzgerald-Lee (1927) p.73.
347. Townshend (1920) p.298.
348. Anderson (1960) p.76.
349. Spackman (1967) p.5.
350. Wauchope (1925) p.224.
351. Barber (1917) p.196.
352. Mousley (1922) p.85.
353. Rawlinson (1941) p.164.
354. Spackman (1967) p.5.
355. Mockler-Ferryman (undated) p.115.
356. Neville (1938) p.189.
357. Neave (1937) p.64.
358. Barber (1917) p.188.
359. Mousley (1922) p.96–97.
360. Barber (1917) p.177.
361. Barber (1917) p.191.
362. Neave (1937) p.63.
363. Mousley (1922) p.118.
364. Ibid p.110.
365. Ibid p.113.
366. Sandes (1920) p.223–224.

Chapter Seven

APRIL 1916 – PRELUDE TO SURRENDER

He knew the state of my troops. He knew I had no food left. He knew that the men were dying, and that disease and scurvy were rife. (Major-General Townshend)[367]

13th Division and Major-General Maude

One of the reasons why the Tigris Corps had failed to defeat the Turks was, quite simply, the lack of British combat power compared to the enemy. Partly for this reason, both Lieutenant-Generals Aylmer and Gorringe had been frustrated by their lack of progress towards Kut. With the arrival of the 13th Division, adding to the 3rd and 7th Divisions, it was believed success was more likely. Blooded in Gallipoli and quickly refreshed and reinforced in Egypt, it was an all-British rather than an Anglo-Indian formation, and was seen to be more potent than the others. Candler, who was on the ground with them, described the soldiers of the Division as a 'cool, hard, determined-looking breed, well seasoned now, and burnt to the complexion of Gurkhas.'[368] However, many of the numerous reinforcements had no combat experience; the Division had suffered sixty per cent casualties in Gallipoli, including ten of their thirteen commanding offic-

ers. Two units, the 9th Battalions of the Warwickshire and Worcestershire Regiments, had lost all of their officers there. So despite the presence of the extra division, other factors such as the strength of Turkish defences and the weather, combined with the lack of food in Kut, did not augur well for quick success in Mesopotamia.

The Divisional commander, Major-General Stanley Maude, was to end up taking command of the Tigris Corps after the surrender of Kut and become Commander-in-Chief in Mesopotamia during August 1916; he was responsible for the victorious occupation of Baghdad a year later. Son of a general, he had been commissioned into the Coldstream Guards and

Lieutenant-General Sir Stanley Maude. (Wilson)

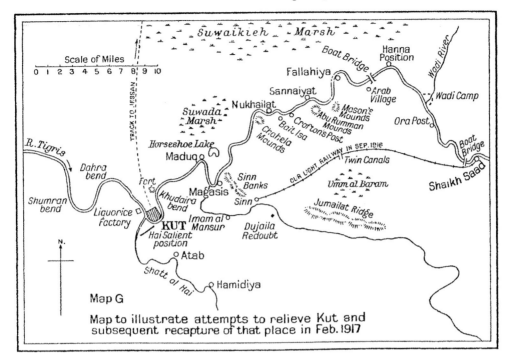

Map G

Map to illustrate attempts to relieve Kut and subsequent recapture of that place in Feb. 1917

Attempts to relieve Kut. (Nunn)

seen service in the Sudan and the South African War, where he had earned a Distinguished Service Order, prior to key staff appointments, with the Brigade of Guards, as Military Secretary to the Governor-General of Canada, and experience in the War Office. As a brigadier-general, he had commanded the 14th Brigade in France during 1915 earning further recognition with the award of Commander of the Bath and, on promotion, took over the 33rd Division (now renumbered 13th Division) in Gallipoli.

He had a fierce reputation for competence. One of his staff officers wrote: 'Our divisional general is a great fellow and very sound. We all have the utmost faith in him.'[369] He was also a stickler for detail and a tough disciplinarian, yet very accessible and always keen to hear advice from his staff, from whom he expected bags of energy and efficiency. In addition, he had the knack of never letting 'the mass of detail obstruct from his vision the big idea.'[370] This latter attribute is the sign of a great commander, even today. He was optimistic of success, writing en route to Mesopotamia: 'At all events it ought to mean fair and square fighting in the open, and manoeuvring, at which we shall beat the Turks.'[371] His optimism was, premature for the defenders of Kut, though he was going to turn the tide of success later, replacing defeat and shame by victory and being described by one historian as 'the ideal soldier in war and certainly the ideal British Commander-in-Chief'.[372] That is a later story. At least for the final attempt to relieve Kut, greater firepower and additional, able leadership was at hand.

Attacks at Hanna and Fallahiya

The defending Turks were well-established on either side of a flooded Tigris, which was now 300 yards wide. Their left flank was still secured by the Suwaikiya and, further west, Suwada

1st Seaforths in trenches.
(IWM Q 71340)

Marshes and their entrenchments at Es Sinn were particularly strong. The Hanna defile was only some 1,000 yards across, whilst the defence had a depth of twelve miles. There was little space for the Turks to be outflanked to the south, as the British still had only limited transport and wanted to ensure that their lines of communication back to Shaikh Saad remained secure. The Turks had about 30,000 infantry spread between Kut and Hanna. On the left bank, the 13th Division faced a wire entanglement followed by five lines of trenches one-and-a-half miles in depth with Turkish guns positioned behind the third line. Four miles further west were the enemy Fallahiya entrenchments and another two miles on was their best defended position of Sannaiyat.

The Tigris Corps Commander, Lieutenant-General Gorringe, planned to attack with the 13th Division seizing the Hanna position on the left northern bank of the Tigris supported by the 7th Division. Meanwhile, the 3rd Division and Corps Artillery would support the assault on the right, southern bank. Bridges across the river would allow quick reinforcement to either bank and a few days after the initial assault, the 3rd Division would have secured Abu Rumman, whilst the 13th and 7th Divisions would have captured the Fallahiya and Sannaiyat positions. The Turks would then be sufficiently weakened for a last bid by the Relief Force to link up with Major-General Townshend's garrison. It appeared as if the floods were already having an adverse effect on the Hanna position, though the British entrenchments opposite were suffering as well.

Gorringe had about 30,000 troops and 127 guns and there were eleven planes and four gun-boats in support. 13th Division, under Major-General Maude, was on the left northern bank of the Tigris with three brigades forward, the 38th, 39th and 40th, and one battalion in the front of each of the brigades. Forty-four guns and the 7th Division, commanded by Major-General Younghusband, were behind. The 3rd Division, under Major-General Keary, was on the right bank with two brigades forward, the 8th and 37th supported by twenty-two guns. The Corps Artillery was concentrated into one grouping of fifty-five guns on the right bank and two on the left. The Commander's intent in his operation order was to

- Assault and capture the enemy's Hanna position at 4.55 am on 5 April
- Seize and entrench an advanced position along a north-to-south line from the Suwaikiya Marsh to the northern extremity of the Fallahiya bend and to push forward along the enemy's communication trenches and the river bund as far as possible, preparatory to attacking the Sannaiyat position.[373]

The attack at Hanna had been planned, initially, for 1 April. The heads of the friendly saps on the northern bank had reached points only 150 yards away from the Turkish front line and the machine-guns from three brigades were concentrated on the southern bank to support the attack on their right. Meanwhile, the Cavalry Brigade was sent to screen the British left flank and help maintain surprise. There was a delay however, firstly because vital reconnaissance planes needed for artillery spotting had not yet arrived, and secondly because of further rain which slowed down the relief-in-place of the 3rd Division by the 13th Division.

Conditions for the waiting infantry were not good, as the History of the South Wales Borderers recorded.

> The 4th [Battalion South Wales Borderers] spent two very uncomfortable days in these trenches, waiting for the ground to dry. The men had no blankets, only their waterproof sheets: no fire-wood was available for cooking, drinking water could only be drawn at one point on which all the Turkish guns seemed trained, and the recent downpours had left the trenches terribly muddy.[374]

A soldier of the 5th Battalion the Buffs recorded on 2 April: 'We are in Venice again, streets of water between the tents, and fields of mud in front. This life is hard enough when the weather is fine, but terrible when wet.'[375]

With the artillery in position on 4 April, the assault was set for the following day. However, despite the best efforts throughout the Tigris Corps and the welcome presence of the 13th Division, the Official History commented 'once again, bad weather and shortage of river trans-port prevented the timely concentration of the maximum available force at the decisive point.'[376] General Lake and Lieutenant-General Gorringe were both taking considerable risks with the latest attack, as there was only three days worth of supplies for the Corps. However, the risk of losing Kut to the enemy was evident.

Major-General Townshend and his beleaguered force were informed of the forthcoming assault on the left bank, Lieutenant-General Gorringe writing

> I quite appreciate that your cooperation must in the first instance be purely passive, but you are the rock on which I hope to split the Turkish forces, and your cooperation by gunfire etc, on his ferry at Magasis, and by containing enemy on left bank on the last day's operations will assist us greatly. I will keep you informed of our progress.[377]

Major-General Maude had used his experience from the Western Front by making the best use of air photographs to ensure that his commanders were thoroughly conversant with the Turkish layout of trenches. His orders emphasised the need for 'discipline, determination and dash'[378] and his 13th Division moved forward to attack at 0455 hours on 5 April. For the South Wales Borderers 'it was a relief to climb out and lie down on the parapet five minutes before the attack started' because of their 'tedious and uncomfortable' wait.[379]

The assault began according to plan, without artillery preparation, in order to achieve surprise. Lieutenant R. Scorer of 5th Battalion the Wiltshire Regiment wrote with a certain sang-froid:

> We went over the top at dawn on April 5th and drove him out of three lines of trenches, advancing to Fallahiyeh where we were held up about noon and suffered a fair number of casualties. I remember on the morning of the 5th it was frightfully cold and we were promised a rum ration.[380]

The guns would open fire on farther enemy trenches once the first ones were attacked by the infantry. Initially, all went according to the schedule and, by 0700 hours, the first five lines of Turkish trenches had been captured. However, the Turks had withdrawn the bulk of their forward troops the night before, possibly because of the effects of the flooding and they were fighting a successful delaying action again, by weakening the British and losing some ground, but not being decisively engaged. Candler commented astutely on the reaction of the 13th Division.

> They thought the Turk was on the run, but we of Mesopotamia knew better. We had learnt from experience that he is the master in the art of retreat. Each separate retirement had been in a manner a victory. Time was all they wanted – to starve out Kut and to wear us down as we advanced. The few barren miles between Shaikh Saad and Sannaiyat was a small price to pay for the best part of two British divisions.[381]

Major-General Maude then pushed forward his brigades towards Fallahiya with the 40th Brigade in the lead; they were soon checked by heavy enemy fire, but he quickly planned a frontal assault onto the position, which was postponed until darkness that evening.

It was during 40th Brigade's move that a Victoria Cross was won by Captain Angus Buchanan of 4th Battalion South Wales Borderers. Captain Stewart Hemingway had fallen wounded and one of his men had attempted to help but he had been hit also. Captain Buchanan leaped out of cover and saved both his brother officer and the soldier under heavy enemy fire. His citation read:

> During an attack an officer was lying out in the open severely wounded about 150 yards from cover. Two men went to his assistance and one of the men was hit at once. Captain Buchanan, on seeing this, immediately went out and, with the help of the other man, carried the wounded officer to cover under heavy machine-gun fire. He then returned and brought in the wounded man, again under heavy fire.[382]

His battalion lost fifty per cent casualties in the assault with three officers killed and seven wounded.

Meanwhile, on the right bank, the 3rd Division had also started the day well and its 8th and 37th Brigades had taken the Abu Rumman positions by midday. Later in the afternoon, a Turkish brigade-sized formation advanced towards them, but they were kept at bay. Meanwhile, reports arrived with the British that the Turks were rapidly reinforcing their Sannaiyat position.

On the left bank, Major-General Maude's attack on Fallahiya began at 1915 hours that evening with concentrated artillery fire from both sides of the Tigris against the position. Led by the 38th and 39th Brigades, the assault began thirty minutes later and, after a hard fight, both had secured their objectives within the hour.

The capture of the Hanna defile and Fallayiha was a significant achievement and Maude stated in his diary that 'Everything went splendidly.'[383] He was commended by Lieutenant-General Gorringe for the success at Fallahiya.

> The highest praise goes to General Maude and his brigade commanders and all under their command for this successful night attack, a difficult operation at all times, requiring dash and good leadership as well as personal bravery among the junior commissioned and non-commissioned ranks.[384]

In addition, General Lake later praised the 38th and 39th Brigades for the action, pointing particular gratitude at the 9th Battalions of the Warwickshire and Worcestershire Regiments. However, it was at a high price, mainly from Fallahiya; there were 1,885 British casualties that day and 1,868 came from the 13th Division.

The Sannaiyat Battle

Major-General Younghusband's 7th Division took over the front line from the 13th Division just after midnight that evening, the 21st Brigade leading. The next objective, Sannaiyat, was under three miles away and Lieutenant-General Gorringe wanted it taken as soon as possible, despite the lack of knowledge about the enemy positions and any prior reconnaissance. Consequently, the 7th Division's orders had been issued at 1930 hours on the 5th ready for an assault, 'zero hour', at 0455 hours on 6 April. The plan was for the 19th and 28th Brigades to pass through 21st Brigade and lead the advance.

The plan sounded simple, but with hindsight it appears complicated and problematic. All movement was taking place during pitch-darkness, whilst the 13th Division conducted a rearward passage of lines through the advancing two brigades. In addition, the 19th and 28th Brigades had to conduct a forward passage of lines through the 21st Brigade in order to lead the assault against an unknown enemy position along what Candler described as 'the most dangerous line of approach'.[385] All this had to take place in a limited amount of time. It is little wonder that things did not go according to plan, despite Major-General Younghusband's demand for 'silence, quickness and dash.'[386]

As the 19th and 28th Brigades' move began, they encountered 13th Division troops withdrawing and had to slow down and change their planned open formation for the advance to one simpler to control. The brigades then became confused amongst the old enemy trenches, now held by the 21st Brigade and, because of the delays, Major-General Kemball, commanding the 28th Brigade, informed Major-General Younghusband that he would probably not meet 'zero-hour' and that the assault should be delayed, especially as there was confusion about how far away the first Turkish trenches were. In effect, the 7th Division, which had already suffered considerable casualties from the actions at Shaikh Saad, the Wadi and the Hanna defile, would be attacking the enemy in broad daylight across open ground.

The Highland Battalion encountered a withdrawing enemy piquet at 0400 hours. At 0530 hours it was becoming light, but both the 19th and 28th Brigades were unable to determine the exact locations of the enemy and they were being concentrated in a gap of about 400 yards between the marsh on their right and on their left boundary, a Turkish communication trench. The Turks knew what was going on, having successfully positioned piquets forward of their location with good communication by telephone line and were, therefore, well prepared. Their machine-gun fire ripped through the two Indian Brigades from both sides of the Tigris – 'It was a torrent of death.'[387] The brigades marched forward to virtual decimation.

The 28th Brigade was hit first, but attempted to continue the assault. The Provisional Battalion of the Oxfordshire and Buckinghamshire Light Infantry and the 51st Sikhs made a further 200 yards before they were brought to a halt. For the former battalion, it was the anniversary of the Peninsula War Battle of Badajoz. Their commanding officer, Major Lindsay Carter, had earlier 'impressed on all ranks the vital importance of silence, quickness and dash, those qualities which go to the making of true light infantry.'[388] However, despite losses of fifty per cent, they were still over 600 yards from the Turkish lines and 'gallant men continually crumpled up with sickening grunts under the impact of solid lead' – all but one officer of this regiment fell in this assault, including four second lieutenants who were killed.[389] The surviving officer, Lieutenant E. Kinghorn was only saved because his belt-buckle had deflected a bullet and he was later to receive a Distinguished Service Order for his actions. A Distinguished Conduct Medal was awarded to a stretcher-bearer, Private Golding. The regiment had suffered eighty-eight per cent casualties in the attack.

The 19th Brigade to their left was stopped also and was even further from the enemy. The Highland Battalion

> continued to advance for a short distance in face of a pitiless hail of shrapnel, rifle and machine-gun bullets. Orders were then given to advance by short rushes, but when a position about 500 yards from the enemy had been reached, the advance was abandoned, only a handful of men having survived; and these few had considerable difficulty in loosening sufficient earth from the hard-baked ground to provide head cover for themselves.[390]

This battalion lost eleven officers and 187 other ranks. The disastrous attack by the 19th and 28th Brigades was seen clearly by their colleagues on the southern bank of the Tigris, the War Diary of the 47th Sikhs recording that 'We on the right bank stood by helplessly watching the slaughter of our old comrades.'[391]

Further advance across the open ground would have been suicidal as the enemy positions were still not identified. Inaccurate friendly artillery fire had already resulted in Allied casualties, but eventually the covering fire improved and the brigades dug in for protection. Following consultation between Gorringe and Younghusband, it was decided to renew the attack the following night with the additional support on the ground from the 40th Brigade.

Unfortunately, the 7th Division was then hit by the effects of flooding. The hastily dug trenches rapidly filled with water. The troops did their best to bale out their defences, but many of the trenches had to be abandoned and the guns struggled to keep operating, as their positions began to flood. Hard-gained ground was lost and the planned night attack was cancelled. According to the War Diary of the 47th Sikhs, 'the Turks, by skilfully manipulating the river bunds, used their position upstream to increase the flood between us and themselves.'[392]

The 19th and 28th Brigades had already lost 1,168 casualties during the day, but at least the arrangement for evacuating the wounded had improved from previous battles. Meanwhile, that evening, elements of the 3rd Division did succeed in gaining ground on the right southern bank of the river. From there, they were able to provide enfilading fire against the Turkish troops on the opposite side in front of the 7th Division.

The pressure was still on Gorringe to seize the Sannaiyat area – the garrison at Kut was running out of food. Consequently, the advance by the 7th Division had to continue with as much supporting fire as possible from the opposite bank of the river and from the artillery and gunboats. Townshend, from Kut, attempted to provide accurate artillery fire on the Maqasis (or Magasis) area to disrupt any Turkish reinforcements. At this stage some ground had been gained, but only at a huge cost and the Turks appeared to be strengthening their position. The situation was not helped by the rising waters of the Tigris, which was flooding both the enemy and friendly trenches, but was also narrowing the area in which the 7th Division was advancing.

At 0700 hours on 7 April, the supporting fire began and the infantry of the 19th and 28th Brigades advanced once more at 0915 hours. Though they managed, amazingly, to move forward 300 yards under heavy enemy fire in vulnerable daylight, they were soon brought to a standstill again and the gap between them and the Turks was still 800 yards. 'It was the same story – a story of sickening waste of life.'[393] The Indian 125th Rifles of 19th Brigade had suffered sixty-one per cent casualties and their three most senior officers had fallen in succession. More digging in was required and reinforcement was impossible because of the enemy's accurate fire. However, that evening, following a friendly heavy bombardment, all three brigades of the 7th Division managed to advance another 200–300 yards.

The next plan was an assault by both the 7th and 13th Divisions the following day and there would be an attempt to outflank the enemy to their left, through part of the Suwaikiya Marsh. A successful reconnaissance of the Marsh, by two staff officers, occurred that night. They calculated that it should be possible for a brigade-size force to cross the Marsh and outflank the enemy – the journey had only taken one-and-a-half hours and the Marsh was only about three feet deep, at worst. The 21st Brigade, with an artillery mountain battery, was allotted the task and it was planned that the Brigade would attack, simultaneously, with the main force at first light on 9 April. However, Gorringe was not prepared to take this risk, because of the fear of rising water isolating the Brigade. Instead, the 7th Division would support the assault of 13th Division.

The second assault by the 13th Division against the Sannaiyat position began at 0420 hours, following a cold night, with 40th Brigade left, 38th Brigade right and 39th Brigade following. The first 400 yards were covered quickly, but then the Turkish defenders fired flares to signal the fire from their guns and machine-guns. Part of the first line of friendly troops reached the forward enemy positions and Major-General Maude recalled in his diary:

> Second line lay down while first line pushed on. Consequently first line, which did splendidly, got into the Turk's trenches in a good many places, North Lancs, King's Own, Welsh Fusiliers, and Wilts especially. But being unsupported by second line had to give way. Officers most gallant in trying to rally second line, but were unable to get men forward more than few yards, and subsequently second line recoiled carrying in a great measure lines in rear of it.[394]

The result was a confused mixture of different regiments and brigades attempting to maintain their bearings under the heavy fire. It was impossible for the officers to provide coherent orders in this muddle, though some battalions, such as the 7th Battalion of the North Staffordshire Regiment of the 39th Brigade kept together.

The 4th Battalion South Wales Borderers' (with 40th Brigade) History described the situation.

> Exactly what happened is uncertain except that the first line went straight on, its survivors actually entering the trenches. The second line, however, seems to have faltered and become mixed up with the fourth and fifth waves which had pressed on. At the same time something started a right incline. Direction was lost and in the din and darkness it was hard to make orders heard or to recover the line of advance. The net result was inextricable confusion and disorder: some men fell back on top of the 39th Brigade advancing in support, and despite all the officers' efforts the whole attack broke down completely.[395]

The Victoria Cross. (Author's Collection)

This regiment won its second Victoria Cross in Mesopotamia on 9 April during the latest relief attempt, through the actions of a stretcher-bearer, Private James Finn. His citation, like Captain Buchanan's, was published on 26 September 1916:

> After a night attack he was one of a small party which dug in in front of our advanced line and about 300 yards from the enemy's trenches. Seeing several wounded men lying out in front, he went out and bandaged them all under heavy fire, making several journeys in order to do so. He then went back to our advanced trench for a stretcher, and, being unable to get one, he himself carried on his back a badly wounded man into safety. He then returned, and, aided by another man, who was wounded during the act, carried in another badly wounded man. He was under continuous fire while performing this gallant work.[396]

The Official History recorded that most of those men who reached the Turkish trenches: 'did not emerge alive'.[397] Candler reported that friendly aeroplanes had identified

> ... a labyrinth of dug-outs, which looked like reptiles with their tentacles fast in the firing trench. 'Snake-pits,' we called them. These were cunningly contrived bombing chambers, and the Turks slipped back into them and, as we rushed the trench, met our thin line with a shower of grenades from hidden positions which we could not locate.[398]

This was the experience of Lance-Corporal S. Blythman of 5th Battalion the Wiltshire Regiment:

> Moved into advance trenches April 8th and made attack at dawn on Sannaiyat position. Was wounded in the shoulder and back, managed to crawl in at night very weak from loss of blood. (It was a slaughter. I heard later that they had had an eight hour armistice to clear up the battlefield.) I was placed in a mulecart and taken to 19 Indian Field Ambulance.[399]

The confusion in the depth of British ranks allowed the Turks to recover and launch a very successful counter-attack. The result was a reorganised 13th Division dug in 400 yards away from the Turkish first line of trenches. The 13th Division had sustained a further 1,807 casualties during this assault and was described by Lieutenant Colonel W. Brownrigg, Assistant Adjutant and Quartermaster-General (Deputy Chief of Staff in today's parlance) of the 13th Division, as 'badly shattered'.[400] The failure of the attack was put down to confusion during the night attack, tired and cold soldiers, a shortage of commanders after earlier actions by the Division and a lack of experience and training.[401]

The bravery and sacrifice of the Relief Force was not in doubt, however. On 9 April, as well as Private Finn's reward, two more Victoria Crosses were won. The Reverend William Addison, Church of England Chaplain to the 6th Battalion Loyal Regiment (North Lancashire), won his for comforting the dying and wounded whilst in the open under fire. Second-Lieutenant Edgar Myles, a platoon commander in the 9th Battalion Worcestershire Regiment, also gained his VC for assisting wounded men in the open and carrying a wounded officer to safety when under fire. The battles around Sannaiyat had yielded a total of five Victoria Crosses.

Second-Lieutenant E.K. Myles carrying in a wounded officer under heavy fire. (*Deeds That Thrill the Empire*)

Corporal S.W. Ware crossing the open under heavy fire to rescue the wounded. (*Deeds That Thrill the Empire*)

Reverend William Addison VC. (Brookwood Cemetery)

The Reverend W.R.F. Addison carries a wounded man to the cover of a trench under heavy rifle and machine-gun fire. (*Deeds That Thrill the Empire*)

Captain Angus Buchanan	4th Battalion the South Wales Borderers, 40th Brigade, 13th Division.
Corporal Sydney Ware	1st Battalion the Seaforth Highlanders (The Composite 'Highland Battalion'), 19th Brigade, 7th Division. Posthumous.
Reverend William Addison	6th Battalion the Loyal Regiment (North Lancashire), 38th Brigade, 13th Division.
Private James Finn	4th Battalion the South Wales Borderers, 40th Brigade, 13th Division.
Lieutenant Edgar Myles	9th Battalion the Worcestershire Regiment, 39th Brigade, 13th Division (attached from 8th Battalion the Welsh Regiment).

It was appreciated by both Lake and Gorringe that the only chance now of relieving Kut would be by continuing the advance on the enemy's right, the southern bank of the Tigris. Any success against Sannaiyat would require more sapping and preparations, which would take at least another four days. Preparations were not helped by a violent thunderstorm on the night of 10/11 April and a hurricane and hailstorm on the 12th. The 2nd Battalion of the Leicestershire Regiment reported the ensuing difficulties:

> Waves actually swept over the extreme right flank of the Battalion trenches and water poured rapidly in. All attempts to block the trenches proved futile, for no filled sandbags were at hand and the loose sand was at once washed away. All hands were busily engaged in clearing the trenches of ammunition and kits, and although by great exertions the whole trench system was saved from being flooded, certain portions on the flanks had to be evacuated. But in rear the bursting of bunds and the washing away of causeways made the matter of supply one of no little difficulty and anxiety.[402]

The battalion was part of the 28th Brigade, 7th Division, which would remain on the left northern bank of the Tigris, whilst the 13th Division was moved to support the 3rd Division on the right southern bank.

At this stage, the Turks had 13,000 troops and 34 guns in Sannaiyat, 5,200 personnel and 21 guns surrounding Kut with 11,000 soldiers, 35 guns and a cavalry brigade in the Dujaila area. The Tigris Corps consisted of 24,000 personnel, a cavalry brigade and 35 guns.[403]

On 10 April, Major-General Townshend was told that his garrison could not be relieved by his cut-off date of 15 April. In Kut, the rations were further reduced and he reported back to General Lake on the 14th that he could hold out until the 29th, though only if some food supplies were air-dropped. Major-General Townshend issued two new important communiqués to his beleaguered command.

COMMUNIQUE NUMBER THREE[404]

10 APRIL 1916

The result of the attack of the Relief Force on the Turks entrenched in the Sannaiyat Position, is that the Relief Force has not as yet won its way through, but is entrenched close up to the Turks in places some 200 to 300 yards distant. General Gorringe wired me last night that he was consolidating his position as close to the enemy's trenches as he can get, with the intention of attacking again. He had had some difficulty with the flood, which he had remedied. I have no other details. However, you will see that I must not run any risk over the date calculated to which our rations would last, namely 15th April, as you all understand that digging means delay, though General Gorringe does not say so.

I am compelled, therefore, to appeal to you all to make a determined effort to eke out our scanty means so that I can hold out for certain till our comrades arrive, and I know I shall not appeal to you in vain.

I have then to reduce the rations to five ounces of meal for all ranks, British and Indian.

In this way I can hold out till April 21st if it became necessary. I do not think it will become necessary, but it is my duty to take all precautions in my power.

I am very sorry I can no longer favour the Indian soldiers in the matter of meal, but there is no possibility of doing so now. It must be remembered that there is plenty of horseflesh, which they have been authorised by their religious leaders to eat, and I have to recall with sorrow, that by not having taken the advantage of this wise dispensation they have weakened my power of resistance by one month.

In my communiqué to you on January 26th I told you that your duty stood out plain and simple; it was to stand here and hold up the Turkish Advance on the Tigris, working hand in hand together, and I expressed the hope that you would make this defence to be remembered in history as a glorious one. I asked you in this communiqué to remember the defence of Plevna, which was longer than that of even Ladysmith.

Well, you have nobly carried out your mission, you have nobly answered the trust and appeal I put to you – the whole British Empire, let me tell you, is ringing with our defence of Kut. You will all be proud to say one day, 'I was one of the Garrison of Kut.' As for Plevna and Ladysmith, we have outlasted them also. Whatever happens now, we have all done our duty; as I said in my report of the defence of this place, which has not been telegraphed to Headquarters, I said that it was not possible in despatches to mention everyone, but I could safely say that every individual of this Force had done his duty to his King and Country. I was absolutely calm and confident as I told you on 26th January and I am confident now. I ask you all, comrades of all ranks, British and Indian, to help now in this food question in the manner I have mentioned.

Charles Townshend
Major-General
Commanding 6th Division

Kut-al-Amarah
10th Apr, 1916

COMMUNIQUE NUMBER FOUR[405]

11 APRIL 1916

General Sir Percy Lake, the Army Commander, wired to me yesterday evening to say: 'There can be no doubt that Gorringe can in time force his way through to Kut; in consequence of yesterday's failure, however, it is certainly doubtful if he can reach you by April 15th.'

This is in answer to a telegram from me yesterday morning to say that, as it appeared doubtful that General Gorringe would be here by the 15th April I had reluctantly still further reduced the rations so as to hold out till 21st April. I hope the Indian officers will help me now in my great need in using common-sense, talk the Indian soldiers [into eating] horseflesh, as the Arabs of the town are now doing.

	Charles Townshend
Kut-al-Amarah	Major-General
11th Apr, 1916	Commanding 6th Division

The defenders of Kut noted that in Communiqué Number Four General Lake had stated that the Relief Force would succeed 'in time'. Major Sandes commented that these words 'naturally suggested to us hungry folk the question "In what time?" No answer could be forthcoming to that query, for none could even guess at it.'[406]

Back in Kut

An anxious Major-General Townshend had received a message from Lieutenant-General Gorringe on 31 March 1916: 'Preparations for your relief are well forward, and you may be assured that I shall not be a day later than is absolutely necessary.'[407] Some optimism remained, despite the hardships, though the relief attempts in the first week of April came to nothing. The General claimed in his book that he had no detailed knowledge of these latest relief attempts, though he was prepared to assist the Relief Force as best he could with his weak garrison.

The garrison was still optimistic, though the rations were now even more scarce and the weather conditions were depressing; thunderstorms, lightning, rain and strong winds were accompanied by hailstones that were 'as large as pigeon's eggs and heavy enough to injure a man seriously.'[408] Captain Mousley commented 'There is always plenty of horse, but vegetables are a great delicacy.'[409]

Townshend was aware that a relief attempt was to be made on 5 April and the garrison heard the initial early bombardment in conjunction with flashes of light in the distant sky. Major Sandes:

> The detonations of the bursting shells, and the distant roar of the guns, shook our houses in Kut and seemed to be absolutely continuous. One could feel the whole atmosphere pulsating with the muffled concussions.[410]

The garrison waited in anticipation of Gorringe's successful breakthrough, listening to the friendly gunfire, which was not so far away. Captain E. Jones, an artillery officer, described his impressions.

> By placing our ears against the trench wall, the heavy guns could be plainly heard. It sounded like a dull thudding, as if someone in bedroom slippers was walking up and down in a room upstairs.[411]

Townshend's artillery did its best to support the attack at Hanna by engaging the ferry at Maqasis and a bridge at Hai, as they were both routes for Turkish reinforcements. However, these targets were both about 11,000 yards away, so the fire was ineffective. On 6 April, Townshend's frustration of not hearing about any progress was illustrated by the content of his telegram to Corps Headquarters:

> Can you give me any news of Gorringe? I have not heard from him since 8.30 yesterday morning, when he wired he had carried the first lines of the Hanna position. I wired this morning asking for news. It is now 4.30pm and I have heard nothing. No news I suppose is good news but it makes my people uneasy. I do not want to bother Gorringe in the midst of work, but he should not keep one like this without news.[412]

His messages were responded to later on the 6th, but no mention was made of the attackers' progress. The same day, the Tigris had risen – three foot two-and-a-half inches in twenty-four hours – and the troops in Kut, once again, found themselves desperately trying to keep their defences intact. Whilst this was going on, Major Sandes observed the concentration of officers on the roof of the post office. They were all peering through their binoculars at the fighting in the distance, desperately trying to work out what was going on and hoping that the garrison might be called on to support a successful breakthrough. Major Barber also described the scene:

> We rested our arms on the house-top walls and gazed and gazed through our glasses till our eyes ached … We walked about restless and irritable, unable to sit still, and feverish with the intolerable suspense.[413]

One particular group of personalities was greatly appreciated by the British troops in the garrison during the siege – the padres. There were three in Kut who were from the Roman Catholic

Kut late in the siege. (Sandes)

Church, Wesleyans and the Church of England. Reverend Spooner represented the latter and had earned a Military Cross for his courage during the withdrawal from Ctesiphon. He gained a special mention from Major-General Townshend:

> He was a great help to me in the siege, for he was always cheery and brave under fire; he was loved by the men. I shall always have the greatest respect and esteem and affection for him.[414]

The General even requested Reverend Spooner to pray for better weather. The padre obliged:

> I went into the Chapel alone and prayed to God. When I came out the clouds were beginning to thin and the sun to break through. Shortly, too, the wind began to veer to the north – a sure sign of fine weather. Thank God for this – it is our only chance of being relieved.[415]

Unfortunately, the improved weather did not last. The padre's collect was appropriately worded for this stage of the siege:

> Grant, we beseech thee, Almighty God, that we, who for our evil deeds do worthily deserve to be punished, by the comfort of Thy grace may mercifully be relieved; through our Lord and Saviour Jesus Christ. Amen.[416]

Though most British soldiers would not have outwardly admitted to being religious, when life was tough it was remarkable how many sought some solace from the padres. Even today, they behave in the same way and commanders value their padres for this reason. They help maintain morale and even if a soldier does not believe in God they provide an alternative source of comfort outside the normal chain of command. As has been mentioned elsewhere, the Indian soldiers were heavily influenced by the guidance of their religious leaders, whether Hindu or Moslem, and Townshend had had to appeal to them in order to encourage the troops to eat horsemeat.

On 7 April 'the housetops were covered with spectators watching the smoke of the shells in the distance down river.'[417] The same day, the mills stopped working for lack of fuel and Townshend reported to Corps Headquarters that his food would run out on 15 April. Meanwhile, the flooding reached its peak, Major Sandes commenting that 'It seemed as if after all we were destined to be flooded out.'[418] The bunds had to be patrolled, inspected and repaired at regular intervals as great sheets of water spread around Kut forming artificial lakes. Once again, the flooding caused problems for both the defenders and the Turks; the riverbank burst 200 yards downstream from the fort and all trenches within fifty yards of the Tigris were flooded: 'The men in the fort suffered much in these strenuous periods from overwork, scanty food, and the enemy's snipers, who prevented much work being done during daylight.'[419]

The news that the second attack at Sannaiyat had failed was a huge disappointment – Townshend reported that, later, Halil Pasha, the Turkish commander told him that the attack by the 13th Division might have succeeded but 'there were no troops following up the attack in support.'[420]

Officially, only one week's worth of rations was left. Townshend wrote: 'It was certain that I would not be relieved by 15th April' and was disappointed when he heard that the Relief Force was digging in once more.[421] Rations were reduced again, to seven then five ounces of barley and the commander believed that he could then hold out until the 21st. He realised, however, that every time he reduced the rations, his garrison became weaker and more ineffective, as in other sieges, 'with the diminished food, you reduce the physical strength of the garrison to an alarming extent, and consequently their courage and hope, and their fighting value to almost nothing.'[422]

He stated that hope was giving way to despair amongst his Indian troops, but that his British soldiers still showed great stoicism.

> The English were as tenacious and brave as ever. They were my sheet anchor. Without the (now – alas! – skeleton) battalions of Norfolks, Dorsets, Oxfords (who showed magnificent courage and bravery at Ctesiphon, where they bore the brunt of the battle), the wing of the West Kents (the old Half Hundred), the Hampshire Territorial Infantry, and the detachment of bluejackets of the Royal Navy, Kut would have fallen, in my opinion, at the end of March.[423]

It has been shown before that Major-General Townshend did not have a great respect for his Indian troops, despite their many examples of outstanding bravery. His comment of the time that Indian troops 'are not constituted by nature to stand misfortune and reverse with the same stoicism as Europeans' would lose him his command today.[424] However, it was recognised that some Moslem Indian troops had difficulty fighting fellow Moslems. The Turks had attempted to encourage desertion from Kut by leaving their propaganda aimed at Moslems on the perimeter of the town and Captain Aubrey Herbert, Member of Parliament, who arrived with the Relief Force in April wrote on the 16th: 'They have brought Indian troops to fight on holy soil for things that mean nothing to them.'[425]

Certainly, Major-Generals Melliss and Delamain believed that the Indian troops performed well and they spent more time with them than their commander. The Official History recognised this differing opinion mentioning that 'General Delamain considers that throughout the siege the Indian troops, like their British comrades, displayed wonderful courage and fortitude' also quoting Colonel Hehir's note of 18 April:

> There is a vast amount of suffering from hunger amongst the troops, which is being borne with admirable patience and fortitude and arouses enthusiastic praise at the pluck and grit displayed by both our British and Indian soldiers. As one is amongst the men daily and speaks with intimate knowledge of the conditions, the behaviour of the men in meeting these unfortunate conditions is heroic.[426]

However, many of the accounts of the siege concur that the Indian troops were suffering the most from the lack of food and were becoming weaker and thinner as the days progressed. Statistics show that the British battalions did remain healthier than the Indian ones, as they did not have the same qualms about food. The former had 30 deaths from disease out of the 1,250 soldiers who began the siege; the twelve Indian battalions had 300 out of 4,000.[427]

Major Barber wrote that 'the gaunt spectre of famine was making itself felt.'[428] Time was definitely running out for the garrison and every possible idea of increasing their food supplies was considered. Communique Number 3 had encouraged more than half of the Indians to eat horseflesh and it is hard to appreciate why the commander had not made such a powerful appeal to them before. He made another direct appeal to this group on 12 April, in which he threatened listing those personnel who failed to eat horseflesh and passing their names to the Indian Government. He claimed that these messages were successful and resulted in ninety per cent of the Indian troops eating horseflesh, but this effect was late. As the medical staff reported,

> The Indian troops and followers are now in state of semi-starvation. The reduction of the grain ration to five ounces per man, which has of necessity been commenced, will, during the course of the ensuing week or ten days, reduce them to a state of great debility and emaciation, and very seriously militate against their utility as a defence force.[429]

Even so, at this stage of the siege, Major-General Townshend signalled the Indian Government and instructed it to inform their various leaders that the garrison was right to eat horseflesh as it had received the permission of its religious leaders and that they should not be castigated for their actions. All troops were becoming weaker; the Regimental History of the 103rd Mahrattas of 17th Brigade stated that 'the troops were literally starving and grew so weak that men going on duty had to have their equipment carried for them to their posts.'[430] The War Record of the 24th Punjabis of 30th Brigade commented:

> Stomach diseases were the most prevalent, and men wasted away for lack of proper food. For instance, there was a man of the Battalion in hospital whose thigh was literally no thicker than an ordinary man's wrist.[431]

But British regiments were also suffering. Within the 17th Brigade's 1st Battalion the Oxfordshire and Buckinghamshire Light Infantry 'the officers and men were now so thin and weak that to walk a few hundred yards required a great effort'[432] and, in the 18th Brigade, Captain Shakescraft of the 2nd Battalion of the Norfolks commented: 'Men are frequently seen sitting down resting in the street. Sentries have to lean against the walls.'[433] Though their commander, Brigadier-General Hamilton mentioned that:

> In spite of all the trying conditions of the prolonged siege, the discipline, good order, and soldierly bearing of the battalion were maintained to the end. The daily guard mounting … was in itself a soul-stirring revelation of the unquenchable spirit of the Norfolk Regiment. Though worn to shadows of their former selves with starvation, constant duty and frequent sickness, though their clothing was grimed and ragged, the men were still punctiliously correct.[434]

The British soldier had plenty of meat, though every other form of food was scarce.

> Every one consumed enormous amounts of horse or mule's flesh, not because he liked it or needed it as sustenance, but merely to fill up an aching void inside him. One would imagine that so much meat would make a person very ill; but it seems that if one's body is starving it can assimilate an excess of any sort of healthy food, though it cannot thrive on a diet of meat alone relieved only by a minute quantity of bread and a few dandelion leaves.[435]

Captain Mousley had to eat his own horse, Don Juan, on 10 April and had the privilege, as his owner, of eating the heart and kidneys.[436] Every last source of food was being identified; Private Hughes:

> A bitch with a litter of five pups, an officer's dog, and two or three disreputable looking donkeys had passed through some of the men's hands and found their way to the cooking pot.[437]

The awful diet was steadily weakening the whole garrison as they increasingly suffered from related medical problems ranging from scurvy and dysentery to cramps. Captain Mousley visited the officers' hospital and commented that it was 'full again to overflowing with dysentery, jaundice and malaria cases.'[438] Some relaxation had been gained from smoking, but by this stage of the siege the troops were left with 'Kut mixture', 'a horrible compound of ginger and dried tea leaves'.[439] As luxuries became more scarce, the prices shot up at the auctions of deceased officers' personal belongings.

Tigris Corps Headquarters suggested the ejection of the remaining Arab population from the town in order to save food, but Major-General Townshend did not want a massacre and did not agree; there were recent examples of civilians trying to escape and being shot on sight by Arab or Turk. An option was to send supplies by boat with towed barges full of food which they could release towards the town, but they would be extremely vulnerable; the *Sumana* only survived because of all its extra sand-bagged protection. Matters were made worse when the local Arabs' grain ran out on 14 April and the mills had already closed down because of the lack of flour. Townshend may now have regretted his earlier decision to allow the Arab population to stay in Kut. Certainly, at this stage, some of the garrison would still have been happy to let them go – an extra 6,000 mouths had to be fed as a result.

There was now an attempt to airlift food into Kut and some of the garrison wondered why this had not occurred before. Though it may have been the first time in war that this had been done and the garrison was grateful for the drops, it was described by Townshend as 'a complete failure.'[440] There were only limited numbers of aeroplanes in good condition and they were not equipped to carry the required food, estimated by the commander's staff to be 5,000 pounds a day. The airlift began on 16 April failing to meet the quantities required and succeeding in dropping two bags in the Tigris, much to the annoyance of the observing garrison. The maximum weight of flour dropped daily was 2,450 pounds with an average of about 1,600 pounds. Major Sandes described the drops:

> The loads were strung below the fuselage and, when released at a height of 6,000 feet, fell turning slowly over and leaving an aerial trail of floor till they plunged with dull thuds on to the plain near the brick kilns.[441]

Unfortunately, as Major Anderson observed that 'It was only in the mornings and evenings that the aeroplanes could fly owing to the heat which overheated their engines and the number of trips per day seemed fearfully disappointing.'[442]

The History of No. 30 Squadron was more positive about its performance, recording that just nine aeroplanes were available for this airlift and, of the 19,000 pounds of food carried, 16,800 pounds made it into Kut.[443] Loads were dropped from 5,000 to 7,000 feet and included 5,000 lira of currency, drugs, and medical dressings. The stores were double-bagged and hung on an improvised bar attached to each aircraft's bomb frame. The records admit that

> A small amount of food was dropped into the Turkish lines or in the river. This was owing to the curious trajectory often assumed by the bags, which lost their forward speed at once and seem to have been blown about by the wind.[444]

The deliveries were better than nothing, possibly allowing the soldiers to hang on for a few more days, and they did provide some entertainment for a tired and bored garrison: 'A plane would be heard approaching; spectators would rush out and stand gaping, laughing and chattering about it like children.'[445]

The Royal Navy pilots were accused of being the most inaccurate with their drops and facetious messages such as 'Would Her Majesty's Navy mind dropping us something now and then instead of to the Turks?' were sent. Fortunately, 'Fritz' and the enemy aircraft were busy elsewhere and did not interfere significantly with these re-supply flights.

Rations were reduced by a further ounce of barley per man and Townshend informed his higher command that the garrison would only be able to survive longer if extra food was sent by river.

As food ran out, the garrison remained subject to another onslaught – from fleas, sand-flies and flies. It was difficult to sleep as these creatures with 'bites like bulldogs'[446] attacked human flesh during the night. Candler, based with the Relief Force, provided a vivid description of this hazard.

> The flies in the tents, dug-outs and trenches, unless seen, were unbelievable. To describe them is to hazard one's own reputation for truth. You could not eat without swallowing flies. You waved your spoon of porridge in the air to shake them off; you put your biscuits and bully beef in your pocket; and surreptitiously conveyed them in closed fist to your mouth, but you swallowed flies all the same. They are settled in clouds everywhere … At night the flies disappear, and the mosquitoes and sand-flies relieve them, completing the vicious circle. In one camp I struck a species which could bite through cord riding-breeches … The sand-fly is another and more insidious plague. A net with a mesh fine enough to exclude him is suffocating, and he will keep one awake at night with a hose of thin acid playing on one's face. He is also the transmitter of a microbe which will lay you by the heels for three days with a virulent fever.[447]

The medical staff coped admirably with casualties during the siege, but they were now struggling to keep up with the volume of sick men, who had great difficulty recovering when they were so weak. Poor diet and a lack of drugs exacerbated the situation. Major Sandes commented on the hospital operating conditions.

> Operations had to be performed in places which would make a London surgeon speechless with disgust, and the wounded and sick had to lie in dark rooms with mud floors, frequently very damp, generally very dirty, and always exposed to shells or bombs. Our doctors did their best in the wretched surroundings in which they found themselves.[448]

On 16 April, Major-General Townshend repeated an earlier suggestion to his superiors about the prospect of some escaping the siege. He planned to do this by running the gauntlet of the enemy defences, along with 600–700 other men from the garrison, on board the gunboat *Sumana*. Major-General Melliss had volunteered to stay with the remainder. The commander of Kut knew that the prospect of success was small, but felt that at least not all of the garrison would go into captivity. As Townshend was such an avid student of Napoleon, who was so criticised for abandoning his troops on the way back to France from Russia, it is hard to countenance this option. Others must have thought the same – his commander replied that if relief failed and food supplies did not reach Kut, then

> … the Army commander is prepared to sanction the proposal contained in your telegram … namely that *Sumana* shall try to run the blockade, taking as many officers and other ranks as possible where services are of most use to the State. Army commander, however, makes this one exception, that he considers you yourself bound to remain behind in command of the garrison, though he would deeply regret loss of your services.[449]

He was told that this should only happen as a last resort and only on a direct order from Army Headquarters. It is notable that Major-General Townshend makes no further mention in his book of his personal role in this planned exploit.

One key personality of the siege, Brigadier-General Frederick Hoghton, commander of the 17th Brigade, died on 12 April after a few days of illness following being poisoned by herbs. Herbs had been eaten by some of the garrison in order to supplement the lack of vegetables, dandelion leaves substituting spinach. A popular character, he was buried after a well attended funeral in a cemetery on the northern edge of Kut, where he still lies today. The Reverend Spooner reported

Commonwealth War Grave, Kut today.
Brigadier-General Frederick Hoghton. (Brigadier
Mark Armstrong)

that there were over 150 officers and 100 men
present, and a special roadway had to be made
for the ceremony because of the poor state of
the ground.[450] Brigadier-General Hoghton
was described by Lieutenant Heawood as 'one
of the nicest men in the whole force'. His
regiments was forthwith ordered not to eat
the vegetation.[451] Colonel W. Evans took over
command of the 17th Brigade.

By mid-April 1916 the garrison was weak
and weary, the last issue of jam had gone and
sugar was hard to obtain. Even Major Sandes,
who appeared to maintain high morale
throughout the siege, commented that 'the
Turks sat around the dying town like vultures
round a dying man, waiting for the end.'[452]
Major Nelson, Commanding Officer of the
2nd Battalion the Queen's Own Royal West
Kent Regiment stated, simply, in his diary on
12 April: 'Very heavy thunderstorm last night.
Trenches in a bad state. Men are weak, and
cleaning trenches has to be done in short spells, with many reliefs.'[453] Though Arthur Kingsmill's
account of the same battalion was that 'everyone was looking thin, but in spite of everything the
troops kept cheerful, making the odd wise-crack now and then.'[454]

Captain Spackman wrote in his diary that 'things are beginning to get rather desperate now.'[455]
Everyone was only receiving five ounces of bread a day:

> We eat a lot of sparrows nowadays as a sort of change. Sorry this history is now mostly about food,
> but it is the one thing that is ever present – as a topic of thought and conversation![456]

The morale of both the defenders of Kut and the Relief Force was, understandably, declining.
Captain Herbert MP, who had just arrived at the Mesopotamia Expeditionary Force Headquarters
commented in his diary on 13 April, when referring to Major-General Townshend's force, 'no
one thinks that he's got a dog's chance of getting out.'[457] Some of the Arab population of Kut
realised that the odds were against the garrison and from mid-April many of them were attempting to escape at night on improvised rafts; few escaped the Turks and each morning revealed
Arab corpses floating on the Tigris.

Last Attempts at Breakthrough – Beit Aiessa (Bait Isa) and Sannaiyat

Dawn of 17 April marked the next stage of the final relief attempt. The plan was for the 3rd
Division to capture the Turkish Beit Aiessa position in order to allow the 13th Division to relieve
them prior to a further 3rd Division march round the Dujaila defences.

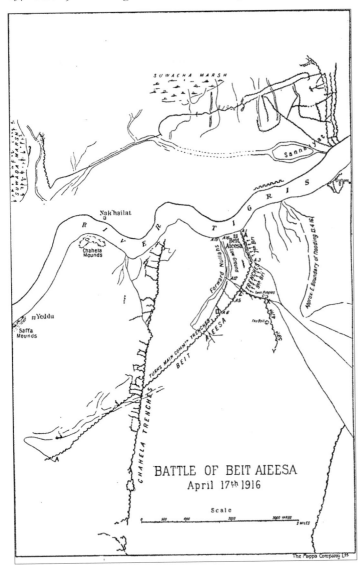

BATTLE OF BEIT AIEESA
April 17th 1916

Scale

Battle of Beit Aieesa, 17
April 1916. (Candler)

Some progress forward on the right southern bank of the Tigris had been made in the previous few days, as the enemy's forward piquet line in front of Beit Aiessa was captured, though the main assault was delayed because of more wet and boggy conditions. The 3rd Division had succeeded in pushing their lines 1,500–3,000 yards further west, but at the expense of another 400 casualties on 12 April, mainly from the 36th Sikhs and 89th Punjabis of the 37th Brigade. The final VC of the Relief Force was awarded to Naik Shahamad Khan of the 89th Punjabis 'for most conspicuous bravery'. He succeeded in beating off three Turkish counter-attacks with his machine-gun section, even when their weapons were knocked out by enemy fire. He also succeeded in withdrawing with his men, one of whom was wounded, together with the weapons and equipment.[458]

Conditions continued to be miserable that evening, as a 'shumran' or north-easterly gale blew up the waters of the Suwaikiya Marsh into waves and proceeded to swamp some of the Tigris Corps defences as well as those of the Turks on the north bank of the Tigris.

It was believed that the floods elsewhere on the front were being made worse by the Turks digging at Beit Aiessa and making inundations to divert the floods. This made it an important objective. However, the poor weather conditions were not only making living conditions difficult for the troops, they were also hampering accurate reconnaissance from both the air and on the ground. Identification of the enemy positions was impossible, ensuring that subsequent artillery supporting fire would be inaccurate. Incredibly, the outpost position of 'Twin Pimples' was captured on 15 April despite bad weather conditions during the 7th and 9th Brigades' night move – and the navigation by compass of some units being affected by the metal of their fixed bayonets! The bad weather allowed surprise and success to be achieved, as described in the History of the Connaught Rangers, who were in the 7th Brigade:

> The advance across the intervening space of 800 yards took three-quarters of an hour, the troops having to wade in the dark through mud swamps and get over deep water cuts in places. A violent thunderstorm with torrents of rain, which burst as the troops were crossing the open, and the blackness of the early morning, helped to conceal the move forward. The Turkish sentries were apparently sheltering from the rain and saw nothing, for the surprise was complete.[459]

In the 9th Brigade, Candler recounted the success of the 1st and 9th Gurkhas:

> With true psychological instinct they went in and killed nearly every man in the trench, cutting and slashing with their kukris, jabbing with their bayonets, or firing a charge pointblank to finish the work of steel. They took three machine-guns and cleared the second line with similar carnage. The Turkish third line rose in a cloud and bolted.[460]

Dorsets in the front line.(Sandes)

The seizure of these enemy positions in front of Beit Aiessa was a feat of endurance as well as courage. The Official History acknowledges that the 3rd Division had been under 'considerable strain' and that although total casualties

> ... had only amounted to 615, the flood and bad weather conditions, combined with the fact that they had frequently been short of rations, had rendered the operations unusually trying; and it was held that the troops had made good progress with considerable skill.[461]

The delays, however, again raised concerns about the ability to relieve Kut in time.

As the friendly artillery barrage began at 0645 hours on 17 April, the objective of the 7th and 9th Brigades was to gain control of six canals, known in the orders as 'Six Water Channel', just west of the feature. Ten minutes later, they advanced across 1,000 yards of open ground, each on a 300-yard front. Fortunately, there was an early morning mist that helped cover them and the timing was perfect; the barrage stopped as they reached the Turkish trenches. The Connaught Rangers recorded the action.

> Again taken by surprise, the Turks made less resistance than was expected. Numbers of them put up their hands as our men approached and surrendered tamely. Altogether, upwards of 180 of the enemy were made prisoners, while their killed and wounded totalled some 300 officers and men. The captured position was at once consolidated and held during the day, two enemy counter-attacks being beaten off.[462]

British commanders were encouraged by this success and the 13th Division prepared to move forward to relieve the 3rd Division and attack further positions, but it did not take long for the Turks to launch a major counter-attack. From Kut, Major-General Townshend reported a major enemy force, about 1,400 strong, moving towards Dujaila, whilst the 7th and 9th Brigades observed a concentration of Turks to their south-west. An enemy bombardment began at 1700 hours and an hour later a massive enemy attack struck their line overwhelming forward Gurkha battalions. The Connaught Rangers:

> The Turks broke through en masse, in a closely formed column, estimated at some ten thousand bayonets, headed by the picked Second Constantinople Division, the corps d'elite of the Ottoman Army, which had arrived at Es Sinn recently, having been sent to Mesopotamia after the allied evacuation of Gallipoli.[463]

Candler commented that 'the Turks did not rely on a surprise. Their plan was to pour in masses of troops and to carry the position by sheer weight of numbers.'[464] By 1930 hours, the 9th Brigade was retreating eastward, pursued by the enemy and there were reports of shortages of ammunition. Quick action by Colonel Campbell and the Highland Light Infantry at Twin Pimples, supported by artillery, stemmed the Turkish advance, whilst the Connaught Rangers and a company of the 27th Punjabis held their positions tenaciously. As some friendly pockets held, Major-General R. Egerton, commander of the 7th Brigade, was forced to withdraw north towards the Tigris before attempting to re-group his command. By midnight he had assessed that the position was critical, especially as communications had broken down with the Connaught Rangers and the 89th Punjabis. Not knowing if any reinforcements were on the way, he ordered their withdrawal despite their success so far.

Elsewhere, the 8th Brigade was being heavily attacked and, because of the fragility of the whole position, the 1st Battalion of the Manchester Regiment, the 47th Sikhs and the 59th

Rifles, supported by the 23rd Mountain Battery, were ordered to hold the line and defend their locations to the last man. This they did, under huge pressure, and they were eventually reinforced by units from the 13th Division later in the night. Candler commented that 'every man who could hold a rifle, clerks, signallers, orderlies, was sent to the firing line to hold the parapet until the attack had failed.'[465] The War Record of the 47th Sikhs recorded:

> The enemy attempted to bomb up our trench from the right but number 1 Company with the assistance of the Manchester's Company, which had come up in the nick of time, held on to its position

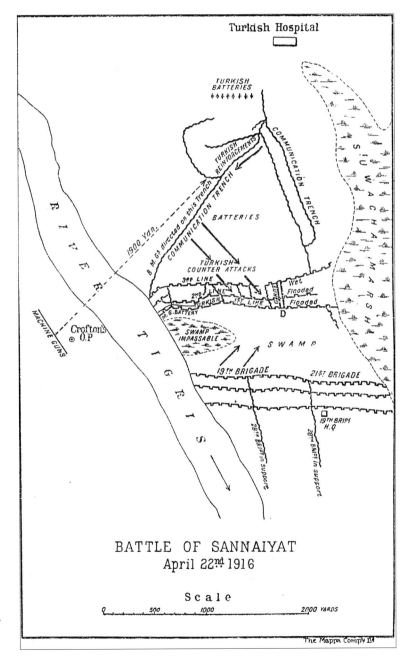

Battle of Sannaiyat, 22 April 1916. (Candler)

and repulsed the attack … The situation on the right of the Brigade, and probably that of the whole force, was saved by the fine stand of Number 1 Company and their company of Manchesters.[466]

A fourth Turkish attack was made at 0300 hours, with a final one at 0400 hours.

Though in some cases they got quite close to the British line, they failed entirely to break the stout defence of the 8th Brigade, who had that night covered themselves with glory and by 5.30 am the Turks in that area were in full retreat under heavy British artillery, machine-gun and rifle fire. By 5.45 all was quiet.[467]

The Turkish assault had been impressive and, though it did not drive all of the British and Indian forces back and was described in the Official History as a 'tactical failure',[468] it did affect the momentum of this latest Allied attempt to break through their lines and relieve Kut. 'It was led with great determination, was well timed, given good direction, and struck our troops at a time when there was inevitable disorganisation owing to relief (by the 13th Division).'[469]

The Turkish decisive action came with a high price; 4,000 men compared with the friendly casualty figure of 1,650.[470] Candler wrote that 'we killed more Turks at Beit Aiessa than at Shaikh Saad, The Wadi, El Orah, and Falahiyeh combined.'[471] However, the 3rd and 13th Divisions were no longer in a position to exploit any weaknesses on the right southern bank of the river. Even at this stage, misplaced optimism still prevailed; Major-General Townsend was informed on 20 April,

You can assure all ranks from me that their relief will be effected shortly. They must not relax their gallant efforts during the next few days, and I am quite sure that you will continue to inspire them by your courageous example.[472]

The deadline for the food to run out in Kut was fast approaching and the food airlifts were either not making it through to the town or were now being harassed by German aircraft. A final effort to break through to Kut was to be made by the 7th Division, supported by the 35th and 36th Brigades, on the left northern side – once more at Sannaiyat. The final attack at Sannaiyat was planned for 20 April, but again weather conditions and local flooding postponed the assault, this time for forty-eight hours. The fate of the Kut garrison was rapidly being sealed.

Major-General Younghusband launched his attack on Sannaiyat on the morning of 22 April against three main lines of entrenched Turkish positions that were at least manned up to his own strength. Bombardments took place on the opposite, left bank, side of the river to help deceive the enemy, but the odds were not in favour of the 7th Division. A patrol of the previous night had reported 'the Turkish front trench seemed to be only weakly held',[473] but the plan of attack had to be changed at the last minute because of the flooding in front of the positions. Instead of a 'two-brigade up' attack by the 19th and 21st Brigades, the 19th had to lead the assault with its sister brigade behind.

The Highland Battalion (Seaforths and Black Watch) and the 92nd Punjabis succeeded in pushing through the first line of enemy trenches, but were stalled at the second. All positions were flooded and the ground was 'a deepish quagmire and the infantry progress was very slow, many men sinking up to their armpits in mud and water'.[474] Also 'men were floundering through and over water-logged machine-gun pits and communication trenches, exposed the whole time to the pitiless hail of bullets and shrapnel.'[475] Some of the 19th Brigade reached the third line, but as the soldiers struggled in the conditions many of their weapons became clogged up with mud, their rifle bolts were stuck and they were not able to engage the enemy effectively.

The Turks had launched a counter-attack within the hour against the exposed flanks of the 19th Brigade, but it was driven off. Their second counter-attack could not be held and the Brigade had been pushed back to its original start line by 0820 hours. The 21st Brigade failed to support the lead brigade despite suffering over 250 casualties and receiving effective support- ing fire from thirty-five grouped friendly machine-guns. The Highland Battalion lost 597 men, including twenty officers.[476] A later analysis summed up the grim situation:

> Owing to the bad weather, the heavy casualties, and the fatigue of the troops, no further attempt could be made to relieve Kut. Since 5 April we had lost 10,000 men, and since January our battle casualties had been 60% of the forces engaged; on neither bank of the Tigris had Turkish resistance been overcome or materially shaken.[477]

Candler, who was observing Sannaiyat reported that 'the fate of Kut was said to hang at Sannaiyata',[478] but even if the 7th Division had been successful, there still remained the well- entrenched Turkish depth positions to deal with and the Tigris Corps was in no shape to make it through to Kut. One deficiency at that stage was the lack of trained and experienced officers, as remarked on by the commander of the 13th Division, Major-General Maude:

> Casualties especially heavy in officers, and we are having bad luck in this respect … some of the bat- talions have only 5 or 6, including the colonel and adjutant, left. Some drafts are however arriving, but not in sufficient numbers to keep pace with casualties.[479]

General Lake sent a telegram to India and London:

> … Gorringe considers that the troops have, for the present, reached the limit of their offensive powers … We are still 12 miles from Kut on the right bank and 15 miles on the left bank. Floods on earth flank limit our power of manoeuvre, and each attack, without several days of artillery prepara- tion which our time limit precludes, is costly …[480]

As the crescendo of fire from friendly guns again faded away, the defenders of Kut sensed that their end was nigh. Major Barber wrote that the situation 'made us long for the end – any end almost, for the sake of the miserable sick.'[481] The Easter church service had a special poignance; Captain Mousley wrote on 24 April:

> What an appalling price we are costing! A calm seems to be stealing over the garrison. It is the reac- tion from suspense extended infinitely far, and we know that we have done all possible to carry our resistance to the last possible day … We have now drifted very near the weir and within a few days will know our fate. A few say it appears already.[482]

Major-General Townshend commented that 'the stormy weather, the rain, the floods, and the mud all in turn assisted the Turk to keep Kut in his clutch.'[483] He knew that he had now to enter negotiations with the Turkish commander, Halil Bey, for surrender. Before that occurred, how- ever, there were two imaginative, though fateful, ideas for relief that were tried: an attempt to run the blockade around Kut by boat – and a move to bribe the enemy.

The *Julnar* Affair

General Lake had been informed by Vice-Admiral Sir Rosslyn Wemyss, the senior Royal Navy officer in Mesopotamia, on 13 April that the chance of a steamer making it through to Kut with supplies was small; the Official History calling it a 'forlorn hope'.[484] However, the decision was made that, in extremis, an effort could be mounted and the *Julnar* was secretly prepared at Amara with sheet steel protection and three weeks of supplies for the Kut garrison on board. The *Julnar* was a twin-screw steamer and reported to be 'faster than most of the river craft, and if any vessel at all could slip through the blockade she was that vessel.'[485] The crew of twelve volunteer, unmarried ratings was to be led by Lieutenant Humphrey Firman Royal Navy, Lieutenant-Commander Charles Cowley Royal Navy Volunteer Reserve and Engineer Sub-Lieutenant William Louis Reed Royal Navy Reserve. Both Cowley and Reed had intimate knowledge of the Tigris from before the War, as they had worked for the Euphrates and Tigris Steamship Company, conducting business on the river under the British flag.

The crew would have to cope with the difficulties of navigating in the dark on a windy and unpredictable river. They would also have to run the gauntlet of the Turkish guns and any potential minefield or submerged obstacle en route. However, as a Royal Navy historian pointed out:

> The Army had appealed to the Navy for help. So long as there was the smallest grain of a chance, so long as it could be said that there was a remote possibility of success, that appeal must not be made in vain.[486]

The attempt to relieve the garrison again generated hope within Kut. One of the besieged, Lieutenant H. McNeal of the Royal Field Artillery, wrote: 'Great excitement prevailed in Kut when it was heard that the relieving force would attempt to send the steamboat *Julnar* through with rations.'[487]

The *Julnar* set off from Fallahiya at 0700 hours on 24 April, making six knots speed and carrying over 250 tons of supplies. Despite an attempt to move through the most vulnerable stretches of the river by night and to disguise her advance with friendly gunfire, she was repeatedly engaged from different Turkish positions along the banks of the Tigris. She may well have been tracked by Turkish spies, as the attempts to keep the mission secret seem to have failed. Near Maqasis, at about midnight on 24 April, a shell killed the captain and wounded Lieutenant-Commander Cowley and one rating. Once at Maqasis, the *Julnar* struck a cable or hawser, which fouled her screw, and she was stopped. The ship had no choice but to surrender.

Both Firman and Cowley were awarded the Victoria Cross for their bravery, whilst others in the crew were also awarded decorations.[488] It is still not certain whether Cowley died from his

The *Julna*. (Black Tab)

Left Lieutenant
Humphrey Firman
VC, Royal Navy.
(Wilson)

Right Commander
Charles Cowley
VC, Royal Navy.
(Wilson)

wounds or was shot by the Turks. He was an interesting character. Although British, with an Irish father, his mother was Armenian. From the Turkish perspective, he was, therefore, a traitor.[489] The *Julnar* affair had been an audacious, wasteful adventure. The 103rd Mahrattas, watching from Kut, recorded:

> On the night 24th–25th , a gallant attempt by the steamship *Julnar* to run the Turkish lines and bring supplies into Kut roused the last flicker of hope, which died out when dawn on the 25th showed the *Julnar* some miles downstream, heeled over and stranded with a thin wisp of smoke coming from her funnel.[490]

Captain Mousley noted, 'It appears that this tragic but obvious end of so glorious an enterprise is a last hope. We have scarcely rations for tomorrow.'[491] Townshend wrote: 'Thus the attempt to run the blockade had failed. I wired to Headquarters my heartfelt sympathy with Admiral Wemyss for the heroic effort of his brave bluejackets.'[492] Lieutenant-General Gorringe was sure that 'this attempt to succour Kut, although unsuccessful, was universally considered in the Tigris Corps to be worthy of the finest traditions of the Royal Navy.'[493]

Only one more faint chance of escape was left.

Negotiations and Lawrence of Arabia

The final attempt to save the garrison of Kut came at the end of April when Major-General Townshend attempted to buy their freedom. The idea was approved by Lord Kitchener and the British Cabinet, though Sir Percy Cox, the Indian Government's political agent in Mesopotamia, 'regarded it with disgust and refused to have anything to do with such a project.'[494] On 7 April, as the idea was being discussed, Sir Percy Cox wrote to Colonel Beach, head of Intelligence in the Mesopotamia Expeditionary Force:

Halil Pasha. (Braddon)

It appears to me to be neither in the interests of Government or of myself as Chief Political Officer that I or my name should be connected with this business in any way. You see, I am not a migrant – I am a permanent official in the Gulf and I may conceivably have to remain here for a time after hostilities are concluded. The project in view is pretty sure to become known sooner or later especially if it proves unsuccessful and I cannot afford as a Political Officer of the Government of India to be identified with it.[495]

His concerns proved to be justified as British prestige in the region plummeted as the world heard of the attempted transaction and the Turks and Germans scored a propaganda victory. Captain Wilson, who was a political officer on Lieutenant-General Gorringe's staff, was also unhappy with the consequences.

> I have heard from many, including Persians, Arabs and Turks, that this attempt to bribe Enver, as it was always described, owing to the extreme secrecy maintained on our side, did us immense harm. Moreover, it was surely bad policy, even in April 1916, to provide the enemy with cash and guns, in order to protect invalids, however gallant, against the fortune of war.[496]

Townshend's first offer was to give the Turks one million pounds and forty guns if his force was released, though Captain Wilson commented that he was not certain whether the money was supposed to be destined for the Turkish officers or their government. He also pointed out that the sum of money was not even readily available either in Mesopotamia or India.[497] The offer was refused by Enver Pasha, General Halil Bey's commander, whose view was that his government did not need the money and they had just sacrificed 10,000 soldiers to gain Kut. A second offer of two million pounds was also refused and the Turkish commanders demanded unconditional surrender. A delegation of three British officers was sent to negotiate: Colonel Beach, Captain Herbert, and a certain Captain Thomas (T.E.) Lawrence. Captain Herbert, who wrote an account of the negotiations with the Turks, knew Turkey well, had some authority and knew various Turkish leaders including Halil Pasha.[498]

Captain Lawrence was sent to assess whether the local Arabs might revolt and join the Arab Movement. From his perspective, a revolt by local Arabs could help save the garrison. The roots of the Arab Independence Movement had indeed begun in Mesopotamia, though its leader had been imprisoned by the British. Earlier in April, Lawrence had approached Sulayman Fayi, a Basra official with connections in Turkey, encouraging him to lead a revolt and claiming that he could provide the funds and the weapons; Fayi 'rejected the proposal'.[499]

Senior officers at the Tigris Corps Headquarters were also mostly not interested in his unorthodox ideas, which was understandable because as officers of the Indian Army they could see the dangerous potential political precedent of encouraging a revolt against an Imperial master. Captain Lawrence commented that 'the local British had the strongest objection to my coming; and two Generals of them were good enough to explain to me that my mission (which they did not really know) was dishonourable to a soldier (which I was not).'[500]

He considered that conditions were ideal for a revolt in the area, but the British authorities were not prepared to pursue his plan. Lawrence believed that if his ideas had been followed and promises of Arab independence announced, then Kut might have been saved, if such an initiative had been coupled with a greater effort to re-supply Kut by air.

By the time the three officers had been led blindfolded into the Turkish lines from 'No-Man's Land' and met General Halil Bey on 29 April, the decision to surrender had been made, unbeknown to them. They attempted to negotiate an exchange of prisoners, but that was also too late. By that stage Townshend had already destroyed his guns and Herbert reported that 'Khalil (Halil) was angry and showed it.'[501] After having dinner with the Turks, they withdrew to humiliation, as the world's newspapers obtained the story. Lieutenant Keeling of the 119th Indian Infantry wrote his impression of the affair:

> … the proposal was made openly and clumsily, and only resulted in sarcastic leaders in the Constantinople Press, proclaiming that the great British people, having failed to conquer the Turks with swords, were now trying to corrupt them with their gold.[502]

Both Captain Lawrence and Colonel Beach were back in Basra by 8 May and Lawrence described Mesopotamia as a 'blunderland'.[503] He compared the Mesopotamian command's 'wood-chopping tactics' with the 'rapier-play' adopted by the British General Edmund Allenby in Palestine.[504] 'The entire episode merely reinforced his contempt for the regular army and the military establishment'.[505]

By the end of April, 15–20 men a day were dying of starvation in Kut. 'I had to get food at once or all my men would lie down and die.'[506] Lieutenant Naylor described the food situation:

> The bread ration had entirely failed, and for the last four days we had what we called emergency rations for two days. These rations differed very slightly and consisted of such odds and ends of stores as had not been large enough for an ordinary issue. Such things as Huntley & Palmer biscuits, a few ration biscuits and a little chocolate were among these scraps. Actually from the point of view of food, Kut could not have held out a day longer than it did.[507]

Townshend met Halil Bey personally on the Tigris on 26 April. He attempted to negotiate, but he had nothing to bargain with as the Turks realised his garrison was so weak and starved it had no option but to surrender. He was offered personal freedom if he did not destroy his guns and supplies, but this deal was refused.

Hostilities ceased at Kut on 27 April. Major Sandes described the unfamiliar silence.

> The stillness after so many months of noise was quite extraordinary. The day was calm, the weather fine, and the river-flood had fallen considerably; the atrocious weather and flood conditions had lasted just sufficiently long to prevent our relief … It was difficult to recognise Kut that morning. Gradually one by one, and then in twos and threes, people wandered out on to the river-front, deserted for so many months in the daytime; and men walked openly on the roofs of the houses, safe from the bullets of snipers for at any rate a few hours.[508]

Townshend's next, optimistic communiqué would ring hollow in the time to come:

COMMUNIQUE NUMBER 5[509]
28 APRIL 1916
It became clear, after General Gorringe's second repulse on 22nd April at Sannaiyat, of which I was informed by the Army Commander by wire, that the Relief Force could not win its way through in anything like time to relieve us, our limit of resistance as regards food being 29th April. It is hard to

believe that the large forces composing the Relief Force now could not fight their way to Kut, but there is the fact staring us in the face.

I was then ordered to open negotiations for the surrender of Kut, in the words of the Army Commander, 'The onus not lying on yourself. You are in the position of having conducted a gallant and successful defence, and you will be in a position to get better terms than any emissary of ours. The Admiral who has been in consultation with the Army Commander considers that you, with your prestige, are likely to get the best terms – we can of course supply food as you may arrange.'

These considerations alone, namely, that I can help my comrades of all ranks to the end, have decided me to overcome my bodily illness and the anguish of the mind which I am suffering from now, and I have interviewed the Turkish General-in-Chief yesterday, which is full of admiration at an 'heroic defence of five months,' as he put it.

Negotiations are still in progress, but I hope to be able to announce your departure for India on parole not to serve against the Turks, since the Turkish Commander-in-Chief says he thinks it will be allowed, and has wired to Constantinople to ask for this, and that the *Julnar*, which is lying with food for us at Magasis, now may be permitted to come to us.

Whatever has happened, my comrades, you can only be proud of yourselves. We have done our duty for King and Empire; the whole world knows we have done our duty.

I ask you to stand by me with your ready and splendid discipline, shown throughout, in the next few days, for the expedition of all service I demand from you. We may possibly go into camp, I hope between the Fort and the town, along the shore, whence we can easily embark.

	Charles Townshend
Kut-al-Amarah	Major-General
28th April, 1916	Commanding 6th Division

The garrison was concerned about their future and wondered whether they would be prisoners or not. The monotony of the siege was relieved on the 28th when weapons, ammunition and equipment were destroyed. Major Barber described the activity:

> Guns were blown up, and bits of them were flying about in a most dangerous way; rifles were smashed up, wagons were burnt; ammunition was dumped into the river at night; field glasses, swords and pistols were broken and thrown away.[510]

Captain Spackman: 'I fired my revolver into the prisma of my beautiful binoculars and then smashed my revolver with a sledge hammer and then burnt my saddlery.'[511]

Only a day later, Major-General Townshend's final communiqué was published. There was to be no parole, which would have meant freedom for his troops, in exchange for a guarantee that they would never fight against Turkey again. Instead, all were about to be subjected to over two years of captivity, the other ranks in particular in appalling conditions. Communiqué Number 6 appears to be incredibly naive when one considers the situation that the British and Indian troops were about to endure. It is noteworthy that neither of these last communiqués appeared in Major-General Townshend's later account of the siege:

COMMUNIQUE NUMBER 6[512]
29 APRIL 1916
The GOC has sent the following letter to the Turkish Commander-in-Chief:
Your Excellency,

Hunger forces me to lay down our arms, and I am ready to surrender to you my brave soldiers, who have done their duty, as you affirmed when you said: 'Your gallant troops will be the most sincere and precious guests.'

Be generous then; they have done their duty. You have seen them in the Battle of Ctesiphon; you have seen them during the retirement; and you have seen them during the siege of Kut for the last five months, in which I have played the strategic role of blocking your counter-offensive and allowed time for our reinforcements to arrive in Iraq.

You have seen how they have done their duty, and I will be certain that the Military History of this war will affirm this in a decisive manner.

I send two of my officers, Captain Morland and Major Gilchrist, to arrange details.

I am ready to put Kut into your hands at once, and go into your camp as soon as you can arrange details, but I pray to you to expedite the arrival of food.

I propose that your chief medical officer should visit my hospitals with my Primary Medical Officer. He will be able to see for himself the state of some of my troops – there are some without arms and legs, some with scurvy. I do not suppose you wish to take these into captivity, and in fact the better course would be to let the wounded and sick go back to India.

The Chief of the Imperial Staff, London, wires me that the exchange of prisoners of war is permitted. An equal number of Turks in Egypt and India would be liberated for the same number of combatants. Accept my high regards.

> Charles Townshend
> Major-General
> Commanding 6th Division
> and Forces at Kut

I would add to the above that there are strong grounds for hoping that the Turks will eventually agree to all being exchanged. I have received notification from the Turkish Commander-in-Chief, to say I can start for Constantinople soon. Having arrived there, I shall petition to be allowed to go to London on parole and see the Secretary of State for war and get you exchanged at once. In this way I hope to be of great assistance to you all.

I thank you from the bottom of my heart for your devotion to duty and your discipline and bravery, and may we meet soon in better times.

> Charles Townshend
> Major-General
> Commanding 6th Division

Kut-al-Amarah
29th April, 1916

The garrison also received a telegram from Captain Nunn, Royal Navy:

> We, the officers and men of the Royal Navy who have been associated with the Tigris Corps, and many of us so often worked with you and your gallant troops, desire to express our heartfelt regret at our inability to join hands with you and your comrades in Kut.[513]

The Padre, Reverend Harold Spooner, held his last service in Kut. The surrender occurred on 29 April 1916.

Notes

367. Townshend (1920) p.336, referring to the besieging Turkish force.
368. Candler (1919) p.177.
369. Callwell (1920) p.199.
370. Ibid p.164.
371. Ibid p.193.
372. Falls (1967) p.707.
373. Moberly (1924) p.373.
374. Atkinson (1931) p.202.
375. *The Great War 1914–1918* Volume II (1991) p.102.
376. Moberly (1924) p.371.
377. Townshend (1920) p.312.
378. Moberly (1924) p.375.
379. Atkinson (1931) p.203.
380. Gibson (1969) p.110.
381. Candler (1919) p.173.
382. *London Gazette* 26 September 1916 and Gliddon (2005) p.74.
383. Callwell (1920) p.207.
384. Ibid p.207.
385. Candler (1919) p.179.
386. Moberly (1924) p.379.
387. Candler (1919) p.180.
388. Neville (1938) p.195.
389. Neville (1938) p.196.
390. Wauchope (1925) p.225.
391. Anonymous (1992) p.157.
392. Ibid p.159.
393. Neville (1938) p.200.
394. Callwell (1920) p.210.
395. Atkinson (1931) p.205.
396. *London Gazette* 26 September 1916 and Gliddon (2005) p.87.
397. Moberly (1924) p.391.
398. Candler (1919 p.183.
399. Gibson (1969) p.110.
400. Callwell (1920) p.211.
401. Moberly (1924) p.392.
402. Wylly (1928) p.161.
403. Figures from unnamed (1930) p.47.
404. Townshend (1919) p.321.
405. Nelson (1918) p.3971.
406. Sandes (1920) p.232.
407. Townshend (1920) p.309.
408. Sandes (1920) p.225.
409. Mousley (1922) p.125.
410. Sandes (1920) p.228.
411. Neave (1937) p.71.
412. Townshend (1920) p.313.
413. Barber (1917) p.210–211.
414. Townshend (1920) p.314.
415. Moynihan (1983) p.19–20.

416. Townshend (1920) p.314.
417. Ibid p.315.
418. Sandes (1920) p.230.
419. Ibid p.230.
420. Townshend (1919) p.318.
421. Ibid p.318.
422. Ibid p.320.
423. Ibid p.320.
424. Ibid p.321.
425. Herbert (1919) p.214.
426. Moberly (1924) p.447.
427. Anonymous (1933) p.217.
428. Barber (1917) p.211.
429. Townshend (1919) p.326.
430. Paltan (1930) p.52–53.
431. Anonymous (1934) p.46.
432. Neville (1938) p.212.
433. Petre (1919) p.93.
434. Ibid p.94.
435. Sandes (1920) p.233.
436. Mousley (1922) p.131.
437. Neave (1937) p.18.
438. Mousley (1922) p.129.
439. Rawlinson (1941) p.166.
440. Townshend (1919) p.325.
441. Sandes (1920) p.239
442. Anderson (1960) p.88.
443. Anonymous (undated). Attached extract from AH 209/24/17. p.1–3.
444. Ibid.
445. Barber (1917) p.222.
446. Herbert (1919) p.207.
447. Candler (1919) p.235–6.
448. Sandes (1920) p.236.
449. Townshend (1919) p.331.
450. Moynihan (1983) p.34.
451. Mockler-Ferryman (undated) p.119.
452. Sandes (1920) p.239.
453. Nelson (1918) p.3970.
454. Kingsmill (1966) p.57.
455. Spackman (1967) p.6.
456. Ibid p.7.
457. Herbert (1919) p.209.
458. *London Gazette* 26 September 1916 and Gliddon (2005) p.96. During the period of the Kut siege, the Relief Force had been awarded twelve Victoria Crosses (Two Royal Navy officers and ten Army personnel).
459. Jourdain and Fraser (1924) p.513.
460. Candler (1919) p.188.
461. Moberly (1924) p.407.
462. Jourdain and Fraser (1924) p.514.
463. Ibid.

464. Candler (1919) p.192.

465. Ibid p.195.

466. Anonymous (1992) p.169.

467. Moberly (1924) p.419.

468. Ibid p.419.

469. *A Study of the Strategy and Tactics of the Mesopotamia Campaign* (1930) p.48.

470. Figures from *A Study of the Strategy and Tactics of the Mesopotamia Campaign* (1930) p.48.

471. Candler (1919) p.198.

472. Townshend (1920) p.333.

473. Moberly (1924) p.427.

474. Ibid p.428.

475. Wauchope (1925) p.228.

476. Figures; Moberly (1924) p.432.

477. *A Study of the Strategy and Tactics of the Mesopotamia Campaign* (1930) p.49.

478. Candler (1919) p.208.

479. Callwell (1920) p.215.

480. Moberly (1924) p.433.

481. Barber (1917) p.226.

482. Mousley (1922) p.148.

483. Townshend (1920) p.332.

484. Moberly (1924) p.435.

485. Cato (1917) p.92.

486. Ibid p.94.

487. Ibid p.98.

488. *London Gazette* 2 February 1917.

489. For a more personal account written by Sub-Lieutenant Reed's granddaughter read Hammond (2006) p.70–74.

490. Paltan (1930) p.53.

491. Mousley (1922) p.149.

492. Townshend (1920) p.334.

493. Nunn (2007) p.228.

494. Graves (1941) p.199.

495. Ibid p.200/201.

496. Arnold (1930) p.99.

497. Wilson (1930) p.97.

498. Herbert (1919).

499. Asher (1998) p.145.

500. Lawrence (1940) p.59.

501. Herbert (1919) p.235.

502. Keeling (1924) p.2.

503. Wallach (2004) p.175.

504. Lawrence (1940) p.60.

505. Rooney (2000) p.85.

506. Townshend (1920) p.335.

507. Neville (1938) p.215–6.

508. Sandes (1920) p.247.

509. Nelson (1918) p.3972.

510. Barber (1917) p.234.

511. Spackman (1967) p.7.

512. Nelson (1918) p.3972.

513. Barber (1917) p.238.

Indian infantry roll-call. (*The Illustrated War News* 31 May 1916, Part 98)

Chapter Eight

CAPITULATION

April 29th (147th Day of Siege). The worst has happened. An unconditional surrender. We have destroyed all guns, rifles, ammunition and stores, so the Turks won't get much – only a starved, sick and worn out Division and a Brigade. Turks took over Kut at midday.
Major Nelson[514]

The Garrison

At 1140 hours on 29 April, General Lake was informed by Major-General Townshend that the guns and most munitions in Kut had been destroyed and that Halil Bey had been told that the garrison was ready for surrender. At 1242 hours another message explained that a Turkish regiment could be seen approaching the fort to take control, and communications were cut off between Kut and the rest of the Mesopotamian Expeditionary Force at 1300 hours when the wireless was destroyed. 'White flags were hoisted on the walls.'[515] Private Hughes wrote: 'What an eyesore. It does not look British. When the Union Jack was lowered it was a ceremony that touched the tender spot in the heart of every one of us.'[516] The garrison was only made aware that they were to become prisoners on the 29th, dashing their hope of a parole, but energising a last hour of destruction, as the remaining weapons and equipment were put out of action.

The day before, Captain Mousley wrote 'we are a sick army, a skeleton army rocking with cholera and disease.'[517] The garrison had been subjected to five months of constant harassment by enemy artillery and sniper fire, the constant, wearing fear of assault, and casualties from disease. They had also suffered from floods, high temperatures, foul smells – and false hopes fuelled by failed relief attempts and over-optimistic communiqués from their commander. However, the troops were also proud to have kept the enemy at bay for so long and to have shown courage and tenacity in the face of great adversity. To their thinking, they had bought time for the rest of the British and Indian forces to consolidate and carry on the fight. They were also still fiercely loyal to their commander, despite his often misinformed criticism of the Indian troops. Townshend surrendered the following personnel in Kut:

British Officers	277
Indian Officers	204
British Other Ranks	2,592

Indian Other Ranks   6,988
Indian followers (non-combatant)   3,248

This was a total of 13,309; 1,025 had died from enemy action, whilst 721 died of disease. 2,500 had been wounded and 72 were missing. 1,450 were in hospital and, of those, in theory, the worst 1,130 cases were to be exchanged with Turkish prisoners and evacuated down the Tigris to the Relief Force. Observers reported, however, that the Turkish doctors were more inclined to allow the Indian wounded to be exchanged or sent downstream, rather than the British patients who were in a worse condition. 345 personnel were later exchanged from Baghdad.[518] Of the civilian population, 247 had died and 663 were wounded.[519] Twenty-six transport mules remained out of the original 1,800.[520] 'The Turks also recorded capturing 40 artillery pieces, 3 aircraft, 2 river steamers and 40 automobiles'[521] though there is no evidence of some of those items in the British Official History.

Both Major-General Townshend and Major-General Melliss were sick when the Turks occupied Kut, so Major-General Delamain handed over the town, as Halil Bey was being granted the Turkish honorific title of 'Pasha'. The new Turkish commandant of Kut, Kaimakam Nizam Bey, lined up the senior British officers outside Townshend's headquarters where they handed over their swords. Private W. Robinson reported that 'They were all treated alike with great courtesy, the commandant shaking hands with them before touching the swords presented to him, which were piled on the table.'[522] Halil Pasha then honoured the Kut commander by refusing to accept Townshend's sword and pistols, saying 'They are as much yours as ever they were.' According to Townsend, he also said 'I should be the honoured guest of the Turkish nation. My force would be sent to Asia Minor to be interned in places in a good climate near the sea.'[523] There was of course great relief amongst the garrison that the siege was over, but as Captain Spackman later wrote, 'We had not realised that really we were jumping out of the frying pan to get into the fire.'[524] Seventy per cent of the other ranks that went into captivity were to die.

Looting by Turk and Arab had begun immediately. They were not part of the best fed, dressed or equipped army and made the most of the opportunity, particularly in the hospital where the patients had little energy to resist the looters. Boots were a favourite prize and even the ill Major-General Melliss had his boots stolen from under his bed. There was also a rumour that the ransom money that had been offered by the British was hidden somewhere in the town, so a feverish search was made.

The Turkish soldiers' attitude towards British and Indian personal property during the forthcoming 'death march' into captivity needs to be placed in context. They were clothed in particularly coarse and cheap material and three-quarters of them did not even own underwear. General Otto Liman von Sanders:

> Therefore, one cannot consider Ottoman soldiers' attempts to strip off the clothes of the dead British and Indian soldiers who fell in front of the Ottoman trenches, after another unsuccessful attack, callousness. It was the only opportunity for the Ottoman soldiers to find clothes, shoes and underwear. The prohibitions issued against seizing the clothing of the dead bore no fruits. In such cases the 'European manners' were of no use; and the Ottoman soldiers were immediately replacing the shabby clothes on their scrawny bodies with the new ones taken from the enemy.[525]

He does not mention the thefts from the living. Initially, relations between the British, Indian and Turkish troops were generally cordial. The worst wounded and sick were exchanged and, as both sides had suffered hardships over the previous months of the siege, they had something

Opposite and above Mosque in Kut and with its minaret damaged later in the War (above).
(Barber and Author's Collection)

in common. The Turkish officers promised the garrison food when they reached Shumran (or Shamran) Camp and Candler wrote:

> The Kut garrison at the time of the surrender were well treated by the enemy. Turkish officers gave every British soldier a handful of cigarettes as he left the camp, and British and Ottoman privates were observed fraternising with friendly and explanatory gestures.[526]

Lieutenant Bishop of the 66th Punjabis was optimistic: 'We believed the Turks would treat all ranks well, as up to that moment they had always fought and behaved like gentlemen … we were inclined to think that all would be well.'[527] This situation quickly changed and Lieutenant-Colonel Frederick Wilson, writing in 1930, graphically described how events unfolded, how the occupation of Kut was accompanied 'by scenes of indiscipline, violence and savage brutality … resistance being met by merciless bludgeoning.'[528] As the columns and boats of prisoners started to move upstream, personal items and equipment were stolen and the practice of exchanging clothes, other belongings and money for scarce food became commonplace.

Major Sandes was more philosophical about Turkish behaviour and acknowledged that 'When the Turks occupied Kut, they found themselves suddenly called upon to take charge of a large number of wounded, sick, and starving soldiers and non-combatants with wholly inadequate arrangements for so doing.'[529]

Unlike Lieutenant-Colonel Wilson, he commented that, despite the temptations, 'the amount of looting which took place was extremely small and does credit to the discipline of the enemy.'[530] Turkish discipline was obviously tough and officers shot offending soldiers. Major Sandes observed that 'the Turkish officer on active service has absolute power of life and death over each and all of his men, and does not hesitate to exercise it.'[531] He anticipated that as the Turks had difficulty sustaining their own troops, let alone the captured, and as they were poorly dressed and equipped; the British soldier would have difficulty surviving on the same rations that Turkish soldiers endured. Major Sandes' comments are echoed by a recent Turkish study

Prisoners of the Turks at Kut. (IWM Q 92609)

on the Ottoman Army, which deals with disease and death on the battlefield during the War. Large numbers of Turkish soldiers were admitted to hospital because of 'the chronic problem of malnutrition, which could not be eliminated despite all efforts.'[532] It is no surprise that any opportunity to ameliotate their own condition was seized.

Some of the Arab residents of Kut, who had stayed loyal to the British, provided the occasional chapatti to the new prisoners, but suffered at the hands of fellow Arabs and the Turkish Army: probably 250 were shot.[533] Staff Sergeant H. Bird reported 'We slept in Kut that night, as there were no steamers to take us up river, and during the night some of our interpreters were badly knocked about by the enemy for having helped us during the siege, and later most of them were hanged in the square in the centre of the town.'[534]

Reverend Spooner recorded that there was no respect for the dead lying in the Kut cemetery, which rapidly had its crosses stolen and became hatched with footpaths cutting across the graves. He also wrote about the hangings:

> Each morning one saw the bodies of dead and dying hanging on tripod gallows set up on the river-banks. The Turks' method was to hang a man by his neck to the top of the tripod and then ease the legs of the tripod until the man's feet were well off the ground, when the victim was left to be slowly strangled to death.[535]

One interpreter, named Sassoon, had attempted to kill himself by jumping off a roof after being tortured and having his legs broken; he failed in this attempt and was then hanged. This account has parallels to today, in Iraq. Interpreters and other locals working for the coalition forces have had to run similar risks.

Norfolk Regiment soldiers. (IWM Q 92608)

The Relief Force

The Relief Force had lost 23,000 casualties. Their sacrifice was recognised formally by a message from His Majesty the King Emperor, George V, in a message sent to the Army Commander on 2 May:

> Although your brave troops have not had the satisfaction of relieving their beleaguered comrades in Kut, they have under the able leadership of yourself and subordinate commanders fought with great gallantry and determination under most trying conditions. The achievement of relief was denied you by floods and bad weather and not by the enemy whom you have resolutely pressed back. I have watched your efforts with admiration and am satisfied that you have done all that was humanly possible and will continue to do so in future encounters with the enemy.[536]

The 13th Division's commander, Major-General Maude, had his own thoughts about the demise of Kut.

> Its fall has been very disappointing, but I do not think that the fault lies with the soldiers, although no doubt an attempt will be made to saddle them with responsibility. The local difficulties, the long line of communications, the water transport (or rather the lack of it), the menace from floods and rains, the barrenness of the country – all these factors rendered the most careful organisation and liberal expenditure necessary as a preliminary to success. The obstacles in our way were enormous, hampered as we were by floods and restricted as our movements were by being tied to the river – but we did our best, as I think will be admitted when the story is known.[537]

It is incredible that, even after this disastrous defeat in the Mesopotamia Campaign and the recent humiliation at Gallipoli, the competence of the Turkish forces was still being underestimated. Townshend stated that 'in our case at Kut we had resisted for just five months, and we were compelled to surrender not by the enemy but by famine.'[538] This totally ignores the fact that the Turkish strategy of isolating Kut and blocking attempts by the Relief Force to raise the siege had been effective and decisive. The adverse terrain and weather were not the only factors that had prevented British success.

Most of the frustration and bitter disappointment in the Relief Force was felt by the regiments who had officers and men, whom they knew personally, in the captured town. In the case of the 1/4th Hampshires, this included relatives, friends and business acquaintances. The wing of the battalion within the Tigris Corps had worked hard to try and relieve its comrades and as its History states:

> No one without experience of trying to negotiate flooded trenches under the climatic conditions prevailing in Mesopotamia during January, March and April, 1916, could fully appreciate the misery and hardship endured by infantrymen, harnessed with all the impedimenta of 'Battle Order' advancing over slippery, swampy ground offering no vestige of cover, against machine-gun and rifle fire directed by a foe expertly entrenched and well versed in the art of defence.[539]

This unit had recognised the enemy's success.

The Relief Force had to get on with its war against the Turks, whilst their comrades went into captivity. The Anglo-Indian force's daily routine was summed up by Major H. Davson of the 82nd Punjabis, 36th Brigade of the Tigris Corps. On 30 April, he wrote in his diary:

> Two more moves, and we are now in another lot of first line trenches. Heat is appalling, and only just begun. Flies bite hard – are in thousands. Cholera has started, so things are very cheery. I was inoculated yesterday against it and then had to march in the heat of the day to relieve trenches. Great fun … We lie and gasp every day under a blanket, which we put up to keep the sun off, which it does indifferently … Kut has fallen. With our forces we could not have got through and 24,000 casualties since December is a lot … In fact, you may say that I am fairly fed up with Mesopotamia. Food is now disgusting. We are short of milk, jam, sugar and exist on bully beef (fly blown) and stale bread. I am thankful to say so far I am very fit on it. I do not eat much, which is perhaps as well in this heat. I can't get at my mosquito curtain, which is annoying in this weather as they have reinforced the flies.[540]

On 1 May, the 7th Division were still dug in on the northern bank of the Tigris opposite Sannaiyat, whilst the 3rd and 13th Divisions remained opposite Beit Aiessa. Some recuperation and reinforcement was required before they reassumed their offensive.

The level of British embarrassment as a result of the Kut disaster, coupled with the Allied failure at Gallipoli, should not be underestimated. The British Empire had been exposed as vulnerable and, at times, weak. It had lost face to both the Turk and the Arab, revealing a fallibility that had not been so obvious before. It was not until 1917 that perceptions changed, as the British General Edmund Allenby or 'El Nebi' ('a promised one of God') began achieving success in Palestine, the Arab Revolt gained strength with Lawrence of Arabia, and General Maude achieved eventual victory in Mesopotamia. The Kut surrender did not have as great an impact on the British public as it might because Mesopotamia was a 'sideshow' compared to the Western Front and the level of sacrifice occurring there; attention would soon be focused on the Somme. However, the disaster was more obvious to the population of the Middle East and elsewhere. The *New York Times* of 30 April 1916 acknowledged that the British public had never lost faith in Major-General Townshend but

Indian Army machine-guns. (*The Illustrated War News*, 20 October 1915)

... the surrender of General Townshend's army to the Turks is one of the few instances of the war in which an entire fighting unit of important numbers has laid down its arms. It is one of the largest body of troops of the Entente Allies which has surrendered at one time and larger than any other captured French or British force.[541]

This was humiliating news for the British Empire.

The Anglo-Indian force eventually marched into Baghdad, led by General Maude, in March 1917. He was to have a well supported army of five infantry divisions amounting to over 166,000 men, whilst Halil Pasha's strength had gradually diminished, but that is in the future.

This chapter ends with British acknowledgement of the sacrifices made by both the garrison of Kut and those who attempted to relieve the town; in Lord Kitchener's speech to the House of Lords on 4 May 1916:

I am glad that the noble and gallant lord has offered me this opportunity of paying a tribute to General Townshend and his troops, whose dogged determination and splendid courage have earned for them so honourable a record. It is well known how, after a series of brilliantly fought engagements, General Townshend decided to hold the strategically-important position at Kut-al-Amara, and it will not be forgotten that his dispositions for the defences of that place were so excellent and so complete that the enemy, not withstanding large numerical superiority, was wholly unable to penetrate his lines. Noble lords will not fail to realise how tense was the strain borne by those troops who, for more than twenty weeks, held to their posts under conditions of abnormal climatic difficulty, and on rations calculated for protraction to the furthest possible period until, as it was proved, imminent starvation itself compelled the capitulation of this gallant garrison, which consisted of 2,970 British and some 6,000 Indian troops, including followers.

General Townshend and his troops, in their honourable captivity, will have the satisfaction of knowing that, in the opinion of their comrades, which I think I may say that this House and the country fully share, they did all that was humanly possible to resist to the last, and that their surrender

Two views of Lieutenant-General Maude riding into Baghdad. (Callwell and Royal Hampshire Regiment Museum)

reflects no discredit on themselves or on the record of the British and Indian Armies.

Every effort was, of course made to relieve the beleaguered force, and I am not travelling beyond the actual facts in saying that to the adverse elements alone was due the denial of success; the constant rain and consequent floods not only impeding the advance, but compelling – in lieu of turning movements – direct attacks on an almost impossibly narrow front. No praise would seem extravagant for the troops under Sir Percy Lake and Sir George Gorringe, and that they did not reap the fruit of their courage and devotion is solely due to the circumstances which fought against them. The last message sent by General Townshend from Kut was addressed in these terms:

'We are pleased to know that we have done our duty, and recognise that our situation is one of the fortunes of war. We thank you and General Gorringe and all ranks of the Tigris Force for the great efforts you have made to save us.'

I think the House, no less the country at large, will endorse these words, and I am sure that those who held and those who strained every nerve to relieve Kut have alike earned our admiration and gratitude. I am glad to endorse what the noble Lord has said in regard to the conduct of the Turkish commander.[542]

The Kut Garrison was about to enter captivity.

Notes

514. Nelson (1918) p.3957. (2nd Battalion the Queen's Own (Royal West Kent) Regiment in Kut).
515. Neville (1938) p.217.
516. Neave (1937) p.92.
517. Mousley (1922) p.151.
518. Wilson (1930) p.99.
519. Moberly (1924) p.459.
520. Sandes (1920) p.251.
521. Erickson (2001) p.151.
522. Neave (1937) p.94.
523. Townshend (1920) p.336.
524. Neave (1937) p.96.
525. Ozdemir (2008) p.39. The German general, Otto Liman von Sanders, had led a German mission to Turkey in 1913 to train and reorganise the Army. The Turks appointed him a corps commander and then a Field Marshal. He became the Turkish 5th Army commander at Gallipoli.
526. Candler (1919) p.213.
527. Bishop (1920) p.34.
528. Wilson (1930) p.99.
529. Sandes (1920) p.262.
530. Ibid p.265.
531. Ibid p.265.
532. Ozdemir (2008) p.34.
533. Neave (1937) p.101.
534. Ibid p.99.
535. Moynihan (1983) p.36.
536. Moberly (1924) p.438.
537. Callwell (1920) p.217.
538. Townshend (1920) P 337.
539. Wheeler (undated) p.17.
540. Qureshi (1958) p.228.
541. *New York Times* of 30 April 1916.
542. Townshend (1920) p.338–339.

Commonwealth War Graves Kut, Cross of Sacrifice today. (Brigadier Mark Armstrong)

Part Two

IMPRISONED

The Trek
No pause, no rest! Forward the column pushes
Across the stern and unproductive plain –
And Thirst, Satan's archfiend, darts at the brain
And the weight of the great heat their spirit crushes
To deeper silence and the tired feet bleed –
While the ruthless Turk with yells and sometimes blows
Urges them on beside his impatient steed
To a future where and how no soldier knows
Beyond the dust-cloud on the horizon's rim,
Beyond the range of Hope – to memories grim.
But neither desert thirst nor fiercest sun
Nor dust-storms, nor the unknown miles ahead
Can touch their heart or clog its valves with dread –
These English lads that fought at Ctesiphon
'Sparkling Moselle'[543]

Chapter Nine

INTO CAPTIVITY

'Yallah! Yallah!'[544]

Shumran

Nothing could prepare the British and Indian other ranks for the conditions that they were about to endure. For them, over two years of horror awaited. Many of the officers, who were separated from their soldiers, had a tough time also, but nothing like the experiences of their subordinates. Meanwhile, Major-General Townshend lived in relative luxury until the War ended – it is no wonder that he received a great deal of criticism on his return to England.

Several officers published their accounts of captivity, the most well known being Captains Johnston and Yearsley and Lieutenant Jones in 1919, Lieutenant Bishop and Major Sandes in 1920, and Captain Mousley in 1922. All tell of hard conditions, the frugal existence, the harsh discipline of their captors and some of failed and successful escapes. However, the most fascinating accounts were those written by or about other ranks, particularly Flight-Sergeant Long's *Other Ranks of Kut* and the story of Regimental-Quartermaster-Sergeant Harvey of 2nd Battalion the Dorsetshire Regiment.[545] Though Flight-Sergeant Long's book was not published until 1938, it is the most evocative of the Kut prisoner stories and contains the harshest of tales. There are many more personal diaries. Whether it is an officer's or soldier's tale, the next stage of the Kut story remains fascinating, but grim. Inevitably, this chapter relies heavily on personal accounts that graphically bring alive the story of the prisoners' journey into captivity.

The first experience of most of the prisoners was being marched, in squads, to the foreshore of the Tigris in readiness for their move to Shumran. This was only eight miles upriver, but took eight hours to march. 'Although only a short distance all ranks were greatly fatigued due to their starved condition.'[546] The garrison was physically and mentally weak after the siege and it soon became obvious that future conditions were not going to be any better and that food was to be limited.

> We found we were not allowed any food, so I gave a Turkish soldier one rupee and eight annas for a dirty black loaf, which my pal and I soon devoured. In the afternoon the Turks gave us some filthy black biscuits, which the men ate at once, as they were hungry and could not wait to have them soaked, as they were advised to do.[547]

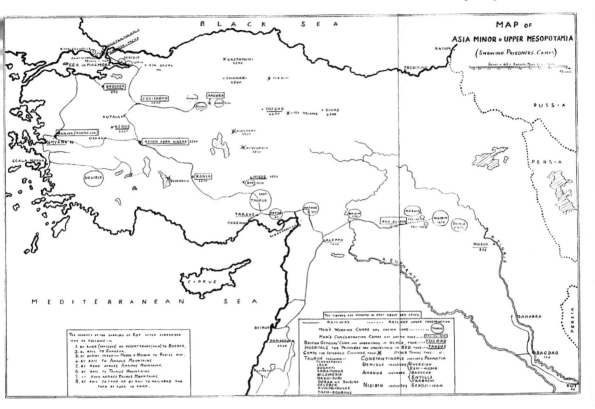

Map of Asia Minor and Upper Mesopotamia, showing prison camps. (*Prisoners of War in Turkey* pamphlet)

Major Sandes provided the best description of the much-maligned Turkish biscuit, which was, initially, the only available food.

> Imagine an enormous slab of rock-like material, brown in colour, about five inches in diameter and three-quarters inch thick, made of the coarsest flour interspersed with bits of husk and a goodly portion of earth, and you have a tolerable idea of the diet on which the Turkish soldier seems to thrive.[548]

The average individual daily issue of two-and-a-half biscuits did not provide much nutrition, particularly as some soldiers had not eaten for thirty-six hours before they were distributed. Sergeant Munn wrote that his soldiers received six biscuits each on arrival at Shumran, but eight of his men died during the first night. 'The doctor put their deaths down to having eaten the coarse biscuit whilst the stomach was in a weak state.'[549] During their week's stay at Shumran, fifty-three of his battalion's men were to die. Sergeant H. Coombes of the Queen's Own Royal West Kent Regiment wrote 'Disease started at Shumran. First cholera, then dysentery, and enteritis.'[550]

River transport was limited and men of the 16th and 17th Brigades had to march to Shumran, 'another great test of endurance and pluck.'[551] This included Second-Lieutenant Ubsdell of the 66th Punjabis, who wrote a unique record of his experiences on rice paper in very small script. He described himself as 'done and very hungry' when he reached Shumran and noticed that soldiers were selling clothes for food.[552] Private Hughes saw the same exchange:

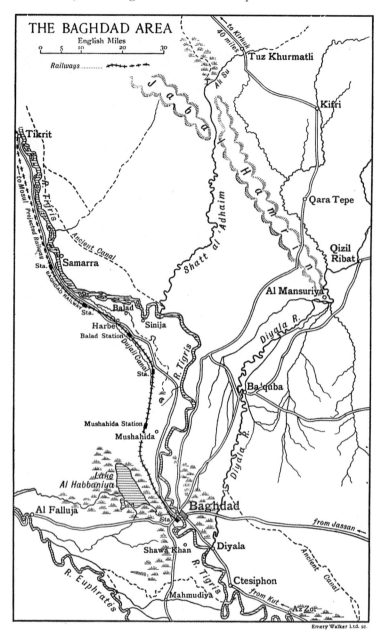

The Baghdad area.
(Lucas)

As we passed through the Turkish lines, some of our men were giving away their overcoats and any-thing they owned that would procure a loaf of bread. It was dark when we arrived at our camping place, and found that no arrangements had been made as regards giving food, so we had to 'grin and bear it'. [553]

The short-term expediency to eat and survive meant that many of the soldiers were to suffer worse later, as they ran out of valuables to barter and money to pay for food. Many were already suffering as they had nothing with which to bargain and had already been robbed of anything of value.

Flight Sergeant P.W. Long. (Long)

Food, or its scarcity, dominated life during the siege and it continued to dominate captivity. The 'earthy' biscuits could not sustain soldiers who were already weakened and illness increased, many of the troops suffering from severe dysentery or enteritis. Fifty per cent of the 76th Punjabis were suffering from diarrhoea and Major Sandes reported that many men were left behind dead when the prisoners left Shumran, 'due to food unfit for dogs to eat.'[554] The Turkish soldiers made the most of the situation and were seen selling food, including official rations supposedly destined to their captives, to the British and Indians. A small respite occurred at Shumran, in the first few days, when a British boat, the *Shuhrur*, under a white flag and towing two barges, arrived with decent rations, including jam, sugar and canned beef, though these meagre supplies did not last long. Lieutenant Elton of the Hampshire Regiment described the food as 'belated Christmas gifts' and soldiers were eating tinned Christmas pudding.[555]

Major Sandes travelled to Shumran from Kut on the Turkish steamer *Busrah* on 30 April with what was known as the '1st echelon' of mixed-rank prisoners. 'We were gazing for the last time on the wreck of our hopes, and silence reigned aboard the ship.'[556] However, the passengers were not sad to see the last of the town and were probably disappointed that this initial journey only lasted two hours so that they could travel further away from the place. Captain Spackman was travelling on the same boat and described seeing the victor, Halil Pasha.

> He is a small dapper young-looking Turk. Intellectual and determined in appearance and manner, evidently pleased with his success in capturing a British-Indian force of 12,000 or thereabouts, including about 270 British officers. There were, however, a very large proportion of sick and followers.[557]

It was quickly evident that the officers were to be more comfortable than their soldiers. They had plenty of their own equipment with them and were able to put up tents for shelter, whilst most of the troops had no tentage or useful accoutrements and were fully exposed to the sun and dust. The Turks did not supply any comforts. Nor did they bury many of those who died on their trek into captivity; at Shumran 'their bodies were cast into a nearby ravine, where in 1917 some of their skulls were found.'[558]

Major-General Townshend was also passing through Shumran, albeit briefly, on his way to Baghdad. A smart launch docked on 3 May, with the General, Colonel Harrington Parr of his Divisional Staff, his aide de camp Captain Walter Morland, two British orderlies, an Indian servant and his Portuguese chef on board. They were escorted by a Turkish colonel, Isakh Bey. There was still a great deal of loyalty toward and respect for Townshend and he arrived and left amidst cheering troops.

As we passed the place where the remnant of the gallant old 6th Division was encamped, officers and men lined the bank and cheered me long as I went by. Tears filled my eyes as I stood at attention at the salute. Never shall I have such a command again. Never had any man a finer command. I loved the 6th Division with all my heart and they gave me their confidence to the last.[559]

However, he did not record any particular concern about the future prospects for his troops and it is not clear whether he made much attempt to ensure that they were being looked after. In his surrender negotiations with Halil Pasha, assurances had been made that the Turks would feed, pay and transport the garrison and General Lake had reminded the Turks about this obligation, but there is no evidence of Townshend's concern. He may have hoped that he would be able to negotiate concessions for his men later and was reported to have called out, 'I hope to be back shortly, boys, with good news,' but nothing came of this.[560] He does mention the fact that his dog, 'Spot', who had stayed with him during the siege, was sent south to safety.

Major-Generals Melliss and Delamain did their best to improve the conditions for the troops and wanted to ensure that a greater proportion of officers accompanied the men, but both of them were ill and their requests had little effect. The only concession given by the Turks was that the unfit would travel by river and that the daily distances marched should not be more than eight miles.[561] This 'eight mile rule' only lasted for one day.

A.J. Barker, who wrote a biography of Townshend, had no doubt that the General could have done more for his troops and should have insisted on greater officer involvement in their well-being. Whilst accepting that the Turkish officers did not really understand why the British officers should be so concerned with their rank and file, Barker believed that if the General had intervened more effectively,

It is possible that the death trek which followed would not have been the appallingly brutal affair that in fact it was. With their officers, the men would probably not have suffered the bestial treatment which was meted out to them by Turks and Arabs alike in the period that followed and there would have been fewer dying men left by the wayside to rot in the sun.[562]

It is difficult not to agree with this judgement, especially as the Turks were always so respectful of officer rank and would have taken notice of their presence and authority. Erroll Sherson, who was related to Townshend, also wrote a biography of the General and was, unsurprisingly, defensive about this issue. As far as Sherson was concerned, the General had done his best and made the ultimate sacrifice by not accepting his 'personal liberty', which had been offered by Halil Pasha.[563]

To Baghdad

It was at Shumran that most of the officers were separated from their men. On 5 May, the British generals, their immediate staff and the first echelon of officers, led by Major-General Delamain, were transported further up river on the *Burhanieh*.

The following day, all of the other ranks began their march, escorted by some Turks, whom Staff-Sergeant Bird described as 'Harry Tate's Cavalry' because of their scruffy state.[564] Only one officer was allowed to remain with each regiment, Major Henley marching with the batch of 253 men of the Oxfordshire and Buckinghamshire Light Infantry, though the rank and file would be on their own from Baghdad. Some sick personnel remained in the hospital at Shumran. Second Lieutenant A. Ubsdell wrote

All except British Officers, Viceroy Officers and their orderlies marched out en route for Baghdad. All they took with them was one blanket and great coat, waterbottle, a haversack and three days rations each.[565]

The officers could see that their soldiers would have a rough time – Lieutenant Bishop commented that 'Our hearts misgave as we watched them go.'[566] They were all weak after the siege and were not fit to march. Despite the protestations of the British doctors, the Turks still insisted that the troops would walk.

After five months of siege these men were as weak as rats from starvation, none of them fit to march five miles; they were full of dysentery, beri-beri, scurvy, malaria and enteritis; they had no doctors, no medical stores and no transport; the hot weather, just beginning, would have meant in those deserts much sickness and many deaths, even among troops who were fit, well cared for and well supplied.[567]

Regimental-Quartermaster-Sergeant Harvey commented that there were no packs in which to place their belongings, so the troops did their best to carry their meagre items – in his case a blanket, coat, three pairs of socks, a spare shirt, shaving kit, tooth brush, soap, notebook and food. Lieutenant Elton and other officers waved goodbye to the column, whilst attempting to keep cheerful.

A batch of 115 British and 240 Indian Viceroy officers with their orderlies and servants left Shumran on the steamer *Khalifa* on 10 May for their three-day journey to Baghdad. Major Barber, from Kut, was already on board the boat as he and other medical staff had been despatching the very seriously wounded down river to the Relief Force. He wrote that a German sailor, who was a fellow passenger, predicted that few of the prisoners would see their homes again:

Our Germans who go to England as prisoners will, we know, be well cared for and will get back again, and so will your English who go to Germany, but those who go to Turks – no, perhaps not so many as ten in a hundred will ever get back![568]

This depressing prediction was not far from the truth. Close to 300 men were reported to have died at Shumran during the first week of captivity.

Not all of the sick from Kut were exchanged. The remaining group, including Flight-Sergeant Long, were put on the ill-fated *Julnar* and despatched to Baghdad. Captain Mousley described the *Julnar* as the 'Death Ship, as on it were all the remnants of the sick.'[569]

Meanwhile, the marching column did not fare well, especially as they began their move at the hottest time of the day. The first twenty-four hours spent trudging the eight miles to Baghela (or Bughaila) ended with hundreds of ill men who could not march any further; many died, though the lucky ones were eventually picked up by boat. The Regimental History of the Oxfordshire and Buckinghamshire Light Infantry recorded that 'Private Carter, 'R' Company cook, died within three miles of the camp and was buried where he fell.' He was not the only one to suffer this fate.[570]

As soon as they were out of sight of Shumran, their Arab guards had begun to steal boots, helmets and water bottles. If a sick man lagged under the burning sun he was either clubbed mercilessly on the head or left to die slowly by the wayside.[571]

Private Hughes was in the column:

With great shouts of 'Yallah! Yallah!' (move along), as the men fell out wholesale, the Arabs came up, knocking them about awfully. Many would get up and plod along through fear, but kept falling out on the roadside and were left to die. A few camels were found for the column to carry the dying men, but the number was quite inadequate for the number required ... With our own eyes we saw many fall off the camels, while others were knocked off by the Arabs to die on the road. Then the clothes were taken off the corpses, which were left absolutely naked to make food for the vultures.[572]

Private A. Goode saw that 'Those too ill to move were just left behind, without food or money or water.'[573] The Turkish officers did not seem to have control and the stronger members of the column and their senior NCOs were usually powerless. Regimental Sergeant-Major Love, who was in charge of the Oxfordshire and Buckinghamshire Light Infantry contingent,

> ... saw the sergeant of the escort, Shiaba by name, beating Armourer Quartermaster-Serjeant Packer, who had fallen out owing to dysentery, he reported the Turk to the Commandant. For satisfaction Regimental Serjeant-Major Love was told that there was no cause for complaint; the Arab had done his duty; this was Turkish discipline, and, while prisoners, the Regiment would be subject to Turkish discipline.[574]

This did not bode well for the rest of their time in captivity.

When they did get the chance to rest at night, more of their few remaining belongings were stolen as they slept and their drinking water came from contaminated sources. Their only initial food supply came in the form of small and mouldy chapattis after two days of marching. Thereafter, the Turkish biscuits appeared again.

> By this time we had found the best way to eat these was to pound them as small as possible with the heel of the boot, soak them for a couple of hours, and then boil for a time. It was impossible to eat them in their dry state, in fact, it was impossible to break them except with a stone or the heel of a boot.[575]

Morale was not helped as, en route, they saw Arabs jeering at them, who drew their fingers across their throats, ululating. Private Hughes was not impressed with the locals and commented that 'these people are a treacherous race and friendly to whichever is the triumphant side.'[576] As more recent operational experience has again shown, occupied populations can be fickle.

Sergeant Coombes recorded one rare opportunity for food that was seized:

> One evening at the end of a march a mule came into camp. It was recognised as one which had been left behind, lame, when we retired on to Kut. It was unfortunate for the beast that it had come at that time among so many hungry people, and its fate can be guessed.[577]

The troops were starving. Lieutenant Keeling noted, at the beginning of their move from Samara, that every man 'carried six of the hard Turkish biscuits as his rations for three days.'[578]

The *Khalifa* arrived at Baghdad on 13 May and the officers were paraded through the streets en route to a nearby cavalry barracks – Lieutenant Bishop called it 'a triumphal procession to impress the inhabitants.'[579] Surprisingly, however, Lieutenant Keeling reported that 'we found the inhabitants extremely civil, and a large proportion of them were Jews and Christians who would have expressed their sympathy openly if they dared.'[580]

The War Record of the 24th Punjabis concurred and recorded that the local population 'displayed no sign of hostility' but that they seemed 'sorry for our plight'.[581] Unfortunately, the sanitation conditions in the barracks were not good, encouraging further sickness, and the only way of procuring food was, again, by paying for it or by bartering. Second-Lieutenant Ubsdell wrote that 'It is infernally hot here and drinking water is scarce.'[582] Fortunately, each officer had been issued four gold lira before the surrender and, in Baghdad, received a further month's pay in gold, so at least some means of survival existed. There was some concern amongst the Viceroy commissioned Indian officers as they thought that they had been paid too much and might have to reimburse the Indian Government after the War! The payment in gold was important, as Lieutenant Bishop pointed out. 'Had this not been so, we should have had a very much harder time on the march, since no Arab would look at Turkish paper money in these days.'[583] The officers had another luxury – colonels were allowed two orderlies to stay with them, whilst other officers were allowed one each. As to the other ranks, some had one five-piastre note given to them as a one-off payment.

Major-General Townshend did not see his old command arrive in Baghdad. Instead, during his short stay before travelling on to Constantinople, he was billeted at the Italianate Embassy and had a dinner laid on in his honour. He was moved on quickly, avoiding contact with his men.

Meanwhile, the troops had halted at Aziziya, where 350 were abandoned later to be transported up the Tigris by boat, but the remainder were still forced to march the 100 miles to Baghdad in eight days.

From the *Julnar*, Flight-Sergeant Long saw the column moving toward Baghdad.

> No words can describe the appalling misery of that scene. Here were men who had suffered and fought through the long months of the siege, although they were gradually starved, and were not fit to do a day's march, yet they were being driven across the pitiless wastes under a scorching sun, herded along by a callous escort of Arab conscripts.[584]

Reverend Spooner was disgusted with what he saw.

> It made my blood boil to witness the treatment of our troops and to hear their horrible stories. I saw great bruises on their sides and backs – they had been driven and beaten for three days, their only food two Turkish biscuits each.[585]

Sergeant Munn recorded that he fell out at least twenty times during the march and was flogged each time until he went back into his place in the ranks. He described the rations:

> Our rations during the march, which lasted 10 days, consisted of two, and sometimes three, biscuits per day (two biscuits would weigh about three ounces). On one occasion we got a handful of dates, once we got a small sheep per company (panned out to about 1 ½ ounces mutton per man), and once we got some Arab chapattis in lieu of biscuits. The chapattis were green with mould, but still a welcome change to the biscuits … We got to Baghdad somehow.[586]

Regimental-Quartermaster-Sergeant Harvey wrote that he saw his Turkish escort flog three prisoners for having bits of biscuits in their pockets, even though they had not eaten for three days – each received twenty lashes.[587]

The state of the marching troops arriving in Baghdad on 15 May 1916 was recorded by Captain A. Shakeshaft:

> The troops soon began to arrive, a dreadful spectacle … to see British troops in rags, many barefooted, starved and sick wending their way under brutal Arab guards through an eastern bazaar …

Number 71 British Stationary Hospital, formerly Turkish barracks. (IWM Q 27351)

> From men in hospital I heard many stories of the horrors of the march from Shumran ... General
> Melliss kept me quite busy writing letters on the subject to those in authority; they were of course
> never answered.[588]

Captain Mousley's account was vivid: 'They were literally walking corpses, some doubled with
the pain of cholera, some limping from blows received en route.'[589] After being marched through
the city, like the officers, the prisoners were grouped by the railway station.

> Instead of taking the road direct along the river front we were hustled all through the bazaars where
> we received every possible insult. Spitting at us was their great delight, and needless to say plenty of
> cameras were levelled at us.[590]

Unlike the officers, they were not placed in buildings. The Sikhs and Hindus were separated
from the Moslems and did not see each other again, as the Turks did their utmost to convert
the Indian Moslems to their cause. When Flight-Sergeant Long arrived in Baghdad, as he was
marched along the streets, he was spat in the face by a woman from the crowd and then received
a blow from a Turkish rifle butt in the shoulders and a cut in his lip from a bayonet lunge. His
wounds were spotted by a Turkish officer, a Mulazim-i-evvel (lieutenant), who, once he had
identified the miscreant, subjected the man to a vicious beating with his rawhide whip. Flight-
Sergeant Long wrote that he felt 'physically sick' during the incident.[591] The soldier's behaviour
had been punished and Flight-Sergeant Long, belatedly, 'protected', but the incident revealed
the different culture existing at that time in the Ottoman Empire and its acceptance of a form
of corporal punishment unacceptable in other countries. He was to be witness to, and victim of,
worse beatings over the next two years.

It was now becoming clear to the officers how their soldiers were suffering. Many had been
forced to sell belongings and most of their clothing so that they could pay for food to survive.
Their boots were valuable and many of the soldiers arrived in Baghdad barefoot having sold the
boots or had them stolen en route. Private Goode remembered: 'A few of those who still possessed their boots were afraid to take them off, knowing they would be stolen as soon as they
were asleep.'[592] A meal of more biscuits and dates is all that awaited them in the city.

Despite being ill, Major-General Melliss attempted to put pressure on the Turkish hierarchy
to improve the prisoners' conditions. He demanded to speak to Halil Pasha, who promised him

that he would move the seriously ill to a Turkish hospital and that the soldiers' makeshift camp would be moved to shade. Meanwhile, Major-General Delamain and Colonel Hehir arranged for eleven British medical officers to remain in Baghdad to help with the sick from the marching column. Lieutenant-Colonel Edgar Baines of the Indian Medical Service was disgusted with the poor sanitation and the state of the Turkish medical care, and he also joined in the effort to improve conditions. Turkish medical officers did help, along with French nuns and the American consul, Mr Brissell, whom Sergeant Munn described as a 'pukka hero'.[593]

Halil Pasha arranged for the soldiers' camp to be moved five miles upstream where there was some shade, but the prisoners still suffered in their weak state and there was an average of nineteen deaths each day. He did appear to care about his captives, responding to Major-General Melliss's protestations, and ordered the issue of new clothing to some of the ill prisoners who were returned to British lines, but seemed to have little say over medical facilities or the onward movement of the troops.

A small group of officers managed to slip away from their captors and were lucky to see Mr Brissell. Major Sandes wrote that he 'was most affable and gave us excellent liqueur, brandy, coffee and cigarettes, and later advanced us each three lira in gold from his small store carefully hidden away in his safe, and apologised because he was unable to give us more.'[594]

Mr Brissell promised to help them and warned them that they would be better off escaping than staying in a Turkish prison. As the months of captivity went by, they realised that his advice was good. He was a great help to the British and Indian troops and organised food, blankets, clothing and some disinfectant to be sent to them. He regularly visited the hospitals, helped direct the work of the American Red Cross Society and arranged for the eventual evacuation to British lines of twenty-two officers and 323 men in August. He also coordinated Christian burials for those who died. Without his efforts, many more of the prisoners would have perished. Unfortunately, he was to contract cholera himself and died shortly afterwards, whilst he was still negotiating exchanges. Major Barber, who was one of the medical officers who stayed in Baghdad, wrote 'we owed him much'.[595]

Sergeant Coombes spent ten days in Baghdad. Water was as scarce as food and 'the only means of water supply was one pump, and thousands of people had to use it. There was many a fight for water around this place.'[596] It is not difficult to imagine the sanitation horrors. Others were luckier; Sergeant Munn had dysentery and was admitted to hospital and 'dieted on five loaves of brown bread and five cigarettes daily',[597] whilst Lieutenant Heawood had contracted typhoid and went into one of the hospitals in Baghdad with fever. After a few months, he was fortunate enough to be exchanged and sent down to Basra.

Before departing Baghdad, the British troops were paraded in front of the Turkish War Minister, Enver Pasha, along the railway station platform. Bands played and aeroplanes flew above. He was making the most of the victory.

Samara

The officers were split into four groups: the generals and their staff, destined for Brusa (or Broussa); two echelons of 100 officers each; and finally the remaining sick, who would move to Asia Minor later. They were forced to shed excess personal belongings prior to moving; Second-Lieutenant Ubsdell wrote that 'no sooner had we begun sorting, than all sorts of queer coves came along to see what they could pick up.'[598] The Turks were shocked when the officers held an after-dinner improvised concert on the night before they left the city. The two echelons entrained at Baghdad station on 16 May and travelled the seventy-five miles upriver to Samara. Private L. Eyres later pointed out that 'for the officers, who were sent as far as Baghdad by boat, then by train and marched on till the next railhead was reached, a few ponies and mules were provided and donkeys for their kit, but the rank and file had no transport of any kind.[599]

At Samara, the officers prepared for their first march, though they had no idea of their destination. They were going to embark on a journey of 370 miles across the Taurus Mountains to the railhead at Ras al Ain. The temperatures were high, water was scarce and rations non-existent, unless the prisoners paid for them – most survived on fruit bought from passing Arabs. They were, however, better placed than the other ranks following behind them and their orderlies knew it. En route, they would pass destroyed or abandoned villages which had belonged to Christian Armenians. They had been massacred or driven out of many areas by the Turks. (The Armenian massacre, during and after the War, is now widely acknowledged to have been an an act of genocide – though not by modern-day Turkey. Thousands died on forced marches without food and water into the desert of what is now Syria.) Many of the prisoners, especially those few who escaped, were later to be helped by Armenians.

The troops set off to Samara about ten days later than their officers, in '40-man' open trucks for a short, two hour journey, but these were packed with 70 men. An anonymous report stated that, at Samara

> We stayed for three days. The food we got was unfit for human consumption; it generally consisted of whole wheat and a few filthy dates, and we were forced to buy any food we could afford from our escort, who charged terrible prices. If we were caught buying food from the natives we were beaten in a terrible manner with sticks and butts of rifles. The sight when we moved out of Samara was terrible. We left sick men lying on the ground groaning in agony, and nothing to lie on with the exception of a few sheep-skins.[600]

They had the prospect of a 200-mile march ahead of them. A quarter of them had already lost their boots and had no money and most were wearing only a pair of shorts and a torn shirt, full of lice. Matters were made far worse by their escort, described by Private Goode as 'the lowest class of Arabs' who treated them with 'infamous brutality'.[601]

As at Shumran, more wounded were left behind at Samara as they could not attempt the march. Captain Reginald Clifford of the Indian Medical Services raised money from the officers, which was enough to buy some food for the debilitated prisoners and Lieutenant-Colonel Baines had many moved into the nearby Turkish hospital – Flight-Sergeant Long, who was at that time temporarily blind, spent a short time there.

Again, Major-General Melliss did his utmost to relieve the suffering of his men. Despite his continued illness, he insisted on travelling to Samara to see what was happening to them. Thanks to his efforts and action by Halil Bey, some food was supplied and slightly better medical support provided. At least some of the prisoners, who had to fall out from sickness and injury on their long march, survived.

Captain Wilson, the political officer, later wrote in 1930 that Major-General Melliss, incarcerated at Brusa, appealed to the Turkish War Minister for better treatment of the other ranks, having seen and heard of some of the appalling misery being endured. 'Enver Pasha replied, with a dignity suited to the occasion, that having given orders for the proper treatment of our prisoners, he could not believe that what General Melliss had reported was true.'[602]

The prisoners were, understandably, not fond of the country in which they had served and were now incarcerated. Author Dorina Neave explained their feelings well:

Mesopotamia has been called the cradle of civilisation, but to our men it was an evil land, full of the plagues of Egypt, and scattered over it men met a dirty, cruel, despicable people, in an empty, barren, scorching desert, laying between two great rivers, ribbed with narrow strips of green fields and unhealthy marshes. Dirt was thick and foul wherever Arabs had a dwelling place, and their scavengers were great beetles of every size and description, as well as jackals, hawks, dogs and ants, and the eating sun which cleaned up the refuse with which man befouled the earth.[603]

Conditions were not going to become any better.

The Trek Continues

Major Sandes marched off from Samara, with 375 fellow prisoners, on the evening of 15 May. They were under the command of Yuzbashi (Captain) Essad Bey, and escorted by twenty Arab gendarmerie, whom the British christened 'Yellahs', because of their favourite order of 'Yallah!' and Second-Lieutenant Ubsdell called 'an awful lot of scallywags'.[604] The group consisted of 88 British officers, 60 Indian officers and 227 orderlies and included Major-General Delamain and other senior officers who travelled on ponies. Captain Spackman wrote: 'I had a big white donkey (which we called the Tetrarch) which I was able to ride most of the way, so we didn't do so badly.'[605]

Major Sandes gives much credit to Major Walter Gilchrist of the divisional staff for his efforts to make sure that the column was reasonably looked after by the Turks. His group marched for ten days to reach Mosul on 25 May and covered 170 miles, but only three British officers and no Indian officers fell out. The heat and terrain were difficult and there was a shortage of water, but they did not suffer from the same harshness and brutality as their soldiers as they passed through Tikrit, Kharinina, Sanaich, Wadi Khanana and Shirgat (or Sharqat). Second-Lieutenant Ubsdell noted that 'our staple food seems to be dates and chapattis, with occasionally a piece of meat if we are lucky. Also had boiled eggs and sour milk.'[606] Lieutenant Bishop recorded that he was able to 'ride for an hour and walk for an hour alternately' and that his column was issued Red Crescent postcards to complete, allowing their folks at home to hear from him, eventually, for the first time.[607] This indicates that if the other ranks' columns had been properly officered, then casualties would have been dramatically reduced. The distinction made between rank was summarised by Lieutenant Elton: 'If we thought we were being marched beyond our powers, unlike the men, we should be able simply to refuse to move farther, and, instead of shooting us, the Turk would shrug his shoulders and acquiesce.'[608]

Whilst in Mosul, some of the officers, including Major Sandes, were briefed by Enver Pasha that 'while we were in Turkish hands we should be treated as precious and honoured guests of the Ottoman Government.' The irony of this statement was not lost on the audience who were increasingly becoming aware that 'our rank and file were treated as slaves.'[609]

The first 3,000 other ranks left Samara on 22 May and reached Mosul on 3 June. Sergeant Coombes marched away from Samara in another column on the evening of 29 May, following the right bank of the Tigris. His column was heading for Tikrit, where more sick personnel fell out. Regimental-Quartermaster-Sergeant Harvey had arrived there a few days before: 'Exhausted and quite willing to quit this life if we could only see a quick way out.'[610] Conditions were desperate: 'Our sanitary conditions were delightful; our latrines were two yards from the bivouac, and any man getting there was promptly stoned by our friends in the villages.'[611]

Sergeant Coombes wrote that it was difficult to eat their rations of flour, because there was no straw to light as fuel. Fortunately, some of the accompanying Gurkhas 'swam downstream, to where there were reeds growing, and brought back, each a load, fastened to his head. They cooked ours as well as their own.'[612] The only slight respite was a change of scenery, as the landscape became less monotonous.

The soldiers knew that it was vital to keep going as they saw what happened to those who ran out of energy or just gave up.

> To drop behind made matters even worse, for the escort behind would ride at anyone who lagged and assist them along with rifle butts. They were cruel and unsympathetic brutes, this escort. How many dropped out and were never seen again, and how many could these Turks account for? They would not leave them behind, or make arrangements for them to be brought along. It was too much trouble, and so they assisted them on the road to death.[613]

Flight-Sergeant Long was an extremely motivated soldier and an expert scrounger, who at least had the advantage of being able to speak Arabic and Hindustani. He acted as an interpreter for the Turks and was a born survivor. He described the horror of the long march, experiencing the punishment from a guard at the rear of his column.

> On two occasions I felt the weight of his whip as I stayed behind to help one or other of the Englishmen who had been compelled to stop to answer the call of nature, suffering as they were from diarrhoea. I burned with an intense hatred of this brutal fiend as I trudged along in the darkness. Scores of mad plans of vengeance formed in my mind, for as yet I was not broken in to the harsh rules that govern the life of a captive. Nor was I ever to be but I learned to take things more calmly and to suffer blows without thinking of murder.[614]

And so the troops progressed to Mosul, daily travel distances varying from twelve to fifteen miles. Sergeant Coombes arrived there on 9 June for a two day 'rest' before heading away from the Tigris and west across the desert. More prisoners had either collapsed or died on the march or were 'lucky enough' to be hospitalised at one of the towns en route. Sergeant Coombes was not looking forward to moving away from the river, as there would be no certain water supply. The soldiers' personal possessions were still being stolen. Flight-Sergeant Long described one thief's determination:

One of them [a prisoner] had used his kitbag as a pillow and had secured the end of it to his wrist. The thief had deftly cut a hole in the kitbag and had removed more than half the contents without wakening the sleeper![615]

Staff-Sergeant Bird recorded his arrival at Mosul:

> The men were in a terrible state, but we were just dumped near the Turkish barracks and no one came near us. We had neither food nor drink and were so desperately hungry and thirsty that those of us who had kept any clothing soon got to work and sold it to buy bread when the Arabs arrived with food to sell. I myself took off my khaki jacket and sold it for 10 piastres, which enabled my two pals to buy some bread. A large percentage of the men were quite done for and could not possibly march another inch. They were lying on the ground suffering from high fever and dysentery, and, needless to say, were smothered from head to foot in filth and covered with flies.[616]

He was rewarded with two days of rest and issued with some black bread: 'It was so good, I really thought I was eating cake.'[617] Food was always scarce and valuable and carefully measured out, monitored by a British, Hindu and Moslem soldier. Long commented that 'we became experts at making a chapatti on a fire of bracken, straw or dried dung.'[618] The water supply was horrendous. 'One dipped a canteen in the water and drank, looked at the spot where it was taken from, and saw excreta floating along on the top; by all laws we should all have contracted enteric or some worse disease.'[619]

Major-General Melliss did not leave Baghdad until 8 June. Unlike Major-General Delamain's column, which had been ahead of the troops' move, the Melliss group's journey from Samara to Mosul was one which his party would never forget, 'for on all sides were traces of the hardships and sufferings of our rank and file who had already marched through this barren wilderness.'[620]

He travelled through Tikrit and Shirgat, and discovered abandoned sick and dying troops, often left unguarded as they were seen as no use or threat to anyone. Captain Shakeshaft, travelling with him, reported seeing men 'dying of dysentery and neglect … It was the same story everywhere – Turkish neglect and absolute indifference to the sufferings of our helpless men.'[621] Some money was distributed and every effort was made to provide some clothing, blankets and medical support, but these were all scarce resources, so the General's efforts had only a limited effect. When he arrived in Mosul on 16 June, he arranged for some carts to go back down the route to Shirgat, pick up as many of the stragglers as possible and bring them to the local hospital. Major Sandes noted that 'many a dying British soldier in the deserts between Baghdad and Anatolia had reason to bless General Sir Charles Melliss'.[622] He later wrote about his observations en route to captivity and his experiences, as a prisoner, in Broussa Camp – his letter to the Secretary of War can be read in Appendix IX.

Thanks to the efforts that were being made by senior British officers and medical officers, such as Lieutenant-Colonel Baines and Captain Spackman, there was some respite for the sick at Mosul. Clean beds and clothing were provided, though only limited amounts of drugs were available for treatment and Captain Shakeshaft described the patients as looking 'half-starved and very ill.'[623] Under pressure, the Turks provided more beds and Lieutenant-Colonel Baines managed to stop at least 100 soldiers from joining the next trek because they were too ill.

There was also the occasional help from German personnel en route. Lieutenant Keeling experienced this at Tikrit:

> The German officer was very civil, remonstrated with the Turkish commandant about our treatment, and did his best to help us. The same may be said of nearly all of the Germans whom we met on the journey. They despised their Moslem ally and seemed to think it their duty to protect us, as fellow Europeans, against him.[624]

The prisoners needed all the help they could get. He went on, 'The small proportion of the British rank and file who survived Turkish captivity mostly owed their lives to German supervision of the working camps and German care of the sick.'[625] Sergeant Coombes concurred and wrote that Germans sent food and wine to some of his regiment who were in the hospitals and gave bread and tobacco to those on the march.[626]

At Mosul, their last point along the Tigris, the troops were told that their next destination was Ras al Ain, nearly 200 miles to the west across the arid land. The route via Dolabia, Rumailan Kabir, Nisibin and Kochhisar (or Kotschissar) would lead many of them to work on the Baghdad railway. As the columns of men stumbled forward, their numbers diminished as more and more succumbed to the poor conditions and fell out. As they began to head west, Regimental-Quartermaster-Sergeant Harvey described their state:

We had dropped a sprinkling of men along the road all the way along the march; these men had fallen out overcome by exhaustion and were never seen again. If they did not die by the roadside the Arabs would very soon be along and cut their throats for the sake of their boots.[627]

Heading West

Lieutenant Bishop had covered the route from Samara to Mosul in ten days thanks to the use of a number of donkeys and horses. For most, the journeys west began at the beginning of June 1916 and Lieutenant Bishop set off on the 1st in a column carrying what food they could buy and scrounge – flour, rice and raisins. He knew that his column's possible destination was the railhead at Ras al Ain, 200 miles away, with the town of Nisibin about 120 miles distant. He was fortunate, because some carts and donkeys were provided and the escort was reorganised. 'In response to our complaints to the commandant at Mosul of the way in which our Arab escort had behaved, these men were changed for Turkish soldiers, who gave us less trouble.'[628]

Lieutenant Keeling left Mosul on 4 June, in similar circumstances to Lieutenant Bishop. In addition, there was little shortage of water: 'Henceforth water was plentiful, though sometimes brackish, and food was not so difficult to obtain as some interested persons in Mosul had led us to believe.'[629]

Once again, one can see how most of the officers were able to obtain better conditions for themselves – if only the same sort of influence could have been exerted on behalf of the other ranks on their march. Lieutenant Bishop only had to walk for half of the journey and commented that 'we had kept tolerably cheerful, apart from a few inveterate grousers; altogether we had survived wonderfully well, and had fared infinitely better than the troops from Kut, who were marching along in our tracks a few days behind us.'[630]

Flight-Sergeant Long and the rank and file were not so cheerful as they left Mosul. 'We knew neither the day, nor the date, and our outlook was bounded by the probable distance of the day's march, the ability to keep going, and the possibility of rations at the end of it.'[631] Regimental-Quartermaster-Sergeant Harvey's perspective was that 'our lives were of no great value those days.'[632]

From Nisibin, where Lieutenant Keeling came across 'the first trees of any sort which we had seen for fully 300 miles',[633] the journey continued to Ras al Ain and then on to Aleppo, where the officers were put in some dilapidated hotels. The rest of Lieutenants Bishop and Keeling's separate journeys into captivity at Kastamuni Camp were by a combination of train, lorry, cart, donkey and foot through the towns or villages of Islahie, Kulek Boghaz, Bozanri, Konia and Angora (now Ankara) and another prison camp at Afion Kara Hissar (or Afiun Qarahisar).

The officers were kept on the move ahead of the columns of other ranks, so unless they had fallen behind because of medical reasons, few saw the conditions that their men were suffering. When Major Sandes reached Nisibin, he experienced the luxury of bathing: 'In the afternoon I had a ripping bathe in the stream at a place where there was good grass on the bank and the water about 4 feet deep, and slept like a top that night in the cold.'[634]

Some doctors were left behind at Ras al Ain to wait to help the troops who were slowly marching along the same route. Their Hindu and Christian orderlies were taken away from them, as those posts had to be reserved for Moslems.

Many soldiers, mostly Indians, were to end up in Ras al Ain, working on the Constantinople to Baghdad railway, under the supervision of a German civilian company. Captain Mousley:

The Hindoos, less favoured than the Mohammedan prisoners are to remain here. We saw their gaunt skeletons at work carrying baskets of gravel in constructing the railway for the Turks back over the desert they had crossed. This outlook to me seemed sufficiently appalling. They had very little food. The British soldier was to move on. We were glad that he was spared this.[635]

Some of the officers did not have such a relatively comfortable journey and saw much worse conditions. These included Major-General Melliss and other officers who followed the columns later, and medical staff left behind to care for the sick at some of the towns. Captain Mousley, who left Nisibin later than Lieutenants Bishop and Keeling, on 29 June, was not in such a good shape as the others and witnessed more hardship than them.

> For the stragglers it was certain death at the Arab's hands. The tail of the column was an awful place … For the most part British soldiers stayed with their friends until they were dead … I shall never forget one soldier who could go no farther. He fell resignedly on to the ground, the stump of a ciga-rette in his mouth, and with a tiredness born of long suffering, buried his head in his arms to shut out the disappearing column and smoked on … I saw another man crawling on all fours over the desert in the dark quite alone.[636]

Those prisoners who did not die where they fell did not always fare better in the hospitals en route. Reverend Spooner visited a 'hospital' in Nisibin on 29 June:

> I thought I had witnessed horror enough in these frightful hospital conditions, but another more terrible sight had got to be seen. There was a small dark dank room, with no windows to it, only a few feet square. Something told me to go inside this room, and there to my horror I saw two British soldiers, absolutely naked, lying in their own faeces, which had not been cleaned up for several days. They were both dying and, thank God, one was unconscious. The other said to me 'Oh, sir, please kneel down and ask God may let me die quickly. I can no longer stand these horrors.[637]

Flight-Sergeant Long recounted his discovery of a group of naked bodies lying side-by-side in the sun outside the hospital at Nisibin. He assumed that they were badly handled corpses, but on closer examination realised that one was just alive, so alerted a guard. He explained what he witnessed:

> The Arab walked round to his head, and, forcing open his mouth, inserted the neck of the [water] bottle inside. A few bubbles, a convulsive twist, and the poor fellow was dead, deliberately choked to death! It was horrible and I stood gaping until the orderly pushed me away and said, 'Hussa moot. Roo, roo' (Now he's dead, go, go').[638]

The horrors and the pain continued. Sergeant Coombes, travelling in an other ranks group reached one stop where

> … a dozen of our fellows were discovered in a hut – all dead. They had probably been left behind sick by some former column, and without medical aid they had died one by one. It fell to us to give them a decent burial.[639]

He described one day's march of fifteen hours:

> We left in the afternoon, marched all through the night and so on to midday the following day. What a terrible march it was too, and to our dismay when we arrived at the expected water, the stream had dried up. How many men we had lost on that march I cannot say, but I know that there were numbers who never reached water, many of them men of our own regiment.[640]

The troops also had to cope with the heat, as not all of the days' marches were in the relatively cooler evening or early morning.

> On we went, reeling, and staggering along a track that was like a red hot grill. The rocks and stony [ground] shimmered with heat, and, when a halt was called to allow the stragglers to catch up, it was more comfortable to stand than to sit, though many dropped from sheer exhaustion.[641]

Regimental-Quartermaster-Sergeant Harvey recorded the monotony.

> Many times during the march I fell asleep while still marching, and at any little check in the column, I walked straight into the man ahead of me. When I woke again I was cursed for it may times, but that did not prevent me doing it again almost at once, and I really could not help it, I was tired out.[642]

Major Sandes described this stage of the march.

> The march of our rank and file prisoners from Mosul to Ras al Ain was a cruel one … A party of 1,700 British prisoners was given seven camels and a dozen donkeys for the transport of the sick – an utterly inadequate allowance … One man stated: 'I saw, about two days before we reached Ras al Ain, the escort burying one of our men who was foaming at the mouth and moving. Seeing this, I and several other men went to help him, but were driven off by the escort with loaded rifles. He was buried alive in our sight.'[643]

Another eye-witness reported that he was 'without boots or helmet, and on the last march into Ras al Ain I fell out from weakness, and was driven along for the last four miles by continual blows from the escort with rifles.'[644]

On arrival at Ras al Ain on 8 June, Major Sandes pointed out what his own column had achieved.

> Except for two uncomfortable days in the large barrack at Mosul, the column had been marching almost incessantly, morning and evening, since May 15th – a period of 25 days – and in that time had covered a total distance by road of approximately 370 miles under very trying circumstances.[645]

His '1st echelon' was fortunate enough to be entrained at Ras al Ain, heading 180 miles to Aleppo. The generals and senior officers were in a passenger coach, whilst the other officers had plenty of space in horse boxes. There, they were accommodated in an old hotel where they were provided with some money from the British Prisoners Relief Fund.

This was not the case for the other ranks. They were crowded into closed railway wagons which ended up with an average of forty prisoners in each. Many had dysentery and had to sit on top of each other and the carriages remained sealed until their next destination, Islahie, was reached the following day. 'The heat and stench were terrible, and several men died during the journey.'[646]

A further concentration of sick soldiers grew at Islahie as the columns passed through and again, Major-General Melliss tried to help them on his journey into captivity. Captain Shakeshaft, who was travelling with the General, wrote that they were approached by a German warrant officer when they arrived at Islahie on 23 June. He had the decency to bring to their notice the state of the sick British prisoners there:

The German had been to see them several times, but the Turks had warned him off and said that the men had cholera – a lie. He said that they were being starved to death. The General sent Baines to investigate this case … The assistant surgeon came up from the prisoners and bore out what the German had told me. I then went with the General to the commandant to expose the case and ask him to have a telegram sent to Aleppo. He agreed to everything and said he would send a wire, but I doubt it … The General sent me off to thank the German warrant officer; I found him … He promised to do what he could for the men.[647]

One of the ill soldiers at Islahie recalled:

I went into the cholera camp at Islahie suffering from dysentery. I received no medicine of any sort. My food was two tablespoons of barley porridge in the morning and the same at night. To wash we had to creep unnoticed to a stream 200 yards away. The patients lay in Arab tents on the ground without bedding, and in some cases absolutely naked, and men were dying three or four a day out of a total of 80. The dead were often laid outside the tent naked, and had to be buried in the evening by the patients.[648]

When Captain Mousley reached Ras al Ain, he remarked 'I am thankful to Providence that I am lucky enough to write this heading … I feel dreadfully ill and weak. The last spurt has drained our remaining vitality'.[649] His column had suffered more than some of the others. Following on some time behind him, Long commented on the state of the non-Moslem Indian troops working there:

Nearly all of them were of the Kut garrison, and all were Indians of various races and religions other than Mohammedans. Their condition was truly pitiful. They resembled animated skeletons hung about with filthy rags. No tents or other shelter had been provided, and they were living in holes in the ground like pariah dogs … Scores of them were too sick to move from their holes, and I saw many who were obviously dying, yet I was told that they received no medical attention whatever. I chatted to a few of those men, and as we talked the tears streamed down their faces. These were loyal soldiers of the British Empire, and it was awful to think that this was the end of their service of devotion.[650]

When one reads an account like this, one can understand why Flight-Sergeant Long wanted to create his own record of the the horror of captivity, especially as previously published officers' accounts just did not effectively describe the pain that the other ranks had suffered. The same applied to members of the 2nd Battalion the Dorsetshire Regiment when they read Regimental-Quartermaster-Sergeant Harvey's diary. He summed up his column's state at Ras al Ain: 'The number we have left looks appalling; no one will ever know how many were left on the side of the road to die.'[651]

The rank and file who continued their journey from Ras al Ain did not cross the Taurus or Amanus range of mountains by lorry – they had to walk. They also did not have what Lieutenant Keeling did at Konia – meals at the Hotel du Chemin de Fer de Baghdad, run by a French lady: 'She produced roast beef, potatoes, beer and whisky, necessaries of life which we seemed not to have tasted for years, and we lay down in a hot bath which recalled vaguely some previous experience.'[652] This was, however, a rare and unique opportunity, even for high-ranking officers.

By the end of his journey, at Kastamuni, Lieutenant Bishop had not slept in a bed for at least eight months and he pointed out that 'our journey altogether had been nearly 1,700 miles, and was probably the longest distance across country any prisoners of war have had to travel to the place of their confinement.'[653]

Lieutenant Keeling was also bound for Kastamuni, arriving there on 4 July 1916 after two months on the move. His party had been reduced to seventy-five officers and twenty-five orderlies.

Final Destinations

Whilst many Indian troops – mainly the Hindus and Sikhs – and some British troops were to labour on the German-supervised railway construction based at Ras al Ain, the majority of other ranks trudged on, over the mountains, to the south-east corner of Asia Minor or farther inland. Dispersed into many working camps, some of them joined fellow-countrymen captured at Gallipoli. Conditions en route did not improve, as described by Captain Wilson:

> The men were forced forward by gendarmes with the butt-ends of their rifles, till of sheer inanition many had dropped and died. A few managed to take refuge in certain German and Austrian military camps in the Taurus; but the main body was somehow beaten and driven across the mountain range. It was like one thing only – a scene from Dante's Inferno; the description was that of an Austrian officer who witnessed it.[654]

Following the example of Mr Brissell in Baghdad, there was some more much-needed help from the Americans. The United States Consul at Mersina appealed for the sick to be collected and taken to Adana and to an American college at Tarsus, though his greatly appreciated efforts only scratched the surface of the suffering being endured.

Major-General Townshend arrived in Constantinople on 3 June after a twenty-two-day journey by train from Baghdad. His account of the journey is more of a travelogue than the reminiscences of a prisoner. He was fascinated by the game and the ancient buildings en route and appeared to enjoy the flattery that he received from various Turkish senior officers. He was met in the city by a guard of honour, the Turkish commander of their First Army and a number of senior military and political characters. Also present was his new Turkish aide-de-camp, Tewfik Bey. The General commented: 'I wondered at this reception of me, a prisoner of war. I was treated with as much respect and honour as if I had come to inspect Constantinople, I thought.'[655] He was eventually housed in what had been the residence of the British consul, on the island of Prinkipo, which overlooked Constantinople. The building was described by A.J. Barker as 'a house that resembled an English country vicarage.'[656]

His command soldiered on. It is difficult to identify the final destinations of what remained of the garrison. The British officers and their orderlies found themselves in the main spread across the camps of Afion Kara Hissar, Kastamuni, Changri, Kedos and Yozgad. Indian Moslem officers were interned at Eski Chehir, whilst the non-Muslims, about 450 of them, were placed in a camp at Konia. The soldiers were more widely spread and were, generally, employed in railway construction at places such as Ras al Ain, Afion Kara Hissar, Mamourie, Yarbashi and Bagtsche (or Bagtche). The Moslem soldiers were taken to the foot of the Taurus Mountains.

Regimental Sergeant-Major Love was in command of the Oxfordshire and Buckinghamshire Light Infantry detachment from Kut. It eventually reached Airan, which was close to Bagtsche, at the end of June 1916, to work under the German railway engineer, Herr Klaus.

> A Swiss, Vogt by name, was appointed medical officer to this hospital by virtue of the fact that he had been a masseur before the war. Of medical qualifications he had none. A cruel sadist, he used to strike the weak and sick without provocation, but Regimental Sergeant-Major Love reported him to the German chief engineer who successfully prevented repetitions of cruelty.[657]

Private Hughes also suffered at Bagtsche.

> The food they gave us consisted of black bread, beans, rice and a little meat. The hours of work were

issued; 4.30 am till 11 am in the morning and 1 pm to 6 pm in the afternoon. Good workers were to get six or seven piastres a day, but the cost of our 'meals' was to be supplied from this.[658]

Regimental-Quartermaster-Sergeant Harvey arrived at the camp and had to report the strength of what was left of his battalion.

It was a terrible surprise to even myself when I answered 140. We had left Kut over 300 strong. The balance had been left mostly on the road either dead or dying, and among the 140 who remained was not one fit man; all were practically skeletons, while many were almost fit to die with dysentery and various other complaints.[659]

Unfortunately, his experience with the 2nd Battalion of the Dorsetshire Regiment was not unique.

The meagre existence at Bagtsche did not last long as the prisoners became weaker and were incapable of work. They were moved on during September to camps further inland, but the dreadful conditions continued.

The Turks were sending the sick and dying away in bullock carts. We saw three men thrown into one of these carts. The first chap was dying, but not dead, and afterwards two dead men were thrown on top of him. The three were taken to be buried together, and we could hardly believe our own eyes. At this time both my pal and I were sick, and we had lain down in shady spot, as the heat of the sun was terrible … Many men fell out on the mountainside and have never been heard of since … Many fell by the wayside, some of them with a Turkish bayonet in their backs, others to be stripped of what little they possessed by marauding Arabs and then to become the prey of jackals and vultures.[660]

Parliamentary Report 9208, November 1918

A British Parliamentary Report concerning the Turkish treatment of prisoners was written in 1918. The following is an extract about the march into captivity and the state of the stragglers, taken from eye witnesses.

The sights they saw, all along the road, hardly bear telling. Parties of men were lying under any shelter they could find, in all stages of dysentery and starvation; some dying, some dead; half clothed, without boots, having sold everything they could to buy a little milk. Only here or there had an attendant of some kind been left to look after them. Generally there was no one but the Arab villagers, who mercilessly robbed them, or the officer of the local police-post, who stared indifferently and protested that he had no authority to help. The dead lay unburied, plundered and stripped of their last clothing. Right across the desert these sights were repeated; dying men, in tens and twenties, lay awaiting their end. Some had to wait long. Many weeks after there was found a group of 6 British soldiers and a dozen Indians who for 3 months had lain on the bare ground, subsisting solely on a few scraps thrown to them by Arabs or passing caravans. The Englishmen had been 14; 8 had died, and of the survivors only one was able to crawl to a place where there was water. It begins to be evident how it came about that of the men who surrendered at Kut more than 3,000, British and Indians, have never been heard at all.[661]

Two years of incarceration had begun.

Notes

543. From *Smoke*, the Kastamuni *Punch* and Mousley (1922) p.6.
544. Meaning 'Get on and Hurry Up'. A word used continually by the Turkish and Arab escorts to the prisoners. Bishop (1920) p.50. 'I have seen men wince at the very sound of it, as too often the word was accompanied by blows.' Long (1937) p.39.
545. See bibliography.
546. Harvey (1923) p.10.
547. Neave (1937) p.99.
548. Sandes (1920) p.269.
549. Mockler-Ferryman (undated) p.132.
550. Coombes (1918) p.4120.
551. Neville (1938) p.219.
552. Ubsdell (undated) National Army Museum 1960-12-398.
553. Neave (1937) p.99–100.
554. Sandes (1920) p.271.
555. Elton (1938) p.136.
556. Sandes (1920) p.268.
557. Spackman (1967) p.7–8.
558. Wilson (1930) p.131.
559. Townshend (1920) p.340–341.
560. Neave (1937) p.102.
561. Moberley (1924) p.462.
562. Barker (1967) p.205.
563. Sherson (1928) p.328.
564. Neave (1937) p.104.
565. Ubsdell (undated) National Army Museum 1960-12-398.
566. Bishop (1920) p.39.
567. Elton (1938) p.134–135.
568. Barber (1917) p.259.
569. Mousley (1922) p.159.
570. Neville (1938) p.227.
571. Elton (1938) p.135.
572. Neave (1937) p.105.
573. Ibid p.119.
574. Neville (1938) p.227–228.
575. Harvey (1923) p.14.
576. Neave (1937) p.122.
577. Coombes (1918) p.4120
578. Keeling (1924) p.7.
579. Bishop (1920) p.41.
580. Keeling (1924) p.10.
581. Anonymous (1934) p.48.
582. Ubsdell (undated) National Army Museum 1960-12-398.
583. Bishop (1920) p.231.
584. Long (1938) p.24.
585. Moynihan (1983) p.37.
586. Mockler-Ferryman (undated) p.132.
587. Harvey (1923) p.16.
588. Moberley (1924) p.534. Diary of 17 May 1916.
589. Mousley (1922) p.168.
590. Harvey (1923) p.18.
591. Long (1938) p.29.
592. Neave (1937) p.125.
593. Mockler-Ferryman (undated) p.132.
594. Sandes (1920) p.288.
595. Barber (1917) p.313.
596. Coombes (1918) p.4120.
597. Neville (1938) p.229.
598. Ubsdell (undated) National Army Museum 1960-12-398.
599. Neave (1937) p.119.
600. Ibid p.147.
601. Ibid p.148.
602. Wilson (1930) p.136.
603. Neave (1937) p.141.
604. Ubsdell (undated) National Army Museum 1960-12-398.
605. Spackman (1967) p.9.
606. Ubsdell (undated) National Army Museum 1960-12-398.
607. Bishop (1920) p.60.
608. Elton (1938) p.138.
609. Sandes (1920) p.319.
610. Harvey (1923) p.21.
611. Harvey (1923) p.22.
612. Coombes (1918) p.4133.
613. Coombes (1918) p.4134.
614. Long (1938) p.50.
615. Ibid p.53.
616. Neave (1937) p.159–160.
617. Ibid p.160.
618. Long (1938) p.58.
619. Harvey (1923) p.29.
620. Sandes (1920) p.310.
621. Moberly (1924) p.534.
622. Sandes (1920) p.320.
623. Moberly (1924) p.535.
624. Keeling (1924) p.25.
625. Ibid p.26.
626. Coombes (1918) p.4150.
627. Harvey (1923) p.29.
628. Bishop (1920) p.61.
629. Keeling (1924) p.32.
630. Bishop (1920) p.67.
631. Long (1938) p.89.
632. Harvey (1923) p.30.
633. Keeling (1924) p.34.
634. Sandes (1920) p.326.
635. Mousley (1922) p.183.
636. Ibid p.181–182.

637. Moynihan (1983) p.38.
638. Long (1938) p.109.
639. Coombes (1918) p.4149.
640. Ibid p.4149.
641. Long (1938) p.63.
642. Harvey (1923) p.35.
643. Sandes (1920) p.343.
644. Ibid p.344.
645. Ibid p.332.
646. Ibid p.344.
647. Moberly (1924) p.535.
648. Sandes (1920) p.356–357.
649. Mousley (1922) p.181 and 184.
650. Long (1938) p.112.

651. Harvey (1923) p.40.
652. Keeling (1924) p.43.
653. Bishop (1920) p.79.
654. Wilson (1930) p.139.
655. Townshend (1920) p.63–64.
656. Barker (1967) p.209.
657. Neville (1938) p.234.
658. Neave (1937) p.171.
659. Harvey (1923) p.46.
660. Neave (1937) p.174–175 and 179.
661. Keeling (1924) p.18–19. From Parliamentary
     Paper Cmd 9208, November 1918.

Chapter Ten

SURVIVAL

The officers fared much better, and the Turks quite evidently considered that if they did their best for us the death of a few thousands of the men would be overlooked.[662]

Constantinople

Major-General Townshend and his small retinue lived on their island overlooking Constantinople in some comfort for the rest of the War. Shortly after his arrival in the capital, he was introduced to Enver Pasha who told him 'that I was to consider myself a guest of Turkey.'[663] He was to be treated as a corps commander; entertainment was to be provided by the Turkish Government; he was going to be allowed to travel freely; and he was asked whether he would like his wife and daughter to join him in captivity! Incredibly, he accepted this offer, though they did not end up accompanying him – the General wrote that this was because the Austrian Government refused permission for them to travel through their territory. In fact, even the British Government was not prepared to authorise her journey – Mrs Alice Townshend received a short personal letter from Prime Minister Asquith apologising for the fact that he was not able to interfere.[664] The following year, in 1917, Enver Pasha claimed that he would have sent the General home after the fall of Kut, but that the Germans had not allowed this.

Despite his comforts, the General wrote that 'owing to the awful misery of mind I went through each morning on waking a prisoner, out of the war through no fault of mine, I was soon in a very bad state of mind, and for some time wrote most bitter letters to everyone.'[665]

As time went on he became increasingly frustrated by his captivity and wrote to Enver Pasha 'that I could no longer live the life of a prisoner of war, the mental strain was too much for me, that if I didn't get home and to work again I should go mad.'[666] He obviously had no idea about the comparative state of the imprisoned soldiers in his old 6th Division.

However, he said that he lost himself in study and wrote a book on strategy and tactics – 'It was my only means of consolation'.[667] His aide de camp, Captain Morland, was obliged to participate in his enthusiasm for Napoleonic warfare and they both analysed the Turkish situation in the current conflict. Meanwhile, Townshend harboured a hope that he could play a part in undermining the relationship between the Turks and their German allies.

Apart from having his close personal staff, British and Turkish, at hand for support, he was able to swim in the sea and walk twice around the island every day, keep close contact with the American Embassy and had regular access to English newspapers. He could play a grand piano

Major-General Townshend as a prisoner of war with Hallil Pasha (on the right). (IWM Q 79344)

in the 'cottage', and was taken out regularly on one of the local Naval School's yachts by his Turkish aide de camp, Tewfik Bey. (Tewfik Bey was later to be replaced by Hussein Bey, who was never held in the same confidence as his predecessor.) According to Townshend's cousin, Erroll Sherson, attempts were made by the King of Spain to extract him from Turkey and let him reside on parole in Spain.[668]

There is very little about the plight of his fellow prisoners in the General's book. He attempts to exonerate himself by writing that he had warned Halil Pasha that his soldiers would not be able to walk out of Kut: 'I said if they were forced to march they would die in such a climate, at such a time of year, and in such a state of health'.[669] He went on to blame the Germans for the cruelty administered to his soldiers in captivity, absolving Halil Pasha of any guilt, an assessment which bore no relation to reality. One can only assume that he could not believe that his captors, who were certainly looking after him well, would not be fair to others. It also suggests that before he published his book in 1920 he had not had much contact with his old command following the end of hostilities and their release. Yet Sherson claimed 'Townshend worked daily for the relief of the British prisoners of war who had been at Kut.'[670] Little evidence is available to support this, though he backed the effort made by the American Embassy in Constantinople to procure warm clothing and better conditions for the Kut veterans.

He claimed that he did make three attempts to escape, but was unable to describe the circumstances in his book, for fear of giving away the identities of some of the people who were prepared to help him. The main idea was to rendezvous with a British seaplane. Another escape plan was to use a boat that had been hidden on the coast and employ a band of 'brigands' for the operation. Neither plan came to fruition. In 1920 the General promised to publish these covert plans 'at some future date'.[671] It was left to Sherson to take up the seaplane story using the General's diaries and he quoted from them. In July 1918

> We managed to leave the house and row off in a little boat unobserved. We waited at the ren-
> dezvous till quite 2 am. It was a beautiful night – moonlight and no wind. Nothing was seen. So
> there was nothing to be done but creep back to Prinkipo, which we reached without having been
> discovered.[672]

There had been a difficulty in getting a message to the British on time. They tried again, twice more, in August and thought that they heard the plane on one occasion, but their ploy was unsuccessful. They were fortunate that their guards did not notice these attempts at escape. A last effort was made in October 1918 when the General despatched a message to the nearest British authorities asking for friendly boats to watch a stretch of part of the coast on the night of 11 October in order to rendezvous with his own secret boat, but this also came to nothing.

Throughout his captivity, Townshend's wife helped maintain his ego. 'His wife never ceased to write him encouraging letters, telling him how he was adored by all the troops who had served with him and equally by those who had never seen him.'[673] On one occasion, he received a sup-porting letter from a widow of his commander Royal Artillery, Mrs Kitty Maule:

> You are magnificent. No man could do what you have done. I am proud my husband has been under
> you. You will always be our beloved General. God bless you and keep you safe. There is no one like
> you. Forgive me writing, but I wanted you to know how we wives love you and pray for you.[674]

Despite the disaster at Kut, Townshend still had a remarkably high level of support from his sol-diers and the British public. In October 1916, he was made a Knight Commander of the Order of the Bath, in absentia.[675]

In October 1918, as the outcome of the War was becoming clear, Townshend wrote that he was asked by the Turks to negotiate with the British Government: 'I was willing to assist the Turkish Government to negotiate with the British, in return for the honourable way in which I had been treated during captivity.'[676] He even, at one point, wrote to Major-General Melliss tell-ing him about the poor state of the Allied treatment of Turkish prisoners in Egypt. One can only guess at Mellis's reaction on receipt of such a communication. Townshend was introduced to the Turkish Marshal Izzet Pasha and was particularly enthusiastic in his desire to assist the Turks, though he said that his personal freedom was essential if he was going to be able to help them. He remained full of his self-importance, having worked out options for negotiation without any reference to the British Government and appearing not to have any major concern for the British and Indian troops in captivity elsewhere.

Townshend left the island of Prinkipo on 18 October, embarking on his negotiating mission. On 20 October 1918 he returned to British hands at Mudros, where he linked up with the British Commander-in-Chief in the Mediterranean, Admiral Sir Arthur Calthorpe. In his dia-ries, Field Marshal Douglas Haig acknowledged the request from the Turkish Government, sent by Townshend, asking for peace talks: 'All the Cabinet were agreed that no time should be lost in discussing terms of armistice.'[677] Turkish and British negotiations began on 26 October. The General wrote 'I remained with the fleet whilst the business proceeded in order to help if mat-ters came to a deadlock.'[678] The armistice between the two powers was signed on board HMS *Agamemnon* on 30 October 1918.

Townshend does not undersell his own perceived importance in creating the conditions for the armistice. He quoted a senior Turkish delegate: 'Turkey will never be able sufficiently to show her gratitude to you for having made peace possible, and we only ask you to visit Constantinople and to bring Lady Townshend with you.'[679]

He also noted that the French Prime Minister, Monsieur Georges Clemenceau (the 'Tiger'), 'congratulated me warmly on my work, and especially on bringing Turkey out of the War, saving as he put it, millions of money and thousands of lives.'[680] Sherson claimed '…if it had not been for him [Townshend], the world might not have achieved peace by November 11th, 1918.'[681]

Whilst Townshend had obtained a role in the peacemaking, it was not seen by the British authorities as critical. The General was expecting more honours after the War, including further employment in the Army and promotion – he received neither and he had no friends in high places. On 22 November 1918, Field Marshal Haig was accompanying the King on a visit to the Western Front. He wrote in his diary:

> His Majesty then went on to tell me how General Townshend of Kut fame should have remained to share the fate of his fellow prisoners, instead of taking his liberty in order to help the Turks to get a satisfactory peace. Townshend, he thought, was 'an advertising sort of fellow'. I agreed, and a semi-lunatic as well![682]

Life had been different in the prison camps.

Broussa (or Brusa)

Broussa, which was not far from Constantinople and served as a health resort for the capital, became the home of the other senior officers from Kut – mainly the other brigadiers and above, their staff officers and orderlies. Major Sandes described it as: 'the best camp in the country, though not very healthy'.[683] Just twenty-seven officers were reported to inhabit Broussa Camp in the *Yozgad, Broussa and Constantinople* magazine.[684] The senior officers were in the '1st Echelon' of prisoners who were separated at Angora railway station, and the bulk of them were imprisoned in Yozgad. The brigade commanders at Kut – Major-General Delamain, Brigadier-General Hamilton and Colonel Evans – were to spend their captivity in Broussa. They were to be joined, eventually, by their fellow brigade commander, Major-General Melliss. Whilst the others were quickly transported into captivity, it was Major-General Melliss who, having been ill, had been transported more slowly than the others and thus had seen the conditions that the troops were suffering on their journeys. Some of his observations and actions and the reaction of Enver Pasha have already been described in the previous chapter and in the reminiscences of Captain Shakeshaft, his principal staff officer.[685]

Major-General Melliss continued to do his best to support the prisoners of Kut and could not have been impressed by the relative lack of effort being made by his old commander on Prinkipo Island – Townshend does not even appear to have made an attempt to visit his old brigade commanders. A.J. Barker wrote that 'After the War there were rumours that a deputation led by Melliss visited the War Office to protest about Townshend's behaviour.' In Barker's opinion, even with the fifty-year rule concerning the release of State Papers, any evidence concerning this meeting would never surface.[686] An author of the same generation, also writing about Kut in the 1960s, commented on Townshend's inactivity: 'His apparent indifference to their fate, and his readiness to exonerate Enver Pasha, did not endear him to General Melliss in Broussa.'[687] Melliss's actual views of Townshend's inaction may never be revealed.

Details about the camp at Broussa are limited, compared with other locations. It was the first capital of the Ottoman Empire and an attractive location at 600 feet above sea level. The population of the town was about 90,000. The prisoners' accommodation was basic and based on 'two overcrowded insanitary houses', though conditions were not too bad – there were no serious shortages of food or heating fuel, unlike in other camps, and the commandant, Mir Ali, was benign. Life was bearable at Broussa and prisoners' letters talk about the local fishing, pleasant surrounding countryside and the varied menu. A letter dated 9 July 1918 from Lieutenant-Colonel Henry Broke-Smith of the Royal Field Artillery described the demiparadise: 'Time seems to pass more quickly here than at Yozgad or Afion Kara Hissar. I suppose it is the little extra freedom we have.'[688]

There were also many Indian Moslem soldiers located at Broussa who were treated well and had few restrictions. Freedom of movement was the main limitation for the senior British officers who were housed in old hotels in the town, but were not allowed to speak to the local population or visit the sick in the hospital.[689] The senior officers' lives were also extremely monotonous. They attempted to apply pressure on the Turkish authorities to improve the lot of their fellow prisoners housed in other camps and plotted to escape. At one stage Melliss managed to exchange covert messages with Admiral Wemyss in order to help set the conditions for an escape, but nothing came of this initiative.

Lieutenant-Colonel Baines established a hospital run by Major E.A. Walker of the Indian Medical Services and it became a destination for some ill prisoners from other camps. At one time, 600 sick men were moved there from another camp at Denzil (or Denizli), though fourteen of them died of pneumonia within a fortnight of their arrival.

Captain Mousley arrived at Broussa for a brief period towards the end of the War, following a failed escape attempt. He made the point of informing the generals about the state of their men elsewhere and wrote about life at Broussa.

> Life here was more possible. They had books and papers not so very old. They had two years of uninterrupted study, and were very proficient in acquired languages.[690]

Broussa was very much an isolated 'sleepy hollow'.

Kastamuni

Roughly 200 British officers and 200 orderlies ended up at Kastamuni. The nominal roll included some of the personalities already mentioned in this book:

- Major H.J. Anderson – Rangoon Volunteer Battery
- Lieutenant H.C.W. Bishop – Indian Army Reserve, attached 66th Punjabis
- Lieutenant H.A. Clifton – 8th Battalion the East Surrey Regiment
- Lieutenant G. Elton – 2/4th Battalion the Hampshire Regiment
- Lieutenant E.H. Keeling – Indian Army Reserve, attached 119th Infantry
- Lieutenant (later Captain) E.O. Mousley – Royal Field Artillery
- Reverend H.A. Spooner – Chaplain
- Second-Lieutenant A.R. Ubsdell – Indian Army Reserve, attached 66th Punjabis.

A key reference to the time spent by British personnel at Kastamuni, and later Kedos, where they were moved to in 1917, is Captain C.L. Wooley's account.

> We chafed beneath the whims of individual commandants, we suffered from the inefficiency and the lack of organisation which characterises everything in Turkey, and at times we had, some of us at least, more serious charges to bring against our captors; but the Turks were not out to inflict on us

systematic bad treatment, and from the time we reached camp and could more or less run our own show we, as officers, were not so badly off. The Turk, who cares little for his own men, cared nothing for ours, and from sickness and neglect, hunger and brutality, three-quarters of them miserably died. Knowing what they endured, it is not for us to make much of our own grievances.[691]

There was a sense of relief as the prisoners filtered into the camp. They had been travelling, in various stages of sickness and in varying degrees of discomfort for over two months for a distance of over 1,700 miles. The officers were placed in two buildings known as 'Upper' and 'Middle' Houses, in the Greek quarter of the town, and they had the luxury of sleeping in beds. The population of the town was about 30,000 and a pamphlet designed to provide help for relatives and friends of prisoners of war in Turkey described it as 'a beautiful city, isolated from the rest of the world by forests and high mountains. Lord Kitchener was vice-consul there in 1880.'[692]

Lieutenant Elton, who arrived there on 3 July 1916, observed 'We had not slept inside four walls for seven months.'[693] When Captain Mousley arrived three weeks later, he wrote 'Oh! The ecstasy of that night with the breeze playing over one's face – sleep that would not be broken at any un-earthly hour by a 'Yellah' for donkeys or by dust-storms or by a stampede.'[694] They were also provided with a reasonable hot meat on arrival, though Lieutenant Bishop complained,

> Unfortunately, this was much the best repast we obtained from the contractor, and when it came to arranging a daily messing scheme we had to be content with a very moderate programme. However, everyone had got so tired of scraping along, cooking and foraging for themselves on the journey up, that any sort of plan by which someone else would do the work was not to be refused, even if we were to be done over it.[695]

He referred to the various 'charges' that the prisoners had to pay to commandant Tewfik Bey. They were paying him for their food, rent for their accommodation and more than they should have been for a stamp that acknowledged their receipt of some monthly pay. Their pay was seven liras a month, but food was six liras a month and there was an additional charge of three liras for hire of furniture!

Remarkably, it was possible for the officers to receive cash from merchants in Kastamuni town even though it was miles from civilization. They wrote undated 'cheques' on blank pieces of paper, which were to be redeemed by the owners after the War. The British pound was held in high esteem, but the dealers were relying on honesty from the officers and would not have fared so well if the British had lost the conflict. Captain Keeling recorded that, after the War, some cheques had been honoured but that there was still £650 due in 1923. The British Treasury honoured the debt, so most of those tradesmen received their money. Keeling points out that 'had the rank and file in Turkey been able to raise money in this way, the mortality among them would have been far lower.'[696]

Personnel at Kastamuni were paid by the Turks who gave them the equivalent each month of what their own soldiers received. The British War Office deducted the equivalent amount from their home accounts and shortfalls of money in the camp were rectified by an allowance provided by the Red Cross. They were, therefore, reasonably comfortable, financially.

The commandant was referred to by Captain Woolley as 'a moth-eaten "dugout" Kaimakam [lieutenant-colonel]'.[697]

> At normal times he probably meant well, but he was ignorant and suspicious, with a violent temper and no ideas of business method or military discipline – he was as dowdy in dress as he was dirty in person; he was also pettily dishonest and a drunkard.[698]

Left Kastamuni Sketches – the castle and houses near the school. (Woolley)

Right Kastamuni Sketch – 'Napoleon', our interpreter. (Woolley)

Tewfik Bey was eventually replaced by a much fairer and more decent officer in early 1917. This was the fat Fallah (or Fateh) Bey. Tewfik Bey was removed from the post after some of the commandant's crooked financial arrangements with the food contractor were discovered by the Turkish authorities. Lieutenant Bishop described the new commandant: 'He proved to be a very good fellow and things were running much more pleasantly.'[699] Inevitably, his period of reign was described as the 'Fatty Regime'.[700]

The guards, or *postas* (known as 'bluebottles' by the prisoners), were mainly elderly reservists, called up to do a poorly-paid and mundane job. Captain Woolley does not reveal much animosity towards them: 'As long as we did not work them too hard they let us do much as we liked, and though there were some surly brutes amongst them with whom we had trouble, the majority were all right.'[701]

Many of the guards, who were armed with ancient rifles and only had two rounds each of ammunition issued, appear to have been 'adopted' by the inmates and given amusing nicknames such as 'Johnnie Walker' and 'Ginger'. There were no stories of brutality in Kastamuni.

The small things in life remained important, just as they had during the siege of Kut. For isolated and often bored groups, sleep, food, exercise, mail from home, keeping warm and keeping busy were the tricks of survival. The personnel incarcerated in Kastamuni had more opportunities to maintain this routine of activities than many other of the 'Kuttites' spread around the prison camps of Asia Minor. A normal daily routine was as follows:

- 0630 hours – reveille, cold wash in bucket, tea and toast
- 0830–0900 hours – breakfast of two eggs, piece of bread, cup of milk
- Morning – sleep, play cards, read books, write diaries, smoke

- 1300 hours – lunch of greasy food
- Afternoon – sleep, play cards, read books, write diaries, smoke
- 1630 hours – tea
- 1730 hours – exercise on occasions; a walk or games
- 1945 hours – dinner, followed by bridge or chess

Captain Mousley commented: 'It may read nicely, but in truth it is a sorry existence.'[702] At least these prisoners had a bearable, if dull, life. They had far more freedom in Kastamuni than most prisoners in other camps.

The food menu rarely varied – a mixture of rice, macaroni, eggs and stuffed vegetables. Captain Woolley described it as monotonous with 'everything served swimming in yellow grease.'[703]

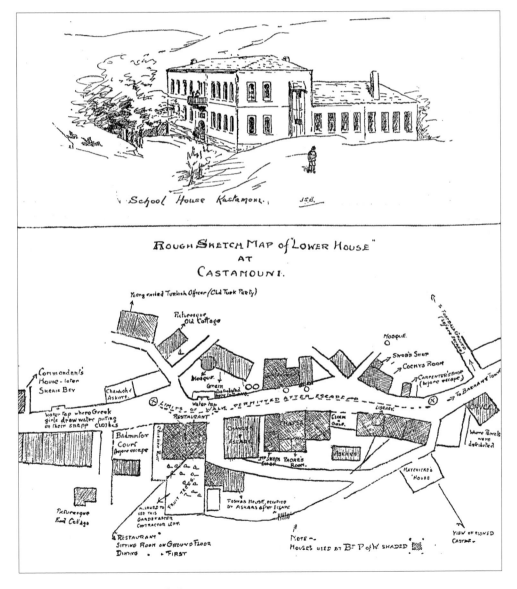

Sketch map of Kastamuni. (Wooley)

However, despite the small size of the courses, it was regular food, something that many other camps did not provide.

Exercise was important, especially after the long, debilitating trek to reach the camp. The prisoners were limited to one short walk a week initially but this restriction was lifted in due course and they were also able to visit the local bazaar and bath, under escort. Captain Mousley was very keen to take exercise as he recovered from malaria. He hated captivity. 'With returning fitness I begin to hate, loathe, detest and abhor this soul-smothering life.'[704] Games were played on a nearby hired rough pitch.

> It was very stony and by no means level, but, nevertheless, was a great acquisition. As a rule, each group of house used it three days a week. To start with, we only had a soccer case and no bladder. We stuffed a case with grass and played a very modified form of rugger, where collaring was disallowed on account of the stones, and punting and place kicking forbidden in order to preserve the life of the ball.[705]

Proper balls eventually arrived in the camp and the rules were adjusted. As time went by, cricket, rounders, soccer, rugby and badminton were played, all watched over by some amateur 'book-

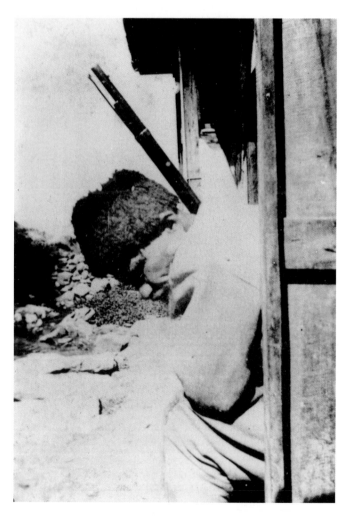

Turkish sentry in camp. (IWM Q 106235)

makers'. Games helped maintain health and took the inmates' minds off their situation. Even boxing took place and, in winter, some improvised tobogganing. The exercise did not take everyone's minds off their situation, of course, as Lieutenant Elton revealed:

> But if the past was still potent, it was the future which haunted us. When in the first place, should we get home? Should we indeed ever get home? Each in his own degree and manner, we thrust the grim misgivings out of our consciousness.[706]

One of his key appointments in helping to keep minds distracted was as sub-librarian. By the end of 1916, he was helping to catalogue and classify over 1,000 books, which had arrived either from home or the American Embassy.

Mail was vital for good morale, and Lieutenant Bishop remembered 'The greatest events in our life were undoubtedly the arrival of a mail or parcels.'[707] News from family and friends, which arrived in batches about every ten days, allowed the reader to lose himself in a dream of home. Letters took, on average, twenty-five days to arrive with parcels taking three to four months if they were not interfered with or stolen en route. Captain Mousley described the arrival of mail in the early months of captivity, when it was at its most precious, on 1 October 1916.

Picture of prisoners. (IWM Q 92617)

Loud shouting and cheering and wild stampede towards the restaurant dining-room announced that another mail had come. We all go quite mad on these occasions, and charge past postas, knocking over chairs or each other, and crowd around the table while the letters are given out.[708]

Some gifts also arrived at the camp via the Red Crescent or organised by the American Embassy in Constantinople. Prized possessions were the warm clothes which were so useful over the winter period, especially as they came in all sorts of strange shapes, colours and sizes, providing some amusement for the inmates. Temperatures dropped, but during the first winter there was plenty of wood to buy for fires. In addition, the officers had their orderlies to look after them.

'What we craved for more than anything else was reliable news.'[709] The prisoners had a thirst for any information, but unlike for some of their successors in the Second World War, there was no secreted wireless to listen to, let alone the large screens of satellite real-time information available today. Any information gained was scarce, inaccurate and old; naturally, as in any closed community, rumours flourished. A German-run paper, *Hilal*, was available and letters from home contained coded information about what was going on. Lieutenant Bishop reported that many stories were picked up by Greek shopkeepers in the local bazaar.[710]

Lectures were organised to keep people busy and a debating society lasted for a short time. Major Saunders lectured on motoring, Lieutenant-Colonel W. Cramer-Roberts instructed on figure-drawing and Captain Woolley gave a course on the 'Evolution of Religion in the Old Testament'. Other topics included the horse, polo, telephones, pottery, law, rubber planting and even the Mesopotamia Campaign. It is remarkable how such obscure subjects can become fascinating to an isolated and bored audience!

However, the most successful of the enterprises was the band, or 'Kastamuni Orchestral Society', the KOS, which started in early 1917. Some musical instruments such as old violins were scrounged from the local bazaar whilst some simpler instruments, like drums and banjos, were homemade – mainly by Lieutenant C. Munroe. The first practice consisted of two violins, one mandolin, one flute, one clarinet, two banjos, one 'cello' and two drums. Second-Lieutenant R. Parsons of the Royal Garrison Artillery became the main conductor and had to write the scores before mail with music arrived from home. Captain Mousley was the first violin and Lieutenant Clifton played the side-drum and, later, the double bass. Lieutenant Bishop enjoyed the concerts.

We even had a little dancing on one or two occasions and one day the commandant brought two or three Greek and Armenian ladies. This was such a success that he became very excited and declared, 'Next veek plenty lady kom'.[711]

It was important to let off steam to maintain morale, whether it was sport or playing in the orchestra. At Christmas 1917, Captain Mousley played in the football matches and then 'consumed a tremendous amount of cognac and mastik, and anything else going, regardless of price, and for a few hours we quite took charge of things.'[712] Activities such as this led to misspelt Turkish orders that provided some mirth amongst the prisoners.

Notice!
1. As some officers drink more than is necessary they pour liquors throughout the windows down to the street upon the people and disturb the neighbours, making great shindy by the effects of much drink. In this way these officers cause complaints to be made by everybody.
2. It is forbidden to keep more than is essential.
3. Liquors will be drunk sufficiently and soberness will be kept.

4. It will not be made for great noise as far as spoiling the others, and good manners and quiet will be maintained.

Signed TEWFIK[713]

The commandant did not allow the officers to share Christmas services with their men, so Reverend Spooner was busy. However, food was reasonably plentiful and the prisoners ran a successful variety show and a party for the local children. On the day, another perk was provided by the Pope who sent the prisoners £40 for Christmas.[714] It was a holiday marked by an inmate's poem:

> A Christmas in captivity,
> Oh what a sorry travesty!
> A song to sing in a minor key
> Of things that are and should not be;
> Yet still I have to comfort me
> The Christmas of my memory.[715]

Dramatic performances began on that first Christmas in captivity and flourished at Kastamuni. Lieutenant Munroe and Lieutenant-Colonel Taylor encouraged the performance of 'The Kusty Minstrels'. The programme included carols, a banjo duet, songs and sketches and a finale of 'God Save The King'.

The prisoners clung to their routine and Lieutenant Elton's comments about how they coped are fascinating:

> It was interesting to observe the variety of ways in which the captives addressed themselves to captivity. Most of them belonged to the pre-War Indian Army, and practically all of them, it was obvious, were first class regimental officers. Some played bridge for the two and a half years. Some gossiped and read light literature. A few learnt Turkish. A number developed unsuspected talents and became carpenters, cobblers, cabinet-makers, or made themselves violins and bassoons and turned musicians. One or two studied the prophecies of Daniel. Two, of whom I saw a good deal, worked assiduously – at Turkish, Persian, Oriental History or French.[716]

Lieutenant Bishop admitted that learning Turkish was not a popular pastime 'as no one expected ever to want it again when once they had left the country' but saw that lectures and participation in the debating society were popular activities.[717] Lieutenant Elton spent his time

> … reading history and classical English fiction, writing inferior poetry and worse prose, talking to Dick Lacy about that borderland between Berkshire and Hampshire from which we both hailed, and striking up a friendly acquaintance with a wider variety of human beings than I had encountered anywhere before.[718]

In fact, Lieutenant Godfrey Elton, later the Labour peer and historian, the 1st Baron Elton of Headington in the County of Oxford – like many other fellow-prisoners – learned a great deal about himself whilst in captivity. 'I acquired a sense of values, too, and learned once and for all that kindness, courage and common sense are worth more than intellect.'[719] He and others had the breathing space to come to such abstract conclusions, perhaps, as they received a remarkable level of freedom. However, even the modern soldier, who may not be in prison but has to serve in dangerous and isolated locations under a great deal of stress, understands his sentiments. He also appreciates the simple things of life, is able to judge what is really of importance and is able to place day-to-day 'crises' in perspective. This is because he has experienced insignificant events being blown out of all proportion within such a tight-knit community with no mechanism to place things in context. Similar circumstances were experienced by the prisoners of Kastamuni. Lieutenant Keeling admitted

> The monotony of our life, though often relieved by the whims of the gaolers, was trying, and we all got bored with one another's society, conversation and mannerisms, and depressed by the feeling that we were ignominiously out of the war.[720]

Another innovation in the camp were the 'underground' camp newspapers – it was vital to keep them secret for fear of Turkish reprisal. There were two amongst the officers, which appear to have been in competition to begin with, the *Mastik* and the *Smoke*. The orderlies produced the *Ekmek*. Lieutenant Elton's other key responsibility, apart from librarian, was co-editor of the *Mastik,* which seemed to be favoured by Captain Woolley who admired the coloured cartoons by Major N. Rybot. Its rival, the *Smoke*, was started by Captain Mousley in the spring of 1917 and he called it 'The Kastamuni Punch and Tatler'.[721] The paper was a popular satirical fortnightly product that contained cartoons, poems and various spoof articles about current affairs. Like similar in-house productions, it was topical and only really understood by the people living at the time and within its sphere of influence. They enjoyed the unique language and 'in-jokes'. When one looks at the articles today, some are incomprehensible; however, to the prisoners of Kasatamuni they were another way to let off steam and provided much needed entertainment. The poems are still moving, like these two verses of 'The Fall of Kut' by 'Sparkling Moselle':

> God grant to us, now captives –
> Who at death's gate boldly dare
> Boast we haven't succumbed to battle –
> Grant us this fervent prayer –
>
> That in our future cheerless,
> We yet shall know o'er Kut
> Our avengers see the Union Jack –
> Tramp the Crescent underfoot.[722]

The *Smoke* did not impress Captain Woolley: 'Unfortunately, it indulged over-freely in those personalities which the editors of the *Mastik* were careful to avoid, and was officially suppressed after a short and eventful career.'[723] Either Captain Woolley had been at the sharp end of some indiscreet comments or he must have fallen out with Captain Mousley at some stage!

What of life outside Kastamuni? A hint of how the other ranks were being treated was given in the spring of 1917, when twenty-five extra orderlies arrived. Lieutenant Bishop reported 'They brought dreadful stories of the treatment of the troops during the first few months, and it became clear that at least two-thirds of the Kut garrison was already dead.'[724] None of them were fit when they arrived at Kastamuni and two of them died soon after arrival. Captain Mousley:

> The reports they brought of the men were simply terrible. Hundreds of them seem to have perished in the cold. The sick were allowed to die without any attention whatever. A daily loaf of bread and one blanket, and often no medical care at all, had counted for hundreds. Whole regiments are wiped out.[725]

The fit and adventurous planned their escape from the camp, despite its isolated position. Success came on 8 August 1917 when four officers broke away – Lieutenants Keeling and Bishop, Captain R. Tipton of the Royal Flying Corps and Captain Sweet of the 2/7th Gurkhas. The latter had already proved his bravery back in Kut when he helped to blow up the bridge. Their story is in the following chapter.

Though they had been successful, things changed for the worse for those left in Kastamuni as a result. Captain M. Johnston of the Royal Garrison Artillery and Captain Kenneth Yearsley, Royal Engineers, who would both escape in due course, wrote in their joint memoir: 'We were confined to our houses without any exercise for 10 days; sentries were more than trebled on the principle of locking the stable door.'[726] The commandant was replaced, the routine was changed and soon after the prisoners were moved from Kastamuni to a less comfortable camp.

In two separate groups during September and October 1917 the prisoners were marched eighty miles south to the village of Changri. They were led by the senior British officer, Colonel H. Annesley of the Supply and Transport Corps Indian Army and escorted by the camp second-in-command, Sherif Bey, making the most of the selection of carts and mules provided to help move stores and personal belongings. From Changri, many of the prisoners were moved to Kedos, 100 miles west of Smyrna, where there was a very liberal regime, whilst some ended up joining other prisoners at Yozgad.

Changri

Changri did not impress the prisoners as they arrived. It was a small town with a population of about 10,000 at 2,500 feet above sea level. Accommodation was a dilapidated two-storey building with long barrack rooms that would house batches of twenty or thirty inmates. Most of the building had been used as a cow and goat stable and the floors were covered in six inches of manure. Everything was filthy and the water supply was contaminated – water had to be brought from elsewhere – and geese, sheep and goats were still roaming the area. The first column of officers and their orderlies did their best to scrape the filth off the floors with bits of wood. Captain Woolley was not impressed: 'The barracks had before the War been condemned as unfit for human occupation: some French prisoners from the Dardanelles had been interned here, and sixty graves on the hillside close by testified to its healthiness.'[727]

Colonel Annesley attempted to stop the second column moving from Kastamuni because of the conditions he had found and wrote to the Netherlands Minister in Constantinople and Osman Bey, the general officer commanding at Angora, in protest. He complained about insufficient space, a lack of glass in the windows, no drinkable supply of water, the disgusting kitchen, and the insanitary rooms and latrines. He demanded that his group should be moved to a different location and that the second column should remain in Kastamuni. He forcefully finished his letter of 2 October:

> Should no notice be taken of this representation and should we be kept here for any length of time, the whole circumstances of the case will be reported to the British Government at the end of the War, and every officer here will make it his duty to let the facts be known to every nation. The officers look to you as the Army Corps commander to see that justice is done, and speedily.[728]

Gradually, his attempts to improve the environment did work, although the second column was not stopped and arrived on the same day that Osman Bey inspected the camp. Following his visit, the prisoners were given more freedom, better and cheaper food, and glass for the windows and firewood; Changri remained unpleasant nevertheless.

The prisoners quickly attempted to re-establish some of their activities and routine to pass the time. The orchestra reassembled, the library was set up again and a new chapel was established by Reverend Spooner. Changri was much more isolated than Kastamuni, conditions were not as good and the prisoners were more strictly guarded.

Colonel Annesley did not want things to become any worse, so he asked the officers to give their word not to escape as he was fearful of potential Turkish reprisals. This request was not popular, especially as it came from the senior British officer rather than the Turks. Following some debate he modified this request, pending guidance from the British War Office, but Enver Pasha promised that all officers who would give their word not to escape should be transferred to 'suitable camps'.[729] The prisoners' response to this offer was controversial and resulted in a certain amount of debate and ill-feeling, as it is a prisoner's duty to try and escape. They were being offered better conditions, but at a high price. A statement was prepared for them to sign:

> On condition that I am moved to a good camp and receive accommodation suitable for officers, with reasonable liberty, I hereby give me word of honour not to attempt to escape while I am a prisoner of war in Turkey.[730]

Seventy-seven officers subscribed and forty-three objected. The seventy-seven were 'rewarded' for their commitment and they were told that they were to be taken to Kedos (or Geddos) and lodged in four comfortable houses. These prisoners moved out of Changri in the third week of November – the previous seven weeks had not been pleasant and they had another five weeks of travelling before they reached their final destination.

Despite the acrimony surrounding the split of prisoners, Captains Johnston and Yearsley, who did not sign the statement and stayed behind, wrote: 'It was very sad parting from many good friends, and when the last cart disappeared round the spur of the hill, one turned away wondering if one would ever see them again.'[731]

Their fellow prisoners had another objective on their minds – escape. Conditions remained poor at Changri with a shortage of food, which was becoming more difficult and expensive to obtain and a scarcity of fuel for cooking or warmth. At Changri, the twenty-five officers and one soldier who were eventually to escape from Yozgad on 7 August 1918 formed their core planning groups. One group consisted of

• Captain V.S. 'Nobby' Clarke – 2nd Battalion the Royal West Kent Regiment
• Captain R.A.P. 'Grunt' Grant – 112th Infantry
• Captain A.B. 'Old Man' Haig – 24th Punjabis
• Captain J.H. 'Perce' Harris – 1/4th Battalion the Hampshire Regiment
• Captain 'Johnny' Johnston and Captain 'Looney' Yearsley, the authors of the book *450 Miles to Freedom*.

Changri was an isolated location and since Captain Keeling's break from Kastamuni, the Turks had ensured that both the prisoners and the potential routes away from the town were well guarded. Thick snow and the cold conditions during the winter of 1917 also prevented action. The prisoners were not allowed away from their meagre accommodation for three months, apart from occasional trips to the woods to cut down some wood for fuel, the odd visit to the local bazaar and a little tobogganing on Christmas day. Their new commandant, Sami Bey, was not as pliable as his predecessors, as he was fearful of any potential escapes and what might happen to him as a result. The British senior officer, Lieutenant-Colonel A. Moore of the 66th Punjabis, had his work cut out maintaining standards for his men. However, morale seemed to remain reasonably high. 'We were all good friends, and united in our determination not to knuckle under the Turk.'[732] Small groups of like-minded prisoners from other camps, who had refused to agree to not escape, gradually reinforced the Changri group as the winter progressed. Imaginative plotting continued, as plans to dig tunnels, take over the camp from the guards and arrange for British aeroplanes to execute a daring rescue were considered. The prisoners, who by then consisted of forty-seven officers and twenty-eight orderlies, had plenty of time to think and become lost in their imaginations. They had also worked out how to send coded messages home, but it would take months to complete the loop of sending a message and receiving a reply.

Plans were well under way for an escape and a tunnel was being dug when the prisoners were told that they were going to be moved again, this time to Yozgad, eighty miles south-east, though 180 miles by road. Prospects for the tunnel looked poor anyway, as one of the shafts struck water and it was extremely unlikely that any Allied aeroplanes would be available for the escapees. One group planned to hide in the roof rafters, but as the time to leave Changri arrived, this intent seemed futile as nominal rolls were called regularly.

The prisoners set off on their twelve-day trek to Yozgad, via Angora, in April 1918.

Kedos

We return to the larger group of Changri prisoners, who had agreed parole terms and were on their way to Kedos. They also walked to Angora, where they saw some of the old Kut garrison working on the railway. Captain Woolley wrote that they seemed to be better off than nine months before:

> They were being better treated than formerly, or at least were doing better. The Turks only gave them a loaf of bread a day and 10 piastres a month, but they were receiving 4 liras a month from the Dutch Embassy, besides private and fund money and a lot of parcels, including those for the dead.[733]

The next part of the journey was by train to Eskishehir, where some Indian officers presented them with gifts of drinks and food. The railway carriages were uncomfortable and cold, but worse for the orderlies as theirs had no glass in the windows. The next destination was Afion Kara Hissar, where they stayed shivering for three weeks amongst a mix of British, French and Russians who did their best to make them comfortable. Captain Woolley noticed that their conditions were worse than his group had experienced – it was extremely cold, but wood for fuel was again scarce. Freedom was limited and the other ranks were not allowed to converse with the officers. He was happy to leave.

They left in three batches and were split during Christmas 1917. Brevet-Colonel H. Cummins of the 24th Punjabis had arrived at Kedos with the Gurkhas to discover that the accommodation was again poor and definitely not as described before they travelled. One group was trudging through the snow heading for Kedos, the remainder were shivering at Afion Kara Hissar. They had all reached Kedos by the end of 1917. The 'Notes for Relatives' leaflet, produced in England, described the town.

> Picturesquely situated about 2,600 feet above sea level, on the Ushak-Broussa road, in a deep hollow surrounded by precipitous hills and intersected by a small but rapid river, which escapes through a narrow gorge. On the east the town is hemmed in by lofty rocks of black basalt, extending in a semi-circular form like the rim of a crater. The neighbourhood produces much opium.[734]

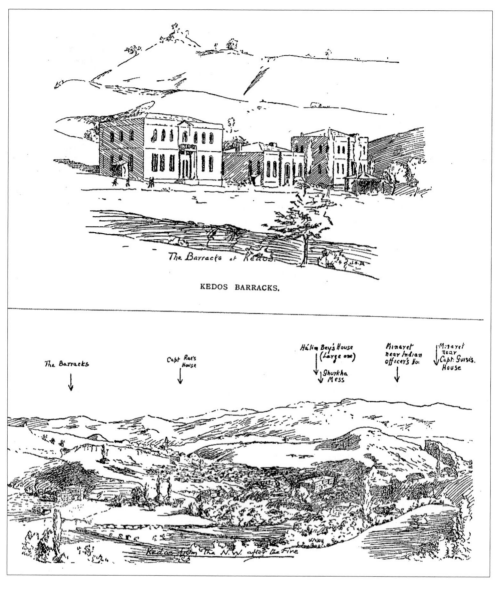

KEDOS BARRACKS.

Kedos Sketches – the barracks and view from River Valley. (Woolley)

Their new commandant was Habib Nouri Bey:

> Commonly know to us as 'Dippy', short for Dippy Dick and meaning an obstinate, ill-tempered old Kaimakam, who, rumour had it, once commanded a division on the Erzerum front but had since descended to the station of a Prison Commandant.[735]

The barracks were clean, but the facilities were poor. Many personal belongings and all money in excess of seven liras were removed as new prisoners arrived. The accommodation was in large rooms into which the prisoners were squeezed. There were no proper beds – just rush mats, which had to be bought by the inmates from the local bazaar. Discipline and rules were

Kedos Sketch – Ali of Kedos, or 'The Second-in-Command'.
(Woolley and Rybot)

rigidly enforced, conditions were sparse and the officers were not allowed any assistance from their orderlies. Freedom was limited and, at first, even reading books was forbidden. Exercise was limited to walking in between a marked off area in front of the main building twice a day for short fixed periods. Some outdoor games were played, though never to the same degree as in Kastamuni. Eventually the prisoners were allowed to sing; 'Dippy' had tough, though often inconsistent, rules.

The camp had been established in the spring of 1917 and one of the first Kut prisoners in April had been Captain Spackman from the Indian Medical Services. He had helped ill Kut prisoners at Mosul from May to November 1916 and had then spent four months travelling through Nisibin, Ras al Ain, Aleppo and Afion Kara Hissar before he reached his destination. The prison gradually expanded as British prisoners arrived from both the Mesopotamia and Palestine fronts. Captain Spackman was a key personality in the camp; as well as his medical expertise, he could speak a little Turkish and often acted as an interpreter.[736] On one occasion, he fell foul of one of the commandant's many rules, as he was caught playing chess. For this sin, he was given twenty-four hours' solitary confinement.

A Sikh subadar had to be operated on, as he had an abscess on the liver. Captain Spackman, assisted by a Turkish doctor, local dentist and some brother officers holding the patient down, carried out the procedure. He had to improvise with equipment – a cut throat razor, some cocaine and clothing for bandages. Perhaps it is not surprising that, although the subadar initially seemed to recover, he died shortly afterwards.

In June 1917, conditions improved as a result of an external inspection from Miralai (Colonel) Yusuf Zia Bey. A carpenter started making beds and other furniture and the area marked out for exercising was enlarged, though the latter perk did not last long.

Many of the activities begun in Kastamuni were resurrected. Mess meetings, a debating society, reading on the new beds, card games and learning languages were all things that kept the prisoners busy, though freedom to roam or play outdoor games was still very limited. Food was dull, but at least available, and meals remained important events:

• Breakfast – bread, crushed wheat (bulgour), salt, pepper and coffee with occasional extra eggs and buttermilk
• Lunch – two boiled eggs or a watery stew with occasional cheese or butter
• Dinner – eggs, stew or cold salad, followed by stewed fruit or 'dog' (boiled bread and currants).[737]

A major event took place in September 1917 when Dippy was replaced by a new commandant, Adhem Bey. Instead of someone who stuck by rules 'we realised that we had at last a man who would look after our interests'.[738] He was also referred to as a 'gentleman'.[739]

A change of policy concerning the conditions of the prisoners was made two months later. They were all offered parole in exchange for relative freedom at Kedos. If they refused they could end up under tight guard in the nearby town and heard that they could be shipped back to Changri Camp. Eventually, all of the prisoners, except Second-Lieutenant F. Sheridan of the

2/9th Gurkhas, Lieutenant T. Jenkins of the 4th Battalion South Wales Borderers and Captain Johnston, agreed to the parole. Captain Woolley wrote 'A few days later the three "diehards" were sent off to Changri, where we hoped that the consciousness of having done the right thing in their estimation would fully compensate them for the rough journey there, and for any further unpleasantness that might fall to their lot.'[740]

He goes on to say that the prisoners at Kedos then had a comfortable time, with few restrictions. They were joined by eighty other British officers from Changri, mainly captured at Kut, who had also agreed to the parole. He avoids any debate about their decision to accept a deal with the Turks, rather than attempt to escape. Conditions at Kedos were extremely civilised compared with all other camps. There was a lot of freedom, the orchestra and drama society thrived and there was even a social calendar of events. When the prisoners were eventually sent home, via Ouchak and Smyrna in October 1918, they even

> ... said goodbye to the Commandant and his staff. He made a little speech and shook hands with us all and we cheered him and sang that he was a jolly good fellow ... he was certainly very pleased; and we for our part were indeed grateful to a man who was a gentlemen himself and treated us as such, and we felt that he thoroughly deserved his musical honours and the piece of plate for which we subscribed.[741]

What a comfortable existence they had compared with other men from Kut.

Yozgad

About 100 miles from the coast, Yozgad was described as 'the most isolated camp in Asia Minor, situated in a town of some 12,000 inhabitants, out of whom all the rich Armenian families had been exterminated.'[742] It was set in a mountainous area 4,500 feet above sea level.

The first batches of officers from Kut, which included Major Sandes, had arrived there on 30 June 1916 after a two-month journey and the camp gradually expanded to hold 100 officers and sixty orderlies. At first, they were squeezed into two surprisingly clean buildings, until Lieutenant-Colonel Baines managed to gain another building for use as a hospital. Mattresses were provided and the prisoners eventually occupied six detached houses divided into two groups, each with vegetable gardens established by the prisoners.

The commandant, Bimbashi (Major) Kiazim Bey, kept a tight guard on the prisoners who had little opportunity to escape and there were plenty of little rules akin to 'Dippy's reign' at Kedos. He was described in the 1918 White Paper on the subject of the Treatment of British Prisoners of War in Turkey as a 'Turk of the old school – polite, honest and silent.'[743] Major Sandes viewed him as aloof but polite, and goes on to describe him from a very nineteenth-century British perspective. 'In my opinion he was a Turk of the old school, poorly educated, only partially civilised, soured by ill-health, and with a rooted dislike for all Europeans.'[744] Fellow captives, Captains Johnston and Yearsley, however, noted that he expected bribes and accepted 'a regular commission from every shopkeeper who wished to supply his wares to the camp.'[745]

There were twenty guards and their attitude changed from hostility to friendliness as they began to know their captives. For the first few weeks the prisoners were confined to their houses, probably because the commandant was concerned that they might attempt to escape. The British senior officer, Colonel Harwood, wrote letters of complaint to both Enver Pasha and the American ambassador in Constantinople – the commandant refused to send them. As in Kastamuni, there were problems with the local contractor who provided most of their meals, and

Two sketches of Yozgad camp. (Johnston and Yearsley)

From a sketch   by Capt. K. F. Freeland, R.A.

UPPER HOUSE, YOZGAD, FROM N.N.E.
(Winter Time.)

A = Sentry's box.
B − − − − C = Track followed by Cochrane and Ellis.
D = Hockey ground.

E·B·BURNS

From a sketch   *by Capt. E. B. Burns, E. Kent Regt.*

YOZGAD CAMP FROM N.W.

A = Hospital House.   C − − − D = Course followed to river bed.
B = Upper House.   E = Market gardens.
C = Position of hole made in fowl-house wall.

the prisoners started running out of money. Some funds arrived in late July from the American Embassy and in September the Turkish Government started to give the prisoners pay. Other good news was that mail and parcels from home eventually arrived at Yozgad, mail first arriving in July. Conditions were vastly improved when the commandant removed some of the restrictions of movement in the camp and the prisoners were allowed to exercise.

Whilst the other ranks elsewhere were kept busy on manual labour tasks, the officers at Yozgad, as at other officer camps, quickly thought of ideas to keep themselves active and to take their thoughts off their captivity. Gambling became popular and as Major Sandes described, 'Any sort of relaxation from the deadly monotony of our existence was welcome, and roulette did its part in distracting our attention from our troubles.'[746] Other activities followed such as carpentry and a lecture programme and the prisoners, now with money, purchased extra food that they stored under the watchful eye of Captain M. Dinwiddy of the Royal West Kent Regiment. Football, hockey and a new library were other distractions that began flourishing in October, and a debating society started in November. Many of the orderlies had even procured pet dogs to keep them amused.

The prisoners in this camp became adept at sending cryptic postcards home, which contained secret messages about their conditions and requested, unbeknown to their censors, international inquiries into their conditions. These were often very simple, such as this extract from a card sent by Second-Lieutenant E. Jones of the Royal Garrison Artillery:

> Send tea and tobacco, Eno's, underclothes, needles, sugar, Antiphon, tabloid ink, soap, Foramint, aspirin, cocoa, toffee, Oxo, razor, Yardley's dental extract, matches, alum, nuts, dates, Euthymol, novels, quinine, uniform. I remain Yozgad for present.[747]

We will allow the reader to crack the fiendish code: use the first letter of each word! Similarly coded messages were sent in response from home, so at least some news was received about families and what was happening in the War. This helped a little to improve morale.

Christmas 1916 passed in relative comfort, with turkey and goose on the menu. The prisoners put on a play for everyone's entertainment, following the success of the pantomime *The Fair Maiden of Yozgad* and Major Sandes accompanied singing with his fiddle. A band was eventually formed of three violins, a guitar and a flute, but it never reached the same standard as the 'Kastamuni Orchestra'. Tobogganing began in earnest as the snow arrived, though the prisoners heard rumours that the conditions at Kastamuni were much better than theirs.

The most fascinating tale to come out of Yozgad was the escape attempt by Captain Elias Jones and Lieutenant Cedric Hill, described in their book *The Road to Endor*. This tale became one of the best known escape stories from the First World War and is described in the next chapter.

Conditions at Yozgad were not too bad. Commander H. Stoker recounted:

> After the long experience of prison, life in the internment camp at Yozgad seemed very delightful that summer. There was companionship, literature, exercise, and comparative comfort.[748]

He had experienced a lot worse at Afion Kara Hissar Camp.

However, as Major Sandes wrote, 'Autumn [1917] came, and we dragged out our monotonous existence from day to day – we ate, we worked, we played, we slept, and we tried not to drown our sorrows too deeply in raki.'[749]

As there was a shuffling around of some of the prisoners and he had had enough of Yozgad, he volunteered, with twenty others, to be moved to Afion Kara Hissar. He does not explain why they volunteered, apart for a desire for change; it was not a wise decision.

Prisoners' band at Yozgad. (IWM Q 106238)

The prisoners from Kastamuni arrived at Yozgad at the end of April 1918, where they met up with some of their Kut compatriots, whom they had not seen for two years. Reverend Spooner decided to forego the relative pleasures of Yozgad and shared the terrible hardships of some of the other ranks at Bor.

As in other camps, the prisoners had done their best to gain concessions from their commandant and similar activities took place at Yozgad that helped pass their time in captivity. An unusual event in this camp was the 'Yozgad Hunt Club'. Twice a week, a hunt was allowed with three pairs of greyhounds. 'Seldom did they fail to account for at least one hare or fox between the hours of 4 and 9 am each Monday and Thursday in the spring and summer of 1918.'[750] Games took place, but because of the rough terrain, hockey was preferred to football. The routine continued until the end of the War. Meanwhile Captains Johnston and Yearsley were busy planning their escape.

Afion Kara Hissar

Afion Kara Hissar was a place where a mixture of British officers, the bulk of the Indian officers and some British soldiers were imprisoned. It became well-known because of the poor conditions and, to quote the Official History, the prisoners 'met with most brutal treatment from its Turkish commandant'.[751] Author Russell Braddon later described the commandant, Bimbashi (Major) Muslum Bey, as 'vicious, perverted and probably insane as well.'[752] He was eventually removed from his post in 1918, once the authorities discovered how he governed his camp, alongside his naval postas. The prisoners had had to suffer for a long time before the arrival of a far more civilised and benign commandant – Kaimakam (Lieutenant-Colonel) Yusuf Usuf Zia Bey.

This isolated location had been used since the beginning of the War and a mixture of mainly French, Russian, Italian, Polish and British prisoners had made it their home. The officers had been placed in a house on the western outskirts of the town and, prior to mid-1916, had a monotonous, though not too unpleasant existence. One of the early prisoners was Commander Stoker, Royal Navy, who had been captured with the rest of the crew of Submarine AE2 at Gallipoli. He described the routine.

> With moans and groans of our life during the first months one could fill pages; one of the chief hardships was being allowed no literature of any sort or description. But a tale of woe is dull writing – and reading; it was just the ordinary ghastly existence of prisoner of war – the living death.[753]

The commandant was ordered to send two officers of noble birth to Constantinople. This order was issued as a Turkish reprisal for the way, they had heard, that their prisoners were being treated by the British in Egypt. Commander Stoker and Lieutenant Fitzgerald, Royal Navy, were the pair. They were not particularly 'well-connected', but volunteered, not unreasonably, as it was an opportunity to leave the camp – they had no idea why. They were immediately placed in a Constantinople prison for one week, had their personal belongings stolen and were given filthy bedding. Solitary confinement followed for a further fourteen days, though Commander Stoker described a new unofficial companion – 'Archibald was the biggest rat I have ever seen or imagined in my life.'[754] Lieutenant Fitzgerald commented that 'one week of solitary confinement in this dark hole on bread and water, which is all the food amounts to, is enough to send one mad.'[755]

Eventually, after another eleven days of captivity, the American ambassador, Mr Henry Morganthau, managed to arrange for them to be released. There followed five days of freedom, living in a hotel and being provided with food, a bath and a decent bed before being sent to Kastamuni Camp. Commander Stoker escaped from there, but was recaptured and was awarded three weeks of solitary confinement. He then spent some time at Yozgad Camp in 1917 before being transferred back to Afion Kara Hissar and then returned to Yozgad again – he had kept his captors busy!

'Men were flogged unreasonably for petty and trivial offences.'[756] Major Sandes recorded that most of the NCOs had suffered from corporal punishment. Captain Francis Yeats-Brown provided a vivid description of his life in the camp.

> Prisoners see war without its glamour. The courage and comradeship of battle is far from them. They meet cruel men, and their own fibre coarsens … A criminal's sentence is fixed, but not that of a prisoner of war. Settled in Afion Kara Hissar, the future seemed an endless avenue, leading nowhere. Spring came, and the days succeeded each other in a pageant in which we had no part, cooped up as we were.[757]

He passed the time using yoga as a way of taking his mind away from his surroundings. He dreamed of freedom and eventually escaped from a Constantinople hospital. The accounts from Afion Kara Hissar are far more depressing than many of the other officers' tales.

Soldiers were beaten and imprisoned for trivial reasons, such as burning lice-ridden filthy clothing, and were seen leaving their cells in a sorry state hardly able to walk when they had been reasonably healthy before their ordeal.

> The first commandant, a Turkish naval officer, was very fond of knocking the men about. He struck me across the face for wearing my slippers in my room. I saw an Australian receive six strokes across

the shoulders with a 'sjambok' from a chaoush [sergeant] for playing catch with bread. The same Turk beat me and two others for going across and shaking hands with two new arrivals. I saw one British soldier receive 10 strokes of the stick on his feet.[758]

The latter practice, not uncommon in many of the other ranks' camps was known as being 'bastinadoed'. Major Sandes wrote that he knew of two officers who had received the punishment – one a Russian, the other Indian.

There were accusations of rape and Colonel Lethbridge, who was the British senior officer in 1917, wrote in his memoirs:

> The Turkish commandant treated our private soldiers grossly, and was a drunkard. When in this state he was not accountable for his actions … There was no crime that this individual was incapable of, including grossly immoral and unnatural conduct.[759]

He helped collect evidence of the commandant's behaviour.

The weakest prisoners, who were hospitalised at Afion Kara Hissar, also suffered cruelly.

> There I saw many weakly men knocked about by the Turkish orderlies simply because they were too weak to attend to themselves. I saw this happen to a Quarter-Master-Sergeant who died within a few days of the beating.[760]

One of the Turkish doctors was nicknamed 'the Butcher' and there were various prisoner accounts about patients who were administered injections of a mysterious brandy-coloured liquid and then died shortly afterwards. Beatings of weak soldiers, who were close to death, regularly occurred in the hospital. Hygiene was poor, with clothing only being changed once every three weeks and some soldiers only getting the opportunity to wash every six weeks.

Typically there was only one blanket and a quilt per man, with no mattress even during winter. Seventeen prisoners shared a room twenty-one feet by fifteen feet. Fuel was only available for three hours heating each day. The mainstay of the rations was the issue of meat, one to one-and-a-half goats, for 400 men every second day.

Lice and bugs of all description failed to defer to rank – Major Sandes recorded one method of fighting back:

> During the summer it was necessary to empty boiling water periodically into all chinks of one's home-made bedstead, so as to slay the budding generations of bugs which bred continually in these nooks and crannies. We found that a bath of water once a week effectually checked the increase of bugs, though it was impossible to eradicate them as the walls and floors were full of them.[761]

Captain Yeats-Brown hated the bugs and explained how annoying they were when he was attempting to sleep:

> One squashes a bug and there is a smear of blood – one's own blood. One lights a candle, and there, scuttling under the pillow, are five or six more of the flat fiends. Having killed every living thing in sight, one lies back, hoping to sleep. But they smell horribly when dead, and keep alive the memory of their itching at neck and wrist … There is no end of them. You kill them on the bed and they jump on you from the walls. You slaughter them by fives and tens, but they still come from the crannies where they have lain for months – years maybe – waiting for the scent of live bodies … They not only suck your blood, but sap your faith in God.[762]

The rank and file knew this discomfort, but also much worse conditions than the officers and their orderlies experienced at Afion Kara Hissar.

The Other Ranks

> Without the medium of radio or television little news reached the ears of the general public as to the true state of affairs existing in Turkish prison camps, and what did manage to seep through normal channels was for the most part suppressed. To this day little is known of the siege of Kut and its disastrous effect upon the minds of the emaciated defenders, called upon at the end of their active military service to face an ordeal of slavish cruelty.[763]

The low chance of survival of the other ranks compared with the officers was demonstrated by the numbers of men from the 1/4th Battalion Hampshire Regiment who were repatriated at the end of the War. All ten officers, including one who escaped, returned home, but only about fifty rank and file, out of the original 178 captured at Kut, survived. Another example of a battalion's attrition was the fate of the other ranks of the 7th Rajputs; only 120 out of the 301 who went into captivity returned to India after the Armistice.[764]

As was recounted in the previous chapter, many rank and file did not make it to the prison camps or they were so weak on arrival and so poorly fed and ill-nourished that they did not last long as they worked on the railways. At least 1,000 prisoners died on the long marches. When the remainder of the 2nd Battalion of the Dorsetshire Regiment reached Bagtsche, there were only 140 left out of the 350 who left Kut. As their Official History put it,

> … when at last the survivors did at last arrive at their destination they were almost without exception put to work on the railway or some similar task, and kept hard at it on inadequate rations, under insanitary conditions, herded together in the filthiest quarters and frequently treated with the utmost brutality. The vast majority of the men taken at Kut had perished of their privations and ill-usage long before the Armistice.[765]

Whilst the British officers were concentrated in the camps already mentioned, most of the other ranks were spread around various smaller camps. They worked for Turks and Germans, mainly on the railways, as at Ras al Ain. The conditions at Bagtsche were notorious and the camp was known to the soldiers as the 'cemetery'. It was eventually closed down in 1917, as a result of information leaking out about it to the outside world. Another camp nearby, Yarbashi, was closed in the same year for similar reasons. Other locations included Hassanola, near Angora, Airan, Entelli, Daridja, Bozanti and Psamatia, which was in the suburbs of Constantinople. All of these camps, most of which are now very difficult to identify on a map, are listed as locations housing members of the 1/4th Hampshires.[766] This was typical of the imprisoned Kut units – officers had been split from their soldiers and the remaining troops had been split again. Work at the camps was described thus:

> At Bagtsche work on the railway line consisted of carrying away broken rock in small trucks after blasting had been carried out by German engineers. The hours of work were from 4.30 am until 11 am in the morning and 1pm to 6pm in the evening; pay, six or seven piastres a day from which was deducted cost of meals. The only food supplied was black bread, beans, rice, and a little meat, with water from a nearby stream.[767]

Sergeant Coombes was at Yarbashi for a short time with a group from his regiment – the 2nd Battalion of the Queen's Own Royal West Kent Regiment. Put to work on the railway, they were not ready for labour – they were too weak.

> After all the hardship of the previous 10 months and the continuous marching, we sort of felt that, as soon as it stopped, and we were settled to regular food and work, something would happen. It did. All kinds of diseases made their appearance. The men died in numbers each day.[768]

The Germans realised that there was no point continuing the work with these prisoners so they were moved on, after further hardships, to Afion Kara Hissar. Sergeant Coombes described the long ordeal: 'It had been a trail of death from Kut onwards. Everywhere death! … For over two years we remained in these various camps – two years of toil and hardship.'[769]

It has been calculated that about fifty per cent of the British rank and file had died by the end of the first year of captivity and fifty per cent of the remainder in captivity were to die before the Armistice.

Most of the Indian soldiers were kept in Northern Mesopotamia but were also found spread across various camps. They had been split into religious groups, as described in the previous chapter, and the Moslems amongst them were better treated than the others. They were located at the foot of the Taurus Mountains helping to build a railway. Conditions in captivity were still not easy – many weakened soldiers died in the first few months and they were not supplied with any warm clothing during the first winter period of 1916/17. Eventually, like the officers, they received extra clothing from the Red Cross Society and the American consul – all the prisoners had much for which to thank the American consuls at Mersina and Aleppo and, later, the Netherlands Minister.

For the Indian Moslem soldiers, who were divided into groups of 300 men, the work routine lasted all of the daylight hours with two short breaks in the day of about two hours in total, during which they received their rations. Food consisted of one loaf of bread and some soup each day and the soup contained meat every other day. It was regular sustenance and probably no worse than a Turkish soldier's allotment. At first they were accommodated in tents and then were moved into huts and the men were all issued a small amount of pay, which at least allowed them to supplement their rations from time to time and to purchase tobacco. Security was not tight and they had relative freedom to move around,

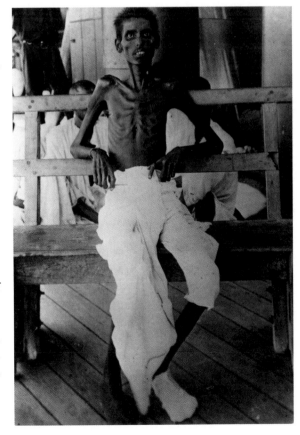

Indian prisoner of war exchanged in June 1916. (IWM Q 79446)

however, no entertainment was allowed in the evening and mail was extremely limited – some soldiers received two letters during their imprisonment. No parcels were received. Thus the conditions for the Moslem soldiers were Spartan and dull, but at least they were survivable.

The Sikhs and Hindus were mainly at Ras al Ain and their life in captivity was far worse than their brother soldiers, as they helped construct the railway towards Nisibin. They were divided up into groups of 100 men, each commanded by five NCOs. Their accommodation remained tented throughout their incarceration.

> Each gang had a Turkish guard of one Non Commissioned Officer and six to nine soldiers. Gangs
> were encamped at approximately 200 yards distance, and when one gang's particular stretch of rail-
> way was completed they were leap-frogged on ahead towards Nisibin.[770]

Life was hard and twenty-five per cent of the Sikh and Hindu soldiers died in the first six months. Although the work hours were similar to those of the the Moslem soldiers, rations were less and only just enough to survive. Disease, especially typhus, was prevalent. Conditions did gradually improve, as Sundays became days of rest and some stores began to arrive from India. These were basic but vital supplies, coordinated by Captain M. Puri of the Indian Medical Service. They included 'cooking pots, clothes, ghi, rice, atta, sugar and tea.'[771]

Many of the regiments retained their proud tradition for good discipline and this helped to sustain their period in captivity. The Official History of the 2/7th Gurkhas recorded this pride following the separation from their officers.

> In the 2nd Battalion there was no straggling; each man took strength from his comrades: cohesion
> and membership were never lost. This essential soundness we owe to three remarkable men whose
> names should appear as illuminated letters in our record. They were Colour-Havildar Fatehbahadur
> Limbu, the Senior Non Commissioned Officer who took command of the Battalion; Colour
> Havildar Bhotri Khattri who assumed the duties of Adjutant; and Havildar Hari Singh Khattri the
> Sikh Quartermaster Clerk. These three ran the Battalion and carried it triumphantly through every
> trial so that when it disembarked from Egypt after the Armistice it bore itself as smartly as it had
> done in 1914 when it first set foot in Suez.[772]

The role of senior NCOs was critical for all of the soldiers in captivity. For example, Regimental-Sergeant-Major Love looked after the remnants of his Oxfordshire and Buckinghamshire Light Infantry battalion, whilst Regimental-Sergeant-Major 'Billy' Leach kept 'A', Headquarters, Company of the 1/4th Battalion Hampshire Regiment motivated. Once the march into captivity was complete, however, many units were dispersed throughout different camps and proved difficult to track.

Regimental-Sergeant-Major Love received great praise for his work in protecting his soldiers.

> Quick to realise the lives of his men depended on him, he enforced discipline and self control
> with all the strength of his character and training at the cost of his popularity, ably supported in
> his endeavours by Quartermaster-Serjeant Burbidge, Distinguished Conduct Medal, Serjeant Ward,
> Distinguished Conduct Medal, and the Non Commissioned Officers. Vilified, insulted and reviled
> by the Turks, he never for one moment surrendered to the enemy, though their prisoner, nor gave up
> the unequal contest.[773]

Regimental-Sergeant-Major Leach was equally revered, as illustrated in the speech by Major Footner at the Welcome to Kut Prisoners at Winchester, in 1919: 'I suppose in the whole of

Regimental-Sergeant-Major Billy Leach. (Royal Hampshire Regiment Museum)

Turkey there was no British officer or man who did not know Sergeant-Major Leach, at any rate by name and reputation, for the work he did for prisoners of war.'[774]

Leach became the senior prisoner of war at Nisibin and was fondly remembered by many soldiers. Flight-Sergeant Long recorded that 'he kept all the records of the British prisoners and was responsible for their administration and the distribution of letters, parcels and clothing etc.'[775] Long goes on to mention his team – Captain Puri, a Sikh havildar and some Indian sepoys – writing: 'Leach was a very efficient man and universally popular, not only with the prisoners but with the Germans and Turks with whom he came into contact.'[776] His small notebook, which recorded every issue of rations to individual soldiers and his regiment's dwindling nominal roll as it marched into captivity, is now held at the regimental museum of the Royal Hampshire Regiment, at Serle's House, Winchester. Long ended up assisting at the Regimental-Sergeant-Major's funeral, as he died from typhus.

> The funeral was the best conducted one that I had witnessed as a prisoner of war, and several Germans attended. Sergeant-Major Leach won respect and popularity by his unfailing courtesy, willingness to help others, and hard work on behalf of the prisoners at Nisibin, from captives and captors alike. His going was a sad loss to the British community at Nisibin and to all the little groups of Englishmen in isolated camps for miles around.[777]

Captain Puri wrote letters of condolence to Leach's regiment and father. This is his letter to Mr Leach, written in Nisibin, on 4 May 1918.

> I am very much grieved to inform you of the demise of your noble son, on the morning (9am) of 26 April. He died of typhus fever. During the earlier part of his sickness I was not here but one of my assistants, Mr Newbold, attended him. During the latter part of his illness however I came back and did what I could and what was possible under the circumstances. He was buried on the morning of 27 April. I, Captain Osmond from next Section, a good many sergeants and over 100 Englishmen and Indians attended his funeral.
>
> I am making an attempt to have a photograph of his grave to be taken – If it is possible I will have a copy sent to you.
>
> Loss of your son has been much felt by all our prisoners here. He was universally respected. I have lost one of my best assistants and workers. He was my personal assistant and I have felt his loss very much. I went out on tour and left him quite fit and strong. We had a photograph taken by a German officer on 12 April. I had to go out on the 13th and he said that on my return we would have a separate photograph of the men of my staff. On my return on the 24th I found him so sick-delirious and showing all the signs of a very serious attack of typhus fever.

Memorial or 'Death Plaque' for Regimental-Sergeant-Major Leach, sent to his next of kin. (Royal Hampshire Regiment Museum)

What was possible was done for him.

Such was the will of the Almighty! We mortals can't pry with his secrets. May He grant peace to the departed soul and courage to you, his mother and his other relations to bear his loss manfully. Please accept heartfelt sympathies on my behalf and on behalf of all the Englishmen and Indian prisoners of war here.[778]

This note represents similar correspondence referring to other deaths. Sadly, many others went unrecorded; the following appeal was made by Mrs Hendley in the Hampshire Regimental Journal of March 1919.

> Mrs W Hendley, of 57, Eastfield Road, Andover, would be very grateful if any returned prisoner of war from Turkey could give her any information respecting 1691 Private W Hendley, 1/4th Hampshire Regiment, of whom she has not heard since the fall of Kut, when he was known to have been taken into hospital at Nisibin. All stamps will be refunded.[779]

Conditions for the other rank prisoners did improve gradually in 1917, as some of the most brutal commandants were moved on and a few of the worst camps closed. Parcels also started to arrive in some locations, donated by Regimental Care Committees. Regimental-Sergeant-Major Love:

> Words cannot express our grateful thanks to the ladies [of the Oxfordshire and Buckinghamshire Light Infantry] who worked so hard for the regiment in keeping us supplied with food and clothes. But for them very few would ever have reached home.[780]

Mrs Esme Bowker, the widow of Lieutenant-Colonel Bowker, who had died commanding half of the 1/4th Hampshires at the Hanna Defile[781] in January 1916, established the 4th Hampshires Comforts Fund, which proved to be a lifeline to the regiment's soldiers. The Fund attempted to locate all of the regiment's men who had been captured and to send them clothes and money. The Fund's nominal roll is retained at their regimental museum. The incarcerated men of the 2nd Battalion of the Dorsetshire Regiment received similar help. Dorchester's population organised a 'Kut Day' on 26 July 1916 to raise funds. The towns of Weymouth and Bridport supported this effort, under the leadership of Colonel Lord Ellenborough, and the three towns had raised over £1,602 by the end of the year.[782] Not all of the parcels made their way to the right recipients, but they did aid the prisoners' conditions and helped to locate many of the men, some of whom had been feared dead.

As well as increased external help, British medical staff gradually took over the well-being of the prisoners in most locations. By 1918, the soldiers were generally much better looked after, with enough clothing, food and money to survive, but they had suffered considerable privations in the meantime.

The War Records of the 24th Punjabis summed up the feelings of the prisoners at the end of the War:

> The lot of an 'Other Rank' prisoner of war is always liable to be a hard one. The lot of the unfortunate Other Ranks in the hands of the Turks was especially hard. There can be no excuse for the death of the large number of prisoners in the hands of the Turks. It was due to callousness and a complete failure to realise their responsibilities for their prisoners.[783]

As the story of the 1/4th Battalion of the Hampshire Regiment concluded, 'any attempt to enlarge further upon the treatment meted out to prisoners of war by Turkish authorities over the whole period of captivity would mean endless repetition of acts of violence, gross neglect of sick and dying men and crimes against humanity.'[784]

Perhaps the last word about the Turkish attitude to the Kut prisoners should go to Colonel Spackman of the Indian Medical Service, who has already been quoted here as a captain. He had been imprisoned for two-and-a-half years after the fall of Kut. He was twice mentioned in despatches and retired in 1945 as the honorary surgeon to King George VI. Writing in the Purnell magazine *History of The First World War* in the 1960s, he stated with impressive constraint:

> The disaster that befell British prisoners in Turkey cannot really be blamed on individuals. It stemmed from the inability of the Turkish High Command to foresee the inadequacy of their civil and military administration to feed and transport so large a body of men of whose deteriorated physical condition they had been warned.[785]

It is no wonder that some prisoners made a bid to escape – many had nothing to lose.

Notes

662. Keeling (1924) p.2.
663. Townshend (1920) p.364.
664. Barker (1967) p.210.
665. Townshend (1920) p.365.
666. Ibid p.369–370.
667. Ibid p.365.
668. Sherson (1928) p.334.
669. Townshend (1920) p.366.
670. Sherson (1928) p.336.
671. Townshend (1920) p.372.
672. Sherson (1928) p.340.
673. Ibid p.334.
674. Ibid p.336.
675. *London Gazette* of Tuesday 17 October 1916. P 10077.
676. Townshend (1920) p.376.
677. Sheffield and Bourne (2005) p.477.
678. Townshend (1920) p.382.
679. Ibid p.385.
680. Ibid p.386.
681. Sherson (1928) p.351.
682. Barker (1967) p.218.
683. Sandes (1920) p.444.
684. A British magazine printed to aid prisoners of war in Turkey (1918) Edition Number 3. p.21.
685. Recorded in Moberly (1924) Appendix XXIX.
686. Barker (1967) p.237.
687. Braddon (1969) p.303.
688. *Yozgad, Broussa and Constantinople Magazine* (1918) Edition Number 3. p.12.
689. Neave (1937) p.283.
690. Mousley (1922) p.327.
691. Woolley (1921) p.V.
692. *Prisoners of War in Turkey* (1918) p.23.
693. Elton (1938) p.146.
694. Mousley (1921) p.205.
695. Bishop (1920) p.82.
696. Keeling (1924) p.70.
697. A facetious term used to describe 'an oldish officer returning from retirement to active service and displaying little efficiency' – Brophy and Partridge (1969) p.94.
698. Woolley (1921) p.3.
699. Bishop (1920) p.86.
700. Woolley (1921) p.27.
701. Ibid p.4.
702. Mousley (1921) p.218.

703. Woolley (1921) p.5.
704. Mousley (1921) p.215.
705. Bishop (1920) p.93.
706. Elton (1938) p.147.
707. Bishop (1920) p.86.
708. Mousley (1921) p.216.
709. Keeling (1924) p.60.
710. Bishop (1920) p.95.
711. Bishop (1920) p.97–98.
712. Mousley (1921) p.225.
713. Woolley (1921) p.15.
714. Keeling (1924) p.63.
715. Woolley (1921) p.17.
716. Elton (1938) p.148–149.
717. Bishop (1920) p.96.
718. Elton (1938) p.150.
719. Ibid p.152.
720. Keeling (1924) p.61.
721. Mousley (1921) p.230.
722. Ibid p.254.
723. Woolley (1921) p.117.
724. Bishop (1920) p.100.
725. Mousley (1921) p.229.
726. Johnston and Yearsley (1919) p.5.
727. Woolley (1921) p.47.
728. Ibid p.49–50.
729. Ibid p.53.
730. Ibid p.54.
731. Johnston and Yearsley (1919) p.11.
732. Ibid p.17.
733. Woolley (1921) p.57.
734. *Prisoners of War in Turkey* (1918) p.23.
735. Woolley (1921) p.61.
736. For Captain's Spackman's full story, read his nephew's book *Captured at Kut* (see bibliography).
737. Woolley (1921) p.76–78.
738. Ibid p.81.
739. Ibid p.90.
740. Ibid p.82.
741. Ibid p.107–108.
742. Neave (1937) p.202.
743. Johnston and Yearsley (1919) p.57.
744. Sandes (1920) p.395.
745. Johnston and Yearsley (1919) p.58.
746. Sandes (1920) p.407.
747. Ibid p.410.
748. Stoker (1925) p.292.
749. Sandes (1920) p.438.
750. Johnston and Yearsley (1919) p.59.
751. Moberly (1924) p.465.
752. Braddon (1969) p.304.
753. Stoker (1925) p.156.
754. Ibid p.200.
755. Neave (1937) p.184.
756. Wheeler (undated) p.32.
757. Yeats-Brown (1930) p.191 and 193.
758. Sandes (1920) p.371–372.
759. Neville (1938) p.235.
760. Sandes (1920) p.372.
761. Ibid p.441.
762. Yeats-Brown (1930) p.193–194.
763. Wheeler (undated) p.26.
764. Rawlinson (1941) p.171.
765. Anonymous (1933) p.218.
766. Anonymous – typed papers at Royal Hampshire Regiment Museum.
767. Wheeler (undated) p.32.
768. Coombes (1918) p.4163.
769. Ibid p.4164.
770. Anonymous (1934) p.57.
771. Ibid.
772. Mackay (1962) p.56.
773. Neville (1938) p.237.
774. The *Hampshire Regiment Journal* (March 1919) p.64.
775. Long (1938) p.263.
776. Ibid p.278–279.
777. Ibid p.320–321.
778. Captain Puri Letter dated 4 May 1918.
779. The *Hampshire Regimental Journal* (March 1919). p.64.
780. Moberly (1924) p.465.
781. See Chapter 4.
782. Details from Anonymous (1933) p.261.
783. Anonymous (1934) p.57.
784. Wheeler (undated) p.32.
785. Spackman (1969) p.1783.

Chapter Eleven

ESCAPE

And from here in the backwater of the world, without news or knowledge, our hearts go out to our countrymen on the other front, and we pray to God that we may soon be amongst them again.[786]

Attitudes

No Kut prisoners wanted to be imprisoned and their fate was made worse by the fact that, in their view, the Turkish enemy had never defeated them in battle. Once some of them had recuperated so far as they were able after the debilitating months of siege and the long trek into captivity and had become used to their new prison environment, their minds turned to escape.

Some, like Flight-Sergeant Long, made early, short and unsuccessful bids for freedom as they decided that the conditions during the march were so bad little could be worse. They had nothing to lose; he was en route to Bagtsche when he made up his mind to go: 'Not knowing what the future held for me I agreed that he [a sergeant] was right, and that I was willing to take a chance.'[787] He did succeed in avoiding Bagtsche, though he was recaptured quickly and placed in the civilian Adana prison, where he was bastinadoed. A determined, intelligent and canny prisoner, after a period in Afion Kara Hissar, he later escaped again from the camp at Bor. His second escape also failed. There were some like-minded soldiers – at Adana prison he became friends with Corporal 'Micky' Dade of the Royal West Kent Regiment, who had attempted to escape with seven others from Entelli camp where they had been working on a railway. They had been recaptured after only a couple of days of freedom with no food or equipment and no realistic chance of success.

Initially, most prisoners became used to the routine of captivity, as described in the previous chapter, rather than concern themselves about escape. Their conditions varied and many resigned themselves to a long period in prison where, if they kept themselves busy and out of trouble, time would pass and they would eventually be reunited with their families and friends at home. Others were in a position which, quite simply, would never give them the means or opportunity to make a bid for freedom; discipline for some was harsh, limited amounts of food meant that they could never build up a reserve of energy and they were so geographically isolated that there was nowhere to escape to, even if they had the will or opportunity to do so. There was also a fear of repercussions if an escape went wrong or was discovered. The debate about whether to make the attempt or not, using Kastamuni as an example, has already been mentioned. In that case, many agreed not to escape and were tempted by a more comfortable life elsewhere.

Kastamuni cartoon, 1917 – 'Captain Smith puts his plan of escape to the test.' (Rybot from 1934 Kut Annual Dinner menu, Royal Hampshire Regiment Museum)

It was a POW's duty to attempt to escape. There were many bored and motivated individuals, especially amongst the officers who were generally living in reasonable, though uncomfortable, conditions. They were extremely frustrated, wanting to fight back against the enemy by escaping and getting home. The situation was summed up by Neave:

> But there were a number of prisoners who had no intentions of escaping and frowned upon the efforts made by others as most disturbing to their own comfort. A good deal of antagonism and ridicule was worked up against rash attempts which had no chance of success. But the only means the prisoners, cooped up under revolting conditions, had of passing the hours of enforced idleness was in making plans of escape.[788]

Attitudes did vary. Commander Stoker's escape has already been mentioned. After eighteen days in the mountains, he and two fellow Royal Navy officers had been recaptured and placed in solitary confinement for two months in Constantinople. Repercussions at Afion Kara Hissar included the locking up of 100 prisoners in the local Armenian church for two months; there was no space and typhus broke out in the building. In addition, a new and more oppressive commandant was appointed to run the camp. This experience influenced attitudes, as Commander Stoker wrote: '70% of officers held that a man had no right to attempt to escape – owing of course, to the apparent hopelessness of success, and the certainty that others would have to suffer for the attempt.'[789]

Following the Afion Kara Hissar Stoker episode, Colonel G. White, the British senior officer, decided that there should be no further escapes. The early relatively harsh conditions at that camp have already been described, so one can understand his attitude. However, the officers' lives were not tough there. Flight-Sergeant Long, who acted as an orderly at Afion Kara Hissar for a short period, commented bluntly:

> the officers had a life of luxury … This is written in no spirit of churlishness or rancour, for I know that there were some very gallant officers at Afion and other camps, and some most amazing attempts to escape were made by some of them, attempts which entailed the possession of indomitable courage and the ability to endure great hardships. But nothing they suffered under the normal state of captivity can be compared in the slightest to the suffering, degradation and hardships that were the portion of the 'Other Ranks'.[790]

The Kastamuni Four

It did not take Lieutenant Bishop long to decide that he was not prepared to remain at Kastamuni. Freedom was more important to him than the steady camp routine and after the depressing experience of tending to the graves of three officers and three orderlies who had died following their march into captivity, he made his escape with three brother officers on 8 August 1917 – Captain Tipton, who had been captured in Egypt, and fellow 'Kuttites' Captain Sweet and Lieutenant Keeling. Lieutenant Bishop had been hatching plans with his roommate, Lieutenant Keeling, since the previous November, but they realised that any attempt to cross the mountains during winter would be doomed to failure. There was also pressure from the British senior officer not to escape and he wrote 'most people gave their parole not to try to escape under present conditions.'[791] Only eleven officers refused to sign and kept their options open.

Like many other potential escapees, they had the choice of either walking across 300 miles of land to reach the Russians or heading to the sea, north or south, at least forty miles away. The coast and boat option seemed the best, but any plan was cloudy when so little was known about the countryside around them. A map was essential, as were appropriate stores, food and clothing. Lieutenant Bishop commented that the best map was in the commandant's office, but impossible to copy; they did however manage to obtain compasses for navigation from local shops. Eventually, a very basic map of a ridiculously small scale was used – a 1:200,000 map of Turkey (thirty-two miles to the inch) taken from a school book called *History of Persia*.

Lieutenant Keeling wanted two key pieces of information:

1. Where are the Russians, and are they coming nearer?
2. What is the best place on the Black Sea coast at which to look for a boat?[792]

He attempted to gain this knowledge through encrypted postcards sent home, but to little effect. Other geographical intelligence was gained, covertly, from friendly aliens interned locally. 'On the whole these allies recommended us not to make any attempt, one saying that had it been possible he himself would of course have gone long ago. Actually they were afraid of trying anything of the sort or being in any way implicated with us.'[793]

At one stage, some funds were passed to a Greek who claimed that he could find out information about a boat on the coast that they could use, but after receiving the money, he was never seen again. The final plan was to head for the Black Sea in the north and the Crimea, 'to strike the coast near Baffra, steal a boat and make our way to Trebisonde, keeping just in sight of land.'[794] Baffra was a challenging 110 miles away, by the shortest route, from Kastamuni, so the practical distance would be at least 200 miles. Captain Tipton was the sailing expert. Their motivation levels were high, as described by Lieutenant Keeling: 'To have a definite purpose in life made us the happiest prisoners in the camp, and the fact that all our plans had to be made in secret did not detract from their zest.'[795]

Preparations continued. Carrying the right amount and type of food was critical. Bombardier Prosser of the Royal Field Artillery, the mess chef, baked large numbers of hard-tack biscuits made from butter, flour, sugar, eggs and raisins for them. Each of the four men carried

- Food – biscuits, dried goat (like biltong), cheese, chocolate, Horlick's powder, condensed milk, tin of meat, soup squares, meat lozenges, sugar and salt
- Stores – matches, compass, knife and spoon, spare socks, cardigan jacket, a fez, piece of soap, toothbrush, water bottle filled with tea
- Money – £20 of Turkish money hidden in clothing.

In addition, some significant – and some downright astonishing – stores were split amongst the team. These included a sail in two sections, forty feet of rope for rigging, an axe-head, candles, two canteens for cooking, frying pan, cup, towel, fishing tackle, needles and thread to repair the sail, boot repair kit, nails, string, scissors, shaving kit, cocoa, tea, first-field-dressing, quinine, vaseline and tablets to keep them awake.[796] The sail was made from a patchwork of a towel, two valises and a sheet. Measuring ten by seven feet it was going to be used as a 'duvet' for the four men, as they rested during breaks on their trek across the hills.

Clearly a great deal of planning went into the escape. Most of the food had been saved from parcels from home and the stores had been improvised from various locally-purchased articles. Lieutenant Keeling had spent time making bags and rucksacks to hold these treasures, which weighed thirty-five pounds per man.

The group was going to pose as a team of German surveyors. As Lieutenant Bishop put it: 'We had decided that our only chance was to pretend we were Germans, since the country people, while seeing we were not Turks, would be too ignorant to know any difference between Briton and Hun.'[797]

Another prisoner, Captain H. Rich of the 120th Indian Infantry Regiment, provided a pass, written in Turkish, for them.

> To all Turkish Military and Civil Officers:
> Give every assistance to the bearers, Hauptmann Hermann von Below, and his party of three soldiers, who are surveying.
> Signed Osman, Commanding Angora Army Corps[798]

This may not have worked if read by German personnel, but they hoped that it would be good enough for the locals and might help them obtain food en route. The escapees were to draw some improvised badges of German rank which they attached to their tatty British khaki uniforms – additional deception was to be achieved by the wearing of their fezes!

8 August 1917 was a darker evening than usual in Kastamuni, with less moonlight. Bombardier Prosser again helped the group by escorting them through part of the town ensuring that their route was clear. He was certainly a vital character in the escape and had developed a habit of walking through the camp and into the nearby town wearing an old coat, a fez and a false beard! A sealed door was easily opened and six other officers sang loudly and proceeded to open and

shut doors and carry out some noisy bed-repairing. In addition, a partially damaged note, which might be discovered, was left in one of their rooms suggesting that they were heading on a different route to the one they were taking. The first night of freedom went well despite the odd barking dog, more light than expected, some carts moving along the main road and the fact that Captain Sweet's absence had, unluckily, been discovered within two hours of their departure. The Turkish commander of the guards, Sherif Bey, announced the escape to the remaining prisoners by shouting: 'Il n'y a pas trois officiers.'[799]

They had covered about ten miles on the first night before they refilled their waterbottles in a stream and settled down to a routine of walking at night and sleeping by day. Despite being seen by a local boy, fortunately the nearby villagers did not appear interested in them.

Lieutenant Bishop became known as the best navigator as their journey progressed. They travelled for eight hours on the second night, dumped some of their stores because of the weight, but annoyingly lost some soap and a knife in the darkness. They continued their march across rough terrain. They became weaker and thirstier as they struggled through the dark nights, scrounging vegetables from fields and sometimes failing to find water. They covered thirty miles in four nights, but Captain Tipton was suffering from stomach pains, developing a fever and becoming weaker than the rest. At one point, a local saw them and, despite Captain Sweet's attempt to tell him that they were Germans, he identified them as prisoners of war.

> We denied it, and he repeated it, again and again. Then he shrugged his shoulders, mounted his pony and took himself, his boys and his cattle off, while we continued our march, wondering whether he would put gendarmes on our track. None turned up.[800]

They were extremely lucky on that occasion.

Having travelled for eleven nights, they reached a crucial point in their journey as their food stocks had dwindled and they needed to know their exact location. The local villagers were very poor but friendly and seemed to accept their story about being German surveyors. The headman, who was a Turkish sergeant who had fought at Gallipoli, served them various dishes: 'These consisted of cucumber sliced up in milk, yoghurt or curdled milk and chapattis – a feast such as we had hardly dared to hope for.'[801] 'It was not luxurious food, but we all ate about three times as much at this sitting as we had eaten in a whole day for more than a week.'[802] The four escapees had been lucky again, aided by Captain Sweet's knowledge of Turkish, a little money and some 'German' tobacco; the sergeant showed them the route toward their destination, which was still ninety miles away, though the coast was within thirty miles distance. More food, including apples and another meal were obtained from another village and their surveying story continued to convince the locals.

A significant morale-boosting milestone was reached on 21 August when the Black Sea was seen for the first time and the following day they calculated that they had walked nearly 200 miles. Two days later they saw a boat which they thought might provide the opportunity to leave the mainland.

Unfortunately, they were discovered by a Turkish sentry and the team had to attempt to extract themselves from this tricky situation with their cover story. It worked up to a point, but they were obliged to travel in the boat, escorted by Turks, to the town of Jerse (or Gerze), which was six miles north along the coast: 'The situation was not hopeful, but even now it was not certain that all was lost.'[803] The Turks were obviously suspicious and took them to the gendarmerie station at Jerse. There, they had to speak, on the telephone, to a senior German officer at a nearby port. Another attempt to bluff the enemy followed, this time led by the German-speaking Captain Tipton:

He could think of nothing to say but 'Sprechen sie Deutsch?' And having repeated this ad nauseam, he threw down the receiver and remarked with well-simulated disgust that the telephone was out of order.[804]

The bluff did not work and the escapees had to admit that they were English. After a night in a cell, the group was sent back to their original prison. They covered eight miles on the first day. After two weeks at large, they must have been particularly depressed at their failure to succeed; but their fortunes were to change again.

> A few days later [27 August 1916] we were being marched across the mountains 20 miles from the coast on our way back to Kastamuni. Our guard consisting of a sergeant and eight men were suddenly surprised one morning by firing from the side of the road. One was killed, two wounded and they threw down their rifles. Within two minutes our rescuers, who were adherents of the old Turkish Party, had disarmed them all.[805]

Four *akhardash* or comrades had come to the rescue of the escapees who would hide with them for four weeks in the woods and mountains before travelling with them, by boat, to safety. Unfortunately, Captain Sweet was nowhere to be found after the successful ambush. Not realising who was attacking them, he had thought that it was an opportunity to escape again and rushed away; despite an hour's worth of shouting, nothing was seen of him. He was recaptured by some Turkish soldiers a few days later, without any food and stores as they had been lost in the ambush, attempting to take a swim in the sea:

> He was shockingly treated. They had a deep-rooted conviction that he possessed some gold, and when he denied it they first beat him and then held lighted resinous pine splinters between his fingers, until he fainted.[806]

He was a brave officer, who had won his DSO for demolishing the bridge at Kut with Lieutenant Mathews. However, having been returned to imprisonment in a civilian jail at Angorra and then sent to Kastamuni, he was to die of influenza at Yozgad in late 1918. As Lieutenant Keeling wrote, 'He was a brave man who deserved a better fate.'[807]

The fortunate three British officers remained with the *akhardash* and embarked on a boat, with a number of their rescuers, on 23 September. By that time they had walked another 150 miles since they had been recaptured. Three days later they were on the Black Sea, nineteen people in two small boats attempting to navigate by the sun and an old book's inaccurate map. At one stage, Captain Tipton had to navigate as they were heading too far east. The strength of the wind varied and the food began to run out, but relief was at hand as land was sighted on the fourth day.

> At 1230 pm after a voyage of three and a quarter days, and on the forty-ninth day after leaving Kastamuni, we grounded on the beach of a town which was evidently a watering place, and which turned out to be Alupka, on the east coast of the Crimea, about 35 miles south-east of Sevastopol.[808]

Three captives from Kastamuni had been successful in their escape. Captain Tipton's freedom was short-lived, however. As an enthusiastic member of the Royal Flying Corps, he was keen to get back into the air and fight the enemy. On 9 March 1918 he was shot down over France and died of his wounds three days later. There was also a negative impact on the prisoners left at Kastamuni, Captain Keeling acknowledging, 'Our escape had a lamentable effect upon the treatment of officers left behind.'[809] However, despite their increased privations, the hope created by this escape amongst the remaining prisoners was immeasurable.

The Yozgad Break-Out

The success of the 'Kastamuni Four' encouraged some prisoners (although not many) to make their own bid for freedom. One group was to become the 'Yozgad Eight', whose six core planners were mentioned in the previous chapter, when they were incarcerated at Changri at the end of October 1917 – Captains Clarke, Grant, Haig, Harris, Johnston and Yearsley. They were to escape from Yozgad with twenty fellow inmates on 7 August 1918 – a quarter of the camp's officer prisoners.

When they began plotting, they were still at Changri and were better guarded than previously because of the Kastamuni escape and the fact that they were the 'hard-core' of officer prisoners who had refused to sign the parole. It was also an extremely cold winter which did not help their aspirations to cross the surrounding difficult terrain. They had a number of options for escape routes:

> Roughly speaking, there were four alternative directions open to us. Northwards to the Black Sea, a distance of 100 miles; eastwards to the Russian front, 250 to 350 miles; to the Mediterranean, 300 miles southward, or 400 miles westward.[810]

Inspired by an old magazine story about the escape of forty officers from a Confederate prison during the American Civil War, the Changri prisoners began to dig a tunnel. Simultaneously, a plan was conceived for the landing of four Handley-Page aircraft in the vicinity of the camp. This would trigger a break-out, though the ability to coordinate this idea through postcards sent between the camp and Britain would be a major if not impossible challenge. All plans were shelved, including an idea of hiding in the building rafters, as the prisoners were moved eighty miles south to Yozgad Camp.

Attitudes about escaping varied at Yozgad. Conditions were bearable for the inmates, as described earlier, and there were a number of privileges that had been hard-won; 'The prospect of anyone attempting to escape and thereby causing their suspension was looked upon by the majority of the original camp almost with horror.'[811] However, the group of six officers was joined by Lieutenant-Commander Archibald Cochrane, the submariner, and Captain F. Ellis of the Duke of Cornwall's Light Infantry. Lieutenant-Commander Cochrane was a real bonus to the team; he had attempted to escape from Afion Kara Hissar, knew the landscape around there and had managed to communicate with England to arrange a friendly boat to be at a certain point off the Mediterranean coast for a period at the end of August 1918. Their eight-man group was one of four that would make for 'Rendezvous X' and their proposed route was a distance of 450 miles. One of those groups included the ubiquitous Bombardier Prosser who had helped the Kastamuni Four break out. Of the two remaining parties, one was to head for the Black Sea, whilst the other planned to head eastward for Persia.

Preparations continued apace, similar to Kastamuni. Again, food, stores, money and documents had to be prepared. The eight men were each to carry forty-three pounds of equipment and the kit-list was remarkably similar to that of the Kastamuni group, though no improvised sail was carried in this attempt. They even copied the idea of posing as a German survey party and ensured that they had fezes to wear, for walking at night, so that their silhouettes would look Turkish. They were better prepared for water collection than the other escapees, having three improvised fold-away buckets, as well as water bottles. Compasses were obtained from the local market and they managed to scrounge a slightly better map than the other escapees; a French one with a scale equivalent to twenty-four miles to the inch. Another prisoner, a technical Royal Engineer named Captain A. Mathews, used his ingenuity to manufacture a sun compass and star charts to aid navigation.

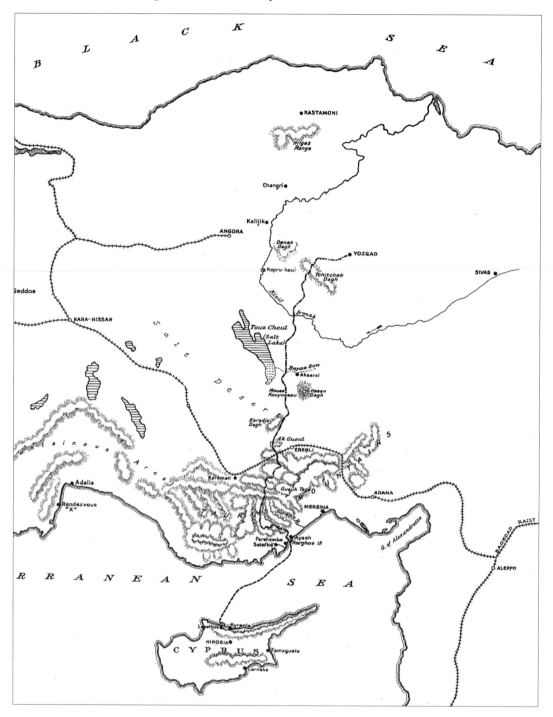

Yozgad to Cyprus. (Johnston and Yearsley)

Cooking pot used in Captain Harris's escape group.
(Royal Hampshire Regiment Museum)

A conscious decision was made not to procure firearms and avoid violence during the
escape, because of the fear of repercussions. The
group started to learn Turkish and took as much
exercise as possible, avoided potentially injuri-
ous contact sports, and built up their fitness and
stamina.

> Running and hard walking round the garden
> became a regular institution in some houses;
> and several cupboards, if suddenly opened at
> almost any hour of the day and at many in the
> night, would have disclosed a member of an
> escape-party loaded up in the most extraordinary
> manner, and performing gymnastic exercises for the strengthening of leg and shoulder muscles.[812]

The break-out was originally planned for 30 July, when there would be little moonlight, but the
date was, frustratingly, missed as there was a rumour that an exchange ship from England was
arriving in Turkey – the prisoners did not want that to disrupt their move. As an escape hole
was prepared in a kitchen building and dummies positioned on beds as a deception measure, the
night of 7/8 August was set for escape. The morning's roll call would be confused by the usual
scramble for the day's sporting 'hunt', hopefully, allowing further valuable undetected time. The
men left the camp at about 2030 hours and despite a barking dog and a crash of crockery that
might have alerted the sentries, a six-and-a-half hour start was achieved before their absence was
discovered. The eight men rendezvoused two miles from Yozgad and then followed a telegraph
line along a ravine; 'Although there was no moon, our eyes rapidly accustomed themselves to the
bright starlight, and hopeful progress was made, but not without occasional alarms.'[813] On their
first morning they saw both a Turkish deserter and some people in the nearby fields, but were
not disturbed. Meanwhile the other groups were breaking out of the camp and setting off on
their own routes in the dark.

They established the same routine as the Kastamuni Four as they rested by day and walked
under cover of darkness. Progress was slow, however, and they were not making the predicted
twelve miles per day. Their first crisis occurred on the fourth night, as Captain Ellis was ill and
had to be left with Captain Grant as the others desperately sought water. After one-and-a-half
miles of walking and having been forced to take Kolas (opium pills) to keep going, they eventually found some stagnant water. Three of them returned to the two officers left behind. Captain
Harris:

> Clarke, Looney and I stayed by a stream all night sharing watches, no sleep, great anxiety, mosquitoes
> and sand flies very bad. About 2.00 am a dog came and stopped about 10 yards from us barking, but
> luckily a man called him off and took no notice of us.[814]

The group gathered together in a cave where they were accosted by a goatherd. In order to
placate him they gave up some spare clothes, tobacco, biscuits and some money. They obtained
some refreshing sour milk and water in return, as well as the hope that he would not give their

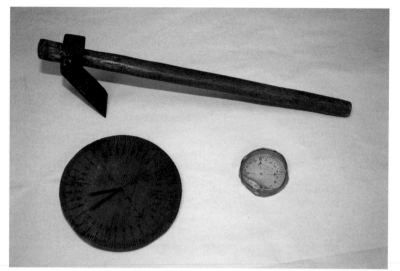

Yozgad escape
equipment –
sun-compass,
compass and pick
(the only potential
weapon carried
by the group).
(Royal Hampshire
Regiment
Museum)

Captain Harris's
cap badge and
'dog-tags' and a
Turkish belt badge.
(Royal Hampshire
Regiment
Museum)

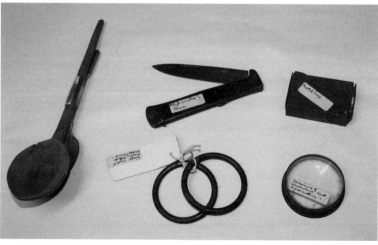

Yozgad escape
equipment
– spoons,
fire-lighting
kit and lens for
lighting fires.
(Royal Hampshire
Regiment
Museum)

position away. On the following night he returned with another shepherd and, to buy his silence, they gave him more money and a watch. They learned, however, that there were a number of gendarmes searching for them in the hills and the shepherds advised that they remain still and hidden for three days. They also offered themselves up as guides, though insisted on receiving more money.

On the morning of 13 August they thought that their luck had run out. One of the shepherds ran down to them and said gendarmes were coming and moments later they were confronted by two tatty looking policemen.

> What was more important than their dress, however, was the fact that we found ourselves looking down the muzzles of a rifle and revolver carried ready for trigger-pressing by Beau Brummel and his seedy-looking friend. These two gentlemen now came to the kneeling position for greater effect.[815]

The shepherd denied any friendly attachment to the British group and one even gave Captain Grant a nasty blow on the head. After a brief discussion with the Turks, during which one of them asked whether the officers wanted to go home or stay imprisoned, a deal was made, money passed hands and the escapees continued their journey.

> We have already had to bribe four people, and there is not much bribing power left. We are likely to be very thirsty in the near future. In fact, in appreciating the situation it cannot in any sense be a hopeful one. Nevertheless, we are still free men![816]

By the eighth night, the group was tiring, moving slowly and sometimes struggling to find water supplies, but they kept going. Food stocks were running low with nine day's worth left and still 180 miles to go. A significant psychological marker, the River Kizil Irmak, was crossed on the tenth night; they enjoyed wading across the 300 yards of water. They ran into some inquisitive shepherds and the following day had to peddle their German survey cover-story, but they seemed to succeed in bluffing their way. On the twelfth night they thought that they saw a group of men waiting to ambush them in the hills and had to take an alternate route to avoid them. They decided to keep walking during the day so that they could cover more distance.

Their next significant incident occurred late morning on 20 August, following their discovery by two men on donkeys and two boys. They had moved 700 yards away when 'a rifle bullet whizzed over our heads and plunked into the higher ground some distance beyond.'[817] Captain Harris:

> Halted. Thought game up, gendarmes, but Cochrane and Grant went back to talk, we followed slowly 400 yards behind, they began moving back, refused to talk. Cochrane told us six to keep in sight of them. Two recognised as two previous meetings. One of men indicated now by acting that we were to de-clothe and go away at which Cochrane and Grant ran back towards us followed by brigands firing, all of us then doubled and walked 100 yards alternately in open order and , although very near, no one hit. Repeated firing. Gradually outdistanced them.[818]

They had been very lucky. They lost some of their water, which was heavy to carry, but they could not afford to drop their packs of precious food and stores and so ran as fast as they could carrying the weight. They were tired, but with the boost of adrenalin they managed to outpace their pursuers. They failed to find more water. Captain Harris noted on the following night: 'Very cold wind, most people rather dispirited, few of us optimistic.'[819] Their food was running out and the conditions were becoming worse, with difficult stony ground to cross and colder nights to endure.

The flight from Moses' Well. (Johnston and Yearsley)

A big decision was made on their seventeenth night, 23/24 August 1918. The next village simply had to be entered to obtain food. The whole group needed revitalising, but Captain Grant in particular was feeling extremely weak from his previous head wound and had even volunteered to be left behind. Captain Harris had his last meal of Quaker Oats before three of the escapees smartened up their appearance as best they could to pose as Germans, and walked into the village. The remainder decided that if the three were caught, then they would give themselves up.

The three entered a shop in the village and were then directed to another building where they were confronted by a Turkish soldier. Once they had told him who they were, he proceeded to speak fluent German, which would have been fine except none of them knew any more than a few words! Further bluffing followed, as they said that they were actually Magyars (Hungarians) and then they were led for an audience with the headman of the village. They were bombarded with many questions and there was every chance their ploy would be discovered because of their poorly-camouflaged British uniform buttons and the fact that they even had to barter with some English-labelled tea, but they managed to get away with it. The three actually enjoyed a quick meal before buying some food from the villagers. The next tricky challenge was returning to their fellow Britons with the headman and two other men from the village in tow. They produced an imaginative solution: 'As soon as the party could get their equipment on we formed up in two ranks. 'Grunt' made some guttural sounds, at which we 'left turned' and started to march off into the blue, leaving three very puzzled men behind us.'[820]

Once again they had been very lucky. They had restocked their food supplies and were able to settle down to a real feast, stopping in a valley described as 'our Paradise' in Captain Harris's diary: 'Beautiful stream under trees at bottom, where we bathed and washed clothes. First time halted one-and-a-quarter hours, passed cave village, scoffed six eggs and four chapattis.'[821]

The group then pressed on over difficult rocky ground for the next four days until they again needed more water and food. They were no longer able to sustain themselves and had lost their independence. On 28 August they approached some Kurdish tents and were able to scrounge more food in exchange for some money. This kept them going until they reached their next psychologically uplifting goal – a view of the sea on the morning of 30 August.

They were exhausted after twenty-three nights of walking. They only had three days of food left and they knew that their next challenge was to find a boat.

> With heads uncovered, and with thankful hearts, we stood gazing, but without in any way being excited. Thus it was that no shout like the 'Thalassa! Thalassa!' of Xenophon's Ten Thousand broke from the lips of our little band that still August morning; although here was the end of our land journey at last in sight after a march of some 330 miles.[822]

A motor boat was seen later that day, but for the next few days they had no energy to find where it had come from. In those first few days of September 1918, they were running out of food and hope. Captain Harris noted: 'People getting very despondent and some practically chucking their hands in.'[823] Captains Johnston and Yearsley wrote that

> Life became a dreary grind, both literally and metaphorically. For the next few days, at any rate, we thought of nothing else but how to prepare and eat as much food as we could. This was not greed: it was the only thing to do. None of us wanted to lie a day longer than absolutely necessary in that awful ravine, but we were at present simply too weak to help ourselves. To carry out a search for another boat was beyond the powers of anyone.[824]

They gradually shook off their lethargy after a week's recuperation and discovered two boats, in their anchorage, on 7 September. A frenzy of activity followed as they procured more food and stores from a nearby village. Reserves of food, mainly chapattis, were prepared for their forthcoming sea journey and three sails were stitched together from lengths of material procured from the village and canvas taken from their packs. Spars and paddles were also improvised.

They made their first bid to obtain one of the boats on the night of 10/11 September. Having taken their boots off to reduce noise, they scrambled in the dark with all of their stores down a ravine to the coast. They failed in their bid, as after hours of trying, they could not set free the anchor of the chosen boat. They attempted to shift it three times, and Lieutenant-Commander Cochrane and Captain Johnston dived into the cold water, but gave up at 0300 hours when a Turkish sentry came to investigate a noise. The group hid amongst the rocks waiting for the following night to try again.

> Our thirty-fifth morning found us in state of great depression. There seemed no chance left of getting out of the country. Lying in our hiding-places we reviewed the situation in an almost apathetic mood.[825]

They were not going to give up at that stage, however. The following afternoon they saw a motor boat towing a dhow and dinghy into the anchorage and hearts lifted immediately. A plan was hatched to bribe the crew to take them to Cyprus. The stores were moved to the beach, as Captain's Haig and Clarke managed to procure the dinghy and bring it back to the waiting group. The eight escapees then paddled the dinghy to the motor boat, as its crew sat on the dhow about fifty yards away. Silently they freed the boat, the thirty-eight-foot *Hertha*, and somehow managed to weigh anchor, muffling any noises with their coats and bits of cloth. They attached the dinghy to the boat and paddled both away from the anchorage without disturbing the nearby crew. Two miles out of the bay, they clambered onboard the boat.

The motor boat used for the escape to Cyprus. (Johnston and Yearsley)

Initially, they could not start the engine and almost lost their stores because no one had secured the dinghy, but they made some headway by sail. 'At about 5, engine suddenly started up. Yells (silent) of joy.'[826] The group was elated and recorded 'it now seemed as if our troubles were nearing their end.'[827] The engine was running and they seemed to have sufficient fuel, water and food to survive the next leg of their journey. They had 120 miles to cover; their fear was being discovered by another boat or by a Turkish seaplane, though at least they found that they were carrying a couple of Mauser rifles and a few rounds of ammunition, should they need them.

Their problems were not over. After eight hours at full speed, the engine seized up just as they thought they could see Cyprus in the distance. Another agonisingly slow hour passed as the engine cooled, and it was another two hours before they succeeded in starting her up again. They reached a small bay in the evening of 12 September. 'And so we had reached Cyprus, but we were all in too dazed a condition to realise for the moment what it meant; in fact, it took many days to do so.'[828] Early on 13 September 1918, they were towed in by twelve Cypriots and made welcome at the Lapithos Police Station.

> Here we stepped on British soil, eight thin and weary ragamuffins. We know our hearts gave thanks
> to God, though our minds could not grasp that we were really free.[829]

Their escape from Yozgad was an amazing achievement. They had spent thirty-six days roaming in enemy territory before sailing to Cyprus. Despite a series of close shaves with the local population, difficult terrain and shortages of food and water, they had succeeded. Luck had been on their side, but Captains Johnston and Yearsley were convinced that a 'higher Power' had helped – 'We feel then that it was Divine intervention which brought us through.'

All of the other Yozgad escapees from 7 August were recaptured, though one other party did succeed in remaining free for eighteen days. Fortunately, the War only had a few months to run.

Madness

Two famous escapers from Yozgad Camp were Welsh gunner officer, Lieutenant Elias Jones, and the Australian aviator, Lieutenant Cedric Hill. Theirs is one of the most famous of the First World War escape stories, indeed of any war. A Second World War escapee, Eric Williams of 'Wooden Horse' fame, wrote:

> Of all these escapes, however, for sheer ingenuity, persistence and skill, [the Jones/Hill escape] is second to none. It has become the classic of 'escape by strategy' as opposed to 'escape by tactics'.[830]

These two officers were to gain their freedom after a very painful deception plan, which began in February 1917 when a number of prisoners set up the Psychic Research Society of Yozgad. This was another way of keeping minds occupied in prison and a couple of groups constructed improvised ouija boards using bits of wood, cut out letters of the alphabet and glass tumblers. Lieutenant Jones managed to memorise the positions of the letters and could locate them blindfolded. He could tell where the letters on the table were in relation to his seat and knew exact places on the table by touch. As some of the rival spiritual groups floundered, he was able to maintain his credibility, claiming that he could contact a spirit medium. He contacted 'Sally' to begin with and admitted 'I had fully intended to tell them that I had steered the glass with my eyes shut, from my memory of the position of the letters. But the talk became too good to interrupt.'[831]

Lieutenant Jones was enjoying himself, making up some amusing stories and gradually persuading his colleagues that he was a genuine spiritualist – the lack of hope existing in the prison probably encouraged credulousness, especially when he seemed to produce results even when put under 'test conditions' by the other prisoners. (It is well known that interest in the occult and spiritualism increases in time of war!) He gradually gained quite a reputation whilst not admitting to anyone that he was actually a fraud.

By April 1917, his skill was well-known in Yozgad and the Turkish interpreter, Moise, began to take an interest, claiming that the commandant, Bimbashi Kiazim Bey, was also aware of his abilities. An idea came into Lieutenant Jones' mind.

> Hitherto spooking had been merely a jest, with a psychological flavouring to lend it interest. But now a serious element was being introduced. If I could do to the Turks what I had succeeded in doing to my fellow prisoners, if I could make them believers, there was no saying what influence I might not be able to exert over them. It might even open the door to freedom.[832]

Ouija board.
(Jones)

Moise asked him whether he might be able to find some Armenian buried treasure in the area so Lieutenant Jones organised a ploy to increase his credibility. Without admitting to fellow-prisoners that he was a fraud, he gained their support in tricking Moise into believing his talent. A rusty pistol and some ammunition had earlier been found, separately, by some of the inmates. These items were placed together and buried. During a séance, witnessed by Moise, Lieutenant Jones went into a 'trance' and guided the interpreter to the cache. The Turk had been convinced about the lieutenant's 'powers', whilst the prisoners had enjoyed the practical joke. For Lieutenant Jones 'it was the first real step in a considered plan of escape'.[833]

News of Lieutenant Jones's achievements was fed to the commandant who summoned him to his office at the end of January 1918. Bimbashi Kiazim Bey wanted the young officer to help him discover the Armenian 'treasure' that was assumed to be buried in the area, following the Turkish persecution of the Armenians. Lieutenant Jones agreed to help and to maintain secrecy and realised, with great satisfaction, that he had 'hooked' the commandant. The next stage was to identify a companion who could be taken into confidence and support the escape bid – Lieutenant Hill was his choice.

Lieutenant Hill had a reputation for being determined to escape, and had been prevented from doing so by the British senior officer in spring of 1917 because of the fear of the consequences for those left behind at Yozgad. He was very fit and was also known to be an accomplished conjuror. Their pact had some simple rules:

- To risk everything and go any length to get away
- On no account to implicate anyone else in the camp. We must so arrange the escape that the Turks would have no excuse whatsoever for 'strafing'[834] the others
- To take nobody into our confidence until it was absolutely necessary
- When possible, to discuss every move beforehand, and to follow the line agreed on
- If circumstances prevented such discussion, Hill was to follow my lead blindly, without question or alteration
- If or when it came to a bolt across country, Hill was to take charge.[835]

The two officers gradually became a team. Together, they learned a code and demonstrated their telepathic 'powers' in a stage-show to the camp's population. Lieutenant Jones was blindfolded in their act and seemed to be able to identify various objects without seeing them. They continued to impress the interpreter and hoped, as well, that they were impressing the commandant. They were hoping, bizarrely, that they would be imprisoned in harsh conditions for their spiritual activity and then eventually achieve a compassionate release from the authorities.

The two officers achieved their first aim on 6 March 1918 when they were charged, following a series of séances, for 'obtaining and sending military information by means of telepathy.'[836] They were to be sentenced to solitary confinement until the end of the War. The previous month had been spent conducting séances with the interpreter during which they claimed that they had knowledge about events outside the camp, through their spiritual contact on the ouija board – the 'Spook'. The Spook also gave them guidance on how they should go about finding the Armenian treasure, but advised them that they should be isolated together in prison, away from any distractions, if they wanted results. Meanwhile, Lieutenant Hill buried two small packages which contained improvised 'treasure' for future use.

On 6 March, both officers and four other prisoners were ordered to see the commandant to talk about their thought-reading and telepathy. Lieutenant Jones acknowledged that he had sent and received messages by telepathy and had discovered war news as a result. The commandant demanded to know who his correspondent was and said that, if he was not given the information within twenty-four hours, then Lieutenant Jones would be placed in solitary confinement. Before both officers were taken away, Lieutenant-Colonel Henry St John Maule, the British senior officer, attempted to discover what was going on and was told by them the same fantastical story. Confused, he placed them on parole, so they were obliged not to escape; they had other plans.

Their new home was not unpleasant as they were placed together in a well-equipped house in Yozgad and their food improved – the commandant still wanted his treasure. Their aim was to gain evidence of the commandant's deal with them and to inform the British authorities of their 'harsh' conditions. For this, they procured a camera and planned to take pictures of their 'tortured' bodies – if necessary harming themselves to provide false evidence. Further séances, in the presence of the interpreter, occurred and the 'Spook' provided more information that seemed genuine, helping to persuade both Moise and the commandant that their spiritual powers were genuine and that the treasure might eventually be discovered. Spook's next move was to demand, through the ouija board, that the two officers should go on a reduced diet 'to increase clairvoyant powers.'[837] This would allow the two lieutenants to appear gaunt and they could use their worsening appearance to encourage the belief that either they were poorly-treated – or to lay the groundwork for another story, that they were insane! Ironically, one of their challenges was trying to avoid receiving too much support from their fellow prisoners – naturally, they were keen to help them and to smuggle food into their house. As the time passed, both Lieutenants Jones and Hill became increasingly confident.

> The Turks were now like children in the Hampton Court maze when a fog has come down. They were properly lost in our labyrinth, and appealed to the 'Spook' to tell them what was happening.[838]

At the end of March and beginning of April, they managed to stage two particularly effective spiritual performances that resulted in the discovery of two of the treasure troves by the Turks. They were able to take a few covert pictures of the commandant to show that he was a participant. They decided to gain the support and non-intervention of the rest of the prisoners by passing a package to the camp's doctor, Captain W. O'Farrell, Royal Army Medical Corps. This included an outline of their plans, plus the camera and negatives showing the commandant's involvement. They still hoped that they had two options – escaping from another camp or being sent home for madness. Their next masquerade had them being attacked by a malignant 'spook'. A large explosion was heard by the Turks (it was actually a trap-door being shut hard) and the two prisoners shouted and raged and succeeded in hurting themselves as if they had been attacked by an invisible force. The Turks thought that the time had come to move them from Yozgad. 'Spook' was encouraging those thoughts and suggesting that they should be moved towards the coast, as that would be where the main treasure would be found.

However, despite their success at hoodwinking the commandant, Lieutenants Jones and Hill were not moved and were about to be released from solitary confinement. They made up their minds to go for option two, to feign madness. Apart from their self-harming, they wrote letters to the Sultan and Enver Pasha claiming that their fellow British prisoners were attempting to murder them, whilst the commandant was extremely kind and looking after them well. They ensured that their appearance worsened by sticking to a meagre diet of bread and tea and remaining unshaven and dirty and they made sure that they were violently sick in their accommodation, which they covered in filth. Their behaviour led to an examination by Turkish doctors in the middle of April. As the two prisoners were being examined, they both acted strangely and illogically and once again duped their audience, who recommended that they should be sent to Constantinople for further examination.

On 26 April 1918, the two officers left Yozgad, escorted by Moise. A few days before they had met some of the prisoners who were to escape from the camp on 7 August and were given the opportunity to join them, however, their path was set. They continued their masquerade of madness on the journey and were seriously considering faking their suicide at some stage – the 'Spook' informed Moise that they were likely to make the attempt.

Two years after the surrender of Kut, 29 April 1918, they were staying overnight at a town called Mardeen when they made their mock suicide attempt. When no one was looking, Lieutenant Hill prepared two nooses amongst their luggage and they signalled to each other that they were ready for their ruse. As they lulled their escorts into a false sense of security by behaving strangely, but quietly, Lieutenant Hill successfully kept them spellbound by some conjuring tricks. He then persuaded them to leave the room that they were in whilst another trick was prepared. As they left, the two officers quickly stepped up on a table and secured the ropes above them. They simultaneously kicked the table away and blew out the candle that was illuminating the room. Lieutenant Jones wrote:

> When we stepped off our table in the dark at Mardeen we simply had to bear it, and though we had arranged to grip the rope with one hand so as to take as much weight as possible off the neck until we heard Moise at the door, the pain was excruciating. Moise did not at once notice that our light had gone out. I revolved slowly on the end of my rope.[839]

They were both suffering a lot of pain but their performance was effective. The Turks were convinced that their act had been genuine and that the prisoners had only been saved from death by the swift intervention of their guards. They had rushed into the room, cut the pair down and then swiftly tipped buckets of water over them. Once the two prisoners had recovered from their dazed state, Lieutenant Jones proceeded to be abusive and noisy and began telling the guards that he was terrified that the British were trying to kill him – a story he continued to peddle as he remained in captivity - whilst Lieutenant Ellis faked unconsciousness complete with dropped jaw and protruding tongue. They continued to act strangely as they proceeded to Angora, where they arrived on 1 May 1918. Their confidence grew and they realised that there was a reasonable chance that they might be released. A few days later, they were admitted to the Haida Pasha Hospital in Constantinople.

Both prisoners prepared themselves for their examination. They ensured that they were as weak as possible by avoiding food and sleep and when they arrived in a ward of ten beds they realised that they would need to stay alert and be very canny if they were to persuade their captors that they had gone mad. They would be under constant surveillance by both the Turkish doctors and their fellow-patients. Captain O'Farrell, the medical officer at Yozgad, had previously advised them that they needed to maintain the 'insane look' at all times.[840]

At first, the doctors appeared to believe that Lieutenant Jones must have had syphilis at some stage in his life and that the disease was causing his current behaviour, though he vehemently denied this. Instead, he continued to act the loon, denied that he had ever attempted to commit suicide and said that he was still terrified of the British. Whilst Lieutenant Jones was noisy and difficult to control, Lieutenant Hill was insular and very quiet, so the Turks had difficulty obtaining any answers to their questions. Both their performances were persuasive. Lieutenant Jones succeeded in sending Madame Paulus, an official representative of the Dutch Embassy, away in tears after she had spoken to him in the ward. Another British patient, Captain Mousley, stayed at the hospital for a while and described his antics.

In the middle of the night I saw a ghoulish figure, wearing a large black mantle and with stark, staring eyes, stalking me from bed to bed … He wore a back overall, a yard of which he had picked into threads, which his busy fingers did incessantly. His hair was long, he wore a beard, and his white, sunken cheeks gave him a ghastly appearance.[841]

However, once he knew that Lieutenant Jones was putting on an act, he was convinced that at least some of the Turks must have realised he was not a genuine case.

They must have been unsure, though, as a highly eminent Turkish doctor, who specialised in mental disorders, Mazhar Osman Bey, was now brought in to help diagnose the two officers. He quickly tested their blood and spinal fluid for traces of syphilis, which proved negative. There was now a pile of evidence that had built up – doctors' reports, written comments from Yozgad's commandant, the spiritualist and telepathic record, the attempted suicides, the interpreter's views and the various letters that had been sent to the Turkish hierarchy.

Our task was 'to keep it up' until the exchange steamer arrived. It was a desperate time for both of us. We were watched night and day. We knew that a single mistake would spoil everything for both.[842]

Lieutenant Hill went through a particularly difficult month when he was held at Gumush Suyu Hospital. His act of severe melancholy continued, but the authorities there decided that he was probably malingering and treated him badly. Lieutenant Jones had been admitted at the same time, but through his continued bizarre performance, after thirty-six hours he was returned to Haida Pasha Hospital. Unfortunately, Lieutenant Hill was suffering from a severe bout of dysentery, was close to death and was handled cruelly. Lieutenant Jones was disgusted by the treatment his friend endured and wrote 'But this I know: they showed a callousness and a brutality in their treatment of Hill which drew violent expostulations from the British patients in the hospital, and for which the doctors deserve to be horse-whipped.'[843]

Hill's maltreatment is an example of why some of the Turkish handling of POWs during the First World War has been compared with Japanese practices during the Second. Lieutenant Hill was only kept alive by efforts made by another British prisoner, Captain T. White, who managed to smuggle milk and medicine to him. Having lost five stone in weight, he was moved to Psamatia Camp, where Lieutenant-Colonel Baines of the Indian Medical Services was persuaded of his madness and wrote to the Turkish authorities demanding that he be repatriated or they would find themselves responsible for his death.

Lieutenant Hill was repatriated in the second week of October 1918 and was joined in Egypt, a few days later, by Lieutenant Jones. Their escape story was quite extraordinary and they had had to endure extreme hardships in order to achieve their aim. They obtained their freedom just two weeks before the Armistice.

Reward

The 'Yozgad Eight' were all to receive Military Crosses or, in the cases of Captain Ronald 'Grunt' Grant of the 112th Indian Infantry and Captain Kenneth 'Looney' Yearsley of the Royal Engineers, bars to existing Military Crosses, for their escape. Captain Harry Bishop, 66th Punjabis of the Indian Army Reserve of Officers and one of the 'Kastamuni Four' was also awarded the Military Cross. Their names were listed, amongst other successful First World War escapers, in *The Times* on 2 February 1920:[844]

The King has been pleased to approve of the following rewards in recognition of gallant conduct and determination displayed in escaping or attempting to escape from captivity, which services have been brought to notice in accordance with the terms of Army Order 193 of 1919.[845]

Notes

786. Captain Mousley at Kastamuni in the spring of 1917. Mousley (1921) p.231.
787. Long (1938) p.123.
788. Neave (1937) p.196.
789. Stoker (1925) p.293.
790. Long (1938) p.198.
791. Bishop (1920) p.105.
792. Keeling (1924) p.75.
793. Bishop (1920) p.109.
794. Ibid p.238.
795. Keeling (1924) p.78.
796. Ibid p.79–80.
797. Bishop (1920) p.112.
798. Keeling (1924) p.84.
799. Johnston and Yearsley (1919) p.3.
800. Keeling (1924) p.98.
801. Bishop (1920) p.155.
802. Keeling (1924) p.101.
803. Ibid p.112.
804. Ibid p.13.
805. Bishop (1919) p.240.
806. Keeling (1924) p.132.
807. Ibid p.133.
808. Ibid p.146.
809. Ibid p.104.
810. Johnston and Yearsley (1919) p.9–10.
811. Ibid p.61–62.
812. Ibid p.77.
813. Ibid p.100.
814. Captain Harris diary (undated) p.2.
815. Johnston and Yearsley (1919) p.125.
816. Ibid p.130.
817. Ibid p.159.
818. Captain Harris diary (undated) p.6.
819. Ibid.
820. Johnston and Yearsley (1919) p.189.
821. Captain Harris diary (undated) p.7.
822. Johnston and Yearsley (1919) p.227–228.
823. Captain Harris diary (undated) p.11.
824. Johnston and Yearsley (1919) p.244.
825. Ibid p.269.
826. Captain Harris diary (undated) p.13.
827. Johnston and Yearsley (1919) p.278.
828. Ibid p.286.
829. Ibid p.288.
830. Jones (1955 edition of 1919) p.7.
831. Ibid p.14.
832. Ibid p.36–37.
833. Ibid p.54.
834. 'Strafing' was the prisoners' term for Turkish punishment of the entire prison population if anyone escaped.
835. Jones (1955 edition of 1919) p.65.
836. Ibid p.71.
837. Ibid p.102.
838. Ibid p.124.
839. Ibid p.191.
840. Ibid p.209.
841. Mousley (1921) p.358.
842. Jones (1955 edition of 1919) p.231.
843. Ibid p.234.
844. Lieutenant Keeling had also been awarded the Military Cross.
845. *The Times* 2 Feb 1920.

Chapter Twelve

FREEDOM

We were proud to receive a gracious message from His Majesty the King, expressing his pleasure at our liberation and his hope that we should have a good time at home among our own people.[846]

Differing Experiences

Freedom for the 'Kuttites' came in different forms. Some of the British and Indian soldiers were lucky enough, as severely wounded personnel, to have been repatriated immediately after the fall of the town, following the bitter disappointment that the anticipated parole for the garrison was not going to happen. A few escaped from Turkish captivity. Others would have over two-and-a-half years of servitude in appalling conditions before they were able to return home. Many never made it. The survival statistics are stark. Of the 2,592 British officers and men that went into captivity, 1,755 died. 10,486 Indians were incarcerated and 3,063 did not survive.[847]

Even these figures are optimistic when one takes into account the lack of accurate information about the Kut prisoners and the 1918 Spanish Flu, which also took its toll on the survivors.[848] In a Baghdad cemetery alone, 1,248 of the dead were collected from camps and roadsides by the Graves Commission.

The prisoners – like all POW survivors – would have felt mixed emotions on their release, which followed the 30 October 1918 armistice with Turkey; guilt, because they had survived when many friends had not, coupled with the ecstasy of gaining freedom and the prospect of seeing their families again. The campaign in Mesopotamia had not always received a great deal of publicity compared with the great battles elsewhere, so whilst some of the Kut survivors were treated as heroes, many of the ex-prisoners quietly and quickly reintegrated into society. From many, there would also be the call for retribution against Turkey.

Arthur Kingsmill of the 2nd Battalion Queens' Own Royal West Kent Regiment was extremely lucky. He had a wound in his right ankle, which was examined by a Turkish doctor at the conclusion of the siege in April 1916 and he was chosen to be repatriated. This surprised one of the British doctors who said to him, 'Kingsmill, you're the luckiest chap the company has in this hospital.'[849] He left Kut on 6 May, heading downstream, in a hospital ship. Once on board, he was offered a bath: 'It was the first for six months and after it I felt as though I was walking on air.'[850] This was the same day that the other ranks began their long march from Shumran to the prison camps; his quick route to freedom was not typical.

Lieutenant Keeling of Yozgad Four fame had his freedom acknowledged at Yalta, in the Russian Crimea, by the local Soviet. Once home, he had the honour of being received by George V and he was to become instrumental in the process for release of other prisoners at the end of the War. Apart from the welcome royal interest, he was not impressed by the official reception of prisoners, writing that 'His Majesty received officers who had escaped a good deal more warmly than did some War Office generals, who wanted to get on with the War and considered us rather a nuisance.'[851]

He was also not impressed by the disparate and uncoordinated departmental approach towards prisoners of war. With that in mind, now as Lieutenant-Colonel Keeling, he pulled together an unofficial 'pressure group', the 'Prisoners in Turkey Committee', mentioned in the previous chapter, in order to influence government departments and improve the lot of those still in captivity. He was also placed on 'special duty' to assist officers in escaping. He eventually returned to Mesopotamia in October 1918 and helped with the repatriation of prisoners.

Major-General Townshend

Townshend returned to England in early November 1918. En route he had met his wife in Paris and been cordially received by the French Premier, Clemenceau, but he did not receive an official welcome at home, despite the popularity and support that had been evident in England in 1916 when he had received his knighthood. His cousin wrote 'in England, only his personal friends made any fuss about his return'[852] and Townshend recorded, disappointed: 'I reached Victoria Station on Saturday 9 November, and had a warm welcome from a few friends and relations.'[853]

Whilst family and friends made the most of their 'hero' and he received applause when he attended a show at a theatre, it was not seen to be appropriate for the Government to make a fuss of him, especially as the Turkish treatment of prisoners was receiving publicity. His lack of friends in high places was discussed in Chapter Ten – he was not going to receive any support from either Field Marshal Haig or General Robertson. He was frustrated and disappointed, writing in a letter to the War Office 'I am utterly cast down and cannot believe that such unjust treatment is intentional.'[854] He was placed on half-pay from 9 January 1919 and his demands for promotion and employment were rejected despite his personal appeal to the Secretary of State for War, Winston Churchill. Churchill told him that his promotion had not been recommended by his previous bosses in Mesopotamia, Generals Nixon and Lake. His position was not helped by rumours that he had offered his services to Austria at the beginning of the War and had made the error of presenting Halil with a horse when he surrendered Kut to him. He had never been politic in his approach to life and now excuses were being corralled to ensure that he faded into the background. The lack of attention given to ex-prisoners of war was spotted by *The Sunday Times,* which used Major-General Townshend's treatment as an example. It stated that even though he had been home for three months, he had been ignored, his recommendations of honours and promotions for his subordinates had not come to fruition and that his promotion had been stopped.[855]

Townshend's book, published in 1920, was one way in which he was determined to regain respect.[856] He made a point of saying that he had received hundreds of letters expressing appreciation of his efforts. One was received from Major-General Kemball, who had commanded 28th Brigade attempting to relieve Kut.

My Dear Townshend,

I was very glad to see in Reuter's that you had arrived safely at home, and had had a great reception in London. I hope that at the end of the War you will receive still higher recognition of your services, and that the gallant 6th Division may also be specially honoured.

Nothing, however, can make up to you and them for your long and terrible captivity, and I can assure you that the fate of the gallant garrison of Kut was deeply felt by all.

I also sympathise with you in having lost all further opportunity to show the great generalship you displayed until you were taken prisoner from no fault of your own. It was unfortunate that Nixon's health broke down when it did, for I felt sure he would have got you out …

However, the elements fought against us, and it was a difficult task under existing conditions. The troops were all right and fought most gallantly, in spite of very heavy losses, especially from machine-gun fire.

Hoping that you are well.'[857]

His cousin's book of 1928 also fought his corner and quoted from a speech by Lord Birkenhead, the Lord Chancellor, in May 1919. 'He said his want of success was due to the inadequate means given him for the work, and spoke of the way the troops had cheered him when he was being taken away into captivity, showing what confidence they had in him.'[858]

The 'authorities' were not so complimentary. An assessment of Major-General Townshend is in Appendix V.

More Typical Experiences

Few prisoners could predict when they might be released, as it had not been long since they had received the bad news about the German spring offensive of 1918 on the Western Front. There was some optimism as September approached, though the camps continued to gather firewood for the coming winter. Many pessimists in Afion Kara Hissar were predicting that release might not arrive until 1920. However, good news arrived at the camp in October and Major Sandes noted the inmates' reaction.

> The joy in our camp in October 1918 was positively delirious at times. The news seemed too good to be true … We scarcely knew whether we stood on our heads or our heels … At last we were free men, though it was difficult to believe it … The camp was no longer the depressing abode of prisoners of war; it was more like a beehive with the bees buzzing their loudest.'[859]

Private Goode's reaction to peace was typical: 'It was the day of our lives when we saw the first armoured car enter Nisibin. We all fairly went mad for a time.'[860] Restrictions were relaxed and groups of ill prisoners were exchanged for sick Turks in British hands. As part of the repatriation process, most prisoners were concentrated at coastal locations, having been moved from the various inland camps. *The Times* correspondent, Mr G. Ward Price, observed that the prisoners that he saw seemed remarkably healthy, but he had missed the point that in a Darwinian sense they were the most robust and had been lucky to survive. Many gathered at Smyrna (now Izmir) and the first batch left the port on the Australian hospital ship *Kanowna* on 1 November 1918. Lieutenant Elton travelled by ship and recorded his feelings:

> Going up that gangway on to the transport in the roadstead of Smyrna I had looked up and seen the British flag fluttering overhead against a blue sky, and thought, 'Now I am a prisoner; and now,' stepping off the gangway on to the deck, 'I am free.'"[861]

Sergeant Coombes also expressed his fellow-soldiers' elation.

> It seemed as if each one had been resurrected. To feel ourselves homeward bound on a British steamer, free once more, was something that cannot be described, but it was true at last. Those of us who came home were indeed lucky, as right to the last some were carried off by Spanish flu and some buried at sea.[862]

Major Sandes arrived at Alexandria, by ship, on 16 November. Many of the men were taken to Egypt and then sent to Calais by train; Private Goode's overland journey across Europe took ten days.

> When we arrived at Versailles we were met by French Red Cross nurses, who gave us Oxo, chocolates and rosettes, and we embarked for Dover on 10 January 1919, having a very rough voyage from Calais, but nobody seemed to mind with the cliffs of old England in sight.[863]

Private Hughes vented his feelings:

> There was not a man amongst us who wished to remain in Turkey one minute longer than was necessary, where we had been through purgatory. It was very sad that at the beginning of our home journey, 10 minutes after we had started, Gunner Illingsworth, of the Bombay Volunteer Artillery Battery, who had struggled through the last four years of adversities, lay down and died and was buried in the Sea of Marmora, adding yet one more to the number never to see home again.[864]

The surviving sepoys of the 3/7th Rajputs, like many of the Indian troops, were gathered together at Alleppo, transported by ship to Alexandria and repatriated to India in January 1919, though

> … many who had been given up for dead arrived from remote parts of Asia Minor weeks and even months later. Of them it may be truly said, 'These are they who came out of great tribulation'.[865]

120 of the regiment returned to India from the 301 other ranks who went into captivity – the rest had 'disappeared'.

Most elation was felt when arriving back at home. Lieutenant Elton believed that it was at Charing Cross Station, London, when he began to feel free, because he was on his own, rather than part of a herd of soldiery. He described his arrival at Winchester station.

> I leaned out of the window and saw my father standing anxiously on the platform in his fur coat. I waved, and by the time the train stopped he was at my door. I tumbled out into the embrace of his fur coat. 'I can't believe it's you,' he said. Tears were streaming down his cheeks.[866]

No one can describe effectively the emotions felt by those released after such a long time of unpredictable captivity. Captain Mousley tried to sum up his feelings, which were also inspired by a final rail journey:

> It was a carriage for the most part of silent men from all fronts. Out of the window, hedges, fields, crows, trees, England flew by. I had a desire to get out and walk every yard. I had an impulse. No, it is too private to record. I was free. England, England, England.[867]

The Reverend Harold Spooner

A hero of the siege, Reverend Spooner, the Anglican padre, was never truly 'free' after his experiences of Kut and subsequent captivity. Major-General Townshend chose to recognise the padre for his skills and he was awarded the Military Cross for his work, which included remaining behind with the wounded on the retreat from Ctesiphon.[868] He continued to do sterling work during the march into captivity, as he did his best to help prisoners at Nisibin and Islahie, and in the prison camps. He was awarded the Most Excellent Order of the British Empire in 1919.[869] He was admired by both officers and the other ranks and even had one of the famous escaper's books dedicated to him.[870] He was also mentioned in many of the personal diaries of the period, as he attempted to bring the conditions of the prisoners to the attention of British and Turkish authorities. After the War he helped record details of all ranks who had died or were still missing.

Like many other victims of the ordeal, he was mentally scarred by his experiences. Though happily married and back in India, a medical officer reported that Reverend Spooner was 'unfitted for work on account of insomnia, depression and irritability'.[871] In 1926 he had a nervous breakdown and was invalided home. He had to spend sixteen years in a Nottingham nursing home, unable to recognise his family, but eventually recovered and took over a parish in the Lake District, living until 1964 when he was eighty-four. His freedom had been harder fought for – and for longer – than most.

Welcome home to 1/4th Hampshires

At this stage, as an example of how a unit was received when it arrived home, it is worth following the return of 1/4th Battalion of the Hampshire Regiment. It was the first Territorial battalion to be deployed to Mesopotamia, having originally been mobilised, like similar units, to garrison India thus relieving regular battalions who were destined for the Western Front. It was re-tasked in Rawal Pindi in March 1915 and joined Indian Expeditionary Force 'D' on the Tigris a month later. Its first action was at the Battle of Shaiba.

Part of this battalion, mainly its headquarters and 'A' Company, had been besieged in Kut within Major-General Melliss's 30th Brigade. The remainder 'half battalion' had been part of the Relief Force, serving in the 9th Brigade, 7th Division, at the Battle of the Hanna defile on 21 January 1916. At this action, the half battalion had lost its commanding officer and adjutant, both killed; thirteen officers and 230 men dead or wounded out of the sixteen and 339 present.

Consequently, as the Regimental History pointed out, 'a mere fragment like the 4th Hampshire was fit for nothing beyond camp duties and guards.'[872] The survivors were transferred to the 35th Brigade as part of the 'Composite Territorial Battalion', the 'Huffs', along with the depleted 1/5th Buffs and continued to attempt to relieve their brothers-in-arms.

Returning to Kut, the Officer Commanding, Major Foster Footner, from Romsey, served alongside nine other officers from the Battalion and 187 other ranks. The officers included Lieutenant Elton, who has already been mentioned and Lieutenant Harris, who was one of the successful eight escapers from Yozgad prison camp. The other ranks included the indomitable Sergeant-Major Leach, who held the unit together on the long march into captivity and kept many other prisoners alive in prison camps before his tragic death. He recorded in his diary the Battalion's strength on 29 April as Kut fell:

Badge of the Hampshire Regiment. (Author's Collection)

• Present – Eight officers and 146 Other Ranks
• In Hospital – Two officers and 28 Other Ranks
• Hospital Guard – Four Other Ranks.'[873]

A total of ten officers and 178 other ranks; nine men had died during the siege and by the time that newly-promoted Regimental-Sergeant-Major Leach marched off from Shumran on 6 May 1916, his group numbered 121. His diary stated, starkly: 'Men still dying.'[874] Whilst all of the officers survived captivity, only about forty rank and file made it home. 'Of those who survived to reach the prison camps of Asia Minor most succumbed to the hardships endured there, hard labour under brutal masters on a meagre diet.'[875]

Whilst in captivity for over two years, the officers and men did not know what had happened to each other as, in common with other regiments, they were scattered throughout Asia Minor. Regimental records show that the other ranks were distributed to Adana, Afion Kara Hissar, Airan, Angora, Baghdad, Bagtsche, Bozanti, Changri, Daridja, Entelli, Kedos, Mosul, Nisibin, Tarsus and Yarbashi. The luckiest ones, who had the greatest chance of survival, served as orderlies for the officers in their camps. Many survived as a result of the good work done by the American and Dutch consuls at Constantinople, the Prisoners of War in Turkey Committee and the Regimental Comforts Fund; they had also had a lot of luck. As the end of the War came, the surviving Hampshires were gathered on the Turkish coast and sent home.

The official welcome home took place in Winchester on 20 February 1919. The reception was arranged by Mrs Bowker, wife of the deceased commanding officer, Mr Reginald Harris, father of the escaped Hampshire officer, and the Mayor and Mayoress. Each soldier was able to bring a relative or friend, whose rail travel was paid for by the Council. The men formed up at the Battalion Headquarters, Castle Hill, where photographs were taken. Led by the Hampshire Depot Band, the forty or so officers and men, all survivors of Kut, marched to the Guildhall.

> It is gratifying to state that there was an excellent response, and the High Street, from the Westgate to the Guildhall, was bright with flags etc., over business establishments, or strung across the roadway. The street, too, was lined with spectators, several deep in places. At half past 12 the men (who by the bye, did not show any marked trace of their privations) marched from Castle Hill to the Guildhall, headed by the Hampshire Band, and they were frequently cheered very heartily by the onlookers.[876]

At 1300 hours they all sat down to a meal in the Banqueting Room. The menu was supposed to be amusing. We cannot know if it was to the guests of honour.

ATTACK ORDERS
Mule Tail Soup
Roast (4th) Hampshire Hog
Steak and Kidney Pie (Basra Flavour)
Kut Grass, Roots etc
Plum Pudding and Tigris Water Sauce
Mespot Jelly
Yesac Blancmange
'Yallah' Cheese

Royal 'welcome home' letter to 2777
Private G. Higgs of the Hampshire
Regiment. (Royal Hampshire Regiment
Museum)

Welcome to Kut prisoners menu of
20 February 1919. (Royal Hampshire
Regiment Museum)

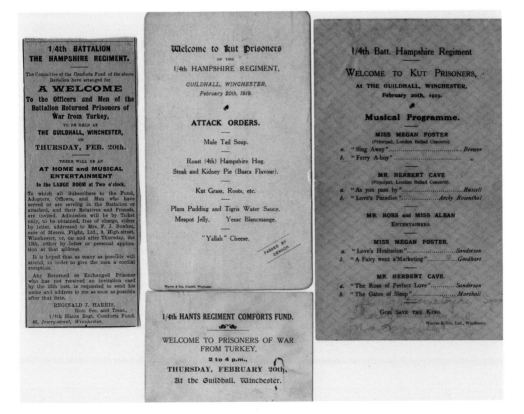

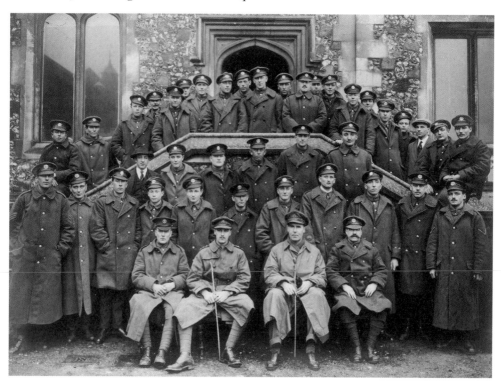

Top row: H. Knight, W. Fry, W. Pritchard, __ Cpl. J.C. Mills, W.T. English, R.C. Plumly, F.J.G. Aldridge, A. Hayden, A.E.W. Crees, E. Vince, F. Prior, __ __ A. Moore, __ E.S.L. Baker, G. Cherrett, G.H. Andrews, T. Savage. Upper middle row: A.J. Beech, W. Tuck, R. Carey, J. Whiting, A. Roberts, T.W. Gullis. Lower middle row: Sgt. A.H. Page, B.W. Adams, G. Higgs, W.A.J. Brown, W. Caine, G.H. Young, A. Windust, E. Burgess, J. Harrison, W. Weeks, W. Smith. Bottom row: Sgt. H. King, Capt. J.H. Harris, Capt. C.E.M. Jones, R.A.M.C., Sgt. A. Hedgeman.

Hampshire Regiment survivors (above) compared to A Company 1/4th Battalion in India, before they deployed to Mesopotamia (below). (Royal Hampshire Regiment Museum)

Musical singing entertainment followed and then Mr Harris gave a welcoming speech.

> We, your relatives and friends at home, watched that siege with the most tense anxiety; we were alter-
> nately hopeful and perhaps, sometimes, a little doubtful. At times we thought Kut would be relieved,
> but at other times it appeared almost impossible, though we knew that where the British flag was
> flying, and the Hampshire Regiment was, the best that could be done would be done … I will not
> dwell on what you suffered during your two and a half years of captivity. I am sure we do not know,
> and probably it never will be known, what sufferings you went through … But we cannot forget the
> gallant fellows who have not come home. They have died like British heroes, their memory will never
> be forgotten, and we tender to those whom they have left behind to mourn, our sympathy.'[877]

Major Footner responded, thanking the Comforts Fund and Committee for their help whilst
they were in captivity and he made the point of praising and remembering the deceased
Regimental-Sergeant-Major Leach for all of his efforts in the prison camps. The group departed;
for many, this was the first reunion that they had experienced with their friends since the long
march into captivity.

The survivors of the 2nd Battalion the Dorsetshire Regiment had been part of a similar
welcoming-home event on 25 February 1916, when they were entertained at the Town Hall,
Dorchester, by Colonel Lord Ellenborough and the Mayor; one of their guests was Major-General
Delamain, their brigade commander at Kut. A contributor to their welfare fund commented:

> He was glad to note that people at home now had a pretty good idea of the treatment meted out to
> the men from Kut. It took a long time to sink in, but it had got there now.[878]

As the Kuttites received some recognition and they dispersed to civvy street, some friendships
endured over the coming years. In 1919, Captain Harris acted as best man for Captain Yearsley's
wedding to Miss Norah Webb at St Nicholas's Church Brighton; other members of the 'Yozgad
Eight' were also present. The *Brighton Herald* described the event as 'A Hero's Wedding'.[879]

As the years passed by a key social event was the Annual Dinner of the Garrison of Kut-Al-
Amara. The President of the Dinner became Major-General Sir Charles Melliss, as the ex-30th
Brigade commander. In 1934, Lieutenant-General Gorringe gave a speech to the gathering. The
Kut Garrison Dinner Club celebrated a 50th Anniversary Dinner on 30 April 1966; their guest
of honour was Field Marshal Sir Claude Auchinleck, who as a young officer had fought with
the 62nd Punjabis in the Relief Force. 'Kut Remembrance Cards' were still being circulated
amongst the survivors in 1976 and the camaraderie continued as the old soldiers faded away. The
annual dinner always included a solemn toast to 'Our Fallen Comrades'. It is fitting to recall the
words of Lieutenant Colonel Basil Peel, who proposed the toast at the Tenth Annual Dinner in
1939: 'Let us lift our glasses to the memory of those gallant spirits, and as we do so let us salute
them by name to remind them of the comradeship unbroken.'[880] Each man then bowed his head
and mentioned the name of one of his comrades who had not survived the Kut experience. This
custom lasted as long as the veterans lived.

Retribution?

Retribution for the disgraceful handling of British and Indian troops by Turkey never came,
though as Flight-Sergeant Long described, some prisoners did their best to punish their captors
themselves. As they were released 'several of the more obnoxious of the commandant's soldiers

The Kut Garrison Dinner, 28 April 1934. (Royal Hampshire Regiment Museum)

were being man-handled by their victims among the prisoners, and the commandant made himself very scarce.'[881]

A British Military Commission did hand the Ottoman Government a list of Turkish personnel who were identified as having committed crimes against the prisoners and sixty of them were arrested and sent to Malta in 1919. A series of charges was prepared against them, including murder, manslaughter, flogging, cruelty and theft, but politics vanquished justice. Lieutenant-Colonel Keeling had done his best to collect evidence concerning the treatment of prisoners and sent this to British authorities in Egypt and Constantinople, but unlike the corroborating documents concerning prisoners written by the Nazis during the Second World War, no Turkish records were available and little action was taken.

Opinions about the prisoners' treatment varied, and of course the officers who were more likely to have an effect on public and government attitudes had not, generally, suffered during their captivity. Whilst some of them such as Major-General Melliss and Lieutenant-Colonel Keeling still sought justice, Brigadier-General Hamilton, the commander of 18th Brigade in Kut, expressed what now seems a bigoted but perhaps typical view of the time: 'Hardships, want of food, sickness, unsympathetic, harsh, and unusually stupid treatment were the experiences common to most travellers in the East among half-civilised and unfriendly people.'[882]

Surprisingly, as the author Braddon discovered when he interviewed survivors in the 1960s, the bulk of Kuttites did not hold a grudge against the Turks; instead they blamed the murders on the Kurds and Arabs.[883]

A peace treaty with the Ottoman Empire, the Treaty of Sèvres, was signed in 1920 and this paved the way for prosecution, but it was never ratified and was superseded by the Treaty of Lausanne in 1923. The Nationalist leader, Mustafa Kemal, was gaining power in Turkey. Whilst his republican ideals were not necessarily welcomed by the British Government, his proposed radical changes to Turkey – which would realign the country to a more western-looking society – were attractive. He had succeeded in capturing a number of British personnel and soon a deal was made to allow their release in exchange for the Turkish prisoners held in Malta. An extremely disgruntled Lieutenant-Colonel Keeling wrote:

Thus were released scot-free, the persons deemed responsible, or partly responsible, for the appalling mortality among our men in Turkey … We were in a commanding position to avenge the British prisoners who died in Turkish hands, but we frittered it away by idle procrastination.[884]

At least the surviving 'Kuttites' were home.

———

Notes

846. Sandes (1920) p.449–450.

847. Figures from various sources including Wilson (1930) p.140.

848. Anderson (1960) p.19. Records five officers and seven other ranks dying of the 'Spanish Grip' at Yozgad in 1918, including Captain Sweet, Distinguished Service Order, 2/7th Gurkha Rifles.

849. Kingsmill (1966) p.63.

850. Ibid p.65.

851. Keeling (1924) p.176.

852. Sherson (1928) p.352.

853. Townsend (1920) p.388.

854. Barker (1967) p.219.

855. Sherson (1928) p.357–358.

856. *My Campaign in Mesopotamia*. See bibliography.

857. Townsend (1920) p.391.

858. Sherson (1928) p.358.

859. Sandes (1920) p.448.

860. Neave (1937) p.289.

861. Elton (1938) p.153.

862. Coombes (1918) p.4164.

863. Neave (1937) p.302.

864. Ibid p.302.

865. Rawlinson (1941) p.170.

866. Elton (1938) p.155.

867. Mousley (1922) p.385.

868. *London Gazette* 19 October 1916. p.10078.

869. Ibid 23 October 1919. p.12980.

870. Johnston and Yearsley – *450 Miles to Freedom*, 1919.

871. Moynihan (1983) p.42.

872. Atkinson (1952) p.164.

873. Leach Diaries (1916) Royal Hampshire Regiment Museum.

874. Ibid.

875. Atkinson (1952) p.159.

876. *The Hampshire Regimental Journal* (March 1919) p.63.

877. Ibid p.64.

878. Anonymous (1933) p.265.

879. *Brighton Herald* 15 November 1919.

880. Wright (1939) leaflet.

881. Long (1938) p.376.

882. Neave (1937) p.317.

883. Braddon (1969) p.334.

884. Keeling (1924) p.233 and 234.

Chapter Thirteen

AN ASSESSMENT

In Mesopotamia a safe game must be played.
Lord Crewe[884]

Arab and Turk

Arab support in the region of the Middle East oilfields had been cultivated by the British in the lead-up to the First World War, much to the dismay of the occupying Turkish power. This included local arrangements with the sheikhs of Mahommerak, Kuwait (or Kuweit) and Ibn Saud. However, more generally, Anglo-Arabic tribal relationships were not good and, in response to the landings in Mesopotamia, the Sultan of Turkey, who was the Khalif of Islam (successor to the Prophet Mohammed) appealed to all Moslems to rise up against the 'infidel' by declaring a Jihad (holy war). Followers in Mesopotamia, Arabia and India were encouraged to kill the Christians by whatever means, as Turkey attempted to galvanise a Pan-Islamic alliance with Afghanistan and Persia. Turkish newspapers declared that 'the killing of the infidels who rule over Islam has become a sacred duty, whether you do it secretly or openly.'[885]

In order to maintain control, British Forces could not afford to lose face either to Arab or Turk in Mesopotamia. However, the British consistently underestimated the enemy, particularly the Turk, who had been adjudged to be weak in the Balkans War of 1912. There, 45,000 Turks had surrendered in Macedonia under the gaze of the British observers who had been attached to Greek forces. In 1914, the British reported that the Turkish Army was 'not in a condition well-fitted to take the field.'[886] Yet a report at the outbreak of the War stated that their army had improved. The warning ignored, 'British misfortune in Mesopotamia and Gallipoli in 1915–16 soon taught them the hard way that their adversary was an enemy not to be dismissed lightly.'[887] In 1914 the Turks had not attached great importance to Mesopotamia and their competent in-country divisions had been diverted to invade Egypt, 'leaving only one in occupation, weak in numbers, ill-equipped and reinforced by mutinous conscripts.'[888] This situation, coupled with the initial British military successes, inevitably reinforced the false intelligence that Johnny Turk was not 'up for it'.

The Arabs were misunderstood, as they had been expected to support their British liberators, a situation perhaps akin to that expected by the Coalition Forces in Iraq during 2003. Lord Crewe, in 1915, wrote to the Viceroy stating that he had been led to suppose that 'there was a general impatience of Turkish domination, and its method of exercise, which could cause many Arabs

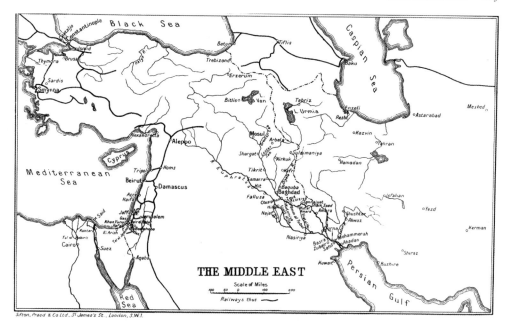

The Middle East. (Eady)

both in Arabia and Mesopotamia to adopt a friendly neutrality even if they did not actually join us.'[889] He was wrong. The battle for 'hearts and minds' was difficult on both sides, as a Turkish General Staff pamphlet stated: 'It was a long time before Turkish Army Headquarters gave up their hopes of extensive support from local levies and realised that the tribesmen of Lower Mesopotamia merely looked upon the war as a means of personal profit and were always ready to back the winning side.'[890]

Preconceived and misinformed attitudes about both the Turkish Army and the local Arabs helped encourage the 'mission-creep' that eventually saw the British forces advance towards Baghdad and overstretch their forces, helping to lead to the debacle at Kut.

The Indian Army

It was the British-led Indian Army which took to the field in Mesopotamia, as the country came within the Indian sphere of influence. The organisation of Expeditionary Force 'D' was typical of the post-1857 Indian Mutiny model designed to ensure loyalty to the crown by providing an integrated 'backbone' of British personnel. Its structure was a balanced mix of Indian and British units within each brigade, whilst each Indian unit had British officers embedded in key appointments. An example of this mix was Brigadier-General Delamain's 16th Infantry Brigade whose main units were:

- 2nd Battalion the Dorsetshire Regiment (British)
- 20th Battalion the Duke of Cambridge's Own Infantry (Brownlow's Punjabis) (Indian)
- 104th Battalion the Wellesley's Rifles (Indian)
- 117th Battalion the Mahrattas (Indian).

Indian despatch riders.
(IWM Q 27318)

Taking into account the various additional combat support and combat service support (logistic) arms, the brigade consisted of about 1,000 British troops and 4,000 Indians.

The Indian Army existed for the defence of India and small-scale operations in places such as the North West Frontier. It operated from static garrisons, rather than as an expeditionary force. The latter required greater logistic support and flexibility than the former. The Indian Army had not been deployed to, or gained the experience of 'the white man's war' between the British and the Boers in South Africa at the beginning of the twentieth century. It was modelled on important reforms generated by Field Marshal Kitchener during his time as Commander in Chief in India from 1902. A staff college had been successfully set up at Quetta, he had reorganised the divisional organisation so that it was established for war and he had encouraged infantry skills competitions, shooting and sports. His changes produced a more efficient army, but he also insituted a weakness: he was convinced that a commander should not be burdened by administration, so efficient deployable logistics were scarce and commanders were barely interested in the subject. In addition, the Indian Army, organised for frontier warfare, was not well established for combat support arms, such as artillery and engineers, and had not trained in combined-arms tactics. This did not bode well for Mesopotamia.

In the years prior to the War, the Indian Army had been reduced in size. There was no motor transport or aircraft and the medical and logistic support was minimal – certainly not able to support a fast moving campaign over great distances with little communications infrastructure. It has been estimated, for example, that the Army was short of perhaps 400 medical officers and 200 assistant surgeons.[891] Nevertheless, in 1914, one cavalry and three infantry divisions were despatched to the Western Front, whilst a brigade was prepared for deployment to German East Africa.[892]

The lack of effective logistic support has long been cited as the main cause for failure in the run up to the disaster of Kut. As the Kirke Report stated:

> The administrative system broke down completely; troops were not sure of supplies; casualties were evacuated after long delays under terrible conditions, and their large number further congested the transport system; the result was that an administrative disaster took place, which was hardly ever been equalled in the history of the British Army.[893]

But there were other problems associated with the Allied force which contributed to the surrender. In recent years, historians have criticised the capability of the Army, describing the 'deteriorating quality of Indian units' as a reason for British defeat. Despite the initial successes, as the campaign progressed the Army's capability declined and Major-General Townshend expressed his concerns about the balance of British and Indian troops, referring to his three British battalions as the 'backbone of the brigade'.[894] The Official History stated that 'regiments were reluctant to attack.'[895] These comments need to be placed in context – no force is as effective as it should be once it has suffered heavy casualties, and the troops were neither appropriately equipped nor trained for the developing operation. There were many examples of Indian bravery and loyalty to the Crown and their leadership came, primarily, from British officers. Matters may not have been helped by certain British officers' attitudes, described as 'an expression of late Victorian upper-class society, rich, snobbish and corseted by etiquette.'[896] The Quetta Report of 1925 denied that there were problems with Indian troops, though the Indian Staff College was unlikely to say anything different! Whatever one's views of the expeditionary force, its successes up until Kut and its high loss of life, which did affect its capability, cannot be denied. The Indian Army had suffered from a lack of investment before the War and this was one of two key reasons for the Kut disaster cited by Sir George Buchanan, the civil engineer who reorganised the port of Basra in 1916; the second was poor command and control of the British force.

Command and Control

Failure to produce clear command and control arrangements for the Mesopotamia Campaign has long been regarded as the trigger for the Kut fiasco. The Indian Vincent-Bingley Commission of 1916, The Whitehall Mesopotamia Commission Report of 1917, and The Staff College Quetta Report of 1925 attempted to explain the disaster very soon after the event, perhaps with limited evidence, but the statement: 'lack of cooperation between India and Britain and between civil and military executives in both countries was the underlying cause of the failures' sums up one of their main findings.[897] Up until Kut, the expedition was commanded from India through the Viceroy. By January 1916, the Chief of the Imperial General Staff, Sir William Robertson, based in London, recommended that the strategic command of the force should come to London, because of the clashes between India and London concerning the value of advancing towards Baghdad. The recommendation was accepted, but too late to avert the Kut disaster. The initial successes encouraged the view that Baghdad could be reached by Townshend. This in turn encouraged 'mission creep' with a force that was not appropriately equipped or supplied to carry out that task. The Secretary of State for India, Lord Crewe, in London after the occupation of Basra, in 1915, said 'Our present position is strategically a sound one and we cannot at present afford to take risks by extending it unduly', but this differed from the views expressed in India.[898] Both Lord Hardinge, Viceroy of India, and Sir Percy Cox, the India Government political service officer with the Army, encouraged the advance and London was not made aware of the force's logistic deficiencies. London was expecting victory, as was Prime Minister Herbert Asquith a few months before the surrender: 'I do not think in the course of war there has been a series of operations more carefully contrived, more brilliantly conducted, and with a better chance of success.'[899]

The situation in Mesopotamia was not helped by the fact that many influential British military and political leaders were not convinced of its strategic importance beyond the securing of oil supplies. Throughout the War there was a clash between the 'westerners', favouring the main effort on the Western Front, and the 'easterners', who saw opportunities for success elsewhere, because of the stalemate in France and Belgium. The 1932 Kirke Report describes the campaign as being 'of little value'[900] and British failures in Gallipoli and Salonika reinforced this view. It was not only the strategy that led to confusion, but also the commanders on the ground who encouraged 'drift'.[901]

For some, the Mesopotamia Campaign perfectly illustrates the judgement that First World War armies were lions led by donkeys. 'Through a mixture of self-interest, personal ambition, ignorance, obstinacy and sheer crass stupidity, this trio sealed the fate of some thousands of British and Indian soldiers.'[902] The trio referred to were Sir Harry Beauchamp Duff, the Commander in Chief in India, General Sir John Nixon, the Army commander at Basra, and Major-General Charles Townshend, commander of the 6th Division and of the Kut Garrison. The Mesopotamian Commission was not impressed by the encouragement given for the Baghdad advance from Sir Beauchamp Duff or the Viceroy, but both men were consistently being sent positive reports about the expedition from Mesopotamia-based Generals Nixon and Cox, so there is little wonder that they encouraged an advance towards Baghdad. The rapid capture of Amara in June 1915 by Major-General Townshend and Major-General Gorringe's 12th Division's seizure of Nasiriya in July encouraged confidence. It was General Nixon who suggested to Lord Hardinge that the advance on Kut should take place, though he did highlight shortfalls in river transport, troops and logistics. Neither London, nor the new Secretary of State for India, Austen Chamberlain, were aware of the shortfalls, and authority was granted for the advance inland during August 1915.[903] This advance, commanded by Townshend, was launched with inadequate support and led to the stalemate Battle of Ctesiphon and the withdrawal to and surrender at Kut.

The generals were considered by many to be unfit and old:

> W stands for the wonder and pain
> With which we regard our infirm and insane
> Old aged generals who run this campaign
> We are waging in Mesopotamia.[904]

Nixon and Townshend were fifty-eight. Generals Barrett and Nixon and Lieutenant-General Sir Percy Lake, General Nixon's successor, all fell seriously ill. The Kirke Report stated that 'in war physical and mental qualifications are of equal importance.'[905] The environment of Mesopotamia demanded fit commanders, as it does today. The 'mental qualifications' of the commander at Kut, Major-General Townshend, will be dealt with later.

Aspersions were also cast against the staff who had to execute their commanders' orders and ensure that the end result was the 'art of the possible'. Many of the best staff had already been sent to France and some feel that the expeditionary force was 'chronically short of officers'.[906] It is also suggested that Nixon 'never equipped himself with sufficient staff to look beyond day-to-day requirements' – this may explain why the planning for logistics was so inefficient.[907]

Logistics

The traditional explanation for the Kut disaster has been the appalling administration and logistic support endured by the garrison. These issues had been resolved by the time Lieutenant-General Maude occupied Baghdad in March 1917. These factors were emphasised in the early criticism and the three reports mentioned earlier, because they were the most obvious reasons for failure at the time. The Mesopotamia Commission recommended a complete overhaul of the Indian Army's administration system. The Second World War commander, Field Marshal Lord Archibald Wavell, once commented that 'a real knowledge of supply and movement factors must be the basis of every leader's plan; only then can he know how and when to take risks with those factors, and battles are won only by taking risks.'[908] This was not General Nixon's way, 'He looked at it purely from the fighting point of view, leaving administration to arrange itself as economically as it could.'[909] At one stage Nixon said that the medical support was working well when it was not, but the Mesopotamia Commission pointed out that the Surgeon-General was reticent and resented criticism. One observer saw two officers running a hospital for 1,000 patients and reported that out of a new batch of ninety doctors, only forty remained in the country after three months, through death and illness.[910]

The waterways were the key to communications throughout the country and became even more important as Townshend's force moved inland. They offered extra manoeuvrability to the advancing force, whilst bringing supplies forward and casualties to the rear. The eventual inspector-general of communications in Mesopotamia, Major-General Macmunn, mentioned that 'people who understood the problem if expressed in terms of camels and mule carts, quite failed to realise that exactly the same data must apply to a river which is to take the place of a road.'[911] However, Major-General Kemball, as Nixon's senior staff officer, clearly identified the importance of suitable boats in June 1915. A special logistics conference followed and a request was sent to India and London in July for six paddle-steamers, three stern wheelers, eight tugs, forty-three barges and six launches.[912] These extra boats were not available to Townshend at the critical time, despite Major-General Kemball's comment that

> … if steps are not taken in good time to meet these requirements there are grave risks of a breakdown at possibly a serious moment. At the present time we cannot make the most effective use of the troops available owing to the want of ships, and in any crisis, insufficiency of river transport would limit the scope of reinforcements, while a breakdown of shipping might have still more serious consequences.[913]

The quantity of river transport did not grow at the same rate as the army in Mesopotamia and the situation was not helped by some prevarication by the military authorities in London and the boat-building firms, which led to further delays. All of the key commanders realised that control of and passage along the waterways was critical and the early successes of 'Townshend's Regatta' proved that. However, even when Lieutenant-General Aylmer prepared to advance with his Tigris Relief Force in an attempt to relieve Townshend at Kut, only three-quarters of his force could be supported and 'no provision could be made for the carriage of water nor of anything except rations and ammunition.'[914] Much of Aylmer's force had to advance more slowly on foot as a result. 'Very severe delay will be entailed by this and the further concentration of the requisite troops for the support of Aylmer's force will in consequence be postponed.'[915] The land transport available was insufficient to make up for the lack of boats. There were enough carts and mules, but a lack of camels.

The supply chain was incapable of meeting the demand. Debarkation at Bombay was inefficient and ships were waiting three weeks at Basra before they were unloaded at the makeshift port that lacked quays. Even by July 1916, it still took six weeks to turn around one ship. Significant improvements only occurred from November 1916, when Sir George Buchanan took control. Earlier that year, he had assessed the situation but received little support from Nixon, perhaps because of his irritating personality. Buchanan pointed out that 'The military expedition to Basra is, I believe, unique, in as much as in no previous case has such an enormous force been landed and maintained without an adequately prepared base.'[916] The situation had greatly improved by the time of Lieutenant-General Maude's successes, but the Kirke Report stated that commanders and their staff should understand the importance of transportation and logistics: 'This campaign shows only too clearly the risk of embarking on any strategic or tactical operation without an assured system of supply: the more prolonged the operation and the longer the lines of communication, the surer must be the system.'[917]

The Environment, Tactics and Morale

Apart from the considerable combat service support challenges in Mesopotamia, the Quetta Report identified the difficulties in coping with the harsh conditions within the country – still a major challenge for any army. Personal comments like 'the excessive heat made military operations impossible' and 'the air was so dry that the dead Turks who still lay out at Beit Aiessa burst into flame if you put a match to them' illustrate the challenges.[918] Commanders could not control the summer heat of up to 130 degrees Fahrenheit (54°C) in the shade or the oppressive sand storms. Flooding occurred at other times of the year, the average rainfall of six-and-a-half inches mainly falling in the months between October and April. The debilitating environment, coupled with the poor supply system, meant that

> Our troops were exhausted with sickness fever, dysentery, boils, cholera, jaundice and scurvy. They
> were often short of rations. Vegetables were not at hand.[919]

It was quickly realised by both General Nixon and Major-General Townshend that the waterways, particularly the Tigris and Euphrates, were critical for success, though the logistic requirement was not fully appreciated. Tracks, roads and railways were lacking and when the rains occurred, great tracts of land were turned to mud making movement across country extremely difficult. River transport and gunboats providing artillery support were used by Townshend with great imagination and, before the Kut disaster, he won a series of skirmishes and battles by making the most of his 'regatta', using the Tigris as the fixed points for his turning movements. He adapted well to the environmental limitations.

The exposed flat and featureless landscape exposed the infantry on both sides and there were no tanks available in the campaign and few aircraft to help break any deadlock. Matters were not helped by poor maps and the occasional mirage. With little protection available in the open, casualties were high and the machine-gun dominated the landscape. Operations at night proved more successful than by day, lessons for the future: 'The campaign in Mesopotamia clearly proved the value of operations at night in a country where landmarks were practically non-existent.'[920] Surprise could be achieved with fewer casualties, the Quetta Report commenting on the battles of Dujeila and Sannayait that 'the part of the operations that took place in the dark was successful.'[921]

As Field Marshal the Viscount Montgomery of Alamein stated: 'High morale is a quality without which no war can be won.' He defined high morale as 'the quality which makes men endure and show courage in times of fatigue and danger.'[922] It is incredible how, in this story, the morale of Townshend's force remained high for such a long time, but there is no doubt that it was ground down over time. The Kirke Report spelled it out:

> The morale of the troops in Mesopotamia was lowered during the early part of the campaign by poor food, inadequate medical arrangements, lack of leave, bad postal services and the effect – especially on the Indian troops – of the loneliness and isolation of the desert.[923]

Conclusion

The Campaign in Mesopotamia is a 'forgotten war' and the Kut story was overshadowed by events elsewhere. For the Allies, Gallipoli was the disaster that was remembered in 1916, prior to the terrible battles of the Somme and Verdun. Mesopotamia was a 'sideshow'. However, the surrender at Kut was an important and embarrassing episode. The 1932 Kirke Report concluded that 'The campaign in Mesopotamia proved clearly that unless strategy, tactics and administration are interdependent, disaster will ensue.'[924] The point has been illustrated throughout this book.

Once Baghdad had been captured on 11 March 1917, the campaign continued in Upper Mesopotamia and West Persia and the Caspian, prior to the ultimate British victory and the subsequent armistice with Turkey in October 1918. The numbers of British and Indian forces

Commonwealth War Graves Memorial at Shaiba to those who died in captivity. (Brigadier Mark Armstrong)

Commonwealth War Graves Memorial at Shaiba. (Brigadier Mark Armstrong)

that had been deployed in Mesopotamia during the War was significant, amounting to 92,501 personnel – not far off the full trained strength of the British Army today. 14,814 were killed or died of wounds, 12,807 died from disease, 51,386 were wounded and 13,494 ended up as either prisoners or missing.[925]

The British suffered 23,000 casualties in the effort to relieve Kut between January and April 1916, including 10,000 in just three weeks of April during the final attempts. The 1st Battalion Seaforth Highlanders, for example, had been winnowed from 962 other ranks to just 103 and had lost forty-three officers killed, wounded and missing: 'Although Kut fell, no man could say that the soldiers did not do all that could possibly be expected of them and more, to break through and relieve their comrades.'[926] The Turks also suffered at least 10,000 casualties in April. Both sides had made many sacrifices.

General Nixon's agreement with Major-General Townshend that a stand should be made at Kut and his subsequent insistence that the 6th Division should remain there, rather than withdraw, was predicated on the ability of his own forces to reach and relieve the town. The British constantly underestimated the effectiveness of the Turks and attacked against well-prepared defensive positions without surprise or darkness in their favour. The improvised command and control arrangements remained insufficient as the Relief Force battled with the terrain and weather as well as a determined enemy. Critically, the British logistic and administrative elements were not up to the task. From General Robertson's perspective: 'The administrative situation was the determining factor.'[927] Lessons were learned and by the time that General Maude advanced again, successfully, towards Baghdad, 'he had an army strong enough and well enough administered to deal with situations in their front.'[928]

KUT~EL~AMARA

5th December 1915 to 29th April 1916

TO THE MEMORY OF

5746 OF THE GARRISON

WHO DIED IN THE SIEGE

OR AFTERWARDS IN CAPTIVITY

Erected by their surviving comrades

Kut Memorial Plaque in the crypt at St Paul's Cathedral. (St Paul's Cathedral)

Having eventually defeated the conventional Turkish enemy, the British were soon to identify that the policing of Mesopotamia was also going to be a challenge. Captain Mousley returned to Kut after the War and saw that

Adequate garrisoning is out of the question for financial reasons, and we are just realizing here, as in Ireland, that to conquer a country is one thing and to police it another … This civilisation, then, must either have an army adequate to protect it or it must conform to whatever standard of efficiency, to whatever degree of perfection, the local inhabitant will tolerate.[929]

These comments are applicable today.

> Freed from the bondage of thy sand,
> My lips are strangely moved to praise
> The loneliness of thy bare land,
> The fiery wind, the noon ablaze.[930]

Notes

884. Secretary of State for India. Message to General Nixon April 1915, quoted in Barker (1967). p.80.
885. Neave (1937) p.4.
886. Handel (1990) p.139/140.
887. Sheffy (1998). p.62.
888. Blaxland (1969) p.442.
889. Wilson (1986). p.276.
890. *The Turco-British Campaign in Mesopotamia and our Mistakes*, by Bimbashi Muhammad Amin. Summarised in Moberly.Vol 1. p.352.
891. Blaxland (1969). p.445.
892. By the end of the War, India had sent 138,000 men to France, 675,000 to Mesopotamia and144,000 to Egypt. Figures from Mason (1974) p.411.
893. Kirke (1932) p.118.
894. Latter (1994) p.161.
895. Moberly (1923) Vol 1. p.66.
896. Barnett (1970) Ch.13.
897. Barker (1967) p.471.
898. Davis (1994) p.56.
899. Strawson (1980) p.137.
900. Kirke (1932) p.117.
901. Liddell Hart (1972) p.117.
902. Dixon (1976) p.96.
903. Davis (1994) p.78/79.
904. From 'The Cynical Alphabet' of 1916. Quoted Barker p.223.
905. Kirke Report (1932) p.125.
906. Latter (1994) p.174
907. Wilson (1986) p.277
908. Army Documents Publication (1996) Volume 3 p.1–1.
909. Evans (1926) p.26.
910. Candler (1919) p.288 and p.290.
911. Quoted in Anglesey (1995). p.34.
912. Moberly (1923) p.341 and 342
913. Millar (1969) p.8.
914. Quetta Critical Report (1925) p.82.
915. Ibid p.80
916. Buchanan (1938) p.210.
917. Kirke Report (1932) p.118.
918. Candler (1919) p.284 and 287.
919. Ibid p.284.
920. Kirke (1932) p.122.
921. Quetta Critical Report (1925) p.329.
922. Both quotations from 'Serve to Lead' p.8 and 17.
923. Kirke (1932) p.123.
924. Ibid p.118.
925. Moberly (1927) p.331.
926. Quetta Critical Report (1925) p.211.
927. Evans (1926) p.69.
928. Anonymous (1930) p.51.
929. Mousley (1922) p.390–391.
930. Griffyth Fairfax (1919) p.80 – 'Glamour – An envoi addressed to Mesopotamia after leaving it'.

AFTERWORD BY LIEUTENANT-GENERAL SIR GRAEME LAMB

Benjamin Disraeli, Earl of Beaconsfield, was reputed to have said that 'there are lies, damned lies and statistics', to which I would add 'lessons learnt', for they seldom are. Military articles, books and regimental accounts are littered with lessons – what is less well known is how few of those lessons are ever learnt. *Kut 1916* is a tale of the hardihood, endurance and courage of the British Army, but it is also a depressing story of political and military foolhardiness. The siege was the final curtain in an Arabian Tale beset by triumph and disaster, Kipling's 'two impostors'. It is a story littered with ambition, ego, ignorance, indifference, failure in communication, double talk and double crossing, a lesson in tactics, the operational art or lack of it and ultimately strategic drift. Colonel Crowley has, in a very soldierly manner, taken an almost forgotten campaign, certainly a forgotten army, and captured the soul of what it must have been like to have fought and won, to have fought and lost, of hopes raised and dashed, of the fortitude of our forefathers and brought it to life nearly 100 years on. It is an honest attempt to record what we think happened in some foreign field at the turn of this last century, it makes for sombre reading and exposes columns of lessons not learnt or likely to be learnt; this is the sorry tale of this book.

It is said the 'Fortune favours the Brave'. I for one am not inclined to that opinion but have seen it written that 'Fortune favours the Competent' for it was competence not bravery that was lacking in Mesopotamia. Soldiering is a passionate and emotional rollercoaster – it demands soul but in equal measure it demands cold logic, dispassionate consideration and the icy laws of calculus. Lord Wavell suggested that things are never as good or as bad as they might seem.

In the early stages of this campaign all went well, with the result that reason and caution became clouded, overlooked, pushed aside by the eagerness for success and yet for those few who were looking, there were signs of the likely outcome that subsequently befell the 6th Division. Could it have been anticipated? Probably, but this cast of actors was not one for quiet reflection and caution. It comprised an ill-informed and wishful chain of command distant from Iraq and drunk with a little tactical success. There were political opportunists for whom the liquor of victory was enticing; they excused threadbare and lacklustre commitment which they considered sufficient, and measured progress in tactical battles whilst operational failure strangled their grand designs and strategic drift secured their ultimate defeat. We should not have found ourselves marching on Baghdad but listening to the intelligence assessments of Turkish force ratios and capabilities whilst recalling that conflict and war is really all about logistics.

Today our emerging Counter Insurgency doctrine talks of working with what you have and demanding what you need. It suggests that tactical success guarantees nothing, it points out the importance of integrity and morality as essential character qualities, the importance of maintaining the initiative and of the dangers of complacency. Soldiering is not a simple science of cause and effect – it is a contest fought by men and women, a battle of wills challenged by luck, opportunity and unfairness seldom in equal measure and it is always beset with uncertainty and complexity. Outcomes in campaigns are not predetermined but they can be loaded in one's favour. The Secretary of State for India, Austen Chamberlain, Sir Beauchamp Duff, the Viceroy, Generals Nixon and Cox and Major-General Townsend can all be held accountable. Ultimately, I would offer it is with the ground commander that the buck must stop for he can lead with the guidance and direction he is given, or resign; Townsend did neither and is damned for all time. Physical courage requires nothing more than the brutal application of willpower and whilst the officers and soldiers who made up the Army were not short of this when closing with the enemy, it was moral courage that was lacking and that is the measure of a general.

Lieutenant-General Sir Graeme Lamb KBE CMG DSO

Commander Field Army

2009

APPENDIX I

The Force Besieged in Kut[1]

Approximately 301 British officers, 2,851 British other ranks, 225 Indian officers, 8,230 Indian other ranks (total 11,607), and 3,530 followers.

Headquarters 6th (Poona) Division's key officers:

Commander – Major-General C.V.F. Townshend
General Staff Officer 1 (Modern title, 'Chief of Staff') – Lieutenant-Colonel U.W. Evans
Assistant Quartermaster General (Modern title, 'Deputy Chief of Staff') – Lieutenant-Colonel W.W. Chitty

16th Infantry Brigade (Major-General W.S. Delamain)

2nd Battalion the Dorsetshire Regiment (Major G.M. Herbert)
66th Punjabis (Lieutenant-Colonel A. Moore)
104th Wellesley's Rifles (Captain C.M.S. Manners)   ·
117th Mahrattas (Major Mc V. Crichton)

17th Infantry Brigade (Brigadier-General F.A. Hoghton)

1st Battalion the Oxfordshire and Buckinghamshire Light Infantry (Lieutenant-Colonel E.A.E. Lethbridge)
22nd Punjabis (Captain A.O. Sutherland)
103rd Mahratta Light Infantry (Lieutenant-Colonel W.H. Brown)
119th Rajputana Infantry (Captain F.I.O. Brickman)

Clockwise from above Major-General Townshend
1914. (Barker)

Major-General Townshend at Kut. (Sherson)

Regimental postcard of the Oxfordshire and
Buckinghamshire Light Infantry, 1916. (Author's
Collection)

Badges of the Dorsetshire Regiment. (Author's
Collection)

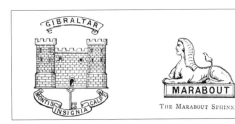

THE MARABOUT SPHINX.

18th Infantry Brigade (Brigadier-General W.G. Hamilton)

2nd Battalion the Norfolk Regiment (Major F.C. Lodge)
7th Rajputs (Lieutenant-Colonel H.O. Parr)
110th Mahratta Light Infantry (Major H.C. Hill)
120th Rajputana Infantry (Major P.F. Pocock)

30th Infantry Brigade (Major-General Sir C. Melliss)

Half battalion of 2nd Battalion the Queen's Own Royal West Kent Regiment (Major J.W. Nelson)
One Company of 1st/4th Battalion the Hampshire Regiment (Major F.L. Footner)
24th Punjabis (Lieutenant-Colonel H.A.V. Cummins)
76th Punjabis (Captain E. Milford)
2nd/7th Gurkha Rifles (Lieutenant-Colonel W.B. Powell)
Half battalion of 67th Punjabis (Major C.E.S. Cox)

Britannia – Norfolk Regiment Badge. (Author's Collection)

Badge of the 7th Rajput Regiment. (Author's Collection)

Badge of The Queen's Own Royal West Kent Regiment. (Author's Collection)

Badge of the 7th Gurkhas. (Author's Collection)

Cavalry

One squadron of 23rd Cavalry (Captain C.H.K. Kirkwood)
One squadron of 7th Hariana Lancers (Lieutenant F.T. Drake-Brockman)

Artillery (forty-three guns in total, including the naval guns) (Brigadier-General G.B. Smith)

10th Brigade Royal Field Artillery (Lieutenant-Colonel HN St J Maule)
63rd Battery (Major H. Broke-Smith) – Six 18-pounder guns
76th Battery (Major O.S. Lloyd) – Six 18-pounder guns
82nd Battery (Major E. Corbould Warren) – Six 18-pounder guns
1st/5th Hampshire Howitzer Battery (Major H.G. Thompson) – Four guns
86th Heavy Battery Royal Garrison Artillery (Lieutenant-Colonel M.H. Courtenay) – Four
    5-inch guns
One section 104th Heavy Battery Royal Garrison Artillery (Major W.C.R. Farmar) – Two
    4-inch guns
Volunteer Artillery Battery (Major A.J. Anderson) – Four 15-pounder guns
One spare 18-pounder
One section 'S' Battery Royal Horse Artillery – Two 13-pounder guns
6th Division Ammunition Column (Captain E.T. Martin)

Engineers (Lieutenant-Colonel F.A. Wilson)

Bridging Train (Captain E.W.C. Sandes)
17th Company Sappers and Miners (Lieutenant K.B.S. Crawford)
22nd Company Sappers and Miners (Lieutenant A.B. Mathews)
Sirmoor Company Imperial Service Sappers (Captain C.E. Colbeck)
Engineer Field Park (Captain H.W. Tomlinson)
Pioneers – 48th Pioneers (Colonel A.J.N. Harward)

Signals

Detachment Army Signals Company (Major F. Booth)
34th Divisional Signals Company (Captain H.S. Cardew)
One brigade section 12th Divisional Signals Company
Wireless Section (two wagons and one pack set)

Chaplains

Reverend H. Spooner (Church of England)
Reverend Father T. Mullen (Roman Catholic)
Reverend A.Y. Wright (Wesleyan)

Logistics

Supply and transport personnel, including elements of the Jaipur Transport Corps and the 13th, 21st, 26th and 30th Mule Corps (Lieutenant-Colonel A.S.R. Annesley). Number 32 Field Post Office

Medical (Colonel P. Hehir India Medical Service)

Number 2 Field Ambulance
Number 4 Field Ambulance
Number 106 Field Ambulance
Number 157 Indian Stationary Ambulance
Number 9 Indian General Hospital
Half of Number 3a British General Hospital
Officers' Hospital
One section Veterinary Field Hospital (Captain Stephenson)

Others

Maxim Battery (Captain CH Stockley) – Six machine-guns
Royal Flying Corps detachment (Captain S.C. Winfield-Smith)

Naval Detachment

His Majesty's gunboat *Sumana* – One 12-pounder and two 3-pounders, two of these guns were
    mounted ashore in March 1916 (Lieutenant L.C.P. Tudway Royal Navy)
Four steam launches (three sunk on 9/10 December 1915)
Two motor launches
Six barges
Four 4.7-inch guns in horse-boats (Lieutenant M.A.B. Johnston Royal Garrison Artillery)
One 12-pounder, mounted ashore in January 1916 (intended for the captured gunboat *Firefly*)

Notes
1. Main figures from Moberly (1924) p.165 and Appendix XIII).

APPENDIX II

The Relief Force

Initially, the 6th (Poona) Division, commanded by Major-General Townshend, the 12th (Lahore) Division, commanded by Major-General Gorringe, and the 6th Cavalry Brigade, commanded by Major-General Melliss, were deployed by the British Empire, under Indian control, to Mesopotamia. The 6th Division formed the basis of the Kut Garrison.

Key Elements of the Relief Force on 3 January 1916[1]

The 7th (Meerut) Division formed the basis of the initial Relief Force.

7th (Meerut) Division (Tigris Corps Headquarters at Ali-Gharbi) (Major-General Sir G. Younghusband)

28th Infantry Brigade (Major-General G. V. Kemball)
2nd Leicestershire Regiment
51st Sikhs
53rd Sikhs
56th Rifles

35th Infantry Brigade (Brigadier-General G.B.H. Rice)
1/5th Buffs (East Kent Regiment)
37th Dogras
97th Infantry
102nd Grenadiers

19th Infantry Brigade (Lieutenant-Colonel Dennys)
1st Seaforth Highlanders
28th Punjabis
92nd Punjabis
125th Rifles

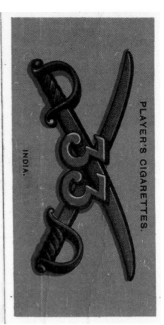

Badges of the Indian Army – Indian Medical Services, 16th Cavalry and 33rd Cavalry. (Player's Cigarettes)

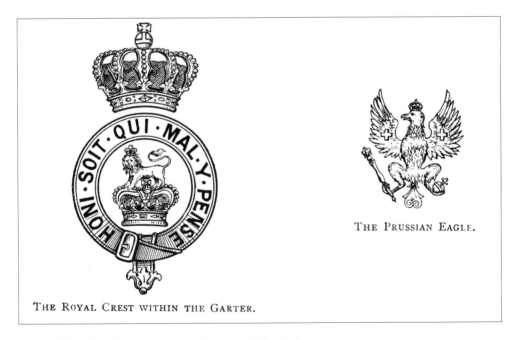

THE ROYAL CREST WITHIN THE GARTER.

THE PRUSSIAN EAGLE.

Badge of the 14th (The King's Hussars). (Author's Collection)

6th Cavalry Brigade of 14 squadrons, including:
14th Hussars
7th Lancers (less one squadron)
33rd Cavalry (less one squadron)
4th Cavalry

Artillery
9th Brigade Royal Field Artillery (eighteen 18-pounder guns)
1/1st Sussex Battery Royal Field Artillery (four 15-pounder guns)
Heavy Artillery Brigade (eight 5 inch howitzers and two 4-inch guns.

Other Units
16th Cavalry (less one squadron)
107th Pioneers
1/4th Hampshire Regiment (less one company)
One company 67th Punjabis

Medical Units
Number 18 Cavalry Field Ambulance of one British and one Indian section
Number 131 Indian Cavalry Field Ambulance of three Indian sections
Number 1 Field Ambulance of two sections
Numbers 5 and 6 Ambulances of two sections each

Transport
1,353 pack mules and 865 carts with draught animals

Royal Flying Corps
Two aeroplanes

Naval
His Majesty's gunboats *Butterfly*, *Dragonfly*, *Cranefly* and *Gadfly*

Arrived Ali-Gharbi 4–7 January 1916
6th Jats (21st Infantry Brigade)
9th Bhopal Infantry (7th Infantry Brigade)
41st Dogras (19th Infantry Brigade)
7th Division divisional staff
9th and 21st Brigades' staff
2nd Black Watch (21st Infantry Brigade)
62nd Punjabis (36th Infantry Brigade)

Key Elements of the Relief Force on 27 February 1916

The 7th Division had been joined by the 3rd Division in the Relief Force
Tigris Corps Commander – Lieutenant-General Sir F.J. Aylmer (in the area of the Wadi)

3rd Division (Major-General H d'U. Keary)

7th Infantry Brigade (Major-General R. G. Egerton)
1/Connaught Rangers (including drafts for 2/Queen's Own Royal West Kent Regiment)
27th Punjabis
89th Punjabis
128th Pioneers

8th Infantry Brigade (Lieutenant-Colonel F.P.S. Dunsford)
1/Manchester Regiment
2nd Rajputs
47th Sikhs
59th Rifles

9th Infantry Brigade (Brigadier-General L.W.Y. Campbell)
1/Highland Light Infantry
1/1st Gurkhas
1/9th Gurkhas
93rd Infantry

Cavalry
16th Cavalry (one squadron)

Artillery
4th Brigade Royal Field Artillery (eighteen guns)

Engineers
20th and 21st Companies of Sappers and Miners
34th Sikh Pioneers

7th Division (Major-General Sir G.J. Younghusband)

19th Infantry Brigade (Brigadier-General E.C. Peebles)
Composite Highland Battalion (2/Black Watch and 1/Seaforth Highlanders)
28th Punjabis
92nd Punjabis
125th Rifles

21st Infantry Brigade (Brigadier-General C.E. Norie)
(The 21st Brigade had replaced the 35th Brigade in the 7th Division. The 35th Brigade was placed in 'Corps Troops')

Composite English Battalion (2/Norfolk and 2/Dorsetshire)
6th Jats
9th Bhopal Infantry
Composite Mahratta Battalion (drafts for Mahratta battalions in Kut)

28th Infantry Brigade (Major-General G. V. Kemball)
2/Leicestershire Regiment
Provisional Battalion, Oxfordshire and Buckinghamshire Light Infantry
51st Sikhs
53rd Sikhs
56th Sikhs

Cavalry
16th Cavalry (one squadron)

Artillery
9th Brigade Royal Field Artillery (eighteen guns)

Engineers
3rd Field Company, Sappers and Miners and 107th Pioneers

Cavalry Brigade (Brigadier-General R. C. Stephen)
'S' Battery Royal Horse Artillery
14th Hussars
4th Cavalry
7th Lancers (only three squadrons strong)
33rd Cavalry (less one squadron)

Corps Troops

35th Infantry Brigade (Brigadier-General G. B. H. Rice)
Composite Territorial Battalion (1/5th Buffs and 1/4th Hampshire)
Composite Dogra Battalion (37th and 41st Dogras)
97th Infantry

36th Infantry Brigade (Brigadier-General G. Christian)
1/6th Devonshire Regiment
26th Punjabis
62nd Punjabis
82nd Punjabis

Artillery
13th Brigade Royal Field Artillery (eighteen guns)
60th and 61st Howitzer Batteries Royal Field Artillery (twelve 4.5-inch howitzers)
23rd Mountain Battery (four 10-pounder guns)
Home Counties Brigade Royal Field Artillery (eight 15-pounder guns)
72nd and 77th Heavy batteries Royal Garrison Artillery (eight 5-inch howitzers)
One section 104th Heavy Battery Royal Garrison Artillery (two 4-inch guns)

Engineers
12th and 13th Companies Sappers and Miners

Medical
Number 18 Cavalry Field Ambulance, Number 131 Indian Cavalry Field Ambulance, Numbers 3 and 20 Combined Field Ambulances, Number 1 Field Ambulance, Numbers 7, 8, 19 and 20 British Field Ambulances, Numbers 111, 112, 113, 128, 129 and 130 Indian Field Ambulances, Number 19 Combined Clearing Hospital and Number 4 Sanitary Section

Air Service
One flight Royal Navy Air Service (one plane serviceable)
'B' Flight Number 30 Squadron Royal Flying Corps (three serviceable planes)

En Route

37th Infantry Brigade (Brigadier-General F.J. Fowler)
Brigade Headquarters
1/4th Somerset Light Infantry
1/2nd Gurkhas
Additional units were also distributed on the lines of Communications at Shaikh Saad, Ali Gharbi, Fulaifila, Amara, Qala Salih, Qurna, Bushire, Band-i-qir, Ahwaz and Basra.

Two formed brigades were part of the Euphrates Line at Nasiriya:

12th Infantry Brigade (Brigadier-General H.T. Brooking)
1/5th Queen's Royal Regiment
44th Infantry
90th Punjabis

34th Infantry Brigade (Brigadier-General E.C. Tidswell)
2/Queen's Own Royal West Kent Regiment (less half battalion)
114th Mahrattas

Naval
Seven gunboats of the 'Firefly' class: Butterfly, Gadfly, Dragonfly, Cranefly, Grayfly, Mayfly and Sawfly. The Stonefly and a large gunboat, the Mantis, arrived in March.

Key Elements of the Relief Force on 5 April 1916

The Relief Force of the 3rd and 7th Divisions had been joined by the all-British 13th Division

3rd Division (Major-General H d'U. Keary)

7th Brigade (Major-General R.G. Egerton)
1st Connaught Rangers
27th Punjabis
89th Punjabis
128th Punjabis
128th Pioneers

9th **BHOPAL INFANTRY**

Badge of the 9th Bhopal Infantry. (Author's Collection)

8th Brigade (Brigadier-General S.M. Edwardes)
1st Manchesters
2nd Rajputs
47th Sikhs
59th Sikhs

9th Brigade (Lieutenant-Colonel L.W.Y. Campbell)
1st Highland Light Infantry
93rd Infantry
1/1st Gurkhas
1/9th Gurkhas

37th Brigade (Brigadier-General F.J. Fowler)
1/4th Somerset Light Infantry
1/2nd Gurkhas
36th Sikhs

Cavalry
33rd Cavalry (Two squadrons)

Artillery
4th Brigade Royal Field Artillery (eighteen guns)
A/69th Battery (Howitzers (four guns))
23rd Mountain Battery (four guns)

Engineers
34th Sikh Pioneers
20th and 21st Companies Sappers and Miners

7th Division (Major-General Sir G.Younghusband)

19th Brigade (Brigadier-General E.C. Peebles)
Highland Battalion
28th Punjabis

92nd Punjabis
125th Rifles

21st Brigade (Brigadier-General C.E. Norie)
English Battalion
6th Jats
9th Bhopal Infantry
Mahratta Battalion

28th Brigade (Major-General G.V. Kemball)
2nd Leicestershire
Provisional Battalion Oxfordshire and Buckinghamshire Light Infantry
51st Sikhs
53rd Sikhs
56th Sikhs

Cavalry
16th Cavalry

Artillery
9th Brigade Royal Field Artillery (eighteen guns)
72nd Heavy Artillery (four guns)

Engineers
107th Pioneers, 3rd Company Sappers and Miners

13th Division (Major-General F.S. Maude)

38th Brigade (Brigadier-General J.W. O'Dowda)
6th King's Own Royal Regiment
6th East Lancashire
6th South Lancashire
6th Loyal Regiment (North Lancashire)

39th Brigade (Brigadier-General W. de S Cayley)
9th Royal Warwickshire
9th Worcestershire
7th North Staffordshire

40th Brigade (Brigadier-General A.C. Lewin)
8th Cheshire
8th Royal Welch Fusiliers
4th South Wales Borderers
5th Wiltshire

Artillery
66th Brigade Royal Field Artillery (thirteen guns)
69th Brigade Royal Field Artillery (four howitzers)

Heavy Brigade Royal Garrison Artillery (six guns)

Engineers
8th Welch Regiment (Pioneers)
72nd and 88th Companies Royal Engineers

Corps Troops

35th Brigade
Composite Territorial Battalion
Composite Dogra Battalion
97th Infantry
102nd Grenadiers

36th Brigade
1/6th Devonshire
26th Punjabis
62nd Punjabis
82nd Punjabis

Cavalry
16th Cavalry (two squadrons)

Engineers
12th and 13th Companies Sappers and Miners
one company 12th Pioneers

Artillery
13th Brigade Riyal Field Artillery (eighteen guns)
69th Brigade Royal Field Artillery (eight howitzers)
Home Counties Brigade Royal Field Artillery (twenty guns)
60 pounder Brigade (eight guns and one howitzer)

Cavalry Brigade
'S' Battery Royal Horse Artillery
14th Hussars
4th Cavalry
7th Lancers
33rd Cavalry (less two squadrons)

———

Notes
1. Moberly (1924) p.490/1 and 510–513 and 526–529.

APPENDIX III

The Turkish Army in and around Kut at the Time of Surrender[1]

6th Turkish Army (35,313 personnel)

13th Army Corps
2nd Division
Composite 35th Division (Included 38th Division)
One Independent Cavalry Brigade
(To the East of Kut)

18th Army Corps
45th Division
(Round Kut)
51st Division
52nd Division
(East of Kut)

Plus elements of the 6th Division (East of Kut)
(The 'Baghdad Group' was part of the 6th Army, but sent to fight against the Russian threat.)

Notes
1. Figures from Murphy (1920) p.100.

Battle of Shaikh Saad –
watercourse. (National Army
Museum 1983-12-72-9)

APPENDIX IV

Key Personalities

Name	Appointment
Asquith, Herbert	British Prime Minister
Aylmer, Lieutenant–General Sir Fenton	British commander of the Tigris Corps and Kut Relief Force before General Lake
Baratoff, General	Russian commander in Persia
Barrett, General Sir Arthur	British 6th (Poona) Division commander for initial operations in Mesopotamia
Beauchamp-Duff, General Sir Harry	Commander-in-Chief India
Bey, Colonel Halil/Khalil	Second Turkish 6th Army commander at Kut
Buchanan, Sir George	British engineer responsible for improving Basra port in 1916
Chamberlain, Austen	Secretary of State for India
Cox, General Sir Percy	India Government Political Agent in Mesopotamia
Crewe, Lord	Secretary of State for India
Delamain, Major-General Walter	British commander of 16th Brigade in Kut
Enver Pasha	Turkish War Minister

Name	Appointment
Goltz, Field Marshal Colmar Von Der	German – Overall Turkish Army commander at Kut
Gorringe, Major-General George	British commander of 12th Division 1915, then commander of Tigris Corps after Lieutenant-General Aylmer
Haig, Field Marshal Douglas	British Commander-in-Chief British Expeditionary Force in France and Flanders
Hamilton, Brigadier-General William	British commander of 18th Brigade in Kut
Hardinge, Viscount	Viceroy of India
Hathaway, Surgeon-General H.	British medical commander
Hoghton, Brigadier-General Frederick	British commander of 17th Brigade in Kut
Keary, Major-General Henry D'Urban	British commander of 3rd Division
Kemball, Major-General George	British senior staff officer to Nixon, then commander of 28th Brigade after Younghusband
Kitchener, Field Marshal Lord Herbert Horatio	British Secretary of State for War
Lake, General Sir Percy	Second British commander of India Expeditionary Force 'D' after General Nixon
Macmunn, Major-General George	British Inspector-General of Communications in Mesopotamia
MacNeece, Surgeon-General	British Director of Indian Medical Services
Maude, Lieutenant-General Sir Stanley	British commander of 13th Division as a major-general, who failed to relieve Kut, but went on to occupy Baghdad in 1917 as commander of British forces in Mesopotamia
Melliss, Major-General Sir Charles	British commander of 6th Cavalry Brigade
Nixon, General Sir John	Initial British commander of India Expeditionary Force 'D'

Name	Appointment
Nunn, Captain Wilfred (later a Vice-Admiral)	British naval captain of HMS *Espiegle* and the Senior Naval Officer of Townshend's Regatta
Nurredin/Nurettin Pasa/Nur-ud-Din Pasha, General	First Turkish 6th Army, XIII Corps commander at Kut
Rice, Brigadier-General Gerard	British commander 35th Brigade
Robertson, General Sir William	British Chief of the Imperial General Staff
Sami, Lieutenant-Colonel Bekir	Turkish commander of 52nd Infantry Division
Suleyman, Askeri Pasha	Turkish commander at the Battle of Shaiba
Townshend, Major-General Charles	British commander of 6th Division and commander of the force besieged at Kut
Wemyss, Vice-Admiral Sir Rosslyn	British Royal Navy Commander-in-Chief of the East Indies Station
Younghusband, Major-General Sir George	British commander of 28th Infantry Brigade, then 7th (Meerut) Division

APPENDIX V

Major-General Townshend[1]

The men love him, and the Turks fear him, for he is lucky and victorious.[2]

To say that Major-General Sir Charles Townshend KCB, DSO[3] was a 'character' is a great under-statement. His eccentric and egotistical personality dominates the story of Kut and his role in the campaign has been considered controversial, as views have varied about his capability to make the right decisions before, during and even after the siege, when he was in captivity.

Charles Vere Ferrers Townshend was born on 21 February 1861 and died on 18 May 1924. He was the great-grandson of the 1st Marquis Townshend, who had taken command of the British troops from a dying General Wolfe at the battle of Quebec in 1759. He was the heir presumptive of the 5th Marquis until 1917 – the embodiment of the upper-middle classes of the Victorian era, though his father was a minor railway official.

His military career began when he was commissioned into the Royal Marine Light Infantry in 1881, transferring to the Royal Fusiliers in 1900 and the King's Shropshire Light Infantry in 1908. He was made captain in 1892, major in 1895, lieutenant-colonel in 1896, colonel in 1904, brigadier-general in 1909 and major-general in 1911.

He gained operational experience in General Wolseley's failed attempt to relieve General Gordon at Khartoum in the Sudan (1884–85) with mounted infantry, and served with General Stewart at the Battles of Abu Klea and Gubat with the Guards Camel Regiment. He distinguished himself in the Dongola expedition to the North-West Frontier in 1895 when he found himself commanding four Europeans and 300 Indian troops in Fort Gupis, near Chitral, besieged by tribesmen for six weeks. He earned the nickname 'Chitral Charlie' and a reputation for courage and good leadership – his successful defence prior to being relieved had resonance with the position in which he found himself later at Kut. However, the defence of Chitral was not an active, aggressive one. Rich, who served in Major-General Townshend's 6th Division, quoted examples of him referring to sallies and the defence of Chitral: 'I will not have sallying parties, the risk is too great … I mean to sit tight until we are relieved.'[4] It is possible that his 'passive' success at Chitral hampered some of his decision making at Kut.

He then commanded a Sudanese battalion in 1898 during General Kitchener's Nile campaign, fighting at Atbara and Omdurman and also served briefly in the Second Boer War. He was a military attaché in Paris prior to commanding territorial divisions in 1911, the Home Counties Division and

Major-General Sir Charles Townshend. (Wilson)

then the East Anglian Division. At the beginning of the First World War he commanded two brigades in India, but was looking for opportunities to serve in France. He had been made a Companion of the Bath after his success at Chitral, an exceptionally high level of reward for such a junior officer, and prior to divisional command had also been mentioned in despatches five times. He received the DSO for the Nile Campaign and after the Kut surrender, was made a Knight Commander of the Bath in 1916.

His impact on the early stages of the Mesopotamia struggle is clear. He resigned his commission in 1920, the same year his book *My Campaign in Mesopotamia* was written. The title alone reveals the hubris of the man. A supportive biography was written by his cousin Erroll Sherson.[5] It was not until 1967 that a more balanced biography was written by Barker.[6] However, following the Kut surrender, and particularly his privileged conditions during captivity, he was obliged to defend his reputation amidst criticism that he had lacked concern for his men. Before his death he served as MP for the Wrekin in Shropshire (formerly Salop) and attempted, but failed, to persuade the Foreign Office to make him an official British representative in Turkey.

Historian John Keegan has described Townshend as 'a dashing and lucky captain, but a bad general and no gentleman',[7] whilst the author Norman Dixon castigated him as a liar, accusing him of not looking after his troops and ambitious at the expense of his command.[8] Another side to the man was revealed by Ronald Millar: 'Townshend had developed a passion for theatrical society and possessed exceptional gifts as a drawing-room raconteur, banjo player and general entertainer.'[9] He was also known to have an obsession with Napoleon and the French art of war, no doubt enhanced by his tour in Paris and his marriage to a member of the French nobility – his troops gave him the nickname of 'Alphonse'[10] at Kut and he managed to die in France. Author Russell Braddon provided a list of recorded examples throughout Townshend's career of him seeking action and promotion at the expense of others[11] and Major-General H. Rich judged that 'he was never satisfied and always convinced that he was not getting on fast enough.'[12] Author James Perry goes even further and calls him a 'louse'.[13]

A number of things are certain. He was brave and intelligent, well-read militarily and enjoyed the good things of life (one of his requests during the siege of Kut was for gramophone needles, which were air-dropped in). Definitely a 'thruster' he was determined to achieve glory and the tactics that he adopted with his 'regatta' worked prior to the stalemate of Ctesiphon. Like many of today's military thrusters, he was always seeking more prestigious appointments and rarely appeared happy in the one he was in – hence the unusually wide variety of regiments and postings. He had also been a lucky

Captain Townshend of the Central Indian Horse. (Sherson)

commander until the siege of Kut – a difficult characteristic to define, but soldiers attach a great deal of value to this attribute and he was popular with his troops. He was one of the first generals to take senior non-commissioned officers into his confidence and allowed them to attend briefings. Captain Mousley, a gunner at Kut, considered that 'One could not but feel the keenest admiration for General Townshend, so steady, collected and determined in action, so kind, quick and confident.'[14] One cannot ignore his charisma and leadership skills, especially when they are described by those within his command rather than by an assessor in more recent times.

He was certainly respected for his early achievements in Mesopotamia by the Turks 'who held him in considerable awe'[15] and, as the Liddell-Hart argues, he was able to beat his enemy without the advantage of numbers and firepower that General Sir Stanley Maude had later in the campaign.[16] It can be argued that he became the 'fall guy' for General Nixon, who had encouraged the advance toward Baghdad.

Dixon is clear about Townshend's legacy 'as the person most responsible for the disaster of Kut and for the misery inflicted upon his troops.'[17] John Laffin, supporting Dixon, stated: 'He was a gratuitous bungler, a calculating man who made decisions deliberately.'[18] Certainly, he was partly to blame for what happened at Kut and appears to have shown little interest in his fellow-prisoners. But it is hoped that this book has identified a number of factors, including the decisions made by all commanders and the actions of the enemy, that contributed to the disaster. We give the last word to an American author: 'An eccentric man even by British Army standards.'[19]

Notes

1. Sources include: *Who Was Who* (1916–1928) p.1049, Dupuy (1992) p.749.
2. Yeats-Brown (1930) p.171. Yeats-Brown was an observer in the Royal Flying Corps, supporting 6th Division.
3. Knight Commander of the Bath and Distinguished Service Order.
4. Rich (1967) p.82.
5. Sherson (1928) entitled *Townshend of Chitral and Kut*.
6. Barker (1967) entitled *Townshend of Kut*.
7. Keegan (1996) p.294.
8. Dixon (1976) Chapter 8.
9. Millar (1969) p.21.
10. Frequent references in Mousley (1921).
11. Braddon (1969) p.28–30.
12. Rich (1967) p.81.
13. Perry (1996) p.246.
14. Mousley (1922) p.15.
15. Rich (1967) p.84.
16. Liddell-Hart (1978) p.148.
17. Dixon (1976) p.106.
18. Laffin (1988) p.60.
19. Depuy (1992) p.750.

APPENDIX VI

Chronology

Date	Mesopotamia	Elsewhere
November–December 1914	Great Britain formally declares war on Turkey Oilfields secured Occupation of Basra and Qurna	Gallipoli – British and French naval bombardment Turkish offensive in Caucasia Turks invade British-occupied Egypt
January 1915	2nd Turco-German Treaty 1st Turkish invasion of Persia	
April 1915	12th Indian Division constituted as General Sir John Nixon takes command of 2nd Indian Army Corps (12–14) Battle of Shaiba (British victory) Major-General Townshend takes command of 6th Division	Gallipoli landings begin Turks withdrawal from Persia Second Battle of Ypres First German gas attack on Western Front Italy joins the Allies Armenian rebellion against the Turks begins British occupy oilfields in south-west Iran
May 1915	(31) British ('Townshend's Regatta') occupy Amara	The *Lusitania* is sunk Allied spring offensive Coalition Government formed in Britain Russian offensive at Tortum and Erzerum, Caucasia Turks counter-attack at Gallipoli

Date	Mesopotamia	Elsewhere
July 1915	(25) British occupy Nasiriya	Germans surrender in south-west Africa Russian offensive north-west of Lake Van, Caucasia Turks defeat British force outside Aden
August 1915	(1) British occupy Ali-al-Gharbi (15) British occupy Sannaiyat	Germans enter Warsaw Further Allied attacks at Gallipoli
September 1915	(27/28) 1st Battle of Kut-el-Amarah (Kut) and occupation of Kut (29)	Tsar takes supreme command of Russian forces French autumn offensive on the Western Front First British use of gas on the Western Front Battle of Loos
October 1915	1st Royal Flying Corps reconnaissance over Baghdad	Austro-German invasion of Serbia Bulgaria enters the War on the Central Powers' side British Machine Gun Corps formed and the formal issue of the British steel helmet on the Western Front Allied advance in Salonika
November 1915	(22–24) Battle of Ctesiphon – British forced to withdraw to Kut	
December 1915	(7) Siege of Kut begins (23) Turks assault Kut occupying north-east corner temporarily	Gallipoli – British evacuation of Suvla and Anzac Marshal Joffre appointed as the new French Commander-in-Chief on the Western Front General Sir William Robertson appointed British Chief of the Imperial General Staff (CIGS) British decision to begin conscription

Date	Mesopotamia	Elsewhere
January 1916 (1st attempt to relieve Kut)	(4) Lieutenant-General Aylmer and his relief force moves from Ali-al-Gharbi towards Kut (7) British victory at Shaikh-Saad. Turks withdraw (13) British attack at Wadi. Turks withdraw (19) General Sir Percy Lake takes over British command in Mesopotamia from General Sir John Nixon (21) British attack at Hanna fails (27) Some Turkish positions around Kut flooded	Gallipoli – British evacuation of Cape Helles Russian offensive on Armenia/ Caucasian Front Austrian offensive in Montenegro British prototype tank begins trials
February 1916	(13) First bombing of Kut from the air (16) Chief of Imperial General Staff takes control from London vice India British 13th Division and 7th Mountain Battery ordered to and begins to arrive in Mesopotamia	Persia – Russian General Baratoff occupies Kermanshah and Erzerum Western Front – Battle of Verdun begins
March 1916 (2nd attempt to relieve Kut)	(8) British Relief Force attack fails at Dujailah Redoubt and Es Sinn (12) British General Gorringe takes over command from General Aylmer T.E. Lawrence begins 'secret mission'	Palestine – Battle of Katia Western Front – Verdun continues Germany and Austria declare war on Portugal
April 1916 (3rd attempt to relieve Kut)	(5) British Relief Force seizes Hanna and Falahiya (17) British Relief Force take Beit Aiessa (6–22) British relief force blocked at Sannaiyat (three attempts failed) (23) SS *Julnar* fails to break Kut block-ade (29) Surrender of Kut to Turkish forces	Ireland – Easter rebellion Persia – Russian General Baratoff cap-tures Karnid after a nine-day march attempt to assist Kut Western Front – Verdun continues
May 1916	(4) 420 officer prisoners are moved by river-steamer from Kut to Baghdad (6) 'Death March' by troops begins from Kut and reaches Tikrit on 23 May. Split into British, Hindu and Muslim groups	Persia – Russian General Baratoff occupies Kars-i-Shrin, only 110 miles from Baghdad British advance in Palestine Turks retake Uzum island in the Aegean Sea from the British

Date	*Mesopotamia*	*Elsewhere*
June 1916	Major-General Townshend reaches Constantinople as prisoner Prisoners of War reach Mosul	Fall of French fort Vaux, Verdun Second Turkish invasion of Persia Arab revolt against Ottoman Empire from Western Arabia
July 1916	(11) Lieutenant-General Maude takes over the Tigris Corps from Lieutenant-General Gorringe	The Somme battles begin Russians capture Erzincan, Caucasus
August 1916	(28) General Maude succeeds General Lake in charge of Allied force	Russian Cossacks link up with Tigris Corps British troops Turks attack Bir Romani, Palestine
December 1916	(13) Allied Tigris offensive resumed	British attack El Arish, Palestine
March 1917	(11) Baghdad occupied	Russian Revolutions 1st Battle of Gaza, Palestine Turks withdraw from Persia

APPENDIX VII

The Defence of Kut and the Failed Attempt to Relieve the
Siege – The British Battle Honours Awarded in 1925 and 1926[1]

Date	Battle Honour	Regiment Awarded to	Current British, Indian or Pakistan Regiment
7 December 1915–28 April 1916	*Defence of Kut-al-Amara*	*British Infantry* The Royal Norfolk Regiment	The Royal Anglian Regiment
		The Dorsetshire Regiment	The Rifles
		The Oxfordshire and Buckinghamshire Light Infantry	The Rifles
		The Queen's Own Royal West Kent Regiment	The Princess of Wales's Royal Regiment
		Indian Army Engineers and Pioneers King George's Own Bengal Sappers & Miners	Bengal Sappers
		Royal Bombay Sappers & Miners	Bombay Sappers
		2nd Bombay Pioneers	Bengal Sappers
		Sirmoor Sappers	
		Indian Infantry Regiments 1st Punjab Regiment	Punjab Regiment
		2nd Punjab Regiment	Punjab Regiment
		5th Mahratta Light Infantry	Maratha Light Infantry
		6th Rajputana Rifles	Rajputana Rifles
		7th Rajput Regiment	Rajput Regiment
		9th Jat Regiment	Jat Regiment

Date	Battle Honour	Regiment Awarded to	Current British, Indian or Pakistan Regiment
		14th Punjab Regiment	Punjab Regiment (Pakistan Army)
		7th Duke of Edinburgh's Own Gurkha Rifles	Royal Gurkha Rifles (British Army)
14 January 1916 – 24 April 1916	*Tigris 1916* (Awarded for the three attempts to relieve Kut-al-Amara)	*British Cavalry* 14th King's Hussars	The King's Royal Hussars
		British Infantry The Buffs (Royal East Kent Regiment)	The Princess of Wales's Royal Regiment
		The King's Own (Lancaster) Regiment	The Duke of Lancaster's Regiment (King's, Lancashire and Border)
		The Royal Warwickshire Regiment	The Royal Regiment of Fusiliers
		The Devonshire Regiment	The Rifles
		The Somerset Light Infantry (Prince Albert's)	The Rifles
		The Leicestershire Regiment	The Royal Anglian Regiment
		The Cheshire Regiment	1st Battalion the Mercian Regiment (Cheshire)
		The Royal Welsh Fusiliers	1st Battalion the Royal Welsh (The Royal Welch Fusiliers)
		The South Wales Borderers	2nd Battalion the Royal Welsh (The Royal Regiment of Wales)
		The Gloucestershire Regiment	The Rifles
		The Worcestershire Regiment	2nd Battalion the Mercian Regiment (Worcesters and Foresters)
		The East Lancashire Regiment	The Duke of Lancaster's Regiment (King's, Lancashire and Border)
		The Hampshire Regiment	The Princess of Wales's Royal Regiment
		The South Lancashire Regiment	The Duke of Lancaster's Regiment (King's, Lancashire and Border)
		The Welch Regiment	2nd Battalion the Royal Welsh (The Royal Regiment of Wales)

Date	Battle Honour	Regiment Awarded to	Current British, Indian or Pakistan Regiment
		The Black Watch (Royal Highlanders)	The Black Watch, 3rd Battalion the Royal Regiment of Scotland
		The Oxfordshire and Buckinghamshire Light Infantry	The Rifles
		The Loyal (North Lancashire) Regiment	The Duke of Lancaster's Regiment (King's, Lancashire and Border)
		The Wiltshire Regiment (Duke of Edinburgh's)	The Rifles
		The Manchester Regiment	The Duke of Lancaster's Regiment (King's, Lancashire and Border)
		The North Staffordshire Regiment (Prince of Wales's)	3rd Battalion the Mercian Regiment (Staffords)
		The Highland Light Infantry	The Royal Highland Fusiliers
		The Seaforth Highlanders (Ross-Shire Buffs)	2nd Battalion the Royal Regiment of Scotland
		The Connaught Rangers	Disbanded 1922
		Indian Cavalry	
		2nd Lancers (Gardner's Horse)	2nd Lancers
		6th Duke of Connaught's Own Lancers (Watson's Horse)	(Pakistan Army)
		17th Queen Victoria's Poona Horse	17th Poona Horse
		18th King Edward's Own Cavalry	18th Cavalry
		Miscellaneous	
		103rd (Peshawar) Pack Battery	
		Indian Engineers and Pioneers	
		King George's Own Bengal Sappers & Miners	Bengal Sappers
		Queen Victoria's Own Madras Sappers & Miners	Madras Sappers
		Royal Bombay Sappers & Miners	Bombay Sappers
		2nd Bombay Pioneers	Disbanded 1920s.
		3rd Sikh Pioneers	

Date	Battle Honour	Regiment Awarded to	Current British, Indian or Pakistan Regiment
		Indian Infantry	
		1st Punjab Regiment	Punjab Regiment
		4th Bombay Grenadiers	Grenadiers Regiment
		6th Rajputana Rifles	Rajputana Rifles
		7th Rajput Regiment	Rajput Regiment
		8th Punjab Regiment	Punjab Regiment
		9th Jat Regiment	Jat Regiment
		11th Sikh Regiment	Sikh Regiment
		12th Frontier Force Regiment	Frontier Force Regiment
		13th Frontier Force Rifles	(Pakistan Army)
		15th Punjab Regiment	Punjab Regiment
		16th Punjab Regiment	Punjab Regiment
		17th Dogra Regiment	Dogra Regiment
		19th Hyderabad Regiment	Kumaon Regiment
		1st King George's Own Gurkha Rifles (The Malaun Regiment)	1 Gorkha Rifles
		2nd King Edward VII's Own Gurkha Rifles (The Sirmoor Rifles)	Royal Gurkha Rifles (British Army)
		4th Prince of Wales's Own Gurkha Rifles	4 Gorkha Rifles
		8th Gurkha Rifles	8 Gorkha Rifles
		9th Gurkha Rifles	9 Gorkha Rifles

Notes

1. References used; Ascoli (1983), Brereton (1985), Baker (1986), Rodger (2003) and The Army List 2006.

Lieutenant H. Baillie's medals. (Dorsetshire Regiment Museum)

Indian Punjabi. (IWM Q 24746)

APPENDIX VIII

Comparable Ranks[1]

British Rank	Indian Cavalry Rank	Indian Infantry Rank	Turkish Rank
Commissioned Officers			_Commissioned Officers_
Field Marshal			Mushir
General			Birinji ferik
Lieutenant-General			Ferik
Major-General			Liva
Brigadier-General			
Colonel			Miralai
Lieutenant-Colonel			Kaimakam
	Viceroy Commissioned Officers	_Viceroy Commissioned Officers_	
Major	Risaldar-Major	Subadar-Major	Bimbashi
Captain	Risaldar	Subadar	Yuzbashi
Lieutenant	Jemadar	Jemadar	Mulazim-i-evvel
Non-Commissioned Officers	_Non-Commissioned Officers_	_Non-Commissioned Officers_	_Non-Commissioned Officers_
Sergeant-Major	Duffardar-Major	Havildar-Major	Bash chaoush
Sergeant	Duffardar	Havildar	Chaoush
Corporal	Lance-Duffardar	Naik	Ombashi
Lance-Corporal		Lance-Naik	
Private/Trooper	Sowar	Sepoy	Nefer

Notes

1. Main references; _Handbook of the Turkish Army_ (1916) p.134/135 and _India's Army_ (1940) p.9.

APPENDIX IX

Major-General Sir Charles Melliss's Letter to the Secretary of State for War – Sent from Broussa on 15 August 1917

This letter was sent via the Netherlands Minister at Constantinople on 5 September 1917.[1]

Sir,

I have long been anxious to inform His Majesty's Government of the following circumstances connected with the march of the surrendered garrison of Kut al Amara to Baghdad and thence to Mosul, Ras al Ain and across the Amanus and Taurus ranges. Hitherto I have had no opportunity to send in this report.

To rightly understand what follows, it is necessary to realise the starved and dysentery stricken state of the garrison when Kut fell. A report on this, and of the suffering and deaths which occurred amongst the men at the camp Shumran outside Kut has no doubt been rendered by Colonel Hehir, I.M.S. [Indian Medical Services] who was eventually released. And in passing I should like to refer to the noble manner in which Colonel Hehir and Major Baines I.M.S. worked amongst the distressing scenes and conditions of that camp. From Shumran all officers were sent up to Baghdad by boat, and the men were made to march. I have heard many painful stories of that march, of how our poor fellows fell from exhaustion by the way, and were kicked and beaten by their Arab escort to rise again, until in some cases they dropped down dead. But this is only hearsay.

On arrival at Baghdad the men were placed in blazing hot camps, without rest and in spite of the protests of our own medical officers as to their unfitness, the men were then despatched (that is all those who were not actually prostrate) in large batches, without any of their own officers on that terrible march of some 500 miles across a desert like country. I should add that all the officers including generals had been sent on in one party ahead of the men.

As I was in a very weak state when I reached Baghdad, I was allowed to remain there a month and followed later in company with Colonel W.W. Chitty I.A. [Indian Army], Major McKenna I.A., Major Baines I.M.S. and Captain Shakeshaft Norfolk Regiment along the same route (in a carriage) as taken by our men.

I feel it beyond my powers of description to convey to you a picture of what I saw at some of the various halting places en route – Arab villages or small police posts commanded by an Arab or Turkish officer or under officer (all alike a mixture of brutish callousness, stupidity and ignorance). At such places I came across parties of our men, who were too exhausted to go further. They were lying about under a shelter or in any mud hovel given to them, some on the bare ground – others lucky to possess a blanket – many half clothed and without boots, which they had sold to purchase milk to keep life within them, there they lay in all stages of dysentery and semi starvation. Many terribly emaciated, some almost living skeletons, some dying, some dead. There were no medicines and only at some places a hospital attendant or hospital assistant had been left to look after them.

Their one cry was for milk and the officer of the post had regarded their sufferings with complete indifference, excusing himself with the plea that he had no authority to spend money to provide milk. A loaf of coarse black bread was, as far as I saw, the only nourishment given to out poor men to keep life in them. I first encountered these scenes at Tikrit, a considerable Arab village having a civil official and military commandant, some 30 miles distant from Samarra. At this place I found about 300 of our men, British and Indian, who could no longer proceed, and many of whom were in the condition I have described above. But there were similar instances in lesser numbers in other places I stopped at along the road; and no doubt at other places, where we did not stop (I was of course under escort). On one occasion I picked up on the road on the Amanus range four British soldiers lying abandoned on the road as they could no longer keep up. They were without food except for some bread given to them by a passing Austrian officer. Further on at a place named Bogli, a considerable village with a post under a Turkish officer, I found 20 other British soldiers. They were lying neglected and utterly exhausted in a large shed. I might say almost that they were lying in their excrement, for they were all so exhausted with dysentery they had scarcely strength to crawl to the door of the shed to relieve themselves. They had arrived early that morning. No food had been given to them, a half baked black loaf was later on given to them. I am glad to be able to say I was able to insist on carts being provided and I took them all on (including the four picked up on the road) with me to Mamouri where they were kindly treated by the German commandant and sent to a German hospital. Indeed I ought to say here that the only humanity shown to our men was by an occasional Austrian or German officer. I need not say that I and the officers with me did all we could to help out unhappy men. We distributed all the gold we had amongst them. I sent back a letter to Halil Pasha at Baghdad from Tikrit inform- ing him of the state of things and asking for English doctors and medicine to be sent along the route. I later heard that a doctor (English) did come to Tikrit. I also saw Shefket Pasha at Aleppo and sent a full report to Enver Pasha, to which I received an answer (as was to be expected) that he could not believe it was true.

Major Walker I.M.S. (a prisoner here) who came along the route shortly after me can testify to the absolute neglect and filth amongst our sick soldiers at the hospital at Nisibin and the brutal indiffer- ence of the Turkish commandant at that place. The civilians Messrs Todd and Cree also came along the same route shortly afterwards. They are now here. Mr Cree has told me the recollections of what he saw haunted him for long afterwards.

If it is true as I hear that at least half of the British soldiers who were alive when Kut fell, are now missing, the above will explain, of course the Indian soldiers suffered too, but not to the extent that the British did.

I am told that a letter has appeared in *The Times* from General Townshend speaking of his good treatment by the Turks. I believe this is so, but if it has given the impression that we are all well treated, it will have created a very wrong one. Our treatment as officers of general's rank is by no means good at the present time and has often been disgraceful.

We have been and still are subjected to much petty tyrannical and often humiliating restrictions. It is impossible to enter into details. Perhaps the following instances may give some idea of what we endure. On two occasions interned Europeans (an Englishmen in one case, a French lady in the other) were arrested in the street by our escort for merely bowing to us as we passed. To speak to anyone is absolutely forbidden and is a serious offence. Indeed I have often been made to feel, as if I was a dangerous political criminal rather than a prisoner of war. Lately we have been forbidden to play any games and even music is forbidden to us. It is true we live in a hotel (in the poorest quarter of the town) and each officer and his ADC [aide-de-camp] has a room to himself, we may walk out twice a day in the streets of the town, always attended by a soldier. We may not enter a cafe or even a shop. We see nothing but Turkish papers (in French) and as you may suppose, there is never anything cheering for us to read in them.

I can give no information as to how our officers at Kastamuni, Yozgad and Afion Kara Hissar are treated as all intercommunication is forbidden. Nor can I tell you anything as regards our men British or Indian.

Nothing could be much worse than the way we receive our letters from the Turkish censor. Here is my own experience, out of some 30 to 40 cards and letters (mostly cards) which I know are written to me by my family each month. I consider myself very fortunate if I get a half dozen or so in a month. For example in the last four weeks I have had but two cards one of date May 11th. The experience of others is more or less the same.

Is there no prospect for an exchange? It is a terrible existence that we lead, <u>especially for men of our age</u>.

As regards myself some months ago I was not far from the breaking down point. My heart and nerves have become badly affected by my captivity. I enclose a certificate from Major Walker I.M.S. who is in charge of us here. I had asked to be interned in Switzerland – you see the result as stated by Major Walker in his certificate. But it was pretty well a foregone conclusion.

Cannot the Government effect my exchange? I am in a pretty bad way in mind and health. I beg you will do what you can for me.

A few words more. We of the unfortunate Kut garrison have never yet heard that the country was well satisfied with us. It would be a great comfort for us to know that. Nor do we ever read in any of the speeches at home (reproduced in the papers here) of any sympathetic recognition of what we endure in our captivity. I feel sure that all our prisoners in this country and in Germany will derive some comfort if some public mention was made of us to show that what we suffer is recognised by our countrymen. For although what we do suffer, is of no service to the country, we suffer for it indeed, far more than people at home, I think, realise. We suffer in mind because we can serve the country no longer, because of many humiliations to endure and from a terrible monotony and blankness of existence, we suffer in health from loss of liberty and many irksome restrictions, we suffer in professional prospects and pecuniarily.

I have the honour, etc.,

(Signed) C.J. Melliss

Major-General

———

Notes

1. From National Archives at Kew, FO (Foreign Office) 383 (formerly File 249) covering 1917.

BIBLIOGRAPHY

Books

Anonymous (undated). Reprint – *History of No. 30 Squadron, Egypt and Mesopotamia 1914–1919.* (East Sussex. Naval & Military Press Ltd in association with The Imperial War Museum Department of Printed Books)

Anonymous (1918). *With a Highland Regiment in Mesopotamia.* (Bombay. The Times Press)

Anonymous (Undated (1919?). *A Short History of The Queen's Own (Royal West Kent Regiment).* (Unknown)

Anonymous (undated). *Deeds That Thrill The Empire.* (London. Hutchinson & Co)

Anonymous (1924). *A History of the 26th Punjabis 1857–1923.* (Aldershot. Gale & Polden Ltd)

Anonymous (1930). *The Campaign of the British Army in Mesopotamia 1914–1918.* (London. Sir Isaac Pitman & Sons Ltd)

Anonymous (1933). *History of The Dorsetshire Regiment 1914–1919. Part 1 The Regular Battalions.* (Dorchester. Henry Ling Ltd)

Anonymous (1934). *War Records of the 24th Punjabis (4th Battalion 14th Punjab Regiment 1914-1920.* (Aldershot. Gale & Polden Ltd)

Anonymous (1935). *Regimental History of the 6th Royal Battalion Scinde) 13th Frontier Force Rifles 1843–1934.* (Aldershot. Gale & Polden)

Anonymous (1989). *Heritage – The History of the Rajput Regiment 1778-1947.* (New Delhi. Rakesh Press)

Anonymous (1992). *47th Sikhs War Record The Great War 1914–1918.* (Chippenham. Picton Publishing Ltd)

Anglesey The Marquess of (1995). *A History of the British Cavalry 1816–1919. Volume 6: 1914-1918 Mesopotamia.* (Barnsley. Pen and Sword Books Ltd)

Anthology (undated). *Serve to Lead.* (Compiled at the Royal Military Academy Sandhurst)

Arthur, Sir George (1920). *Life of Lord Kitchener.* Volumes I and II. (London. Macmillan and Co Ltd).

Army Documents Publication (1996). Volume 3 – Logistics (MOD)

Ascoli David (1983). *A Companion to The British Army 1660–1983.* (London. Harrap Ltd)

Asher (1998). *Lawrence – The Uncrowned King of Arabia.* (London. Penguin Books Ltd)

Atkinson (undated). *A History of The 1st (PWO) Battalion the Dogra Regiment 1887-1947.* (Southampton. The Camelot Press)

Atkinson (1931). *The History of the South Wales Borderers 1914–1918.* (London. The Medici Society Ltd)

Atkinson (1952). *Regimental History The Royal Hampshire Regiment Volume Two 1914–1918.* (Glasgow. Robert Maclehose & Company Ltd, The University Press)

Baker, Anthony (1986). *Battle Honours of the British and Commonwealth Armies.* (London. Ian Allan Ltd.)

Barber, Major Charles H. (1917). *Besieged in Kut and After.* (Edinburgh and London. William Blackwood and Sons)

Barker, A.J. (1967). *The Neglected War; Mesopotamia 1914-1918.* (London. Faber & Faber.)

Barker A.J. (1967). *Townshend of Kut. A Biography of Major-General Sir Charles Townshend, KCB, DSO.* (London. Cassell)

Beharry, Johnson VC (2006). *Barefoot Soldier.* (London. Sphere)

Birch Reynardson, Captain H. (1919). *Mesopotamia 1914–15, Extracts from a Regimental Officer's Diary.* (London. Andrew Melrose Ltd)

Bishop, Harry C.W. (1920). *A Kut Prisoner.* (London. Bodley Head)

Black Tab (1917). *On the Road to Kut – A Soldier's Story of the Mesopotamian Campaign.* (London. Hutchinson & Co)

Blaxland, Gregory (1969). *History of the First World War.* (Bristol. Purnell and Sons Ltd).

Braddon, Russell (1969). *The Siege.* (London. Jonathan Cape)

Brereton, J.M. (1985). *A Guide to the Regiments and Corps of The British Army of the Regular Establishment.* (London. The Bodley Head.)

Brophy, John and Partridge, Eric (1969). *The Long Trail.* (London. Sphere Books Ltd)

Buchanan, George Sir (1938). *The Tragedy of Mesopotamia.* (Edinburgh and London. William Blackwood & Sons Ltd.)

Callwell, Major-General Sir C.E. (1920). *The Life of Sir Stanley Maude.* (London. Constable and Company Ltd)

Candler, Edmund (1919). *The Long Road to Baghdad.* (Two volumes) (London. Cassell and Company Ltd)

Cato, Conrad (1917). *The Navy in Mesopotamia.* (London. Constable and Company Ltd)

Condon, Brigadier W.E.H. (1962). *The Frontier Force Regiment.* (Aldershot. Gale & Polden)

Davis, Paul K. (1994). *Ends and Means. The British Mesopotamia Campaign and Commission.* (London and Toronto. Associated University Presses)

Depuy, Trevor N., Johnson Kurt and Bongard David L. (1992). *The Encyclopedia of Military Biography.* (London. IB Tauris & Co Ltd)

Dixon, Norman F. (1976). *On the Psychology of Military Incompetence.* (London. Jonathan Cape Ltd)

Eady (1930). *Historical Illustrations to Field Service Regulations, Operations, 1929.* (London. Sifton Praed & Co Ltd)

Elton, Lord (1938). *Among Others.* (London. Hutchinson &Co (Publishers) Ltd)

Erickson, Edward J. (2001). *A History of the Ottoman Army in the First World War.* (London. Greenwood Press)

Erickson, Edward J. (2007). *Ottoman Army Effectiveness in World War 1.* (London and New York. Routledge)

Etherington, Mark (2005). *Revolt on the Tigris. The Al Sadr Uprising and the Governing of Iraq.* (London. Hurst and Company)

Evans, Major R. (1926). *A Brief Outline of the Campaign in Mesopotamia 1914–1918.* (London. Sifton Praed & Co Ltd)

Farndale, General Sir Martin (1988). *History of the Royal Regiment of Artillery. The Forgotten Fronts and the Home Base 1914-1918.* (Royal Artillery Institution)

Fitzgerald-Lee, J. (1927). *The 'D' Force (Mesopotamia) in the Great War.* (Aldershot. William May & Co)

Gibson, Tom (1969). *The Wiltshire Regiment.* (London. Leo Cooper Ltd)

Gliddon, Gerald (2005). *VCs of The First World War. The Sideshows.* (Stroud. Sutton Publishing Ltd)

Graves, Philip (1941). *The Life of Sir Percy Cox.* (London and Melbourne. Hutchinson & Co Ltd)

Griffyth, Fairfax Captain (1919). *Mesopotamia.* (London. John Murray)

Hailes, Lieutenant-Colonel W.L. (1938). *War Services of the 9th Jat Regiment.* (Aldershot. Gale & Polden Ltd)

Handel, Michael I. (1990). *Intelligence and Military Operations.* (London. Frank Cass and Company Ltd)

Harvey, Regimental-Quartermaster-Sergeant and Hewick J.S. (1923). *The Sufferings of the Kut Garrison.* (Ludgershall, Wiltshire. The Adjutants Press Ltd)

Herbert, Aubrey (1919). *Mons, Anzac and Kut. By an MP.* (London. Edward Arnold)

Holmes, Richard (2006). *Dusty Warriors – Modern Soldiers at War.* (London. Harper Press)

Johnston, Captain M.A.B. and Yearsley, Captain K.D. (1919). *Four-Fifty Miles to Freedom.* (Edinburgh and London. William Blackwood and Sons)

Jones, E.H. (1955 edition of 1919 book). *The Road to Endor.* (London. Pan Books Ltd)

Jourdain, Lieutenant-Colonel H.F.N. and Fraser Edward (1924). *The Connaught Rangers.* (London. Royal United Services Institute)

Keegan, John and Wheatcroft, Andrew (1996). *Who's Who in Military History.* (London and New York. Routledge)

Keeling, E.H. (1924). *Adventures in Turkey and Russia.* (London. John Murray)

Kingsmill, Arthur (1966). *The Silver Badge.* (Ilfracombe. Arthur H Stockwell Ltd)

Laffin, John (1988). *British Butchers and Bunglers of World War One.* (Gloucester. Alan Sutton)

Lawrence, T.E. (1940). *Seven Pillars of Wisdom.* (London. Jonathan Cape Ltd)

Liddell Hart, Sir Basil (1972). *Liddell Hart's History of The First World War.* (London. Pan Books Ltd)

Liddell Hart, Sir Basil (1978). Through the Fog of War. (London. Faber and Faber Ltd)

Long, Flight Sergeant P.W. (1938). *Other Ranks of Kut.* (London. Williams and Norgate Ltd)

Lucas, Sir Charles (1926). *The Empire at War, Volume V, Chapter VIII, Mesopotamia* (London. Humphrey Milford Oxford University Press)

Mackay, Colonel J.N. DSO (1962). *History of 7th Duke of Edinburgh's Own Gurkha Rifles.* (Edinburgh and London. William Blackwood & Sons Ltd)

Mason ,Philip (1974). *A Matter of Honour – An Account of the Indian Army its Officers and Men.* (London. Jonathan Cape)

Millar, Ronald (1969). *Kut, the Death of an Army.* (London. Secker and Warberg)

Mills, Dan Sergeant (2007). *Sniper One.* (London. Penguin Books)

Moberly, F.J. Brigadier-General (1924). *History of The Great War. The Campaign in Mesopotamia 1914–1918. Volumes I and II.* (HMSO)

Moberly, F.J. Brigadier-General (1927). *History of the Great War. The Campaign in Mesopotamia 1914–1918. Volume IV.* (HMSO)

Mockler-Ferryman (undated). *The Oxfordshire & Buckinghamshire Light Infantry Chronicle 1915–1916.* (London. Eyre and Spottiswoode Ltd)

Mousley, Captain Edward O. (1922). *The Secrets of a Kuttite.* (John Lane and Co)

Moynihan, Michael (1983). *God on Our Side.* (London. Leo Cooper)

Neave, Dorina L. (1937), *Remembering Kut.* (London. William Clowes and Sons Ltd)

Neville, Captain J.E.H. (1938). *History of the 43rd and 52nd (Oxfordshire and Buckinghamshire) Light Infantry in the Great War, 1914 -1919.* (Aldershot. Gale and Polden)

Nunn, Wilfred (2007). *Tigris Gunboats.* (London. Chatham Publishing Lionel Leventhal Ltd. Reprint from Andrew Melrose Ltd 1932)

Ozdemir, Hikmet (2008). *The Ottoman Army 1914–1918, Disease and Death on the Battlefield.* (Salt Lake City. The University of Utah Press)

Paltan, Jangi (1930). *The 1st Battalion 5th Mahratta Light Infantry.* (Calcutta. Government of India Press).

Perry, James M. (1996). *Arrogant Armies. Great Military Disasters and the Generals Behind Them.* (New York. John Wiley & Sons Inc)

Petre, F. Loraine (1919). *The History of the Norfolk Regiment 1685–1918. Volume II.* (Norwich. Jarrold & Sons Ltd, The Empire Press)

Qureshi, Major Mohammed Ibrahim (1958). *History of The First Punjab Regiment 1759–1956.* (Aldershot. Gale & Polden Ltd)

Rawlinson, H.G. (1941). *The History of the 3rd Battalion 7th Rajput Regiment (Duke of Connaught's Own).* (London. Oxford University Press)

Rodger, Alexander (2003). *Battle Honours of the British Empire and Commonwealth Land Forces 1662–1991.* (Marlborough. The Crowood Press.)

Rooney, David (2000). *Military Mavericks. Extraordinary Men of Battle.* (London. Cassell & Co)

Sandes, Major E. W.C. (1920). *In Kut and Captivity.* (London. John Murray)

Sheffield, Gary and Bourne, John (2005). *Douglas Haig. War Diaries and Letters 1914–1918.* (London. Wiedenfeld & Nicholson)

Sheffy, Yigal (1998). *British Military Intelligence in the Palestine Campaign 1914–1918.* (London. Frank Cass)

Sherson, Erroll (1928). *Townshend of Chitral and Kut.* (London. William Heinemann Ltd)

Stoker Commander H.G. (1925). *Straws in the Wind.* (London. Herbert Jenkins Ltd)

Strawson, John (1980). *Gentlemen in Khaki. The British Army 1890-1990.* (London. Secker and Warburg)

Townshend, Major-General Sir Charles (1920). *My Campaign in Mesopotamia.* (London. Thornton Butterworth)

Von Der Goltz, General Colmar Freiherr (1899). *The Conduct of War.* (London. Kegan, Paul, Trench, Trubner & Co Ltd)

Wallach, Janet (2004). *Desert Queen. The Extraordinary Life of Gertrude Bell.* (London. Phoenix)

Watson, Bruce Allen (1993). *Sieges A Comparative Study.* (Westport, Connecticut, London. Praeger)

Wauchope, Major-General A.G. (1925). *A History of The Black Watch (Royal Highlanders) in the Great War, 1914–1918.* (London. The Medici Society Limited)

Who Was Who 1916–1928 (1929). (London. A & C Black Ltd)

Wilson, Trevor (1986). The Myriad Forces of War. (Cambridge. Polity Press)

Wilcox, Ron (2006). *Battles on the Tigris.* (Barnsley. Pen & Sword Ltd)

Wilson, Lieutenant-Colonel Sir Arnold T. (1930). *Loyalties Mesopotamia 1914-1917.* (London. Oxford University Press. Humphrey Milford)

Woolley, Captain C.L. (1921). *From Kastamuni to Kedos.* (Oxford. Basil Blackwell)

Wylly, Colonel H.C. (1928). *History of The 1st and 2nd Battalions The Leicestershire Regiment in the Great War.* (Aldershot. Gale & Polden Ltd)

Wylly, Colonel H.C. (1925). *History of The Manchester Regiment (Late the 63rd and 96th Foot).* (London. Forster Groom & Co Ltd)

Yeats-Brown, F. (1930). *Bengal Lancer.* (London. Victor Gollancz Ltd)

Younghusband, Major-General Sir George (1917). *A Soldier's Memories in Peace and War.* (London. Herbert Jenkins Ltd)

Articles / Papers

Afion, Kara Hissar Camp leaflet. 'Notes for relatives of British Prisoners of War in Turkey'. (Cambridge University Press)

Anderson Major A.J. (1960). Anderson Paper's Notes. (National Army Museum. 1960-12-29)

Bishop Lieutenant H.C.W. Indian Army (1919). Kut and Kustamuni. (Simla. *Journal of the United Service Institution of India.* Vol XLVII January–October 1918)

Coombes (1918). The *Queen's Own Gazette.* After Kut. (Unknown)

Falls, Cyril (1967). 'Lieutenant-General Sir Stanley Maude'. *History Today,* Volume XVII (London)

Hammond, Josephine (2006). 'Three Heroes of Kut – Ninety Years Ago', *Royal United Services Journal.* April 2006.

Harris Captain J.H. (undated). Escape diary of Captain J.H. Harris from prisoner of war camp, Yozgad, Anatolia, Turkey to Lapithos, Cyprus 7th August 1918 – 13th September 1918. M958. Diary held at Royal Hampshire Regiment Museum, Serles' House, Winchester.

His Majesty's Stationery Office (1917). Mesopotamia Commission Report

Latter, Edwin (1994). 'The Indian Army in Mesopotamia'. *Journal of The Society of Army Historical Research.* (London. The National Army Museum)

Leach, Regimental-Sergeant-Major (1916). Diaries and Notebooks. (Unpublished)

Melliss, Major-General Sir Charles (1917). Letter to Secretary of State For War August 1917. (National Archives FO 383 covering 1917)

Murphy (1920). *Journal of the Royal United Service Institution.* Volume LXV, February to November 1920. (London. J J Keliher & Co Ltd)

Nelson (1918). The *Queen's Own Gazette.* A Monthly Record of Regimental Doings of the Queen's Own (Royal West Kent Regiment). (Unknown)

Officers of the Staff College, Quetta (1925). 'Critical Study of the Campaign in Mesopotamia up to April 1917.' (Calcutta. Government of India Press)

Prisoners of War in Turkey (1918). 'Regulations and Notes for the help of relatives and friends'. Issued by the Prisoners in Turkey Committee, August 1918. (London. St Clements Press Ltd)

Puri Captain, Indian Medical Service (1918). Private letter to Mr Leach. Held at Royal Hampshire Regiment Museum, Winchester.

Rich Major-General H.H. (1967). 'The Enigma of Townshend and Kut Al Amara'. *The Army Quarterly and Defence Journal* Vol LXXXXIII (October 1966 and January 1967) (London. William Clowes & Sons Ltd)

Rimington, Brigadier J.C. (1923). *The Army Quarterly,* Volume VI (April and July 1923). (London. William Clowes & Sons Ltd)

Spackman, Captain William Collis (1967). Journal of Captain W.C. Spackman IMS relating to the Siege of Kut, December 1915 to April 1916. (National Army Museum. 1967-09-16-2)

Spackman Colonel W.C. (1969). *Purnell's History of The First World War.* Volume 4, Issue 64. (London. BPC Publishing Ltd)

Spackman, Colonel W.C. (2008). *Captured at Kut, Prisoner of the Turks.* (Barnsley. Pen & Sword Books Ltd)

The Great War 1914–1918. (1991). The illustrated journal of First World War history. Mesopotamia Diary. With The 5th Buffs along the Tigris 1915–1916

The Times – 2 June 1920

Commonwealth War Grave at
Amara today – Cross of Sacrifice.
(Brigadier Mark Armstrong)

Commonwealth War Graves, Indian
Army Memorial at Amara today.
(Brigadier Mark Armstrong)

Ubsdell (undated). Diary on rice paper of Second Lieutenant Ubsell, 66th Punjabis. (National Army
    Museum. 1960-12-398)

Various authors (undated). *Deeds that Thrill the Empire*. (London. Hutchinson & Co)

War Office (1932). Report of the Committee on the Lessons of The Great War (The Kirke Report). PRO
    WO33/1297

Wheeler Harold V (undated). *War Time Wanderings of the 1/4th Battalion, Hampshire Regiment, (Territorial
    Force) 1914–1919* (Winchester. Private)

Wright Pop (1939). Report of the Tenth Annual Dinner of the Garrison of Kut-al-Amara on April 29th
    1939. (Putney. Patchings)

Yozgad, Broussa and Constantinople Magazine. Editions 2 and 3. (Cambridge University Press)

Regimental Journals

The *Hampshire Regiment Journals* from the First World War period.

The *Queen's Own Gazette*. A monthly record of regimental doings of the Queen's Own Royal West Kent
    Regiment.

Websites

Commonwealth War Graves Commission – www.cwgc.org

First World War site – www.firstworldwar.bham.ac.uk

INDEX